Reflections on Chomsky

'Chomsky speaking on Israel and the occupied territories, May 1988.' Photograph: Michael D. Grossberg/*The Tech*. Reproduced by kind permission.

Reflections on
CHOMSKY

Edited by
Alexander George

Basil Blackwell

First published 1989
Reprinted 1989
First published in paperback 1990

Basil Blackwell Ltd
108 Cowley Road, Oxford, OX4 1JF, UK

Basil Blackwell Inc.
3 Cambridge Center,
Cambridge, Massachusetts 02142, USA

British Library Cataloguing in Publication Data

A CIP catalogue record for this book is available from the British Library.

Library of Congress Cataloging-in-Publication Data

Reflections on Chomsky/edited by Alexander George.
p.   cm.
Essays prepared to honor Noam Chomsky on the occasion of
his 60th birthday on December 7, 1988.
Bibliography: p.
Includes index.
ISBN 0–631–15976–2   0–631–17919–4 (pbk)
1. Linguistics.   2. Chomsky, Noam.   I. Chomsky, Noam.
II. George, Alexander.
P26.C53R44 1991
410'.92'4—dc19

Typeset in 10 on 11 pt Ehrhardt
by Opus, Oxford
Printed in Great Britain by Bookcraft Ltd., Bath, Avon

Contents

Introduction   vi

Acknowledgements   xi

List of Contributors   xii

1 Why Should the Mind be Modular?   1
Jerry A. Fodor

2 Meaning and the Mental: the Problem of Semantics after Chomsky   23
Norbert Hornstein

3 Logical Form and Linguistic Theory   41
Jaakko Hintikka

4 Types and Tokens in Linguistics   58
Sylvain Bromberger

5 How Not to Become Confused about Linguistics   90
Alexander George

6 When is a Grammar Psychologically Real?   111
Christopher Peacocke

7 Tacit Knowledge and Subdoxastic States   131
Martin Davies

8 Knowledge of Reference   153
James Higginbotham

9 Wherein is Language Social?   175
Tyler Burge

10 Language and Communication   192
Michael Dummett

11 Model Theory and the 'Factuality' of Semantics   213
Hilary Putnam

12 Wittgenstein's Rule-following Considerations and the Central Project of Theoretical Linguistics   233
Crispin Wright

Select Bibliography of Works by Noam Chomsky   265

Index   269

Introduction

This volume of essays was prepared to honor Noam Chomsky and his work on the occasion of his sixtieth birthday on 7 December 1988. Through his original, deep, and fruitful contributions to the systematic study of language over the past thirty years, Chomsky has become one of the century's greatest linguists.[1] It is difficult to honor adequately such an illustrious figure and really an honor itself to do so. I once heard a well-known linguist describe her response to a letter inquiring whether she would be willing to recommend Chomsky for some award. She wrote back, replying simply that she had now added to her *curriculum vitae* that she had been asked to write a letter of reference for Noam Chomsky.

The impact of Chomsky's work has extended beyond academic linguistics to psychology and cognitive science; indeed, Chomsky is among the founders of the latter discipline. But both his linguistic research and the scientific setting in which he places it have also provoked much reflection among philosophers. This volume testifies to the philosophical stimulation his work continues to provide.

Chomsky's own attitude to philosophy, and to the philosophical relevance of the linguistics he has pioneered, deserves a more extensive discussion than I can offer here. It is clear that he has always been attracted to the discipline: Chomsky has spoken of the lasting impression left on him by an introductory course in philosophy taken in his freshman year at the University of Pennsylvania (1945), and by his encounters there with Nelson Goodman and Morton White, and later with W.V. Quine at Harvard while a member of the Society of Fellows (1951–5) (Peck (ed.), 1987, pp. 7 and 8; Chomsky, 1979, p. 72).

Consonant with Quine's views, Chomsky does not find useful any sharp distinction between philosophy and natural science (Chomsky, 1988, p. 2). It is hardly surprising, then, that he spends almost as much space responding to the relevant philosophical literature as he does to current work in linguistics; these activities are, for him, of a piece.

This is not to say that he finds himself in agreement with much contemporary philosophical work. On the contrary, he discerns in it strong currents that he believes are impediments to explanatory accounts of linguistic use, understanding, and acquisition. Recently, he has declared that 'there is very little to say of a constructive nature' about most questions in what is sometimes called the theory of meaning (Chomsky, 1988, p. 192). On other occasions he has been less pessimistic, praising much current work as 'very fruitful', 'very interesting', and 'promising' (Chomsky, 1979, p. 72). At any rate, whether positively or negatively, Chomsky insists that Anglo-American philosophy has been an important stimulus for him: 'My own work, from the very beginning,' he acknowledges, 'was greatly influenced by developments in philosophy' (Chomsky, 1979, p. 72).[2]

As for influence in the other direction, Chomsky finds that generative linguistics is indeed relevant to philosophical concerns, but he does not think that these have always been correctly identified. On his view, 'certain well-founded conclusions about the nature of language do bear on traditional philosophical questions,' in particular, on 'the problem of how knowledge is acquired and how the character of human knowledge is determined by certain general properties of the mind' (Chomsky, 1972, pp. 167–8). Chomsky has argued from the very beginning that if anything like present-day linguistics is on the right track, then there is a clear sense in which the Rationalists will have been shown to have won out over the Empiricists on the question of the origin of significant components of human knowledge.[3] Perhaps it is of some significance that that debate is not taken up by any of the following essays. It is a worthwhile question whether Chomsky's assessment of the import, on that score, of his and his colleagues' work is faulty, or instead so obviously correct that his views about that debate have been thoroughly absorbed by the philosophical culture.

The essays in this volume are concerned with a number of different, though interrelated topics. Chomsky has met with great success in his inquiry into the structure of human languages, an inquiry that explicitly adopts a conception of 'the language faculty' as one of several independent though interacting 'mental organs'. This has not gone unnoticed in cognitive psychology generally. Today, the idea that the mind is composed of modules is one that has great currency, even if there is not yet any consensus as to the precise content of this claim. Jerry Fodor, in his contribution, argues that perception is a form of cognition carried out by specialized mechanisms that are not privy to information available to cognitive mechanisms in general, and he explores the possibility of a teleological argument for this version of modularity.

Chomsky would agree that the 'language faculty' is modular, at least in the sense that it operates according to quite specific principles, ones that will not be found to play a role, or have obvious analogues, in other domains of cognitive functioning. Some of these specific principles are brought out in Norbert Hornstein's and Jaakko Hintikka's discussions of Logical Form, the level of linguistic representation that is intended to capture certain features of the meanings of expressions. Hornstein argues that Chomsky's approach to providing explanations for interpretive phenomena adverts only to the syntactical properties of representations at Logical Form, thereby avoiding possibly irresolvable problems besetting accounts that appeal to semantic notions, like reference, truth, etc. Hintikka finds himself in sympathy with the motivation of the current Government-Binding type theories introduced by Chomsky in 1981, but presses two objections: that it is not satisfactory to derive Logical Form solely from the Surface Structure of a sentence; and that there will be explanatory losses if representations at Logical Form restrict themselves to the resources of first-order extensional languages.

While these two chapters focus on particular features of current linguistic theories, the next two are concerned with what these theories are theories of. Sylvain Bromberger formulates, and then answers, the question of how linguistic theory, much of whose evidence consists in the properties of observable tokens, can discover the properties of abstract types, determined by the psychological constitution of speakers. In my chapter, I investigate the question of the subject-matter of linguistic theory and attempt to disentangle various actual and possible objects of inquiry. Failure to distinguish among these objects, I argue, is often a response to misguided reflection and a common source of confusion and of spurious arguments about method in linguistics.

Assuming that some clarification of the status of the grammar is attained, the next question Chomsky's work raises is what is involved in tacitly knowing such a structure. The thesis that Chomsky introduced and has defended vigorously over the years, that speakers of a language have tacit knowledge of a grammar for that language, is one that has excited and disturbed many philosophers. The next three essays are concerned with the question of tacit knowledge. Christopher Peacocke asks what could make one grammar rather than another psychologically real, or the object of a speaker's tacit knowledge, given that different grammars can be equivalent overall in respect of their classifications of expressions as sentences or non-sentences. He argues that a grammar has a psychological existence insofar as it specifies information drawn upon by some processing mechanisms of the individual speaker. Martin Davies explores the suggestion that, *contra* Chomsky, there is a distinction to be drawn between states of tacit knowledge and ordinary belief states (over and above the former's being inaccessible to consciousness); his discussion illustrates the difficulty of drawing that line in any straightforward or principled manner.

In his paper, James Higginbotham also explores issues about tacit knowledge, and links these to another debate: that between those who find a certain priority to the notion of an individual's idiolect at a particular time and those who instead find this notion subordinate to that of a community's language. In this context, he also discusses the status of the familiar disquotational data for semantic theory; how much does one know, he asks, when one knows that 'red' applies to the red things? Tyler Burge accepts the plausibility of focusing on the usage and psychology of individual speakers, as Chomsky urges, but he argues that individuation of an individual's idiolect depends on the language of others with whom he or she interacts; Burge then isolates several senses in which idiolects are social. And Michael Dummett explores these issues by considering the debate between those who take the primary function of language to be a vehicle of thought (he numbers Chomsky among these) and those who take it to be first and foremost an instrument of communication (here he places Grice and Strawson). He argues that this debate is not a significant one and that, once the lines of battle are more insightfully drawn, a deficiency of truth-conditional theories of meaning becomes visible.

The final two essays offer much more general challenges to the factuality or explanatoriness or even the intelligibility of the kind of account that Chomsky has championed. Hilary Putnam, in his contribution, expounds and defends one of his model theoretic arguments against realism. He compares and contrasts it with Quine's argument against the factuality of semantics and in favor of indeterminacy, and discusses in this context the longstanding disagreement between Quine and Chomsky. Crispin Wright explores the extent to which Wittgensteinian reflections on rule-following yield conclusions compatible with what he calls the Central Project of linguistics, namely, to provide a cognitive-psychological explanation of our apparent ability to assign semantic and syntactic representations to expressions never before encountered.

The range of themes covered in this volume reflects the breadth of Chomsky's interests and the variety of philosophical nerves his work touches. In addition, these essays show that Chomsky's work, whether or not one agrees with its conclusions, has raised the level of precision of many philosophical debates, including those about the structure of language and the nature of mind and meaning.

Chomsky has advanced philosophical understanding not only through his published writings, however. There is another, less public, more personal, avenue through which he has fostered intellectual development, an avenue known and deeply appreciated by the countless individuals whose work, published or unpublished, Chomsky has read and discussed with them at length. As an undergraduate, I remember being bothered about what Chomsky then called 'evaluation measures' operating in the Language Acquisition Device; somebody suggested that I write to him, which I did. I was astonished to receive a swift reply that contained a long and helpful explanation and defense of the notion. Many others will have had similar experiences: correspondents, visitors, and students, at MIT and beyond, graduates and undergraduates, Chomsky's and others'. Because his commitment to pedagogical responsibility easily matches his commitment to intellectual responsibility, there is more than one sense in which Chomsky cares deeply about the nature of minds and the growth of knowledge.

Alexander George
Wolfson College, Oxford
May 1988

Notes

1 Chomsky's written output over the years has been torrential and there is simply no room here for even a moderately comprehensive bibliography. I have tried, however, to collect at the end of this volume references to books and articles by Chomsky that should be of most interest to philosophers. For further references, the reader is advised to consult Salvatore Claudio Sgroi, *Noam Chomsky: Bibliografia 1949–81*, Padova, Italy, CLESP editrice, 1983, ix, 361 pages; or E.F. Konrad Koerner and Matsuji Tajima, *Noam Chomsky: A Personal Bibliography, 1951–1986*, Library and Information Sources in Linguistics, Volume 11, John Benjamins Publishing Company, Amsterdam/Philadelphia, 1986, xi, 217 pages. The latter contains an informative essay by Carlos P. Otero on the sixty-odd Ph.D. theses that Chomsky supervised from 1964 to 1986.

2 Citing Goodman and Quine, in particular.

3 There is another way in which Chomsky is a rationalist, and that is through his constant emphasis on reason in the study of language (and everything else). In a recent interview, Chomsky captured well his own uncompromising reliance on reason when he declared: 'There are no arguments that I know of for irrationality' *The Chomsky Reader*, p. 22.

References

Chomsky, Noam 1972: *Language and Mind*, enlarged edn. New York: Harcourt Brace Jovanovich.

—— 1979: *Language and Responsibility*. New York: Pantheon.

—— 1988: *Language and Problems of Knowledge: The Managua Lectures*. Cambridge, Mass.: MIT Press.

Koerner, E.F. Konrad and Tajima, Matsuji 1986: *Noam Chomsky: A Personal Bibliography, 1951–1986*. (Library and Information Sources in Linguistics 11.) Amsterdam and Philadelphia: John Benjamins Publishing Company.

Peck, James (ed.) 1987: *The Chomsky Reader*. New York: Pantheon.

Sgroi, Salvatore Claudio 1983: *Noam Chomsky: Bibliografia 1949–81*. Padova: CLESP.

Acknowledgements

I am fortunate to have many good friends who helped in many different ways in the preparation of this volume. James Higginbotham, especially, has been a mine of good advice. For their support and counsel, I would also like to thank J. S. Baum and John Brennan, Daniel Isaacson, and Sue Vice. This collection was prepared while I was a Junior Research Fellow at Wolfson College, Oxford, a position for which I will long remain grateful. I hope the warmth and light of that institution survive the darkness falling over education in Margaret Thatcher's Britain.

A.G.

List of Contributors

Sylvain Bromberger	Professor of Philosophy at Massachusetts Institute of Technology
Tyler Burge	Professor of Philosophy at the University of California at Los Angeles
Martin Davies	Reader in Philosophy at Birkbeck College, University of London
Michael Dummett	Wykeham Professor of Logic at Oxford University and Fellow of New College, Oxford
Jerry Fodor	Professor of Philosophy at Rutgers University and the Graduate Center of the City University of New York
Alexander George	Assistant Professor of Philosophy at Amherst College
James Higginbotham	Professor of Philosophy at Massachusetts Institute of Technology
Jaakko Hintikka	Professor of Philosophy, Boston University
Norbert Hornstein	Associate Professor of Linguistics at the University of Maryland, College Park
Christopher Peacocke	The Susan Stebbing Professor of Philosophy at King's College, London and Waynflete Professor-elect of Metaphysical Philosophy at Oxford University
Hilary Putnam	Walter Beverly Pearson Professor of Modern Mathematics and Mathematical Logic at Harvard University
Crispin Wright	Professor of Logic and Metaphysics at the University of St Andrews and Professor of Philosophy at the University of Michigan, Ann Arbor

1

Why Should the Mind be Modular?

Jerry A. Fodor

Danny Kaye once described the oboe as 'an ill wind that nobody blows good.' Much the same could be said – and with more justice – of teleological explanations in psychology. There is an irresistible temptation to argue that the organization that one's favorite cognitive theory attributes to the mind is the very organization that the mind ought to have, given its function. One knows that such arguments are, in the nature of the case, *post-hoc*; one knows that the cognitive theories they presuppose invariably come unstuck, leaving the teleologist with a functional explanation for mental structures that don't exist; one knows that there are, in general, lots of mechanisms that can perform a given task, so that inferences from a task to a mechanism are up to their ears in affirmation of the consequent; one knows about the philosopher who, just before they discovered the ninth planet, proved from first principles that there have to be exactly eight. One knows all this; but the temptation persists.

In this paper, I propose to offer some teleological excuses for the modular organization of perception. In particular, I'll raise some functional considerations that might favor modularity in perception even if – as I'm inclined to suppose – the organization of much of the rest of cognition is nonmodular in important ways. Some of the arguments for modularity that I've seen in the literature – for example, that modular processes are especially debuggable – don't do this; so they suggest that, insofar as teleology rules, the mind ought to be modular all over. My line, by contrast, is that given the specifics of what perception is supposed to do, and given internal constraints on processes that do that sort of thing, modular structure in perceptual systems is perhaps what you'd expect.

What *is* perception supposed to do? Psychologists have tended to disagree about this in ways that have deep consequences for the rest of what they say about cognition. There are, for example, those who take it for granted that the primary function of perception is to guide action. (Illustrious psychologists who have held this view include Piaget, Gibson, Dewey, Vygotsky, and surely many others.) It is no accident that such psychologists invariably take the reflex to be the primitive mode of psychological organization, to which cognitive functions must somehow be reduced (phylogenetically, ontogenetically, or otherwise).[1] In reflexes, specific perceptual events are lawfully connected to correspondingly specific behavioral outcomes. To take the reflex as the paradigm psychological process is thus to see perceptual mechanisms as detectors which function to monitor an organism's environment, looking for occasions on which the associated behavior is appropriately released.

I am going to assume (without argument, for the moment) that this picture is profoundly misled. On my view, behavior is normally determined decision–theoretically; namely, by the interaction of beliefs with utilities. In the interesting cases, perception is linked to behavior only *via* such interactions. Specifically, perception functions in belief fixation (in ways that we are about to explore) and perceptually fixed beliefs, like any others, may eventuate in behavioral outcomes. Whether they do so depends on what the organism wants and on the rest of its cognitive commitments. I was once told (by a Gibsonian) that this decision-theoretic understanding of the relation between perception and behavior won't do for flies, since it's plausible that their behaviors really are all reflexive. If this is true, it is another contribution to the accumulating evidence that flies aren't people. Perhaps minds started out as stimulus-response machines. If so, then according to the present view the course of evolution was to interpose a computer – programmed, as it might be, with the axioms of your favorite decision theory – between the identification of a stimulus and the selection of a response.

So my working assumption is that perception is a species of cognition; it's one of the psychological mechanisms whose main job is the fixation of belief. If, therefore, you are looking for a teleological story about the design of perceptual systems, the first step is to get clear about just what perception contributes to belief fixation. You can maybe then go on to show why mechanisms that make *that* contribution to belief fixation ought to be modular. That, in any event, is the game plan for what follows.

To get started, we need a general story about belief fixation within which to locate perception's role. Here's an old-fashioned story – assembled as much from epistemology as from psychology – that strikes me as reasonable as far as it goes. Beliefs have two main kinds of causes: other beliefs and organism/environment interactions. So, for example, one way that you may come to believe that Q is as a causal consequence of believing $P{\rightarrow}Q$ and P. Being in the first mental state is approximately causally sufficient for being in the second.[2] In principle, such chains of mental causation can be as long as you like, bounded only by the inferential capacities of the organism. But I suppose that, as a matter of fact, they rarely get *very* long. Its prior cognitive commitments impact upon an organism's present cognitive state; but so too do its causal transactions with the world. In consequence of such transactions, chains of thought are forever being supplemented by underived premises.

The typical nonmental cause of a belief is an interaction between the body of an organism and something in its environment. Bodily states register – and are thus informative about – the effects of local environmental causes in exactly the way that thermometers register ambient temperature and tidemarks register encroachments of the sea; in fact, in exactly the way that *any* effect registers – and is thus informative about – its cause. Changes in states of the retina, for example, register changes in the properties of incident light, which are in turn caused by alterations in the arrangement of the distal objects that radiate and reflect the light. To the extent that such proximal effects are specific to their distal causes, cognitive processes with access to the one have grounds for inference to the other.

So, the picture is that certain organic states register the proximal stimuli that cause them, and that certain cognitive processes infer the arrangement of local distal objects from the organic effects of these proximal stimulations. In particular, I assume that it's the function of perceptual mechanisms to execute such inferences.[3]

So much for the function of perception. The modularity thesis for perception is accordingly the claim that the mechanisms that perform this function are (a) dedicated, and (b) encapsulated. And the teleological question is whether there is something about inferences from representations of proximal stimuli to representations of distal layouts that makes dedicated and encapsulated devices especially appropriate for executing them. Before I turn to this question, however, I want to say a word about the thesis that perception is a species of inference – dedicated, encapsulated, or otherwise. The way that I've been setting things up, this thesis turns out to be next door to a truism; by contrast, some psychologists (and many philosophers) have taken it to be extremely tendentious.

Discussion of this issue in the cognitive science literature has tended to center – misleadingly, in my view – on the question whether 'poverty of the stimulus' arguments are reliable. It's worth taking a moment to dissociate these issues.

The first step in developing a poverty of the stimulus argument is to claim, on empirical grounds, that proximal stimulation typically contains 'less information' than the perceptual beliefs that it engenders (sensation underdetermines perception, to put this in an older vocabulary). The phenomenon of perceptual ambiguity – Necker cubes and the like – is one sort of evidence for this premise. The second step is to note that this extra information has to come from somewhere; presumably it comes from the organism's store of background knowledge. The last step is to *identify* the claim that perception is inferential with the claim that it exploits cognitive background. In effect, the completed argument is that perception must be inferential because it is 'top down'. Correspondingly, psychologists who don't like the inferential story about perception have generally undertaken to show that proximal stimulation is actually informationally richer than poverty of the stimulus arguments suppose; that – at least in 'ecologically valid' circumstances – there is, in principle, enough information in the light impinging at the retina – and hence enough information registered by the retinal effects that this impinging light produces – to determine a unique and correct perceptual analysis of the distal layout. [4]

Whatever one thinks of this argument, however, it is important to see that the claim that perception is inferential is distinguishable from the claim that it is underdetermined by its psychophysical basis. In particular, it is *not* required of an inference that its conclusion must be stronger than (that it must be 'underdetermined' by) its premises. Demonstrative inferences are, of course, all counterexamples; $P\&Q \rightarrow P$ is a paradigm case of an inference though, on any reasonable measure, P contains less information than $P\&Q$. Similarly, the mental process that gets one from the thought that John is an unmarried man to the thought that he is a bachelor presumably counts as inferential, though in no sense is the second thought 'stronger than' the first. Similarly again for the perceptual case: even if the information in the proximal light uniquely determines the visible properties of the distal layout, the inferentiality of the mental process that proceeds from representing the one to representing the other would not be impugned.

The core argument for the inferentiality of perception derives from two considerations, both of which are quite independent of claims for underdetermination. On the one hand, perception fixes beliefs about *distal* objects; objects typically at some spatial remove from the perceiving organism.[5] And, on the other hand, there is no causal interaction at these distances; all the intentional effects of distal stimuli must be mediated by the organic effects of proximal stimuli (by retinal states, and the like). I assume that, if these organic effects represent anything, then they represent their proximal causes (see n. 3). On this assumption, it follows that perception is a process in which representations of proximal stimuli causally determine beliefs about distal layouts. But that *is* what's claimed when it's claimed that perception is inferential.

I am not, by the way, taking it for granted that every causal chain of intentional states is an inference; for example, associative chains aren't. But then, association doesn't eventuate in the fixation of belief, and perception does. Nor do I hold that perceptual inferences differ in *no* important ways from paradigms of explicit reasoning. For one thing, explicit reasoning is explicit; and that may be important. For another thing, in paradigm cases where *the thought that A*'s causing *the thought that B* counts as the agent's inferring B from A, the agent accepts the proposition *if A then B* in whatever sense he accepts the propositions A and B.[6] This is, however, unlikely to be true in perceptual inference, especially if perception proves to be modular. It's generally assumed that modular systems are 'hardwired', that is, that the principles of inference according to which they operate are 'inexplicit': not just not conscious, but also not mentally represented. A hardwired system that 'accepts' the principle 'if A then B' may thus do so *only* in the sense that it is disposed to accept Bs when it accepts As. By contrast, the sense in which it accepts the As and Bs themselves is much stronger; it involves the tokening of representational states of which they are the intentional objects.

So there are these (and perhaps other) legitimate respects in which the causal chain from representations of proximal stimuli to representations of distal layouts may differ from paradigm cases of inferences. Whether this makes these chains noninferential depends on whether the missing properties are among those that are *essential* to inference. And, for us Realists, that depends in turn on what inferences *really are*, a question that only a developed cognitive science could reasonably be expected to answer. For present purposes, I propose to beg these sorts of issues. All I care about is that there are mental processes in which representations of proximal stimuli cause representations of local distal layouts. I treat it as a stipulation that perceptual inference is modular if and only if – or rather, to the extent that – these processes are executed by dedicated and encapsulated systems.

Why should perceptual mechanisms be dedicated?

Why should perceptual inferences be carried out by specialized mechanisms? Or, to put it another way, why should the mind treat the problem of inferring local distal layouts from proximal stimulations as a different *kind* of computational task than the problem of figuring out the next chess move from the current board state; or the problem of figuring out your account balance from your check stubs; or the problem of diagnosing a disease from a display of its symptoms? For that matter, precisely *which* proximal-to-local-distal inferences are supposed to be executed by dedicated mechanisms? Perhaps, on noticing a sudden increase in the volume of the street noise, I infer that someone has opened a window. Surely there isn't a mental faculty that is dedicated to doing *that*?

I'm going to consider these questions first as they apply to the special case of language perception. I'll then say a little about how the morals might generalize to other perceptual capacities.

I assume that language perception is constituted by nondemonstrative inferences from representations of certain effects of the speaker's behavior (sounds that he produces; marks that he makes) to representations of certain of his intentional states. As a rough approximation, I'll say that such inferences run from premises that specify acoustic properties of utterance tokens to conclusions that specify the speaker's communicative intentions. A speaker makes a certain noise (e.g. the sort of noise that gets made when you pronounce the sentence 'it's going to rain tomorrow'), and, in consequence of hearing the noise, one is somehow able to infer something about what the speaker intends that one should take him to believe (e.g. that he intends that one should take him to believe that it's going to rain tomorrow). The question before us is: why should there be dedicated mechanisms devoted to the execution of such inferences?

I think the crucial consideration is that inferences from acoustic properties of utterance tokens to intentional properties of the speaker's mental state – unlike almost all of the rest of the mental processing that mediates the intentional interpretation of the behavior of one's conspecifics – are algorithmic. That is, they are effected by employing a mechanical computational procedure that is guaranteed to deliver a canonical description of a speaker's mental state given a canonical representation of his behavior. (More precisely, you're guaranteed a canonical description of a communicative intention in exchange for a canonical description of the acoustic properties of a token of any expression in the language that the speaker and hearer share.)[7] If the computations that mediate speech perception are indeed specialized in this way, then familiar teleological arguments for the computational division of labor would favor cognitive architectures in which they are implemented by dedicated processors.[8]

Whether there is an algorithm for inferring the mental state of a speaker from the acoustics of his speech clearly depends on which acoustic properties are specified in the premises and which intentional properties are specified in the conclusion. It may be that it's the speaker's desire to startle Granny that causes him to speak so loudly; but, patently, there is going to be no general form of inference that will connect that sort of acoustic property of an utterance to that sort of intentional property of a mental state. By contrast, there may be a routine procedure whereby someone who hears an utterance of the acoustic form 'it's going to rain' can infer a description of the speaker as intending to communicate his belief that it's going to rain. If so, it would be natural to view the ability to execute this procedure as part of knowing English.[9]

Notice that, on this view, it is quite possibly a mistake to assume – as many psychologists like to do – that ' . . . the function of the [the language comprehension mechanisms] is to project the speech input onto a representation of the world – onto, for example, a mental mode' (Marslen-Wilson and Tyler, 1987, p. 58). No doubt, what the hearer wants from the speaker *in the long run* is news about the world; news that he can integrate with the rest of what he knows. But the way that he contrives to get the news, according to the present view, is by first effecting a more or less algorithmic construction of a canonical representation of *what the speaker said*. And the price of the algorithmicity of this construction may be precisely its encapsulation from information garnered from the preceding dialogue or, for that matter, from information garnered from any sources other than the speaker's phonetic output.

The idea, then, is that speech communication exhibits a tradeoff in which the algorithmicity of a computational procedure is purchased at the price of severe constraints on the sorts of inferences that it can mediate. On the one hand, there are properties of the speaker's state of mind that can be inferred *just from the noises that he makes*; and the speaker has a guarantee that (*ceteris paribus*) any of his colinguals who hear the noises will be able to draw the inferences, *just in virtue of their being his colinguals*. That speakers *can* rely on this is really quite remarkable, considering how tricky inferences from behaviors to their mental causes are in the general case. One expects them to go wrong, often enough, even with the spouse of one's bosom. One expects them to go wrong proportionately more often where the background of shared experience is thinner. What is usually required in the intentional analysis of behavior is a kind of hermeneutic sophistication that's as far as can be from the execution of a rote procedure. The notable exception is inferring intentional content from utterance form. Show me an English-speaker who utters 'it's about to rain' and I'll show you an English-speaker who is thinking about the weather. This sort of inference is enormously reliable even though its premises are strikingly exiguous. *All* you have to know about an English-speaker is that he made a certain sort of noise, and the intentional interpretation of his behavior is immediately transparent.

On the other hand, one buys this transparency at a price. There appears to be something like a procedure for the intentional interpretation of verbal behavior; but all that executing the procedure gives you is a specification of the propositional object of a communicative intention. The only intentional information about a speaker that his colinguals are *ipso facto* able to recover from his verbal behavior is the literal content of what he says. For all the other sorts of things that you might want to know about the speaker's state of mind ('Why did he say that?' 'Did he mean it?' 'What did he mean by it?' 'Why does he believe it?' 'What's he trying to get away with?') you're on your own; hermeneutic sophistication comes into play, mediated by heaven knows what problem-solving heuristics. The good news is that a shared language approximates a guaranteed channel along which a speaker may indicate the contents of his thoughts; the bad news is that it's a very narrow channel.

If much of this is right, it's clear why you might expect the mechanisms of speech perception to be discontinuous from the mechanisms of cognitive problem solving at large. Real problem solving generally has two parts: first there's the business of figuring out how to solve the problem, and then there's the business of proceeding to solve it that way.[10] But speech perception has only part two; it consists entirely of executing an algorithim for the intentional analysis of verbal behavior. One doesn't have to invent the procedure before one applies it because one finishes inventing it when one finishes learning the language. One doesn't have to worry about whether to employ the procedure, because speech perception isn't voluntary. And one doesn't have to worry about what to do if the procedure fails, because its success is guaranteed (*modulo* notes 7 and 9). Speech perception really isn't thinking; it's just computing. Inferring communicative intentions from verbal behavior is a solved problem; so why should the mind treat it as problem solving?[11]

It's instructive to contrast the present treatment of language perception with the approach favored in Fodor, Bever, and Garrett, 1974. They are enthusiastic about the analogy between perception and the process whereby a detective infers the identity of a criminal from his information about the clues. The force of the analogy is that both kinds of mentation involve nondemonstrative inferences from effects to causes: they're presumably both species of hypotheses formation and confirmation. But what Fodor *et al.* missed – and what now strikes me as important – is that the first sort of inference is plausibly algorithmic in a way that the second certainly isn't. Holmes has to *think* to figure out that it was Moriarty who did it; whereas in perception, you don't think, you just open your eyes and look. For the perceiver, but not for Holmes, the space of hypotheses that's available to be confirmed is determined *a priori* (it's just the set of well-formed canonical descriptions of distal objects); and, given the data as canonically described, the choice of one of these hypotheses is, by assumption, approximately mechanical. It's wrong to suppose that because perception is phenomenologically instantaneous it must be noninferential; but it's equally wrong to suppose that if perception is inferential, then it must be computationally just like thought.

We've been seeing that the teleological argument for a dedicated speech processor depends on the plausibility of the claim that speech perception is algorithmic. And that might lead one to wonder about the generality of this line of argument. After all, if there's an algorithm for the perceptual analysis of utterances, that's presumably because speakers and hearers abide by the same conventions for correlating forms of utterance with mental states. None of this applies, however, to computing the correspondence between distal arrangements and proximal stimuli in, for example, vision. So why should one suppose perceptual mechanisms to be dedicated in the *non*linguistic cases?

But, in fact, the conventionality of language is inessential to the algorithmicity of speech perception. What really matters is this: *For any perceptually analyzable linguistic token there is a canonical description (DT) such that for some mental state there is a canonical description (DM) such that 'DMs cause DTs' is true and counterfactual supporting.* (For tokens of 'it's raining,' there is a canonical description – namely 'token of "it's raining"' – such that 'tokens of "it's raining" are caused by intentions to communicate the belief that it's raining' is true and counterfactual supporting.)

Which is to say that speech perception can be algorithmic because certain of the acoustic properties of linguistic tokens bear regular relations to certain intentional properties of their mental causes. It happens, in the case of language, that this relation is largely supported by conventions. But it would work just as well if it were supported by natural laws.[12] As I suppose that the corresponding relation often is in the case of other sorts of perceptual systems. For example, certain aspects of visual perceptual processing can be algorithmic because: *For any perceptually analyzable pattern of proximal excitation of the retina, there is a canonical description (RD) such that for some distal layout of visible objects there is a canonical description (DL) such that 'DLs cause RDs' is a law* (and hence true and counterfactual supporting).

Thus, there are laws relating the two-dimensional shape and orientation of retinal images to the three-dimensional shapes and orientations of their distal causes. Because, in such cases, the relation between being RD and being caused by a DL is quite regular, the procedure that infers DLs from RDs can be approximately fail-proof. And because there is a DL for *every* perceptually analyzable RD, it can be general. If, moreover, the function from RDs to DLs is mechanically computable, then the lawful relation between distal layouts and proximal arrays opens the way to an algorithmic solution to these aspects of visual perception.

All of this makes perception seem rather special among the varieties of problem solving that can effect belief fixation. In perception one is often guaranteed a description of the problem and a description of its solution such that given the former there is a mechanical procedure for computing the latter. And access to the data for this computation is itself nomologically guaranteed for any (normal) organism that bears the appropriate psychophysical relation to a distal stimulus. All you have to do is turn up the lights and point your eyes, and all the retinal information required for (e.g.) visual perception of three-dimensional shape is *ipso facto* available. For auditory perception you have to do still less; all that's required is (what they call on the Continent) *being there*.

Needless to say that nothing like this holds for cognitive problem solving at large. Thinking is *hard*: there need be no description of the terms of a problem from which a (nontrivial) specification of its solution follows mechanically. And, even if there is such a description, there need be no guaranteed procedure for getting access to it. So perception – but not thinking – can often be carried out by 'canned' computational procedures. So, it wouldn't be very surprising if many perceptual mechanisms were dedicated. So, so much for that.

Why should perception be encapsulated?

An unencapsulated (or 'penetrable'; see Pylyshyn, 1984) psychological mechanism is one that has unconstrained access to cognitive backgound. The limit of perceptual penetrability is reached when information that is available to *any* cognitive mechanism is *ipso facto* available as the premise of any perceptual inference. That perception actually approximates this limit has been a main tenet of most post-behaviorist cognitive science and of most post-positivist epistemology. The support for this view of the perception/cognition relation derives partly from empirical evidence, but also partly from a widely accepted teleological argument that is supposed to show that unencapsulated perception makes ecological good sense. Let's now consider this argument.

The *locus classicus* is Bruner (1957) 'On perceptual readiness', a psychological work so influential that even philosophers have heard of it. Here's the kernel of Bruner's teleological argument for the cognitive penetration of perception: 'Where accessibility of categories reflects environmental probabilities, the organism is in the position of requiring less stimulus input, less redundancy of cues for the appropriate categorization of objects' (p. 19). That is, the more perception exploits the organism's background of cognitive commitments, the less proximal information the organism requires to identify a distal layout. Penetration buys shallow processing of proximal stimuli; shallow processing of proximal stimuli buys speed of perceptual identification; and speed of perceptual identification is a desideratum. Thus Bruner on the teleological argument for penetrated perception.

Whether this argument is any good, however, depends on a couple of empirical questions that Bruner largely ignores; and, unfortunately, answering these questions involves quantitative estimates that nobody is in a position to make.

What is the relative computational cost of processing the proximal stimulus vs. processing the background information?

It's all very well to emphasize, as Bruner does, that penetration allows perceptual analysis to proceed with 'fairly minimal' proximal information. But this is valuable only if it achieves a reduction of computational load *over all*; and whether it does so depends on how much processing is required to bring the cognitive background to bear.

The cost of computing the background depends on two unknowns:

(a) The cost of achieving access. Background information must be *located* before it can be *applied*. Depending on the search mechanisms employed, this process may become more costly in proportion as the potentially available background gets larger. If it does, then – all else being equal – the prediction is that perception gets *slower* as cognitive penetrability increases.

This consequence may be avoidable on the assumption that cognitive background is accessed by 'massively parallel' memory searches, as in associative networks. But here too the issues are unclear. In network systems, the computational cost of access is reduced because the possible search paths are fixed antecedently: They are determined by the character of the connectivity among the nodes in the network, which is in turn determined by the stochastic properties of the network's 'training'. In such architectures, memory search is cheap because it's quite insensitive to the details of the perceptual task in hand. (In particular, you don't get the recursive loops that are so characteristic of classical top-down models of perceptual processing: A candidate analysis of the input determines the initial direction of a search, which in turn produces a new analysis of the input, which in turn modifies the subsequent direction of search . . . until some success criterion is achieved.) The consequence – for all the network models so far proposed, at any rate – is that a lot of perceptual preprocessing is required to start them running: They achieve the cognitive penetration of perception by assuming the perceptual penetration of memory search. Nobody knows whether there is some optimal balance in which the right kind of preprocessor conjoined with the right kind of network memory produces computational savings relative to encapsulated perceptual systems. Unless there is, Bruner's speed argument for the penetration of perception looks to be unreliable.

(b) The cost of computing confirmation levels. Whatever background information is accessed must be applied to the analysis of the current proximal display. If you insist on the cognitive penetration of perceptual inference, you have to bear the cost of determining *how much confirmation* the background information that you recover bestows on your current perceptual hypothesis. The problem is that the more background information you access, the more such confirmation relations you will have to compute.

This is rather different from the worry that the more cognitive background you have access to, the more expensive it may be to find the piece of information that you want. As we've just seen, the way out of *that* problem may be to fix the search paths antecedently and then explore them in parallel. But that kind of solution is implausible for the problem of computing confirmation relations. They can't be decided ahead of time because what degree of confirmation a given piece of background information bestows on a given perceptual hypothesis depends not just on what the information is and what the hypothesis is, but also on a bundle of local considerations that change from moment to moment.

Could the yellow, stripey thing I've just glimpsed be a tiger?

But this is the middle of New York.

Yes, but the Bronx Zoo is in the middle of New York.

Yes, but I can see the Empire State Building, and you can't see the Empire State Building from the Bronx Zoo.

Yes, but tigers sometimes escape from zoos.

Yes, but *The Times* would have mentioned it if a tiger had escaped from the Bronx Zoo.

So, in *some circumstances* it can matter to deciding whether a yellow, stripey thing is a tiger that *The Times* really does tell all the news that's fit to print in the Bronx. In other circumstances – if I'm in Budapest, say, or if I'm in a yellow-stripey-chair store – the inductive relevances are quite different. The moral is that it's just about inconceivable that confirmation relations could be 'hardened in' once and for all in the way that the structure of memory search might be. Our estimates of what confirms what change as fast as our changing picture of the world.

What, you might reasonably ask, is the bearing of all this on Bruner's argument? It's that if (*a*) and (*b*) are large with respect to the cost of bottom-up processing of proximal stimuli, *you may gain time by encapsulation.* This was, in fact, the line I took in *The Modularity of Mind,* where I argued that since perception is clearly specialized for the fixation of belief about local distal objects, and since it's the local distal objects that one eats and gets eaten by, it is biological good sense for perceptual systems to be fast. All that agrees with Bruner. But I then made the reverse assumption from his about the relative computational costs of bottom-up proximal analysis as compared to the exploitation of cognitive background; I took it for granted that memory searches and computations of confirmation relations cost a lot. I thus arrived at a teleological conclusion exactly opposite to Bruner's: MOM says that if you want speed, make perception as much like a reflex as possible.[13] That is, make it as encapsulated as you can. The real point, I suppose, is that *neither* Bruner's argument nor mine is empirically warranted in the current state of our science.

How the teleology goes depends on estimating empirical tradeoffs about which, in fact, almost nothing is known.

What is the relative payoff for being fast when your background assumptions are right vs. being accurate when they are wrong?

I've been saying that Bruner's teleological argument for the cognitive penetration of perception ignores the computation-theoretic costs of top down processing. The next point is that it also ignores the game-theoretic costs of misperception.

To be sure, Bruner notices that 'the more inappropriate the readiness, the greater the input or redundancy of cues required for appropriate categorizations to occur' (1957, p. 20). That is, if you let your expectations run away with your perceptions, then you're likely to do worse than an encapsulated perceiver when your expectations are wrong (just as you're likely to do better than an encapsulated perceiver when they're right). What he doesn't notice, however, is the consequent tradeoff between speed and accuracy: *Ceteris paribus*, penetrated perceivers are relatively fast when their background beliefs are true but they're relatively inaccurate when their background beliefs are false; *ceteris paribus*, encapsulated perceivers are relatively slow when their background beliefs are true, but they're relatively accurate when their background beliefs are false. Assuming that the choice is exclusive, which sort of perceiver would you prefer to be?[14]

Alas, it's simply not possible to estimate which cognitive architecture is better overall; still less to guess which one would have bred most or lived longest in the conditions in which the brain evolved. Suffice it that it's easy to imagine cases in which the cautious – namely, encapsulated – nervous system clearly wins. Consider my belief that there *isn't* a tiger salivating in my word processor. This is a belief that I cleave to firmly; I haven't a doubt in the world that it's true. Do I want it to bias my perceptions? Well, what are the probable payoffs?

If I'm right about the tiger not being there, I'll get certain gains from cognitive penetration: If I'm looking for a tiger, I won't start by looking in my word processor; and, since there *isn't* a tiger in my word processor, this will save me time. Similarly, if I'm mucking around in my word processor, trying to figure out what's gone wrong with it, I will not entertain the hypothesis that the bug is a tiger; and that too will save me time. These gains are real but they are modest.

On the other hand, if I'm *wrong* about whether there's a tiger in the word processor, then what I want is for my tiger-perception to be accurate in spite of my expectations. In fact, I want my tiger-perceptions to *correct my expectations*, and I want this very much. Tiggers bounce (as Pooh remarked) and they also bite (a point that Pooh failed to stress). For this sort of case, given an (exclusive) choice between a penetrated perceptual system that is fast when my biases are right and an encapsulated perceptual system that is accurate when my biases are wrong, I opt for encapsulation.

What's the situation when what I believe is that there *is* a salivating tiger in the word processor? Here, whether I'm right or wrong, neither perceptual speed nor perceptual accuracy buys me much. That's because, unless one is absolutely bonkers, what one *doesn't* do if one believes that there is a salivating tiger in one's word processor is look and see. What you do instead is: You tiptoe *very quietly* out the door, which you then lock behind you. Then you run like stink.

The upshot is that in the payoff matrix if you're a *possible edible*, the cell where penetration matters is the one where you think that there is no eater around and you're *wrong*. And what you want in the cell is encapsulation. As you might expect, the situation is roughly symmetrical, but with the signs reversed, if you're the tiger. In the payoff matrix for possible eaters the cell that matters is the one where you think there is an edible around and you're *right*. What you want to be if you're in that cell is fast, since what you don't eat someone else is likely to.

As for the remaining possibilities: Perceptual accuracy in *dis*confirming the hypothesis that there's a local edible doesn't buy you much; you're just as hungry after you look as you were before. How much might perceptual accuracy buy you in the case where you think there are *no* edibles on offer and you're *wrong*? Probably not much because probably – as in the case where you wrongly believe that there's a tiger in the word processor – the more firmly you hold the belief, the more you don't bother to look.

So much for the payoff matrix. There's a case where it is very desirable to be fast if you're right even at the cost of not being accurate if you're wrong (i.e. you'd want your perception to be penetrated) and there's a case where it is very desirable to be accurate if you're wrong even at the cost of not being fast if you're right (i.e. you'd want your perception to be encapsulated). Whether Bruner has a teleological argument for penetration depends primarily on the relative payoffs associated with these two conditions. The trouble is that what these payoffs are is not an *a priori* issue; it depends entirely on how the world is arranged. And neither I nor Bruner is in a position to estimate the relevant facts. Perhaps the only way to tell which architecture is worth more is to argue the other way around: infer the cost benefits by finding out which architecture selection actually endorsed.

It looks like the standard design arguments for penetrated perception aren't actually very convincing; I propose presently to sail off on a different tack. First, however, a digression: Some epistemologists have exhibited great enthusiasm for the perceptual penetration of observation in science, and this appears peculiar in light of the previous discussion. Here is Paul Churchland (forthcoming) for example, feeling quite rhapsodic about perceptual bias:

> even the humblest judgement . . . is always a speculative leap. . . . In the case of perceptual judgements, what the senses do is cause the perceiver to activate some specific representation from the . . . conceptual framework . . . that has been brought to the perceptual situation by the perceiver. A perceptual judgement, therefore, can be no better, though it

can be worse, than the broad system of representations in which it is constituted . . . The journey of the human spirit is essentially the story of our evolving conception of the world . . . The human spirit will continue its breathtaking adventure of self-reconstruction, and its perceptual and motor capabilities will continue to develop as an integral part of its self-reconstruction.

Well, if so then so be it. But one wonders *just* what it is that Churchland thinks perceptual bias buys for the scientist. We've seen that the standard (Bruner) argument for penetration comes down to an assumption about the relative payoffs in speed/accuracy trades. And we've seen that it's perfectly conceivable that selection may have favored speed in the conditions under which the nervous system evolved (just as it's perfectly conceivable that it may have favored accuracy). But, surely, there is no question about which to choose in the circumstances that obtain in scientific investigations; surely what one wants there is observational *accuracy even if accuracy takes a lot of time*.[15] And what you *particularly* want is that your observations should be accurate when your theories are wrong, because then your observations can correct your theories. But if, in science, the smart money is on observational accuracy, then it's an *encapsulated* perceptual psychology that a scientist should want to have. There's no point trying to build bias out of scientific instruments if it's built into the guy who reads them.[16]

The upshot seems to be that nature may have equipped us with cognitively penetrated perceptual systems; but if she did, there is nothing in that to gladden the heart of an epistemologist. On the contrary, if we have unencapsulated perceptual architecture, that's just another respect in which we are not a species ideally endowed for the scientific enterprise.

Encapsulation and objectivity

We seem not to be getting anywhere; after all the talk about cost accounting, we're still in want of a plausible teleological argument for (or against) encapsulated perception. Let's, however, make one last try.

Early on in this discussion, I endorsed what I called a 'decision-theoretic' account of the etiology of behavior, according to which behavior is caused by the interaction of beliefs and utilities. I remarked that this decision-theoretic picture is to be distinguished from the view that the model for the etiology of behavior is the reflex. On the reflex story, an organism's behavioral repertoire is make up of perception-action pairs. On the decision-theoretic story, by contrast, there is nothing special about the relation between perception and action: Perception affects behavior in much the same way that other cognitive processes (e.g. thinking) do; namely, via the fixation of belief. (The only difference is that perception typically gives rise to beliefs about relatively *local* distal layouts, so – given reasonable utilities – the demands that perceptual beliefs make on action are likely to prove pressing. As I observed above, it's the local distal layouts that one eats and gets eaten by.)

Now, this difference between ways of understanding the perception–action relation implies corresponding differences in the way one understands the function of perception, and thus affects the status of teleological arguments from function to design. Presumably, an organism that is built to act on its beliefs will do best, on balance, if the beliefs that it acts on are *true*. If this is so, then a good way to illuminate the teleology of cognitive mechanisms might be to consider what design constraints the quest for true beliefs imposes on the process of belief fixation. The architectural organization of perception might then be understood by reference to its contribution to the truth-seeking process.

What, then, should the design of perception be if our perceptual inferences are generally to lead us from true premises to true conclusions? This way of framing the question suggests an approach to teleological arguments in which normative epistemology provides design hypotheses for theories of cognitive architecture. You tell me something about what good nondemonstrative inference is like and I'll tell you something about what the computational structure of cognition ought to be, assuming that the function of cognition is the fixation of true beliefs.

The trouble with this research strategy in practice is that very little is known about good nondemonstrative inferences. Still, there are some considerations on which practically everybody seems to be agreed, and I think these may bear on the teleological justification of perceptual encapsulation. So I propose first to enunciate a few epistemological truisms and then to see what support they may offer for the view that perception is modular.

First truism: A good empirical inference is subject to at least two constraints: *observational adequacy* and *conservatism*. On the one hand, one wants the hypotheses one accepts to be compatible with as much of one's data as possible; and, on the other hand, one wants accepting the hypothesis to do the least possible damage to one's prior cognitive commitments.

Second truism: Observational adequacy and conservatism are *independent* constraints on nondemonstrative inference. There is no guarantee that the hypothesis that fits most of the data will be maximally conservative or, conversely, that the maximally conservative hypothesis will be the one that fits most of the data. It's too bad that this is so; if the most conservative theory were always best confirmed, we'd never have the nuisance of having to change our minds.

Third truism: We have repeatedly remarked upon the special role that perception plays in the fixation of beliefs about the spatio-temporally local environment. But it isn't, of course, the concern with locality *per se* that distinguishes perception from other processes of belief fixation: Some of your beliefs about stars are perceptual, and most of your beliefs about your appendix are not. The essential difference between perception and other modes of cognition is that perception provides the *data* for the inferences by which we construct our theories of the world; perception is our only source of underived, contingent premises for such inferences.[17] If it isn't a truth of logic, and if it doesn't somehow follow from what you already know, then either perception tells you about it or you don't find out. If this be Empiricism, make the most of it.

So much for epistemological truisms. Now let's put this all together. We've got so far that the data for our empirical hypotheses – the underived contingent premises of our nondemonstrative inferences – are mostly information about the layout of spatio-temporally local distal stimuli; and these data are supplied largely or entirely by perception. And it is a constraint on rational belief fixation that the hypotheses that we select should be as compatible with these data as may be consonant with a simultaneous and independent requirement to maximize conservatism. The following design question thus arises: According to what architecture should one construct a primate nervous system – considered, now, as a machine for drawing sound nondemonstrative inferences – if one is concerned that empirical hypotheses should be simultaneously and independently constrained by observational adequacy and conservatism? There are, no doubt, lots of possible answers to this question; you will remember that I complained in the opening paragraph that teleological arguments have the form of affirmations of the consequent. Still, for what it's worth, *one* sort of architectural scheme that would work would be to modularize perception.

Roughly, the idea would be to make two estimates of levels of empirical confirmation in the course of hypothesis selection: First, decide which hypothesis you would accept given just the current evidence about the layout of local distal objects; then decide what hypothesis you would accept given this evidence plus solicitude for cognitive commitments previously undertaken. This procedure would have the desirable consequence of insuring that both observational adequacy and conservatism have their voices heard in the course of belief fixation. Such a two-step approach to hypothesis selection would be supported by an architecture in which perceptual estimates of the local proximal layout are encapsulated, since encapsulated perception *just is* perception that's minimally varnished by conservatism. Conversely, the more cognitively penetrated perception is, the less it honors the injunction that rational confirmation should reconcile estimates of observational adequacy and conservatism that are *independently* arrived at.

So there's a teleological argument for modularity from plausible epistemological premises, for whatever teleological arguments may be worth. It bears emphasizing that this argument might hold even if the cost-accounting arguments don't. If the function of perception is its role in the fixation of true beliefs, then we would have epistemological reasons for wanting perception to be encapsulated *even if encapsulated perception is slow and expensive*.

Summary and conclusion

In psychology – especially under the Bruner/New Look influence – teleological arguments about the design of perceptual mechanisms have generally assumed that the function of perception is to guide behavior. We have seen that such arguments are largely equivocal: Whether penetrated or encapsulated systems would guide behavior most efficiently depends on empirical estimates that nobody knows how to make.

But why should we prefer the reflexological idea that the function of perception is to modulate action to the decision-theoretic idea that the function of perception is the fixation of belief? One needs, at this point, to resist the siren song of pop-Darwinism. No doubt the cognitive architectures that survive are the ones that belong to the organisms that contrive to generate ecologically valid behaviors. No doubt the computational structure of our perceptual mechanism was shaped by selection processes that favor behavioral adaptivity. It would be perfectly natural to infer that the function which perceptual systems are designed to perform – the function which perceptual systems are selected for – is therefore the production of this self-same adaptive behavior. Perfectly natural, but utterly misled.

The inference involves a sort of distributive fallacy. To see just how utterly misled it is, consider: 'Selection pressures favor reproductive success; the design of the heart was shaped by selection pressures; so the function of the heart is to mediate reproductive successes.' Parallel arguments would show that the function of all organs is to mediate reproductive success; hence all organs have the same function.

Poppycock! The function of the heart – *the function that its design reflects* – is to circulate the blood. There is no paradox in this, and nothing to affront Darwinian scruples. Animals that have good hearts are selected for their reproductive success as compared to animals that have less good hearts or no hearts at all. But their reproductive success is produced by a division of biological labor among their organs, and it's the function of the *heart relative to this division of labor* – namely, its function *as a pump* – that teleologically determines its design.

Analogously in the present case. It's entirely possible that the kind of mental architecture that maximizes behavioral adaptivity is one that institutes a computational division of labor: A perceptual mechanism that is specialized to report on how the world is provides input to a decision mechanism that is specialized to figure out how to get what you want in a world that is that way. If this is indeed the means that nature uses to maximize the ecological validity of the behavior of higher primates, then the function that determines the design of perceptual mechanisms is their role in finding out how the world is. Specifically, what determines their design is their function in providing contingent premises for nondemonstrative inferences to true empirical conclusions.

Compare (and contrast) some recent comments by Patricia Churchland (1987): 'There is a fatal tendency to think of the brain as essentially in the fact-finding business. . . . Looked at from an evolutionary point of view, the principle function of nervous systems is to enable the organism to move appropriately . . . The principle chore of nervous systems is to get the body parts where they should be in order that the organism may survive. . . . Truth, whatever that is, definitely takes the hindmost' (pp. 548–9). It looks as though Churchland is arguing: 'Organisms get selected for getting their bodies to be where they should; only nervous systems that belong to organisms that get selected survive; so the function of nervous systems – the function in virtue of which the design of nervous systems is teleologically intelligible – is to get the bodies of organisms to where they should be.' But as we've just been seeing, that is a distributive fallacy, hence not a good way to argue.

Alternatively, it may be that Churchland is committing a version of the genetic fallacy against which Gould and Lewontin have recently warned us: '[There are cases where one finds] adaptation and selection, but the adaptation is a secondary utilization of parts present for reasons of architecture, development, or history. . . . If blushing turns out to be an adaptation affected by sexual selection in humans, it will not help us to understand why blood is red. The immediate utility of an organic structure often says nothing at all about the [original] reason for its being' (1979, p. 159). If this is true, it follows that the *current* function of an organ cannot be securely inferred from the function in virtue of which its possession initially bestowed selectional advantage. Apparently, the original use of feathered wings was not flight but thermal insulation. Correspondingly, it may be that the original use of nervous systems was the integration of movements. Nothing would follow about what they are used for *now*.

It is, in short, unclear just what about the evolutionary point of view rules out the hypothesis that the way that nervous systems effect the ecologically appropriate disposition of the body parts of (anyhow, higher) organisms is by mediating the fixation of largely true beliefs and the integration of largely rational actions. *Thinking* – specifically, thinking *true thoughts* – is arguably the best way to achieve adaptivity that evolution has thus far devised.

On this story, the biological demands on perception are exactly analogous to the epistemological demands on scientific observation: In both cases, what's wanted is procedures that yield accurate data about local distal layouts. Correspondingly, the demands that cognition places on perception favor encapsulation for the same reason that rational scientific practice favors unbiased observation. In both cases, the goal of the exercise is to draw good inductive inferences; and good inductive inferences require independent estimates of conservatism and observational adequacy. The bottom line is that – unlike the teleological arguments from cost-accounting – teleological arguments from epistemology are reasonably univocal on the question of modularity. They suggest that perception ought to be encapsulated.

On the other hand, how many things have *you* heard of recently that are the way they ought to be?

Notes

1 For a recent attempt to understand cognition in terms of its phylogenetic connections to sensori-motor reflexes, see Llinas, 1987.

2 I assume that it's a psychological law that, all else being equal, organisms that believe $P \rightarrow Q$ and P believe Q. The '*ceteris paribus*' clause constrains both the character of the beliefs (e.g. their complexity) and the values of 'performance' variables (e.g. motivation, attention, available memory, etc.).

3 I don't want to argue the very complicated question whether the states of sensory mechanisms should count as representing – as well as merely registering – their proximal causes (in the way that perceptual states surely do count as representing their *distal* causes). I don't for the life of me see why they shouldn't; and, given a good theory of representation, it may turn out that the options are forced. For example, theories that construe representation in terms of causal covariance would surely imply that states of the retina represent the properties of incident light by which they are lawfully determined; that states of the tympanic membrane represent the spectrographic properties of acoustic proximal stimuli, etc. (See, e.g., Dretske, 1981; Fodor, 1987; Stampe, 1977.) But the issues about modularity are presumably independent of the issues about representation, so I propose to beg the latter in what follows.

4 What I'm calling the poverty of the stimulus argument isn't the one that Chomsky uses that term for, though the two arguments are structurally similar. Chomsky's poverty of the stimulus argument infers the top-downness of language learning from its underdetermination by data (specifically from the underdetermination of the child's grammar by his corpus); analogously, the present argument infers the top-downness of perception from its underdetermination by sensation. Both sorts of underdetermination raise the question where the added information comes from. In the perceptual case, the obvious candidate is the perceiver's cognitive background; in the learning case, the obvious candidate is the child's innate cognitive commitments. So Chomsky argues from underdetermination to innateness; he doesn't, however, offer underdetermination as an argument that learning is a species of inference. He just takes that for granted.

5 Or objects *parts of which* are at some spatial remove from the organism. I touch part of its surface and thereby acquire the belief that there's a table in the landscape.

6 This is different from saying that, in such cases, the thought that if A then B must mediate the causal relation between the thought that A and the thought that B. Any such requirement would lead to the well-known Lewis Carroll regress.

7 Since the inference is nondemonstrative, there is no promise that the canonical description of the speaker's communicative intention that it delivers will actually be *true* of him. It's another question whether you're guaranteed that it will be true of him *if he is obeying the linguistic conventions*. The answer to this question depends, of course, on what linguistic conventions are. I'm inclined to think that they are something like pairings of acoustic types with mental state types; they specify the acoustic properties of the noise you should make if and only if you intend to communicate the belief that P. If that's right, then the inference from the acoustical properties of the utterance to the intentional state of the speaker *is* apodictic (up to ambiguity, of course) when he observes the conventions.

8 For example, the elementary operations can often be larger in a dedicated processor than in a general-purpose one, thereby eliminating redundant computations. Since you always wear socks two at a time, it makes sense to buy and sell them in pairs. (Compare mix and match.)

9   Chomsky (1986, p. 14) denies the algorithmic character of speech perception on the grounds that there are 'garden-path' sentences which speakers regularly misparse; 'the horse raced past the barn fell' is the classic example. I doubt, however, that such cases show the nonmechanical character of speech perception. Rather, they suggest that the class of structures that perceptual algorithms recover fails (slightly) to correspond to the class of well-formed sentences; there is a degree of mismatch between what they can parse and what the grammar of the language generates. Phenomenological (to say nothing of chronometric) considerations make it plausible that, when he encounters a garden-path sentence, the hearer goes over into a problem-solving mode of processing that is quite different from the usual smooth functioning of perceptual parsing.

10   I suppose this corresponds, roughly, to the distinction between the 'declarative' and the 'procedural' stage in problem solving (see Anderson, 1983, chap. 6); or, in a slightly older idiom, to the difference between formulating a plan and executing it (see Miller, Galanter, and Pribram, 1960). I'm not, however, convinced that the psychological theorizing in this area has gotten much beyond Granny's common-sense intuitions. Until it does, I propose to continue to talk in Granny's terms.

11   In these respects speech perception resembles other overlearned and routinized cognitive skills. For example, in solving physics problems, 'novices use painful means–end analyses, working with equations they hope are relevant to the problem. In contrast, experts apply correct equations in a forward direction indicating that they have planned the whole solution before they begin. . . . The schemata in terms of which experts organize their knowledge . . . enable them to grasp the structure of problems in a way that novices cannot' (Carey, 1985, p. 3, summarizing Larkin, 1983). This is not, however, to say that the mechanical character of speech perception is plausibly an effect of overlearning. So far as anybody knows, the ontogenesis of speech perception exhibits nothing comparable to the 'novice/expert' shift. In the exercise of their linguistic competences, children are never novices; all normal children behave like expert users of the characteristic dialect of their developmental stage. Thus, a 4-year-old's prattling is nothing like a neophyte's hesitant grappling with a hard computational task. Analogous observations would appear to hold for the ontogenesis of other perceptual capacities like, for example, the visual detection of three-dimensional depth.

12   In fact, even in the linguistic case it's only roughly true that the connection between the psychophysical properties of utterances and the intentional properties of their mental causes is conventional. Part of the perceptual problem in decoding speech is to infer the speaker's phonetic intentions from a representation of the spectrographic structure of his utterance. Such inferences are reliable because phonetic intentions have regular acoustic consequences. But the regularity that connects phonetic intentions to types of sounds is not a convention but a law. The speaker realizes such intentions by activating his vocal tract, and the acoustic consequences of his doing so are determined by the physical structure of that organ.

13   More exactly, I argued that perception should exploit only such background as dedicated mechanisms require for algorithmic computations of very general properties of proximal–distal relations; see the preceding discussion.

14   At one point, Bruner remarks that 'the most appropriate pattern of readiness at any given moment would be that one which would lead, on the average, to the most veridical guess about the nature of the world around one at the moment . . . And it follows from this that the most ready perceiver would then have the best chances of

estimating situations most adequately and planning accordingly. It is in this general sense that the ready perceiver who can proceed with fairly minimal inputs is also in a position to use his cognitive readiness not only for perceiving what is before him but in foreseeing what is likely to be before him' (1957, p. 15). But having the most veridical guess *on average* doesn't, in fact, entail 'having the best chances of estimating situations most adequately and planning accordingly' unless you're indifferent about how your right and wrong guesses are distributed. Most people would be prepared to trade lots of wrong guesses about the weather for just a few right ones about the stock market.

15   Notice how much accuracy is what we want even if accuracy costs a lot of money; notice how much we are often prepared to pay for sensitive instruments of scientific observation.

16   That a certain degree of theoretical bias is unavoidable in observational instruments is perhaps a moral of Duhemian philosophy of science (just as it is perhaps a moral of Kantian philosophy of mind that a certain amount of theoretical bias is unavoidable in perception). But an *a priori* argument that there *must* be penetration is quite a different thing from a teleological argument that there *ought* to be. And, of course, it's compatible with both Duhem and Kant that observation, though inevitably biased in some respects, should be neutral with respect to indefinitely many hypotheses that scientists investigate.

17   Unless, of course, there are contingent beliefs that we have innately.

References

Anderson, J. 1983: *The Architecture of Cognition*. Harvard University Press.

Bruner, J. 1957: On perceptual readiness. *Psychological Review*, 65, 14–21. Repr. in Anglin, J. (ed.) *Beyond The Information Given*, 1973. W.W. Norton Co.

Carey, S. 1985: *Conceptual Change in Childhood*. MIT Press.

Chomsky, N. 1986: *Knowledge of Language: Its Nature, Origin and Use*. Praeger.

Churchland, Patricia 1987: Epistemology in the age of neuroscience. *Journal of Philosophy*, 84 (10), 544–55.

Churchland, Paul forthcoming: Perceptual plasticity and theoretical neutrality. *Philosophy of Science*.

Dretske, F. 1981: *Knowledge and The Flow of Information*. MIT Press.

Fodor, J. 1983: *The Modularity of Mind*. MIT Press.

1987: *Psychosemantics*. MIT Press.

Fodor, J., Bever, T. and Garrett, M. 1974: *The Psychology of Language*. McGraw–Hill.

Gould, S. and Lewontin, R. 1979: The spandrels of San Marco and the Panglossian paradigm: a critique of the adaptationist programme. *Proceedings of The Royal Society of London*, B 205, 581–98.

Larkin, J. 1983: The role of problem representation in physics. In D. Gentner and A. Stevens (eds), *Mental Models*. Lawrence Erlbaum.

Llinas, R. 1987: 'Mindedness' as a functional state of the brain. In C. Blakemore (ed.), *Mindwaves*. Blackwell.

Marslen-Wilson, W. and Tyler, L. 1987: Against modularity. In J.L. Garfield (ed.), *Modularity in Knowledge Representation and Natural Language Understanding*. MIT Press.

Miller, G., Galanter, E. and Pribram, K. 1960: *Plans and The Structure of Behavior*. Holt, Rinehart and Winston.

Pylyshyn, Z. 1984: *Computation and Cognition*. MIT Press.

Stampe, D. 1977: Towards a causal theory of linguistic representation. In P. French, T. Euhling and H. Wettstein. (eds), *Midwest Studies in Philosophy*, vol. 2. University of Minneapolis Press.

2

Meaning and the Mental: the Problem of Semantics after Chomsky

Norbert Hornstein

One of the foci of work in twentieth-century philosophy has been the theory of meaning. Starting with Frege and Russell, modern analytic philosophy has been preoccupied with the problem of characterizing the nature of linguistic meaning. The work initially concentrated on rendering explicit the syntax and semantics of mathematical language. However, it was not long before the insight and technical knowledge gained in pursuing this specialized task was extended to the study of language as such. The *Tractatus*, the work of the Positivists, the writings of Quine and Austin and the later Wittgenstein, constitute a sustained body of work aimed at elucidating the complexities of the phenomena associated with meaning. In this paper, I will argue that the work on 'logical form' which is currently being done by generative grammarians constitutes an important contribution to these more traditional concerns. However, in my opinion, this work does much more than this. When seen against the background of the larger linguistic enterprise as elucidated in Chomsky's work, this body of research significantly recasts the older issues and brings into sharper focus the many concerns that have been lumped together under the study of meaning. This work can be seen as both accommodating the later Wittgenstein's critique of semantical approaches to meaning while at the same time retaining many of the theoretical intuitions of the work that he criticized. In fact, I will argue that Chomsky's great *philosophical* contribution to meaning theory has been to elaborate a framework of assumptions that would allow syntactic devices to substitute for the obscure semantic apparatus that the later Wittgenstein justly criticized. This syntactic shift provides the means for rendering the later Wittgenstein his due without succumbing to the anti-theoretical nihilism that his writings often engender.

The chapter will be organized as follows. In the first section I will outline the basic framework of a Chomskyan approach to language. In the next two sections I will contrast this approach with semantical approaches and pragmatic approaches to the study of meaning in natural language. This contrast will hopefully make clear why it is that Chomsky's syntactic approach has been able to evade the epistemological problems which have beset theories which have relied on semantic and pragmatic theoretical devices in investigating such issues. Section four will be a brief conclusion.

1 The object of linguistic research

The Chomskyan research program rests on the observation that several salient facts are characteristic of natural languages (NL) and speakers of natural languages and that these facts can be used to significantly constrain the set of 'reasonable' grammatical theories.

First, NLs are unboundedly large. This means that the number of sentences that native speakers can use and understand is for all practical purposes infinite.

Second, people attain linguistic competence of the language community in which they grow up. Thus, Americans in Iowa learn to speak a brand of American English with distinctive Mid-West characteristics. Those from Georgia acquire a Southern dialect and persons growing up in countries like Spain learn Spanish. This seems true regardless of parentage or any other genetic factors. Barring pathological cases, any child can learn any NL if brought up in the right linguistic environment.

Third, the course of acquisition takes place under less than optimal inductive conditions considering the competence actually attained. There are four sorts of difficulties with the input. First of all, it is somewhat degenerate. This means the linguistic input available to the child in the course of language acquisition is not perfect. It includes slurred speech, slips of the tongue, exaggerated accentuation, cooing noises, half thoughts, nonsense syllables, and more. This does not mean that *all* of the input is BAD. Of course it isn't. However, a significant percentage of the linguistic input available to the child is less than perfect. This fact requires the child to sift through the good and bad data and attend only to the well-formed material. Otherwise the child may be badly misled in acquiring the grammar of its language.

Second, the input the child is able to 'intake' is limited. It is not the case that all of the possibly relevant linguistic data that the child is exposed to is usable by the child in the course of language acquisition. The reason is that the child cannot absorb linguistic constructions that are too complex. Memory limitations and other cognitive constraints may make it difficult for the child to take in any more than a small part of linguistic data it is exposed to and use it in acquiring the grammar of its native language.

A third feature of the linguistic data is that they are finite. However, as we saw, the acquired capacity extends to an unbounded number of sentences. Thus, on the basis of exposure to finite data the child becomes adept at dealing with an unbounded number of sentences.

Last of all, and most importantly, many of the features of the child's mature capacity are simply *unattested* in the data that the child is exposed to. For example, there are many principles of grammar that linguists have argued characterize complex multi-clausal constructions. If not obeyed, they result in ill-formed linguistic structures. However, evidence for the existence of these well-formedness conditions is absent from the data that it is reasonable to suppose that the child uses in acquiring its NL. The reason is that the relevant evidence is only manifest in sentence types too complex to be generally used.

Furthermore, even if used, the child's capacities to intake the relevant structures are too limited, plus the relevant data will not be deliberately uttered by parents because they consist of ungrammatical sentences. People do not use such sentences to communicate, precisely because of their complexity and unacceptability. This means that a child will have no access to the relevant data, as adults will not utter the relevant sentences due to their infelicity. As 'negative' data, data that a certain linguistic structure is ill-formed, are often crucial evidence for the nature of these complex constraints and because 'negative' data are not, by hypothesis, presented in the normal course of linguistic behavior to children, it is reasonable to conclude, that for a large range of cases, linguistic data of the relevant type will be simply unavailable to the child. It is this last basic feature of the acquisition process that dooms any simple inductive account of language learning.

The last major feature of NLs that Chomsky observed is that NLs are acquired regularly and easily by virtually all humans regardless of intelligence, motivation, or even desire. This contrasts with virtually every other known biological entity. Birds may fly and fish may swim, but humans alone talk.

These characteristics of NLs do tightly constrain the sorts of theories that will be adequate linguistic theories. The fact that sentences are essentially unbounded in number together with the fact that speakers master this unbounded set indicate that what people learn is a grammar: a set of rules that can be repeatedly applied to 'generate' more and more complex structures. The fact that the data the child has access to are deficient in certain important respects indicates that language acquisition is aided by innate constructs that supply the information absent from the data. These innate structures also mitigate the effects of degeneracy as they release the child from a tight dependency on the environmental input. The fact that any child can learn any language 'like a native' indicates that whatever these innate structures are, they must not be so specific as to facilitate the acquisition of English at the expense of making Swahili unlearnable. The virtual 'reflex' character of NL learning seems to indicate a special linguistic capacity, a linguistic faculty whose function is to facilitate linguistic performance insofar as it is specifically linguistic.

These broad factual features of NL indicate that adequate theories of NL will most likely involve the postulation of a language faculty, richly endowed with innate structure which constrains the form of possible grammars of NLs but which is flexible enough to be applicable to any NL. The Chomskyan perspective might be summed up in the following five commitments:

(1) a belief in the existence of a modular language faculty richly endowed with innate constraints delimiting the range of NL grammars;

(2) a belief that human linguistic capacities are explicable in part by reference to the structure of linguistic representations, that is, the structures that the grammar of the relevant NL generates;

(3) a belief that the central aim of a theory of grammar is to explicate the fine structure of human linguistic capacities insofar as these capacities are specifically linguistic;

(4) a belief in the poverty of the stimulus as the key aspect of language acquisition;

(5) a belief that linguistics is a subpart of theoretical psychology.

These five points will be explored below in trying to explain why Chomsky's syntactic view of logical form is so philosophically important and why and how it is able to circumvent the problems that are characteristic of non-syntactic approaches to interpretation in NL.

2　The central problem

From a Chomskyan point of view, there are several key factors that undergird theorizing in linguistics. The most important one for our purposes is the assumption that a native speaker's judgments about the relative acceptability of a sentence of his language can ultimately be traced back to some structural features of that sentence; at least in a significant number of cases. To help focus discussion, let's take a concrete example or two:

(6) a.　John believes himself to be a fool
　　 b.　*John believes himself is a fool
　　 c.　John was believed to be a fool
　　 d.　*John was believed was a fool

What accounts for the unacceptability of (6b,d)?[1] They are taken to be unacceptable because they violate certain conditions on well-formedness that the language faculty places on grammatical representations of sentences, that is, phrase markers. These phrase markers are taken to underlie (6b,d) and therefore these sentences are judged unacceptable. The sentences in (6) have the structures in (7):

(7) a.　[$_S$ John $_i$ believes [$_S$ himself$_i$ to be a fool]]
　　 b.　[$_S$ John $_i$ believes [$_S$ himself$_i$ AGR/Pres be a fool]]
　　 c.　[$_S$ John $_i$ was believed [$_S$ t_i to be a fool]]
　　 d.　[$_S$ John $_i$ was believed [$_S$ t_i AGR/Past be a fool]]

In (7b), 'himself', an anaphor, must be bound in its domain so as to meet the requirements of the Binding Theory. Binding principles require elements that fall within its purview to meet certain structural requirements. For purposes of this example, the relevant principle is principle A:

(A) An anaphor must be bound within its domain.

The domain for 'himself' is the embedded clause. The AGR marker acts to make the embedded clause the relevant domain for 'himself'. Within this clause it has no binder and therefore the sentence violates principle A of the binding theory.[2] As compliance with principle A is a condition on the well-formedness of phrase markers, this binding violation in (7b) renders the phrase marker ill-formed. Consequently, we predict that the sentence (6b), which has (7b) as a phrase marker, will be judged unacceptable by a native speaker of English within whose grammar 'himself' is catalogued as an anaphor.

A similar story underlies the unacceptability of (7d), with the exception that in this case 't_i' not 'himself', is the element that must be bound. Unlike 'himself' NP-t, the residue of NP movement, is presumably catalogued by native speakers as an anaphor universally. It is part of the structure of the language faculty that the empty categories left behind by NP movement are anaphors and fall under principle A of the binding theory. If so, then in (7d), 't_i' must be bound in the embedded S. As it has no binder in this domain, the sentence is judged to be unacceptable.

(7a,c) contrast with (7b,d) in that their domain is the matrix clause rather than the embedded one. They have the matrix clause as their domain due to the absence of AGR in the embedded S; this is a feature traceable to the fact that in (6a,c) the embedded verb is not finite. In the matrix, 'himself' and 't_i' have a binder, namely, 'John$_i$', and so the phrase markers are deemed to be well-formed. Their corresponding sentences are predicted to be judged acceptable.

Observe, futhermore, that the representations (7a,c) that underlie the acceptable sentences (6a,c) also provide cues for how the sentences are interpreted. In (6a), 'John' is taken to be the antecedent of 'himself', while in (6c), 'John' is interpreted as having the logical object role, despite its position in logical subject position. There is, in other words, a systematic interpretive connection between the subject position and the coindexed position of the anaphor or the NP-trace. As indicated, just what this interpretive dependency comes to is not only a function of the indicated indexing, but of the items involved as well. The 'John$_i$' ... 't_i' relation is quite different from the 'John$_i$' ... 'himself$_i$' relationship despite the fact that both cases fall under principle A of the binding theory.

Is there a unitary *interpretation* for indexing provided by the theory of grammar? Not one more specific than saying that some elements are interpretively dependent on others. What the grammar represents is what is dependent on what, *not* what the nature of this dependency is. The empirical facts seem to be that which interpretive relationship that dependence instantiates is highly sensitive to the nature of the relata that are formally related. In short, full interpretation is not only a matter of structure or grammar, but a matter of lexical content of the relata as well.

None of this should be surprising, nor is it very difficult to formulate fuller principles of interpretation in *specific* cases. Thus, in (6a), the interpretive dependence marked by the syntactic binding is coreference. In (6c), the relationship is one of 'theta' role transmission, that is, the logical role of the NP-trace object is transmitted to its binder. Other dependencies also occur. Thus binding obtains between NPs and reciprocals, quantifiers and variables, quantifiers and pronouns, etc. These do not encode a unitary interpretive relationship despite the syntactic similarities. However, in each case the nature of the dependency is a function of the form of the relationship and the relata involved.

These are the familiar characteristics of linguistic explanations. However, it is worth spelling out the fine points a bit more so that we can see in somewhat more detail than is customary how it is that the theoretical apparatus that drives the explanations we typically offer in linguistics maps onto the kinds of capacities that we are tacitly ascribing to native speakers. After all, to explain the fact that native speakers judge sentences such as (6a,c) better than (7b,d), we are tacitly ascribing to such native speakers the wherewithal to make such judgments. So too with the capacity to interpret the syntactic object as the logical object in (6c) or as coreferential with the anaphor in (6a). A successful linguistic explanation adumbrates the· fine structure of a native speaker's linguistic competence. What is important for our purposes is not the details of the competence theory but the view that ultimately underlying any bit of linguistic theorizing is a bit of psychological description. In effect, any linguistic description tacitly ascribes certain capacities to native speakers. These capacities are what underlies their performance in linguistic tasks we ask of them, for example, the judgments that ·we ask them to make. Consequently, the descriptions and principles offered in our linguistic accounts must have some sort of 'reasonable' or 'natural' psychological interpretation. In particular, the powers and capacities we ascribe to native speakers must meet two conditions: (i) they must be capable of explaining their performance and (ii) they must not be as much in need of explanation as what they are intended to explain. When both these desiderata on linguistic explanations are explicitly brought to mind, the inherent virtues of Chomsky's syntactic approach to issues of linguistic interpretation become most apparent.

In the cases above, the story we would tell to meet these background requirements is straightforward. Part of being a native speaker of English consists in being able to assign sentences such as (6) their corresponding structures in (7). It is a property of the language faculty universally that anaphors must meet certain binding requirements. These are not met in (7b,d), so the structures are rejected as being ill-formed. In short, the language faculty requires that phrase markers be a certain shape to be well-formed and these structures fail to meet these requirements.

Observe that for such a story to run we need not ascribe very exotic capacities to native speakers. In fact, all we must presume is that humans have a language faculty in the same sense that they have a visual faculty. This faculty is taken to impose certain conditions of structural well-formedness on sentences. Native speakers, we postulate, are able to translate strings of sounds into phrase markers such as those in (7). And last, native speakers check to see if these phrase markers have the right sorts of 'shapes', that is, conform to certain specified conditions on well-formedness.

We also attribute to native speakers the ability to relate lexical items to one another. However, the full interpretation that obtains here outpaces the resources of the grammatical capacity. It involves lexical semantics as well. This latter capacity is not well-understood in the general case. For a variety of lexical items, such as anaphors, NP-traces, pronouns, etc., the rules can be stated in a relatively perspicuous way. However, there is, as yet, no general theory of lexical meaning, nor any very good general theory of linguistic content. What is important (and surprising) is that one is not really needed to account for many linguistic capacities characteristic of native speakers.[3]

What is important is that the capacities that we ascribe above to native speakers to make this sort of explanation run do not appear to be very exotic or opaque. Actually, we have little reason to doubt that everything that we are asking of our ideal speaker/hearer we could just as well program a computer to do. In fact, if we were asked to explain why a KAYPRO could not read an IBM PC file, we would give essentially the same sort of explanation. The KAYPRO with a CPM operating system cannot read strings coded in the MS-DOS format. Thus it 'rejects' these strings as ill-formed. Our account relies on little more than the capacity to parse a string and check it against a list of well-formedness requirements.

One of the things that makes explanations such as these satisfying is that these explanations break down complex linguistic capacities into far less complex and epistemologically transparent subcapacities that it is reasonable to suppose humans could have. The subcapacities in cases such as these are neither recondite nor surprising. In fact, the subcapacities are 'dumb' in the sense that Dennett (1978) has observed is required from a successful psychological explanation.

This 'analysis' of the complex capacity is due to a related feature of these forms of explanation. They tie complex linguistic behavior to *locally surveyable* properties of the sentence. What I mean by this is that all the information required to perform the linguistic task demanded of the informant is present within the sentence and made syntactically explicit in the representation of the sentence. Because this is possible, we need not impute extraordinary powers to native speakers to perform as asked. Once the form of the representation is made explicit and the conditions on well-formedness are clearly articulated, it is transparent that checking a sentence's well-formedness can be done quite mechanically.

This is in sharp contrast with many other types of problems where the information required to perform the task is not locally surveyable. However, philosophers are well acquainted with many examples from the study induction in which forms of non-monotonic reasoning play such an important role. In AI, the same problem appears as the 'frame' problem. As we shall see below, a similar, if not identical, set of difficulties besets semantic and pragmatic theories of interpretation.

I have just argued that a key virtue of standard accounts of linguistic competence is that they key linguistic capacity to local features of linguistic representations. In other words, they key specific psychological capacities to the capacity to check the syntactic properties of a finite representation. Chomsky's conception of NL interpretation as tied to representations in 'logical form' extends these sorts of syntactic conditions to less traditional terrains. In conjunction with the general requirements that he has argued linguistic theories must meet, and that we surveyed above, logical forms allow the emergence of largely syntactic explanations of many kinds of interpretive phenomena.

An example will help us see the intended point. Consider the properties of epithets in English. It seems that such expressions are pronominal in certain important respects. Like pronouns, they can be interpreted as anaphoric with another expression:

(8) John$_i$ met Ronny$_j$ before he$_i$ punched the SOB$_j$

They share other interesting similarities with pronouns. They can act as bound variables in many of the places that one can find bound pronouns and they obey the Leftness Condition which prohibits a pronoun from being bound by a quantifier to its left:

(9) a.   John met every senator$_i$ before Frank criticized him$_i$/the SOB$_i$
     b.   *The woman who knows no senator$_i$ kicked him$_i$/the SOB$_i$
     c.   *The SOB's$_i$/his$_i$ father hates every hood$_i$

However, these sorts of pronominal expressions are far more restricted than those of regular pronouns.

(10) a.   Ronny$_i$ believes that he$_i$/* the SOB$_i$ is a fool
      b.   John persuaded every senator$_i$ that he$_i$/* the SOB$_i$ was a fool

In the sentences in (10), one can find pronouns where epithets are not possible. Why not? The reason is that epithets have the form of definite descriptions. They have the shape 'the N'. Definite descriptions, unlike pronouns, fall under principle (C) of the Binding Theory. This principle forbids elements that fall under it to be 'bound' by an antecedent. In other words, it forbids an epithet from being coindexed to a Noun Phrase in an argument position that C-commands it. In (10), the epithet is in just this configuration and therefore it cannot appear in the indicated positions. Pronouns do not fall under principle (C) and so they are not similarly restricted.

(11) a.   [Ronny$_i$ believes [$_S$ that [he$_i$/the SOB$_i$ is a fool]]]
      b.   [Every senator$_i$ [John persuaded t_i [$_S$ that [he$_i$/the SOB$_i$ was a fool]]]]

Examples such as these are of particular interest for they clearly show that the syntax of expressions is crucial to determining their interpretive properties. As the sentences in (8) and (9) indicate, functionally, definite descriptions behave just like pronouns. What the sentences in (10) show is that the ability of definite descriptions to so function is limited by their shape. Pronominal expressions like epithets that have shapes which make them liable to principle (C) are restricted in their distribution. This is true regardless of their semantic functions.[4]

I hope that these sorts of examples clarify how it is that the syntax of logical form can play a significant role in explaining the interpretive features of sentences. I stress 'syntax' for, as we have seen in the case of epithets, in purely functional terms epithets can function just like pronouns. They enter into conditions of anaphora and they can be bound by quantified expressions. Their syntactic requirements explain their limited distribution. Moreover, it is the basic syntactic nature of the explanations which allows us to provide the reasonably straightforward accounts of native speakers' capacities that a reasonable theory of competence requires of linguistic explanations.

There are two virtues to syntactic explanations. First, it is relatively clear what it is to have one. Second, it is relatively clear what it is to employ one. For syntactic accounts, the machine analogy serves us well. The predicate 'being of shape X' is an easily verified property of a string. As we shall see below, this is not true of purely semantic predicates such as 'refers to X' or pragmatic properties such as 'is appropriate in X'. For these latter two predicates later Wittgensteinian considerations arouse more than a little skepticism concerning their true value.

I stress these points because it will be important to contrast these standard sorts of syntactic cases with what we get when we examine indexical theories of interpretation of the sort that we find in certain current semantic-cum-pragmatic theories. The syntactic turn allows us to tie general competence to local features of the phrase marker. Semantic and pragmatic theories, theories that exploit non-syntactic features of language, are not able to provide similar accounts in general. It is a consequence of this, that in these cases, in stark contrast to the one above, the capacities that such theories tacitly impute to the native speaker, that is, the ones needed to make their stories run, are every bit as puzzling as the capacity that we wished to have explained in the first place. Or so I will argue.

3   Indexicality and efficiency

Barwise and Perry (1983) point out that one of the most remarkable features of natural languages is their property of 'efficiency'. 'Efficiency' refers to the fact that 'expressions, whether simple or complex, can be recycled, can be used over and over again in different ways, places and times by different people, *to say different things*' (p. 32). Efficiency is the property that gives force to pragmatic concerns. Consider a simple sentence with indexicals such as (12):

(12) I saw Cal Ripken

(12) can be used to make very different statements. It can be used to convey the information that I, Norbert Hornstein, saw the shortstop for the Baltimore Orioles. Or if said by Peter Murrell it would convey the information that he, Peter Murrell, saw Cal Ripken. This, of course, is not all. As we all know 'Cal Ripken' is not an unambiguous referring expression. It might designate the shortstop for the Orioles or (12) might be saying that I saw the former manager of the Baltimore Orioles. In the first case, I was referring to Cal Ripken Jr, while in the second case it was Cal Ripken Sr. More exotically, perhaps, (12) can be used to convey the information that I think that, contrary to rumours, it is doubtful that Cal Ripken has been traded, or that I believe he was starting the game, or that he was not injured by his last diving catch. All of this is commonplace and I leave it to your imaginations to concoct ever more complicated messages that uttering (12) might send.

How is this linguistic flexibility effected? A most important vehicle of efficiency is the overt indexical expressions present in all natural language. In (8), 'I' refers to the utterer of the sentence (12). In our discussion it referred to either Norbert Hornstein or Peter Murrell depending on who was doing the talking. Other indexicals include the words 'here', 'now', 'tomorrow', 'you', tenses in general, and perhaps even modals of various sorts, though this last case is far less clear, in my opinion.

However, as even the brief discussion above already makes clear, these overt indexical expressions will not suffice to explain how sentences might be dependent on context for the messages that they convey. Overt lexical indexicals do not exhaust the ways that context can be brought to bear on interpretation. Aside from standard indices such as time, place, and person, all of which are salient features of the discourse situation, Barwise and Perry (1983) suggest that a further group of less prominent types of indexicality obtains. Following Tyler Burge, they point out that names are somewhat indexical. Who a speaker associates a name with at a given time is itself a feature of the context broadly construed. As we noted above, 'Cal Ripken' can be used to refer to father or son depending on who is doing the uttering, when, where, and for what purpose. Who the speaker 'connects' the name with is important in determining an utterance's interpretation.

A further feature of linguistic efficiency results from our capacity to exploit 'resource situations'. Consider an example discussed by Barwise and Perry:

> If we wanted to describe Jackie's biting Molly, but did not know Jackie's name we might say something like 'The dog that just ran past the window is biting Molly'. (1983, p. 36)

In this sort of case, Jackie's running past the window is used to refer to Jackie without naming her. Or, as Barwise and Perry might put it, Jackie's running past the window is a *resource* situation which a person in the discourse situation could exploit to refer to Jackie.

It is important to see how open-ended the potential resource situations are which can be used to interpret an utterance. Potentially relevant information includes what is perceived, known, believed by those in the discourse situation, what is pretended to obtain, what one hopes might obtain, and what one even incorrectly believes obtains. In a word, anything at all that might act as background information is a potential resource situation relevant to the interpretation of an utterance.

Barwise and Perry are obviously correct in this. As the most cursory reflection indicates, the background information and assumptions that suffuse a discourse setting can exercise substantial influence on how utterances are interpreted. After all, (8) uttered in the appropriate circumstances can be taken to signal many widely different things, as we saw above.

However, the introduction of resource situations and speakers' connections as possible indices should *not* be seen as an innocent extension of the traditional indexical apparatus. There is a qualitative difference between noting that words like 'I' and 'now' are interpreted relative to the discourse context and the observation that speakers' connections and resource situations are also context-sensitive devices important to determining the interpretation of an utterance. In fact, Barwise and Perry's robust use of these expanded indexical mechanisms should be very troubling to those linguists who adhere to the credo embodied in (1–5) above (pp. 25–6). The reason is that once one exploits general knowledge, beliefs, desires, hopes, dreams, etc., as vital parameters in one's linguistic theory, then the theory becomes intractable.

For the standard indexicals such as 'me', 'here', 'now', etc., how the interpretation of the indexical is established is not particularly puzzling. The referents are both available in, and salient features of, the discourse situation. Consequently, there seems to be nothing particularly mysterious about how speakers use the meanings of these expressions in conjunction with specific features of the context to determine their full interpretations.

Consider 'I' for example. The linguistic meaning of 'I' is something like 'refers to the utterer'. The utterer is a salient overt presence in a given discourse situation. In fact he/she is sensorily accessible, that is, he/she is seeable or touchable or hearable or tasteable. Given this sensory accessibility, it seems easy enough to pick out the utterer in any given discourse context. So it is easy enough to fix the interpretation of the standard indexical 'I'. In short, the capacities that we must attribute to speakers to explain what their mastery of the standard indexicals consists in do not seem to be particularly recondite. As with the anaphor or epithet cases above, we could imagine getting a computer to do this, supplemented perhaps with sensory systems enabling it to pick up sensory information from its local environment which would enable it to determine such things as who is speaking to whom, what the time is, etc. Whatever the particulars, however, in the case of the standard indexicals, the capacities we are tacitly ascribing to native speakers are keyed to local, relatively explicit, properties of the actual context of utterance. In this way, they are quite analogous to the cases discussed in section 2. Consequently, the capacities we must ascribe to speakers to enable them to exploit this sort of information, though not identical to the cases discussed in section 2, seem rather bland.

This changes dramatically when we consider resource situations. As we have seen, virtually anything is a possible resource situation. After all, almost anything one can imagine might be relevant in some context in determining the import of some uttered sentence. Consequently, resource situations are neither tightly tied to the discourse situation nor even identifiable in any straightforward way. The way beliefs, desires, hopes, dreams, etc., are salient features of a discourse situation is very different from the way that the speaker and the addressee are. The big difference is that once knowledge, beliefs, desires, etc., are brought in, interpretation ceases to be a local affair concentrating on exploiting relatively well-defined and sensorily accessible parameters and becomes, instead, a holistic enterprise of hermeneutics. And this is the problem. For how this holistic enterprise is carried out is a total mystery. Though as a practical matter we have no trouble picking up, weighing, juggling, and using vast amounts of information relevantly, quickly, and appropriately in many varied contexts, we simply do not understand how this sort of holistic enterprise is carried out. We simply do not understand *in general* what sorts of capacities a person must have in order to make all-things-considered judgments and effortlessly exploit beliefs in drawing the conclusions that are regularly drawn in the way relevant to the situation at hand. And though we may have a story to tell in any given case, we have no inkling of a theory that would subsume these particular instances within a general framework.

It is worth noting that these sorts of observations are not very novel. The capacity to 'judge' in this holistic manner (as well as the capacity to act freely and the capacity to act strategically) has been considered a hallmark of the mental since the seventeenth century. It was because such 'mental' characteristics did not seem to be amenable to the standard forms of explanation characteristic of the natural sciences that they were separated off from the latter and taken to imply the existence of a different kind of stuff. The deficiencies we have encountered concerning pragmatic accounts simply reiterate these concerns in a slightly different setting.

I argued in section 2 that what makes a linguistic explanation powerful is that it can break a complex capacity down into subcapacities, each of which is less complex than the capacity that we wish to have explained. Behind Barwise and Perry's indexical theory lie capacities that are no less mysterious than the pragmatic capacity that we want to have explained. In this case, the explanation proffered stands in need of just the same sort of explanation that we were seeking in the first place. If Barwise and Perry are correct about the pervasive indexicality of interpretation, and I tend to think they are, then this is not something to be happy about. What it means is that we have no idea how to explain people's pragmatic capacities.

The reason for this is also clear. Establishing connections and exploiting resource situations are not analogous to establishing the interpretation of the more standard indexicals or the grammaticality of sentences. In the latter cases, the determination of well-formedness or appropriateness is tied to local explicit features of the discourse situation. It is dependent on features of the sentence or on sensorily accessible aspects of the discourse situation. This 'locality' is lacking in the expanded types of contextual influence that speakers' connections and resource situations introduce. The *global* nature of the information that must be deployed, weighed, and exploited leaves it a mystery as to how this is, or even could be, accomplished.

To sum up then, I have argued that the large-scale indexical theories which attempt to expand the range of indices to accommodate pragmatic features of language use should not be seen as continuous with standard linguistic accounts of grammatical competence or even the sorts of accounts that explicate the overt indexicals. Whatever their merits, they do not succeed in explaining how it is that we are so pragmatically adept.

4   Semantical concerns

The problems noted in the last section pertaining to the theoretical apparatus of a pragmatic theory such as Barwise and Perry's extend to the standard forms of explanation that exploit in some rich manner the theoretical notions of semantics. Thus, I would like to suggest, the types of concerns that someone committed to (1–5) manifests when considering pragmatic indexical theories should carry over to accounts that exploit standard semantic techniques of explanation. As I have discussed these sorts of concerns elsewhere (Hornstein, 1984), I will be brief.[5]

What is a semantic theory? It is a theory that exploits semantical notions such as 'truth', 'reference', 'properties', etc. in explicating an individual's interpretive competence. A semantical theory of interpretation aims to explain our linguistic capacities in terms of our capacities to refer to objects, discern truth conditions, and pick out properties. It aims to explicate the notion 'content of a sentence' and suggests that these semantical notions alluded to above are relatively well-defined and can serve as useful theoretical constructs for explicating the notion of content. I believe that this optimism is misplaced. Though a notion of content is clearly required it is far from clear that semantical theories are of any use in explicating it.

What is the notion 'content of a sentence' in opposition to? Clearly, the structure of a sentence. Why is the former notion necessary? Because many sentences that should clearly be distinguished from one another nonetheless all share a common structure. Consider, for example, the sentences in (13):

(13) a. Mary kissed John
      b. Mary touched John

These sentences clearly differ from one another. How so? Syntactically they share a common structure. The difference is that in one case Mary is the kisser and John the kissee and in the other case Mary is the toucher and John the touchee. In short, though structurally similar, they have different contents because they have different main verbs. Moreover, we all know that they are different and that they are different for the reasons mentioned. The problem is to explain in what this difference consists without collapsing into triviality.

A trivial explanation, but one that enjoyed considerable popularity for a while, went as follows.[6] Words are related to semantic markers. Different words, by and large, relate to different markers. (13a) differs from (13b) in that in (13a) the verb is related to the semantic marker for 'kiss' while in (13b) the verb is linked to the semantic marker for 'touch'. In understanding a sentence, we 'translate' sentences into representations and in these representations different words are mapped onto different markers. The phrase marker with its relevant semantic markers is what we understand when we understand a sentence. Thus, to sum up, the content of (13a) differs from that of (13b) because their representations differ in the verbal position. We explain our capacity to differentiate them by pointing out that, in our translation of the sentences in (13) into mentalese, we give these sentences different representations.

This sort of account was attacked as question-begging. It was asked in what sense this explained anything. The problem might be summed up in the following question: how does saying that in understanding a sentence we map them into mentalese help explain anything unless we understand what it is for someone to understand mentalese? In short, we have explained precious little unless we can convince ourselves that understanding mentalese is any less opaque as a basic capacity than understanding sentences or words is. Is knowing the marker for 'kiss' a capacity any less involved or opaque, indeed any different in any helpful way, than simply knowing the meaning of 'kiss'? What do semantic markers add?

The conclusion that was drawn from this line of criticism was that postulating semantic markers only pushed the problem back one step. Instead of explaining what it was for a word to have a content, the problem was to explain what it was for a marker in mentalese to have a content. As the same answer looked like it would suffice to answer either question, semantic markers were deemed to be superfluous to the real concerns of semantics. It was suggested that, in place of mentalese translations, understanding what the content of a word is is simply to understand what it refers to. In short, in place of the word/mentalese marker connection, we should substitute the word/world connection. The content of an expression is the object/property/thing it denotes/refers to/picks out in the world.[7]

Unfortunately, on closer inspection this sort of explanation gets us no farther than the first, at least if one's concerns are those of (1–5) above.[8] Why not? The problem, recall, is to characterize what it is that a speaker knows in virtue of which she/he knows the meaning of 'kiss' or 'touch'. The answer the mentalese story gave was that the native speaker had a mental representation. The problem with this account was that it was not clear how saying this said anything different from saying that she/he knew the meaning of the word. But, as what we want to know is what it is for a native speaker to know the meaning of a word, it is not clear how being told it is like having a mental semantic marker helps us if it is unclear what it is to have a mental semantic marker and unclear, moreover, in the same way.

However, the same sorts of concerns beset the story that critics urged as the replacement for mentalese. On this account, the meaning of a word is the thing it stands for. Different kinds of words stand for different kinds of things. There are two questions worth asking: (i) what is it for a word to stand for something in general, that is, what sort of capacity is it that persons have which is the capacity to know that some expressions stands for some sort of entity? (ii) how does our capacity to use and understand a given word 'flow' from our knowing that the word stands for some entity or other, that is, how does a referential semantics help us to understand what it is that knowing the meaning of an expression comes to?

These two points have been raised again recently by Michael Dummett in several of his papers on meaning (see Dummett, 1974, 1976). They echo the sentiments of the later Wittgenstein. He was among the first to challenge the explanatory utility of semantic explanations. The core problem is that semantical explanations fail to break down semantical capacities into comprehensible subcapacities. Consequently, the research program that we might dub 'progressive homuncularization' cannot be applied as we are not able to discharge the puzzling capacity in terms of progressively 'dumber' subcapacities. After all, does it really help to be told that the meaning of 'life' is a function from possible worlds to life on those worlds or that the meaning of 'life' constrains the situations which it partially describes to have life in it, if one's worry is what semantic competence comes to? Is it not the problem that explaining what capacities underlie knowing the relevant function or understanding how situations are constrained is just the very same problem as adumbrating the capacities that lie behind knowing what a word means? Is this any less circular than the mentalese story, given the concerns of (1–5)?

Semantical notions such as reference/truth/denotation/property, etc. enjoy a fabled obscurity. I have argued that it is an obscurity of a very special kind. If we ask what psychological properties of speakers these notions tacitly invoke when deployed, then I think it becomes clear that their explanatory potential is rather low. If what we want from our semantic theory is that it explain what knowledge of words amounts to, then it is not very illuminating to be told that it is knowledge that they stand in the reference relation to certain things if we have no idea what having this knowledge comes to.

5 Conclusion

I have argued in the earlier sections that a syntactic theory of interpretation of the sort that Chomsky's work has made possible succeeds in explaining what interpretive competence might amount to without falling prey to the standard later Wittgensteinian criticisms of meaning theory. Unlike semantic or pragmatic theories of interpretation, syntactic theories allow one to key semantic competence to local properties of the sentence. This further allows the complex interpretive capacity to be 'homuncularized' and thereby explained. This same strategy will not work with semantic or pragmatic theories. A major accomplishment of the Chomskyan notion of logical form was to give logical syntax a new range. By integrating more traditional concerns into the broader framework of linguistic theory of the kind Chomsky developed, it has become clear that certain traditional issues dealing with quantifier scope, pronominal binding, opacity, topic/comment, etc. could be easily accommodated. Moreover, they could be integrated in an interesting way; a way which revealed additional complexity and nuance when combined with more traditional logical analyses.

However, Chomsky's work is important for a second major reason. By showing how questions of sentential semantics might be treated, he has implicitly highlighted certain deep and abiding differences between phenomena that have been often lumped together. I touched on this briefly above. The problems that are endemic to semantic and pragmatic modes of analyses are not new. They were first clearly recognized in the seventeenth century and have made an appearance every time issues of 'creativity', linguistic or otherwise, have become the object of theoretical concern. The 'holistic' capacities that are implicated by pragmatic theories and semantic approaches have long fascinated philosophers and students of human psychology in the broadest sense. One of Chomsky's more important contributions has been to cast doubt on the optimistic attitude that pervades much technical formal work on language, that, once we understand that languages involve rules, all that is left is the relatively trivial problem of finding out which ones. By taking syntax further and deeper than anyone might have expected possible, Chomsky has also shown us how little we understand those human capacities that are most distinctively human.

Notes

A version of this paper was presented in Madrid, April 1986 at a conference organized by *Revista Teorema*. I would like to thank the organizers, especially Carlos Otero, for their input.
1   Observe that I use the term 'unacceptability' not 'ungrammaticality'. These two notions, though often used interchangeably, are not the same. The former is a descriptive term: native speakers judge sentences to be more or less good. The latter is a technical term: some unacceptable sentences have this status because they are ungrammatical, i.e. they violate grammatical prohibitions of various sorts. Other sentences might be unacceptable because they violate other sorts of requirements such as plausibility, parsability, etc. It is the aim of a linguistic theory of the sort outlined in section 1 to explain those judgments whose properties reflect the language faculty, i.e. the grammar. Those that are unacceptable for other reasons are not the primary concern of this focus of research.
2   A binds B if and only if A is coindexed with and c-commands B. For present purposes, A c-commands B if A is 'higher' in the tree than B. This is not strictly

correct but it will do for the examples discussed here. For technical details see Chomsky, 1981.

3   Many linguists and philosophers appear to think that this vitiates linguistic theory. This is simply incorrect. If we can parse a given capacity between the structural contribution of the grammar and the lexical contribution of the words then we might well advance on one front without having very much to say about the other.

Second, no one doubts that it would be nice to have a theory of lexical content. What is more controversial is that this theory, any more than any other branch of linguistic theory, will have to make much use of semantic primitives. When I deny that semantics is relevant to linguistics I do not mean to suggest that sentences have no interpretations. I simply deny the specific claim, raised at times to the level of a truism, that an interpretation theory must be a semantic theory. James Higginbotham, 1985, p. 586, n. 34, seems to misunderstand this point. If he is using 'semantics' as coextensive with 'interpretation' then what he claims is uncontroversial. However, if what he means by semantics is a particular theory of interpretation which proceeds by relating language to extra-linguistic objects and it is in this mapping that interpretation consists, then what he says has rarely, if ever, been defended. Furthermore, unless he means this, then his interpretive theory is *syntactic*, not semantic. I believe that Higginbotham intends his interpretive theory to be semantic in the strong sense. I do not see that anything he says requires this, however.

Indeed, it has recently become somewhat conventional to agree that semantics realistically construed is really irrelevant for questions of psychology: see Jerry Fodor, 1984; Steven Stich, 1983; Stephen Schiffer, 1987. A similar point was made in Hornstein, 1986. I think that the conventional wisdom is correct. Theories of linguistic interpretation need not be semantic. There is little reason to give pride of place to real semantic notions like 'truth', 'reference', 'denotation', 'satisfaction', etc. except in an anemic disquotational sense.

4   Cf. Norbert Hornstein and Amy Weinberg 1988 for further discussion.

5   Some have argued with the technical proposals put forth in *Logic as Grammar*; see the review by Scott Soames, 1987. Here is not the place to respond to details of his technical critique. However, Soames seems to accept the wider point that real semantics (and what other kind is there?) is of very indirect relevance to a psychologically concerned linguistic theory. He argues as much in J. J. Katz (ed.) 1985 and in S. Schiffer and S. Steel (eds), forthcoming. Nonetheless, he seems to think that there remains a connection, albeit a tenuous one. However, he fails to indicate what the relevance of his view of semantic theory might be to the Chomskyan project discussed above. I can see none. If semantics is concerned with truth conditions, and this is construed as correspondence, then I can see no reason for thinking that there is *any* link between semantics so defined and theories of linguistic interpretive competence. Moreover, this is all for the good as far as the latter enterprise is concerned, for semantic theories seem to require the ascription of powers and capacities to native speakers which are as mysterious as those capacities that we wish to explain. Syntactic theories, those types of theories that eschew language-world relations, are not similarly problematic. It is for this reason that syntactic theories are *methodologically* preferable.

Let me add one more point. It has never been clear to me what the point of Soames's semantic concerns is. What is the problem he intends these sorts of theories to solve? To answer that it aims to explain how language conveys information does not help unless we are told what information is and how truth-based theories are able to explain this property in a non-trivial way. It has not proven to be easy to provide full-blooded semantic accounts that discharge the semantic primitives in a physicalistically respectable way. This is a long-standing challenge for semantic theory, dating back to Hartry Field, 1972. As I read him, Soames does not explain how this is possible so much as *presuming* that semantic accounts are crucial. For some recent reflections on these points, see Schiffer, 1987.

6   The criticism that I advance is not intended to suggest that markerese explanations are valueless overall. I merely wish to argue that they contribute nothing to explaining the notion of semantic content. Markerese theories might be an important part of any attempt to explain how vocabulary acquisition is able to proceed as quickly as it does in the early years of language acquisition.

7   This line of criticism can be found in D. Lewis, 1972.

8   The following is based on arguments first advanced by G. Harman 1974. Similar arguments have been advanced in N. Block, 1986.

References

Barwise, J. and Perry, J. 1983: *Situations and Attitudes*. Cambridge, Mass.: MIT Press.

Block, N. 1986: Advertisement for a semantics for psychology. In P.A. French, T.E. Uehling Jr., and H.K. Wettstein (eds), *Midwest Studies in Philosophy*, vol. 10.

Chomsky, Noam 1981: *Lectures on Government and Binding*. Dordrecht: Foris.

1986: *Knowledge of Language: Its Nature, Origin, and Use*. New York: Praeger.

Dennett, Daniel 1978: Why the law of effect will not go away. In Dennett, *Brainstorms*. Cambridge, Mass.: MIT Press.

Dummett, Michael 1974: What is a Theory of Meaning? (I) In S. Guttenplan (ed), *Mind and Language*. Oxford University Press, 97–138.

1976: What is a Theory of Meaning? (II) In G. Evans and J. McDowell (eds), *Truth and Meaning*. Oxford: Clarendon.

Field, Hartry 1972: Tarski's theory of truth. *Journal of Philosophy*, 69 (13).

Fodor, Jerry 1984: Methodological solipsism as a research program. In Fodor, *Representations*, Cambridge, Mass.: MIT Press.

Harman, G. 1974: Meaning and semantics. In M.K. Munitz and P.K. Unger (eds), *Semantics and Philosophy*, New York: New York University Press.

Higginbotham, James 1985: On semantics. *Linguistic Inquiry*, 16 (4), 586 n. 34.

Hornstein, Norbert 1984: *Logic as Grammar*. Cambridge, Mass.: MIT Press.

Hornstein, Norbert and Weinberg, Amy 1988: The necessity of LF. Ms. University of Maryland at College Park.

Lewis, D. 1972: General semantics. In D. Davidson and G. Harman (eds), *Semantics of Natural Language*. Dordrecht: Reidel.

Schiffer, Stephen 1987: *Remnants of Meaning*. Cambridge, Mass.: MIT Press.

Soames, Scott 1985: Semantics and psychology. In J.J. Katz (ed.), *The Philosophy of Linguistics*. Oxford University Press.

1987: Review of Hornstein, Norbert 1984. *Journal of Philosophy*. August.

forthcoming: Semantics and semantic competence. In S. Schiffer and S. Steele (eds), *The Second Arizona Colloquium on Cognitive Sciences*.

Stitch, Stephen 1983: *From Folk Psychology to Cognitive Science*. Cambridge, Mass.: MIT Press.

3

Logical Form and Linguistic Theory

Jaakko Hintikka

The concept of logical form has had almost as many ups and downs in language theory as the Dow Jones in Wall Street. It played an important role in the early decades of this century in the philosophy of language of the middle period Russell (1914) and of the early Wittgenstein (1929).[1] Later, it has been appealed to by Davidson (1984) and Quine (1960).[2] It was not much in evidence in Chomsky's published *œuvre* before the late seventies. Recently, however, it has been restored to a place of honor in the linguistic work inspired by Chomsky or carried out by him. Indeed, most of the work that has been labelled 'Government and Binding Theory' can be viewed as dealing essentially with the logical forms of natural-language sentences.[3]

Now what is logical form supposed to be and why has it been such an intensive concern of both philosophers of language and – of all people – syntacticians? There are in fact excellent reasons for their preoccupation. Let us perform a simple thought-experiment. Let us assume that someone addresses a well-formed English sentence to you, which you (usually unreflectively) understand. Let us assume further that your feat in understanding the sentence is not based (partly or wholly) on the conversational situation but merely on the message you received. Admittedly, actual language understanding normally relies to a considerable extent on contextual clues. But the kind of meaning that language theorists are mostly concerned with is precisely the component of the force of an utterance which is independent of the situation in which it is uttered.

What was given to you when you received the message was a physical (acoustical or optical) structure, a sequence of noises or scratches on paper. Now let us concentrate (for simplicity) on the second case only and let us call the structure given to you a *syntactic structure*. Somehow from this structure you managed to derive a semantical representation of the sentence in question.[4] This derivation was largely independent of the particular words used, and hence depends indeed crucially on the given structure. Its outcome is what can be called *logical form*. The role of this form is to facilitate the understanding of the sentence. Indeed, the process of deriving the logical form from the syntactical form is obviously a major part of the process of understanding the sentence in question.

This account is crude and oversimplified. It nevertheless helps us to perceive the peculiar position of the idea of logical form in linguistic theorizing. It explains why the concept of logical form has played such an important role in meaning theory, at least on the philosophical side of the fence. But it also helps us to appreciate why the idea of logical form is of great interest to syntacticians.

First of all, even if one could not care less about syntax, there remains the massive fact that what is given to the recipient of a linguistic message is merely a sequence of symbols, essentially a syntactical form. As Wittgenstein once put this point in his inimitable way:[5]

> But if one says 'How am I supposed to know what he means, all I can see are merely his symbols,' then I say: 'How is *he* supposed to know what he means, all that he has are merely his symbols.'

It is for this reason that the logical form of a sentence must be derivable from its syntactical form.

In recent philosophy and partly also in recent linguistics there seems to prevail a tendency to underestimate the difficulty of this derivation, which is sometimes called 'logic translation' (Otto, 1978; cf. Hintikka, 1987a). This difficulty is sometimes obscured by a failure to appreciate what is involved in the logic translation. What is needed is a *rule-governed* translation. Now quite frequently it is possible to see what the translation of a sentence into a logical language (usually, first-order language) is, without having any real idea of the mechanism of the translation, that is, of how the logical form is derived from the syntactical one. If examples are needed, the so-called 'donkey sentences' will fill the bill.[6] Consider, for example, the sentence

(1) If Peter owns a donkey, he beats it.

Everyone will agree that the logical form of (1) is

(2) $(\forall x)((\text{Donkey } (x) \,\&\, \text{Owns (Peter, } x))\rightarrow\text{Beats (Peter, } x))$

Yet there is very little agreement, in spite of numerous discussions, how it is that (2) is derived from (1). I shall return to this matter later.

It is also significant that even in the most serious attempts to formulate actual rules for 'logic translation' (e.g. in Montague, 1980) little attention is paid to the more difficult cases, such as those involving the English quantifier word 'any'.[7]

Hence the task of spelling out precisely how the logical form of a sentence depends on its syntactical form is not trivial, and has to be faced by any serious overall linguistic theory. Moreover, the informal explanations given above show that this problem is closely related to the problem of language understanding.

As was mentioned, one can view certain central parts of Chomsky's so-called 'Government and Binding' (GB) Theory as an attempt to spell out in realistic detail how the logical form of a natural-language sentence depends on its syntactical form. To have made this attempt is to Chomsky's great credit. It means that he has faced squarely a problem which most philosophers have denied or else swept under the carpet. Moreover, Chomsky's theory is far more realistic than the ideas of those few philosophers who have taken the problem of logic translation seriously.

It is well known how GB-type theories operate, at least in their main features.[8] A central part of such theories is an attempt to specify precisely how two important ingredients of the logical form of a sentence, for instance, of a sentence containing quantifier expressions, namely, the relations of scope and coreference (binding, coindexing), depend on the syntactic structure of the sentence in question. The precise forms of such dependence are somewhat controversial and do not concern us here.

What is there to be said of the kind of conception of the role of LF on which the GB-type theories are based? It seems to me that two major criticisms are in order here, although both of them concern more the way the GB program is carried out than the fundamental idea itself.

The first concerns the dependence of LF on the surface form of a sentence.[9] Even though Chomsky does allow some input from the earlier stages of the syntactical generation of a sentence S into its logical form LF(S), this form is predominantly determined by the surface form of S. A comparison will make my meaning clear. In my game-theoretical semantics[10] what in effect is the logical form of a sentence S is not determined by its surface form directly, but by the entire structure of the semantical game G(S) associated with S. In the course of such a game, the surface form of S will change drastically in a way which is ultimately based on the structure of S but whose regularities are in practice hopelessly difficult to anticipate on the basis of the surface structure of S. In contrast, in GB-type theories LF is, in Chomsky's words, 'derived directly' from the surface structure. It turns out that this is not feasible in all cases.

A closely related flaw in the GB approach is what I can only consider a hopelessly restrictive and distorted idea of what the logical form of a sentence realistically looks like, at least if we stray a little bit further from oversimplified examples. Logical forms are for a GB theorist essentially like the logical formulas of quantification theory (extensional first-order logic, lower predicate calculus, or whatever your favourite term for this basic type of logical language is).[11] When Chomsky's followers speak of logical form, this is what they have in mind, plus or minus a few minor extensions which I and others have forced them to consider, such as branching quantifiers.

In considering first-order logic as the typical framework representing logical forms, Chomsky is of course but a link in a grand tradition that encompasses Frege, Russell, Quine, Davidson, Lakoff, etc., all of whom used something like a first-order language as their 'canonical notation'.[12] When I am here challenging this conception, I am thus not challenging Chomsky alone but what looks almost like the mainstream tradition in the logical analysis of language.

Before indicating my reasons for finding first-order logic inadequate as a medium for representing logical form, let me first try to get some potential misunderstandings out of the way.

First, I am not concerned here at all with the absence of intensional and modal concepts from the idiom of quantification theory.[13] It is the use of certain notions, such as scope and binding (coreference), as the key explanatory concepts that bothers me in linguists' reliance on first-order languages.

Second, I do not doubt that for a majority of actual examples of English sentences there are first-order formulas which capture their respective logical forms and that the relatively few concrete examples where first-order representation is impossible do not look very impressive *prima facie*. But the case would not be closed even if the logical form of each and every natural-language sentence admitted of a representation in the language of lower predicate calculus. For, as was emphasized above, we would even then face the formidable problem of specifying the precise rules for the translation.[14]

Furthermore, I am not claiming that no formalized discourse can capture the semantical structure of natural languages. Indeed, I believe that a suitable canonical notation can serve to display the semantical structures of the sentences of a natural language like English. In that sense, I believe that the idea of logical form is viable. My claim is a more modest one; I claim that the usual first-order logic (quantification theory) is not the right canonical notation for the purpose.

But if intertranslatability is not the main issue here, what is? I counter this question by returning to my fundamental question: why introduce the notion of logical form in the first place? Why associate with the surface form of each natural-language sentence S another structure LF(S), its logical form? Even if different linguists' and logicians' motives differ from each other, the main answer is plain. It is the answer indicated above in my preliminary considerations. LF(S) is supposed to show how S is to be interpreted semantically. Its function is to lay bare the semantical structure of S. Davidson (1984) spelled this out at one time by suggesting that the assignment of a logical form to each sentence of a given language amounts to a semantical theory for that language. More specifically, that logical forms of different natural-language sentences show how their meanings depend on the meanings of their simpler constituents. However, one does not have to subscribe to the details of Davidson's sometime view in order to agree that somehow or other LF(S) is supposed to exhibit the semantical structure of S.

But if so, and if one uses first-order logic as the notation for logical forms, one is committed to maintaining that the natural language for which the logical forms are set up *operates semantically essentially in the same way as a first-order language*. Otherwise the transition from S to LF(S), that is, the translation or paraphrase of natural language sentences into a first-order ones, does not help us to understand the semantics of the natural language in question, as it was in effect calculated to do.

It is in this sense that I suggest that the use of first-order logic as the framework of logical form is ill-advised. From what has been said it also follows that it is unlikely that there exists a single knockdown argument to show this. The most I can hope for is to call your attention to a syndrome of many different discrepancies between the ways in which natural languages like English operate semantically and the ways in which first-order languages do.

But how do natural languages in fact operate, when it comes to semantics? What are the crucial assumptions on which the usual logic of quantification is based? Your favorite answer depends on the perspective from which you are looking at the concept of logical form, but it seems to me that the following three ideas are likely to be accepted by all the supporters of quantification theory:

(1) The Frege–Russell thesis that verbs for being (like the English 'is') are ambiguous between the 'is' of identity; the 'is' of predication; the 'is' of existence (at least in such locutions as 'there is'); and the 'is' of class-inclusion (as in 'a whale is a mammal').[15]

This assumption is built into the first-order notation in that the allegedly different kinds of 'is' have to be expressed in different ways in the logical notation, indeed, by means of three irreducibly different symbols corresponding to the first three Fregean senses. This brings out the crucial feature of the Frege–Russell ambiguity thesis. What they claim is not only that 'is' or '*ist*' is used in three or four different ways. Pretty much everybody would agree to that. They claim that what distinguishes at least three of these different uses is that in them the word *is* has a logically different meaning, not that it occurs, for example, in a different kind of syntactical environment.

(2) The crucial role of the notions of scope and coreference. This assumption is seen at work in the usual formal notation for quantifiers like $(\forall x)$, $(\exists x)$: each of them comes with a number of occurrences of the variable '*x*' *bound to* it, and also comes with a pair of parentheses which shows the segment of the formula in question in which such 'binding' or 'coreference' can take place. This segment is known as the *scope* of the quantifier in question.

To use this notation, which relies heavily on the ideas of binding and scope, for the purpose of representing the logical forms of natural-language sentences presupposes that natural-language semantics operates essentially by means of the notions of binding and scope. In fact, one of the main thrusts of GB theories is precisely to find the syntactical conditions in which an expression of a natural language can be bound to another (more generally, coreferential with it) or occurs in the scope of another ('governed by it').

It seems to me that neither of these two crucial features of formal first-order languages plays a significant role as basic feature of the semantics of natural languages.

(i) I have discussed the alleged ambiguity of 'is' in an earlier paper (1979). It turns out that in at least one viable framework of semantical representation, namely, that provided by game-theoretical semantics (GTS), the Frege–Russell thesis fails. It fails not only because the different uses of *is* can be told apart contextually, but because in some cases the very Frege–Russell distinction cannot be made. I do not have much to add to that earlier paper. A few remarks may nevertheless be in order.

The main argument can in any case be appreciated without much detailed knowledge of GTS. The crucial idea is that the meaning of sentences containing quantifier expressions must be expressed by reference to suitable instantiation rules. This idea is very much part and parcel of quantification theory in all its forms, perhaps especially in the so-called natural deduction systems. In GTS, this idea takes *inter alia* the form of a game rule which leads from a sentence of the form

(3) X-some Y who Z-W

(where *who* occupies the subject position in *who* Z) to a sentence of the form

(4) X-*b*-W, *b* is an Y, and *b* Z

where *b* is the name of an individual chosen by one of the players (the initial verifier, 'Myself'). An analogous rule governs the indefinite article *a(n)*. As a special case we have a move from

(5) Jack is a boy who jogs

to

(6) Jack is John Jr., John Jr. is a boy, and John Jr. jogs.

Here the two underlined occurrences of *is* are identical semantically, being part of X. But the first would have to be, according to Frege and Russell, an *is* of predication and the second an *is* of identity, which is contradicted by their semantical identity.

Again, a game rule can lead from

(7) There is a schoolgirl who can beat anyone at tennis

to a sentence like

(8) Steffi is a schoolgirl, and Steffi can beat anyone at tennis.

Here there is no reason not to consider the two underlined occurrences of *is* semantically identical. But the former is an *is* of existence, according to the traditional way of thinking, whereas the second one is one of predication. Hence the two cannot always be distinguished from each other. Thus another part of the Frege–Russell thesis fails here. I see little hope of defending it as a serious principle of natural-language semantics.

In a wider perspective, it may be noted that my criticism (Hintikka and

Knuuttila (eds), 1986) of the Frege–Russell thesis has *inter alia* had a liberating influence on the study of the history of philosophy where discarding this anachronistic thesis has enabled scholars to look at several important issues in a new light.[16] I am hoping that a similar liberating influence will materialize also in linguistics.

(ii)(a) I have also subjected the notion of scope to a scrutiny in an earlier essay (1987b). It turns out not to be a useful explanatory concept in natural-language semantics. It represents, when applied to natural languages, a mixture of at least two different notions. One of them is the relative logical priority of different semantically active ingredients of a sentence. The other is a kind of interim availability as a potential reference which can only be explained by reference to the semantical games of GTS and is in fact relative to a given play of such a game (Hintikka and Kulas, 1985, esp. pp. 47–50, 90–4, 113–16). Neither idea can be captured simply by delineating a continuous segment of a sentence or discourse.

An additional example of the failure of the concept of scope in natural languages is provided by the famous Bach–Peters sentences (cf. Karttunen 1971) like the following:

(9) The boy who was fooling her kissed the girl who loved him.

Here, according to the conventional ideas, the reference of *the boy* depends on that of *her*, wherefore *the boy* must be within the 'scope' of *her*. But *her* is 'bound to' *the girl*, and hence in its 'scope'. Since scope is supposed to be transitive, *the boy* must be within the scope of *the girl*. But, by symmetry, the reverse relation must also hold, which is impossible in the usual quantificational notation.

In brief, the usual quantificational notation is (at least if we try to apply it directly) useless for the purpose of exhibiting the 'logical form' of a Bach–Peters sentence like (9).

In GTS, there is no problem about (9), as I have shown before (Hintikka and Saarinen, 1975).

Often, what is meant by scope is really relative logical priority. (An expression having another one in its scope is logically prior to the latter.) But there is no reason why such a priority should go together with a longer segment of a sentence or of a discourse in which other expressions (e.g., anaphoric pronouns) can be 'bound' to the given one. Logically speaking, to run the two together is merely a solecism. The independence of the two notions of scope and logical priority can perhaps be brought home by recalling the phenomenon of informational independence. In such a case, two expressions (of the kind that trigger a move in a semantical game) have the same scope, but neither one precedes the other logically. There are even cases of nontransitive 'scopes', as in the following logical form of the simple English sentence 'I know whom everybody admires' (J. Hintikka, 1982):

(10)

$$\text{I know that} \atop (\exists y) \longleftarrow (\forall x)\Bigg\} \ (x \text{ admires } y).$$

There is not the faintest hope of being able to handle the 'logical form' of (10) by the sole means of the ideas of scope and coreference.

(2)(b) What I have not argued equally systematically before are the shortcomings of the notion of coreference. They are nevertheless quite blatant.

One kind of failure of the notion of coreference takes place in a sentence S whose logical form cannot be spelled out merely by specifying the coreference relations between its several ingredients. In practice, the failure of the notion of coreference often means in such cases that a GB-type analysis of coreference relations in S does not work properly.

The inadequacy of the concept of coreference (at least in the form in which it has been used recently in GB-type theorizing) for the purpose of uncovering the logical form of an English sentence can be shown by means of examples. Thus, consider the following sentences:

(11) Tom and Dick admired each other's gift to him.

(12) Tom and Dick admired each other's gift to himself.

(13) Tom and Dick admired each other's gift to them.

(14) *Tom and Dick admired each other's gift to themselves.

(15) Tom admired Dick's gift to him.

(16) Tom admired Dick's gift to himself.

Consider, first, (11)–(13). They are all well-formed English sentences with a clear meaning. Indeed, they are equivalent with the following respective paraphrases:

(17) Tom admired Dick's gift to Tom, and Dick admired Tom's gift to Dick.

(18) Tom admired Dick's gift to Dick, and Dick admired Tom's gift to Tom.

(19) Tom admired Dick's gift to Tom and Dick, and Dick admired Tom's gift to Tom and Dick.

The question is how structures tantamount to (17)–(19) can be derived from (11)–(13). There does not appear to be any way of doing so by means of the GB-type ideas. Consider first (12). A comparison with (16) shows that *himself* in (12) must be coreferential with *each other*.[17] Likewise, a comparison with (15) shows that in (11) *him* must be coreferential with *Tom and Dick*, with *Tom*, or with *Dick*, if it is to be anaphoric.[18] But since *him* is singular, the first possibility is excluded. But if it is (possibly) coreferential, it is by the symmetry of the situation (possibly) coreferential with the other, too. Being singular, *him* cannot be coreferential with both simultaneously. If so, (11) should be ambiguous, with two different possible coreference relations. But of course (11) is not ambiguous in the least.

Another interesting problem here is to explain why (14) is unacceptable. A comparison with (12) and (16) suggests that on any account which relies on the syntactical structure of (14) alone, (14) should be acceptable (*themselves* could be coreferential with *Tom and Dick*). Yet clearly (14) is not acceptable, or at least is much less so than (11)–(13).

In particular, a comparison with (16) shows that in (14) *themselves* must be coreferential with *each other*. But then there cannot be any reason why (14) could not be well-formed. For *each other* is frequently 'coreferential' with a plural NP, as in

(20) Tom and Dick admired each other.

There are other dire problems here. For instance, in each of (11)–(13) *Tom and Dick* must be coreferential with *each other* on a GB type account. But then it becomes unintelligible that there should be any difference between the logical form of (12) and that of (13). For if *each other* and *Tom and Dick* must be coreferential, then it will make no difference to the logical form of (12) or (13) whether an anaphoric pronoun is coreferential with the one or with the other. But this violates the unmistakable difference in meaning between (12) and (13).

Furthermore, in (13) we have the paradoxical situation that the singular NP *himself* must be coreferential (coindexed) with *each other* which must be coreferential with the plural NP *Tom and Dick*. This makes it impossible to assign a reasonable interpretation to the idea of coreference (coindexing) here.

These problems cannot be eliminated by reference to lexical meanings (or Chomsky's theta-structure), for the lexical ingredients (other than pronouns) are the same in (11)–(14).

As Wittgenstein might have said, the surface forms (11)–(14) do not have the sufficient 'logical multiplicity' to create satisfactory semantical representations for themselves if they are dealt with by means of notions like coreference and scope applied to their surface forms.

This does not mean that it is impossible to explain the respective logical forms of (11)–(13) by means of a rule-governed procedure. However, this procedure has no use for such notions as the head-pronoun relation (relation of coreference). Such a procedure is offered by game-theoretical semantics (Hintikka and Kulas 1985). In it, (11)–(14) are first transformed by a game rule into (21)–(24):

(21) Tom admired Dick's gift to him, and Dick admired Tom's gift to him.

(22) Tom admired Dick's to himself, and Dick admired Tom's gift to
      himself.

(23) Tom admired Dick's gift to them, and Dick admired Tom's gift to
      them.

(24) Tom admired Dick's gift to themselves, and Dick admired Tom's gift
      to themselves.

At a later stage of a semantical game, after the conjuncts have been split up,
the genitives will be dealt with.[19] This will produce from (21)–(24) outputs of
the following respective forms:

(25) Tom admired g, and g is a gift by Dick to him.

(26) Tom admired g, and g is a gift by Dick to himself.

(27) Tom admired g, and g is a gift by Dick to them.

(28) *Tom admired g, and g is a gift by Dick to themselves.

Clearly, (25)–(27) lead to the assignment of the correct logical form to
(11)–(13), respectively. Also, the unacceptability of (28) shows why (14) is not
acceptable. In the clause

(29) *g is a gift by Dick to themselves

the reflexive pronoun is out of place by anybody's token. In game-theoretical
semantics, it will violate the general restriction codified in what has been called
the Exclusion Principle.

In this entire treatment, the notion of coreference (as relying on coindexing
or some equivalent notation) does not play any role.

The game-theoretical treatment also shows why sentences like (11)–(14)
serve their purpose as counter-examples, that is, why their logical form cannot
be spelled out merely by specifying the coreference relations obtaining between
their different ingredients. The reason is that in the course of the gradual
explication of their logical form – for that is in effect what happens in the course
of a semantical game – some of their NPs are split into several NPs with
different 'coreference relations'. *Inter alia*, the pronoun in (11)–(14) is split into
two in (21)–(24), with different coreference relations.

What we have discovered here is a case in which the logical form of an
English sentence is not derivable directly from its surface form. Insofar as the
analysis of a sentence S in the course of a semantical game can be considered as
an inverse of a suitable syntactical generation of S, this means that we have to go
back to earlier stages of the derivation of the surface form of S in order to find
its logical form (cf. Hintikka and Kulas, 1985, pp. 163–90). But, as was pointed
out earlier, Chomsky does not think that we have to do so. Examples of the kind
just given serve to show that he is not altogether right.

Another expression whose game-theoretical treatment can result in a
pronoun's splitting into two is *the only*. Accordingly, suitable sentences

containing this expression can be predicted to illustrate the same difficulty of explicating their semantics by reference to coreference relations holding among their constituents. Some such sentences, including (30), were evoked in the course of a criticism of the idea of coreference (Hintikka and Kulas, 1985, pp. 150–5, 170–2).

(30) Peter is the only man who loves his wife.

Very briefly, the two readings of (30) cannot be explained, as it might be tempting to do, by saying that in them *his* is coreferential with *Peter* or *the only man*, respectively, for these two refer to the same person.

Now we see that such examples as (30) are merely instances of a more widespread pattern.

But there is an even more striking discrepancy between the way natural languages like English operate semantically and the way formal first-order languages operate. This difference strikes at the very heart of the quantificational notation. In elementary logic texts, the nature of bound variables is typically explained by saying that they operate like (anaphoric) pronouns in that they refer to the same entity as their antecedent. Such explanations presuppose that anaphoric pronouns operate, as it were, through their grammatical antecedents (heads) to which they are 'bound' in the same way as a quantificational variable is bound to its quantifier. Plenty of evidence has nevertheless been marshalled to show that this assumption is not acceptable (Hintikka and Kulas, 1985, esp. pp. 98–108). According to the theory developed there, a pronoun is not bound to its head. In fact, the anaphor–head relation does not play any role as a semantical primitive in our theory. (Thus one major reason for employing the concept of coreference is eliminated.) Instead, a pronoun is a free term, rather like a Russellian definite description, with the exception that its Russellian quantifiers range over a choice set *I* which is relative to a play of a semantical game and changes in the course of the game. (The part of a sentence or discourse in which an individual stays in *I* is one of the many ideas that are assimilated to each other in the traditional concept of scope.) Roughly speaking, *I* consists of those individuals that the players of the semantical game have introduced during the game so far. There are nevertheless special rules governing the way *I* changes in the transition from one subgame to another.

Moreover, individuals can be introduced into *I* also by the environment. This explains why anaphoric and deictic pronouns behave in the same way.[20] An application of the game rule governing pronouns is 'blind' to the ancestry of the members of *I*; all that counts is what there is in *I* at the time of the application.

The theory so obtained involves a radically new way of looking at the way in which pronouns operate in natural language. It seems to me that it offers better accounts for various phenomena of natural-language semantics than its rivals.

For details, the reader is referred to Hintikka and Kulas, 1985.[21] The details nevertheless do not matter greatly here. What matters is the massive fact that in the kind of theory just adumbrated the traditional notion of binding (pronoun–head relation) plays no role whatsoever as a primitive. Its role is taken over by various stipulations as to which individuals there are in I at different stages of a semantical game.[22] Accordingly, the way in which the logical form of an English sentence S unfolds in the course of the semantical game G(S) connected with it does not use the notion of coreference or binding at all. The logical forms obtained in this way are also quite unlike the usual translations into a first-order language.

What is this logical form like, then? Here game-theoretical semantics reveals a general reason why first-order languages are in principle inadequate as a medium for representing logical forms of natural-language sentences. What is the logical form of a sentence S according to GTS? This form is expressed by the sentence that says there exists a winning strategy for the original verifier ('Myself') in the correlated game G(S).[23] This is a higher-order sentence, involving quantification over the functions and functionals which codify the strategies of the two players.

In most of the relatively simple cases considered by linguists and philosophers, this higher-order translation admits of a first-order equivalent. This explains the temptation to think that first-order languages are in general an adequate medium of semantic representation for languages. However, there is no general reason to expect that such a reduction back to the first-order level is possible in all cases. In fact, it is not difficult to find examples of possible translations which do not allow for such a reduction. If a quick example is needed, the game-theoretical translation into higher-order language on which Gödel's functional interpretation is based does not reduce back to first-order logic (Gödel, 1958, pp. 280–7).[24] As I have pointed out, there are other possible rules not unlike the ones Gödel uses which do not allow for a first-order reduction, either (Hintikka, 1983, esp. pp. 57–9). Moreover, when informational independence is in operation, we frequently get irreducible higher-order translations (Hintikka, 1974; Barwise, 1979). In fact, as I have recently shown (jointly with Gabriel Sandu), informational independence is not the marginal phenomenon it is often taken to be, but a ubiquitous one which is important in many different parts of the semantics of natural languages (Hintikka and Sandu, forthcoming).

If the game-theoretical account is right in its main features, the 'logic translation' offered by GB-type theories cannot be fully adequate, for it provides no framework in which the higher-order interim translation or the conditions of its reducibility back to the first-order level can be discussed.

What are some of concepts which the GTS account uses?

They include prominently the logical ordering of various ingredients (especially different logical concepts): more generally, their informational dependencies and independencies. These can be handled by means of the concept of scope only when that dependence is transitive and linear. Moreover, the game-theoretical translation into a higher-order notation depends often on the precise rules which govern the information flow from one subgame to another, that is, govern what each of the players can be assumed to 'remember' of what happens in other subgames. There is simply nothing in the current versions of GB-type theories which enables them to take into account the phenomena captured by such 'information transfer' stipulations.

All told, I do not see any realistic hope to use first-order languages (in anything like their traditional formulation) as a framework for the semantics of natural languages like English. Hence GB-type theories are not so much wrong as misguided: they are trying to accomplish what is not on the agenda of a satisfactory theory. Whether the different forms of the GB theory actually assign the right representation to all the particular examples they are supposed to handle is a different question which I shall address separately.

It seems possible to pinpoint the methodological reason why the protagonists of GB-type theories have been led in effect to favor first-order representation. The reason is their idea of linguistic theories as generalizations from particular examples. As was noted earlier, most relatively simple examples can be handled by means of first-order ideas such as binding and scope. Hence it is tempting to try to rely on these ideas in all cases, if one follows the methodology of using particular cases only as material for a generalization. But one can try to use particular examples in a different way, namely as case studies which reveal under analysis the operative factors that determine the situation. This is how the basic ideas of GTS are intended to be defended. In fact, I have recently suggested that something like the game-theoretical way of looking at dependent quantifiers is implicit in any model-theoretical approach to them. And from a game-theoretical vantage point it is only to be expected that we have to go beyond conventional first-order logic.

As was also indicated, GTS encourages looking at the logical form of a sentence as being determined by the entire game connected with it, and not just by its surface form. In this respect, too, GTS serves as a corrective to GB-type theories.

Notes

1 Cf., e.g., Bertrand Russell, 1914 (especially his idea of 'logical constructs'); Ludwig Wittgenstein (1929, pp. 162–71).
2 Cf., e.g., W.V. Quine, 1960, where the idea of logical form enters mainly in the form of the translation of a natural-language sentence into a formal (but interpreted) first-order sentence; Donald Davidson, 1984, *passim*, especially 'Truth and Meaning', originally published in *Synthese*, 17 (1967), 304–23.
3 See Noam Chomsky, 1986; 1980; 1977; Peter Sells, 1985. Cf. also Robert May, 1985 and Norbert Hornstein, 1984.
4 Thus whatever syntactical structure a linguist ascribes to different natural-language sentences must be capable of serving as a starting-point of the derivation of the logical forms of these sentences. This imposes a tacit (and usually totally unacknowledged) constraint on even the most autonomous syntactical theories. This constraint helps in understanding the relevance of the concept of logical form even for pure syntacticians.

5   Wittgenstein, 1974, I, sec. 2.

6   There is an extensive literature on these sentences; see, e.g., Irene R. Heim, 1982; Hans Kamp, 1981; G. Evans, 1977.

7   In his textbook with Kalish and Mar, Richard Montague (1980) actually describes a procedure which is supposed to lead from an English sentence to its paraphrase in a logical notation. If this procedure works in pedagogical practice, what is taught to the students is an art and not a science, for the actual rules Montague presents are full of holes. For instance, the differences between different English quantifier words ('every', 'any', 'each', 'some', 'a(n)', etc.) are not paid any realistic attention, nor are so-called 'donkey sentences' (cf. below) nor cases of informational independence. But even in Montague's logico-linguistic work, these problems are not discussed in any real detail. See Richmond Thomason (ed.), 1974).

   For an example of how tricky the rules are that have to be followed in translating English quantifier words into a logical notation, see Jaakko Hintikka (1986).

8   The crucial concepts used in these theories include such notions as commanding, governing, and local domain, which are all closely related to the logical concept of scope, and binding, which is a generalization of its namesake notion in logic.

9   Thus Chomsky writes:

   It has, however, become clear that other features of semantic interpretation having to do with anaphora, scope, and the like are not represented at the level of D-structure [abstract underlying structure generated by phrase structure rules, *née* 'deep structure'] but rather at some level closer to surface structure, perhaps S-structure or a level of representation derived directly from it – a level sometimes called 'LF' to suggest 'logical form,' with familiar provisos to avoid possible misinterpretation. (1986, p. 67)

10 See in the first place Hintikka, 1983 (with a bibliography), and also Saarinen (ed.), 1979.

11 Thus Chomsky writes (1977, p. 197): 'This analysis is pretty much along the lines of standard logical analysis of the sentences of natural language'. The 'standard logical analysis' which Chomsky envisages here is unmistakably quantificational. In fact, his sentence occurs in the midst of a discussion of 'quantifier scope and variable binding'.

12 *Prima facie*, it might seem that I am distorting history (or terminology) here by calling these languages on the one hand Frege–Russell languages and on the other hand first-order languages, for the actual languages Frege and Russell operated with were higher-order ones. Basically, this does not make much difference. What makes a crucial difference is not whether one's notation includes a higher-order component, but whether one imposes what is known as the standard interpretation on this higher-order component. Now the idea of a standard interpretation was spelled out by Leon Henkin only in 1950. Furthermore, most of the early users of Frege's and Russell's logic, e.g., Russell himself and Wittgenstein, unmistakably assumed in effect a nonstandard interpretation of the higher-order component of their logical language. Hence they might as well have been doing (many-sorted) first-order logic.

   As to the commitment of these philosphers to quantificational languages, cf. e.g., Davidson (1984, p. 151): 'A satisfactory theory [of natural-language semantics] cannot depart much, it seems, from standard quantificational structures or their usual semantics.'

It is no accident that many of these friends of first-order logic belonged to the tradition I have called language as the universal medium. This tradition favors first-order languages as one's preferred *Begriffsschrift*. See Jaakko Hintikka, forthcoming (a), and Merrill B. Hintikka and Jaakko Hintikka, 1986, chapter 1.

13 This restriction to extensional idiom is in fact another symptom of the universalist syndrome mentioned in the preceding note. It does not concern us directly here, however.

14 There is an especially subtle methodological fallacy threatening us here. The fact that people can in most cases provide a translation of a given English sentence into a first-order language encourages a linguist to assume that somehow we language-users have tacit knowledge of suitable rules for the purpose, and hence that there must be such rules. I do not necessarily quarrel with this line of thought. But what would be mistaken is the idea that such rules must operate on the syntactical structure of the given sentence. Now fairly clearly the way language-users actually translate from English to a formal language is by means of some suitable informal *semantical* representations. They envisage what the English sentence *means*, and then reproduce the same meaning in the formal idiom. But then the translation is worthless as a means of studying how language-users actually understand their sentences, and people's ability to come up with first-order translations is no proof of the existence of syntax-based translation rules.

15 Neither Frege nor Russell actually presents the ambiguity thesis in its full generality in any one place. Its presence for the two logicians is nevertheless unmistakable. For its philosophical background in Frege, see Haaparanta 1985.

16 Of course, this palace revolution in the study of the history of philosophy has not been carried out by myself alone, but in concert with a number of other scholars, several of whom are contributors to *The Logic of Being* (1986).

17 According to GB theories, an anaphor like *himself* must be bound in its minimal governing category. The only expression in the minimal governing category of *himself* with which it could be coindexed is *each other*.

18 Instead of arguing directly in terms of analogies with unproblematic cases. The reason is that a GB-type argument presupposes the ascription of some one syntactical structure to the sentence in question. There is usually some amount of uncertainty about such an ascription. In contrast, as long as the analogy I am relying on really holds at the level of syntactic form, my conclusions follow no matter what the details of the analogous syntactic structures are.

19 For the rule for genitives, see Hintikka, 1983; Saarinen 1979, and Hintikka and Kulas, 1985. Note that a fully explicit rule for genitives must clearly be sensitive to semantical differences between different uses of the genitive. In the examples considered here, 'X's gift' means in effect 'gift by X', and is treated accordingly. This point does not affect my argument here, however.

20 None of the competing theories of anaphora offer a satisfactory explanation of this massive fact. Likewise, in GTS we can treat sentential anaphora and discourse in the same way without any additional assumptions.

21 One can of course re-introduce a notion of (possible) coreference into a game-theoretical theory of anaphora. A pronoun can be coreferential with a NP in this sense if the individual initially introduced by an application of a game rule into *I* can be chosen by the initial verifier in one of that player's winning strategies when it comes to the treatment of the pronoun. There is no harm in using the term 'coreference' in this sense. However, not only is it no longer a primitive concept in

one's semantic theory. Not only is it a derived and a rather complex notion. Since it involves a reference to particular winning strategies, it belongs to the theory of (what I have called) strategic meaning and not only to the theory of abstract meaning. See Hintikka, 1987c, pp. 497–529.

22   There are in fact not likely to be a full set of sharp syntax-based rules for membership in I. Speakers in effect 'conveniently forget' members of I. Such fluctuations in the membership in I can only be handled pragmatically, as a part of the dynamics of actual discourse. Cf., e.g., Hintikka and Kulas, 1985, pp. 137–8.

23   This is the most fundamental idea of GTS. It is deeply rooted in the very meaning of dependent quantifiers and in their uses in actual reasoning, as I have argued (Hintikka, forthcoming(b)).

24   As Dana Scott pointed out as early as 1968 (unpublished), Gödel's translation of first-order logic and arithmetic into a higher-order one is most naturally motivated game-theoretically.

References

Barwise, Jon 1979: On branching quantifiers in English. *Journal of Philosophical Logic*, 8, 47–80.

Chomsky, Noam 1977: *Essays on Form and Interpretation*. Amsterdam: North-Holland.
   1980: *Rules and Representations*. New York: Columbia University Press.
   1986: *Knowledge of Language: Its Nature, Origin, and Use*. New York: Praeger.

Davidson, Donald 1984: *Inquiries into Truth and Interpretation*. Oxford: Clarendon Press.

Evans, G. 1977: Pronouns, quantifiers and relative clauses. *Canadian Journal of Philosophy*, 7, 467–536.

Gödel, Kurt 1958: Über eine bisher noch nicht benützte Erweiterung des finiten Standpunktes. *Dialectica*, 12, 280–7.

Haaparanta, Leila 1985: *Frege's Doctrine of Being*. (Acta Philosophica Fennica 39.) Helsinki: Societas Philosophica Fennica.

Heim, Irene R. 1982: The semantics of definite and indefinite noun phrases. Unpublished dissertation, University of Massachusetts at Amherst.

Henkin, Leon 1950: Completeness in the theory of types. *Journal of Symbolic Logic*, 15, 81–91.

Hintikka, Jaakko 1974: Quantifiers vs. quantification theory. *Linguistic Inquiry*, 5, 153–77. Repr. in Saarinen (ed.) 1979: *Game-Theoretical Semantics*.
   1979: 'Is', semantical games, and semantical relativity. *Journal of Philosophical Logic*, 8, 433–68. Repr. in Hintikka 1983: *The Game of Language*.
   1982: Questions with outside quantifiers. In R. Schneider, K. Tuite, and R. Chametzky (eds), *Papers from the Parasession on Nondeclaratives*. Chicago: Chicago Linguistic Society, 83–92.
   1983: *The Game of Language*. Dordrecht: Reidel.
   1986: On the semantics of 'a certain'. *Linguistic Inquiry*, 17, 331–6.
   1987a: Logic translation – an impossible dream? *LMPS '87: Abstracts*, 5 (3), 30–2.
   1987b: Is scope a viable concept in semantics? In Fred Miller *et al.* (eds) *ESCOL '86*. Ohio: Ohio State University at Columbus, Dept of Linguistics, 259–70.
   1987c: Language understanding and strategic meaning. *Synthese*, 73, 497–529.
   forthcoming(a): Is truth ineffable?
   forthcoming(b): On the development of the model-theoretical tradition in logical theory. *Synthese*.

Hintikka, Jaakko and Saarinen, Esa 1975: Semantical games and the Bach–Peters paradox. *Theoretical Linguistics*, 2, 1–20. Repr. in Saarinen (ed.), 1979: *Game-Theoretical Semantics*.

Hintikka, Jaakko and Kulas, Jack 1985: *Anaphora and Definite Descriptions: Two Applications of Game-Theoretical Semantics*. Dordrecht: Reidel.

Hintikka, Jaakko and Sandu, Gabriel (forthcoming): Informational independence as a semantical phenomenon. Paper presented at the 1987 International Congress of Logic, Methodology, and Philosophy of Science (Section on the Foundations of Linguistics). *Proceedings of the Congress*.

Hintikka, Jaakko and Knuuttila, Simo (eds) 1986: *The Logic of Being: Historical Studies*. Dordrecht: Reidel.

Hintikka, Merrill B. and Hintikka, Jaakko 1986: *Investigating Wittgenstein*. Oxford: Basil Blackwell.

Hornstein, Norbert 1984: *Logic as Grammar*. Cambridge, Mass.: MIT Press.

Kamp, Hans 1981: A theory of truth and semantic representation. In J. Groenendijk *et al.* (eds), *Formal Methods in the Study of Language*. Amsterdam: Mathematical Centre.

Karttunen, Lauri 1971: Definite descriptions with crossing coreference. *Foundations of Language*, 7, 157–82.

May, Robert 1985: *Logical Form*. Cambridge, Mass.: MIT Press.

Montague, Richard, Kalish, D. and Mar, G. 1980: *Logic: Techniques of Formal Reasoning*, 2nd edn. New York: Harcourt Brace Jovanovich.

Otto, Herbert R. 1978: *The Linguistic Basis of Logic Translation*. Washington. D.C.: University Press of America.

Quine, W.V. 1960: *Word and Object*. Cambridge. Mass.: MIT Press.

Russell, Bertrand 1914: *Our Knowledge of the External World*. London: Allen and Unwin.

Saarinen, Esa (ed.) 1979: *Game-Theoretical Semantics*. Dordrecht: Reidel.

Sells, Peter 1985: *Lectures on Contemporary Syntactic Theories*. Stanford, Calif.: CSLI.

Thomason, Richmond (ed.) 1986: *Formal Philosophy: Selected Papers of Richard Montague*. New Haven: Yale University Press.

Wittgenstein, Ludwig 1929: Some remarks on logical form. *Aristotelian Society Supplementary Volume* 9, 162–71.

1974: *Philosophical Grammar*. Oxford: Basil Blackwell.

4

Types and Tokens in Linguistics

Sylvain Bromberger

Introduction

Generative linguistics[1] is a perplexing field of inquiry when looked at with philosophic issues in mind. This is so not only because perplexing paradoxes bedevil the naive notions of rule, meaning, truth-condition, reference, or because a multiplicity of interests and beliefs conflict over how its subject-matter should be disentangled in a principled way from other things that influence speech, but also because simple truisms on which its very possibility depends seem problematic on close scrutiny. In this chapter, I want to consider three of these truisms:

(1) Linguistics rests on information about types such as word types and sentence types. Since these are abstract entities, it therefore rests on information about intrinsic properties of abstract entities.[2]

(2) Some – possibly all – of the information about types that is relevant to linguistics is empirical information, that is, information that must be obtained by attending with one's senses. Typically that information is obtained by attending to utterances, that is, to tokens.

(3) Linguistics must concern itself with psychology since the intrinsic properties of types, and their arrangements under various languages must follow – in part at least – from facts about people's mental makeup.

Many linguists are apt to dismiss qualms about these truisms as contrived or frivolous. Their attitude is easy to understand: if (1), (2), and (3) were not true (and hence compatible), linguistics research would be impossible. But linguistics research is obviously not impossible, as attested by ongoing progress and many results, explanations, and predictions. So (1), (2), and (3) must be true and compatible. Why raise doubts about them? They have analogues in other successful disciplines. Why pick on linguistics?

And yet, consider (1) and (2). That we can get information about abstract entities at all is puzzling. It is a problem that philosophers of mathematics must also face. But the conjunction of (1) and (2) raises a problem not pertinent to mathematics but pertinent to linguistics. Philosophers of mathematics face a problem of *a priori* knowledge, that is, a problem raised by the possibility (or at least apparent possibility) of *non-empirical* knowledge about abstract entities. The conjunction of (1) and (2) raises a problem of *a posteriori* knowledge, that is, a problem raised by the possibility (or apparent possibility) of *empirical* knowledge about abstract entities. Empirical information – mentioned in (2) – is based on perceptions and perceptions require causal interactions through which the things observed affect sensory organs. But abstract entities – mentioned in (1) – cannot causally affect anything. They are not in space or time and hence do not participate in spatio-temporal episodes. Causal interactions are spatio-temporal episodes. If linguistics rests on information about abstract entities, how can that information be empirical? How could perception of anything yield information about intrinsic properties of types?[3]

Tokens can be observed. Spoken tokens[4] are events (or aspects of events) that impact our ears, produce kinesthetic sensations, involve detectable movements, and embody occurrent intentions. But according to (1), tokens are not what linguistics is primarily concerned with. Types are. However, according to (2) tokens can yield information about types. But how? It cannot be in the way facts about invisible things are accessed in the physical sciences by observing visible ones, that is, the way physicists reconstruct aspects of invisible electron–neutron collisions from visible repercussions in a cloud chamber, or astronomers infer the rate of motion of galaxies beyond their view from spectrometer readings. Those achievements rely on causal links between things that impact senses (for instance, vapor condensing in a cloud chamber) and things thus 'indirectly' observed (for instance, electrons colliding with neutrons). Causal links between spatio-temporal events make them possible. But, as already noted, types, being abstract entities,[5] cannot be – or participate in events that are – causally linked to anything, including tokens.[6]

Now consider (1) and (3). How can these two be true together? Whatever psychology is about, it is not about abstract entities. It is about mental states, mental structures, mental competences, physiology, neurology, perhaps behavior; and its procedures are designed to yield nomological generalizations and explanatory theories about these. But how can generalizations or explanatory theories about such things have any bearing on intrinsic properties of any abstract entities, or on the ways they group? Or, conversely, how can intrinsic facts about abstract entities have any bearing on generalizations or explanations about things like mental states and the like? In short, how can intrinsic properties of types (or groupings of types) follow from anything about historically contingent configurations at all, be they mental, neurological, behavioral, or anything else? The link, for the reasons given above, cannot be causal. What other link could there be?

Could (2) be false? That seems incredible. The facts that linguists ferret out are contingent facts,[7] and contingent facts – except perhaps for some *recherché* and controversial metaphysical principles – are accessible only through empirical investigation. And in any case, it is undeniable that linguists attend to tokens in the course of their investigations, produce them, judge them, or have informants produce them and judge them. This is not to say that only empirical information about tokens matters to them, or that they perform statistical inductions from observed cases. Nor is it to say that they consider every token, no matter when or how produced, to be evidence. But their inductive procedures – however analyzed – do include the canon that linguistic hypotheses are refutable by empirically supported counterexamples and are corroborated by empirically confirmed consequences.

Could (3) be false? Though widely taken for granted, (3) has been denied and ignored in practice. Many linguists reject the suggestion that their theorizing should be responsive to learning theory or other branches of psychology. Linguists, like philosophers, are also still divided between supporters of versions of Platonism and supporters of versions of psychologism. Chomsky's arguments against E-language approaches and in favor of I-language ones are but a recent episode in that debate, and will not end it. Psychologism has an air of realism, but Platonism simplifies discourse. And Platonism sounds plausible. Think of English. It is a language that happens to be spoken by certain people during a certain historical period across a certain region. But those are contingent facts about English. Linguists are after essential facts. English might not have been spoken by these people. In some possible worlds it is not. It might not have been spoken by anyone: in some possible worlds it is not. In the first of these worlds no facts about English follow from any facts about actual speakers of English,[8] and in the latter ones no facts about English follow from any facts about any human beings. Since pure linguists – as opposed to psycholinguists – working on English are after essential facts, that is, facts that hold in any possible world, including worlds in which it is not spoken, they can disregard that some of them happen to follow from facts about human beings in this world, and they can therefore ignore possible connections to psychology. The same argument for Platonism can be repeated about any language. However, it is not conclusive. It assumes the problematic thesis that English types, like numbers, exist in every possible world. More important, it leaves open whether English would be of any interest to linguists or could even be discovered if no one spoke it, that is, in a possible world in which no one does. Later I will argue that facts about English, or other languages, are of interest and are discoverable only because they follow from facts about the minds of speakers in this world.

Could (1) be false?[9] Could linguistics turn out not to be about types even though linguistics books and journals seem full of facts (or alleged facts) about types, and even though typical linguistic claims seem to mention types? For instance, it is claimed that the underlying phonological representation of 'serene' is identical to the underlying representation of the stem of 'serenity' (although their tokens are phonetically very different), that the last morpheme in 'ungrammaticality' takes adjectives into nouns (although none of the tokens is used to make an adjectival modification), that the phonetic shape of 'Flying planes can be dangerous' is associated with two different sets of thematic role assignments (although no token is), that 'He loves herself' violates gender agreement (although tokens occur probably only to mention this fact), and so on.

According to one view, mention of types is perhaps dispensable. Chomsky (1985, ch. 2) can be read as advocating a version of that view; he urges that linguistics be construed as about I-language and not about E-language. Chomsky here contrasts two approaches to linguistic study. Linguistic approaches that take E-language as their subject-matter presuppose that each language is a system of expressions – or expressions paired with meanings – that is, a system of types[10] – and take on the task of characterizing these systems, that is, of discovering rules or principles from which the types of a given language can be generated, in terms of which their interconnections and individual attributes can be predicted, and through which their kinship to other languages can be made explicit. Linguistic programs that take I-language as their subject-matter assume a different ontology. They start from the position that brain states are real, and that to know a language (to have an I-language) is to be in a certain brain state. And they take on the task of characterizing such states (under idealizations and by abstracting from physiological mechanisms). Thus I-language linguistics needs to admit only certain spatio-temporal things: utterances (and judgments elicited by utterances), which are spatio-temporal events, and brain states, which are states of spatio-temporal entities. The former can inform about the latter, and the latter can account for features of the former. But types play no role in I-languages.

But even subscribers to the I-language approach can, without inconsistency, subscribe to (1): (1) does not require that linguistics be concerned with anything like E-languages, nor does it rule out I-languages as legitimate subject-matter. They can admit types, while denying that languages are properly individuated as sets of types. Chomsky himself actually writes of I-languages as generating classes of expressions (1985, ch. 2). And they probably should subscribe to (1). Claims made by linguists – including claims by Chomsky in technical sections of *Knowledge of Language* – almost always mention types, and only exceptionally mention tokens. Thus in practice, if perhaps not in theory, linguistics must be concerned with facts about types.

So we are stuck with the problems raised by (1), (2), and (3). If (1) and (2) are both true, it is despite the fact that inferences from tokens to types do not presuppose causal links. What then is the nature of these inferences? And unless better reasons are found for denying (3), we need to understand how features of the mind can have repercussions in a realm of abstract entities.

In what follows I propose a solution to these problems. That solution hinges critically on the presumption that theory construction proceeds on a foundation of questions. Such questions are sometimes stated but are more often simply taken for granted. Therefore their role is easily overlooked. They are nevertheless fundamental constituents of the various classificatory systems on which theories rely, and they define the domain in which any given theory operates. In this respect linguistic theorizing is like that in any of the other natural sciences. I do not defend that presumption in this chapter, but by discussing its operation and by juxtaposing linguistic examples with others I hope to make it credible.

My solution hardly qualifies as a theory. It consists mostly of definitions and some illustrations to make these concrete. The relevant facts are clear. What we need are clear ways of envisaging them.

The Platonic Relationship Principle

One reason for believing that (1) and (2) can be reconciled is that linguists, in practice, often impute properties to types after observing and judging some of their tokens, and seem to do this in a principled way. Let us call the principle on which they (implicitly) rely the *Platonic Relationship Principle* to underline that it guides their attention from worldly to abstract entities. How does the Platonic Relationship Principle operate? We know that it cannot assume that types and tokens are causally related. But it must assume that they are related in some way. What way? The answer I will propose in this section is that

(4) Tokens of a type make up a quasi-natural kind, and their type is the archetype of that quasi-natural kind.

I now turn to an explanation of that answer.

Quasi-natural kinds

Quasi-natural kinds, as I use the term, are groupings, classes, assemblages, that are in many – but not all – respects like natural kinds. The notion of natural kind – insofar as it is clear at all – is loaded with historical and parochial connotations that are irrelevant for present purposes. The notion of quasi-natural kinds discards most of these connotations and preserves what I regard as essential for investigative purposes. It is free, for instance, of any association with 'nature', whatever that may be; artefacts can make up quasi-natural kinds.

Quasi-natural kinds satisfy three conditions which I will label 'the modeling condition', 'the explainable differences condition', and 'the individuation condition'.

The modeling condition is that each member of a quasi-natural kind must be a model of every other member of that kind. That condition enables inferences of facts about any arbitrary member from similar facts about any other member.

The notion of model on which I rely here is the notion of model appropriate for artefactual models. An artefactual model is an object so designed that, by finding the answer to some questions about it, a competent user can figure out the answer to questions about something else. So, for instance, by counting the number of smokestacks on a model of the *QE II* an initiated user can figure out the number of smokestacks on the real *QE II*; by counting the number of black spheres on a wire and wood model of methane, an initiated user can figure out the number of carbon atoms in a methane molecule. Or take maps. A map is a model of the territory it represents. By getting the answer to, for instance, (5) and (6) about the map

(5) What is the distance between point *a* on the map and point *b* on the map?

(6) How many contour lines occur between point *a* and point *b* on the map?

one can get the answer to the following questions about the territory mapped:

(7) What is the distance between place *A* in the territory and place *B* in the territory?

(8) What is the difference in altitude between place *A* in the territory and place *B* in the territory?

But there are usually limits to what even an initiated reader can find out in this way. Though one can find the answer to

(9) What is the name of the publisher printed on the map?

by looking at the map, the rules of map reading will not turn that answer into the answer to any question about the territory. And conversely, few maps, if any, yield the answer to such questions about the territory as

(10) How many stones are there in the northern half of the territory?

or

(11) How many bicyclists were riding in the northern half of the territory on 4 July 1984 at noon?

In short, ignoring artefactness, the idea of a model comes down to the following:

(12) M is a model of O relative to a quadruple $<Q_m, Q_o, P, A>$ if and only if, in that quadruple, Q_m is a nonempty set of questions about M, Q_o is a nonempty set of questions about O, P pairs members of Q_m with members of Q_o, and A is an algorithm that translates answers to any member of Q_m into answers to the member of Q_o paired with it by P, and translates correct answers to the former into correct answers to the latter.

Note that this concept of a model is that of a diadic relation: no object is intrinsically a model. It takes a pair. Note also that it is a relativized notion. No pair of objects stands (or fails to stand) in the model/modeled relation absolutely, but only relative to specific sets of questions, pairings of questions, and algorithms.

but only relative to specific sets of questions, pairings of questions, and algorithms.

Things not usually called models of each other nevertheless stand in the relation described in (12): samples of mercury, for instance. Let 'm_1' and 'm_2' designate two samples of mercury, then (13) will hold:

(13) m_1 and m_2 are two good samples of mercury only if m_1 is a model of m_2 with regard to the quadruple consisting of:
   a. Q_{m_1}, a set of questions about m_1 that includes 'What is the boiling point of m_1?', 'What is the freezing point of m_1?', 'What is the molecular weight of m_1?';
   b. Q_{m_2}, a set of questions about m_2 that includes 'What is the boiling point of m_2?', 'What is the freezing point of m_2?', 'What is the molecular weight of m_2?'
   c. The pairing P_m that matches each question in Q_{m_1} with the question in Q_{m_2} exactly like it but for the switch from reference to m_1 to reference to m_2.
   d. The algorithm A_m that matches identical answers but for the switch from reference to m_1 to reference to m_2.

In satisfying (13), samples of mercury do more than just satisfy (12). Those additional features are important in what follows. I will shorten their description with the help of the following convention on which I will also rely throughout the rest of this paper:

(14) *The Related Questions Convention:*[11] When some $Q(n_1)$ is a question that is about something n_1, and some $Q(n_2)$ is a question that is about something n_2, and $Q(n_1)$ can be turned into $Q(n_2)$ by substituting n_2 for n_1, do not distinguish unnecessarily between $Q(n_1)$ and $Q(n_2)$ but refer to them as one and the same question about both n_1 and n_2. And when the (right) answer to $Q(n_1)$ can be turned into the right answer to $Q(n_2)$ by again substituting n_2 for n_1, do not distinguish unnecessarily between these two answers, but refer to one single answer that holds for both $Q(n_1)$ and $Q(n_2)$.

So, for instance, the point about the boiling point in (13) can now be made by saying that m_1 and m_2 bear the same answer to

(15) What is the (or its) boiling point?

Let us now return to those additional features:

A.   The universal generalization of (13) with respect to the positions occupied by m_1 and m_2 is also true. In other words, though any two samples of mercury are mutual models relative to many quadruples over and above those sketched in (13), the quadruples sketched in (13) work for every two samples of mercury. B.   The universal generalization of (13) is true when construed as a nomological, law-like, generalization. Counterfactuals instantiated from it are

true. If the water in the glass before me right now were a sample of mercury, it would be a model of any sample of mercury relative to the quadruple in (13).
C. P_m and A_m combine to match identical answers to identical questions.
D. Some of the questions mentioned in (13) bear answers that are amenable to explanation, that is, that can serve as object to sound why-questions,[12] and these why-questions in turn get identical answers. So, for instance,

(16) What is its boiling point?

gets the same answer for every sample of mercury

(17) 356.6°C

and that answer is the object of the sound why-question (that is, a why-question that has a true 'because' answer)

(18) Why is the boiling point 356.6°C?

which, in turn gets the same answer for every sample of mercury (something about molecular bonds).

The modeling condition on quasi-natural kinds incorporates these additional features A–D. Fully stated, it then becomes:

(19) Every member of a quasi-natural kind is nomologically a model for every other member relative to some questions askable of each and to which each bears the same answer with the same explanation.

If we use *questions projectible for N* to mention the questions that render (19) true for a quasi-natural kind N, we can restate (19) as follows:

(20) If N is a quasi-natural kind, then there is a nonempty set Q_p of projectible questions for N, and if the answer[13] to any of them gives rise to a why-question[14] then that why-question is also projectible for N.

The explainable differences condition requires that some differences among the members of a quasi-natural kind be systematic differences, that is, differences that follow from laws, or principles, or theories, and kinds of circumstance that pertain to all its members. So, for instance, samples of mercury differ in temperature, but the temperature of each at any given time is accounted for by laws and kinds of boundary conditions common to all samples of mercury at all times. The second condition, more fully stated, is that

(21) If N is a quasi-natural kind then there is a nonempty set of questions Q_a
   a. whose presuppositions are satisfied by every member[15] of N;
   b. to which different members of N bear a different answer;
   c. whose right answer in each case – that is, for each member – is the object of a sound why-question;
   d. whose answer, in turn, in every case, follows from common nomological principles, supplemented by contingencies peculiar to the case but of a kind applicable to all.

The point of the condition on presuppositions is to allow for failures of presupposition. An example will show what is going on: 'What is the age of the person who was king of France in 1987?' has no answer because no king of France existed in 1987. That is a failure of existential presupposition. 'How fast did Julius Caesar fly when he crossed the Rubicon?' has no answer, not because Julius Caesar did not exist but because Julius Caesar did not fly when he crossed the Rubicon – or for that matter at any other time. That is a failure not of existential presupposition, but of something I have called elsewhere attributive presupposition. Different sorts of things satisfy different sorts of attributive presuppositions. Thus samples of mercury satisfy the attributive presupposition of 'What is its boiling point?' but not of 'What is its limit?' The situation reverses for mathematical series.

Actually this condition has to be further qualified. What I should really say is that there is a nonempty set of presuppositions which are satisfied by every member of N modulo reference to locations in space or in time, that is, if we abstract from certain specification of places and times. So for instance the sample of mercury in the dish before me right now may not satisfy the presupposition of

(22) What was its temperature on 7 July 1924 at noon?

because it did not exist on 7 July 1924. But it must satisfy the presupposition of some questions of the form 'What was its temperature on . . .? However, since (21) will play only a minor role in what follows, I will leave it in this relatively crude state for the present.

Let us call questions that satisfy (21) *w-projectible questions for N*. Then, returning to our example, (22) is a *w*-projectible question for samples of mercury, since (a) every sample of mercury satisfies its presupposition,[16] that is, has a specific temperature at specific times; (b) different samples of mercury have different temperatures at specific times; (c) whatever the temperature of a sample of mercury at a certain time may happen to be, the question

(23) Why did it have that temperature at that time?

has a correct answer, and at least one right answer to (23) for each sample follows from the same general principles (for instance, of kinetic theory) supplemented by boundary conditions peculiar to the sample but of a sort common to all (for instance, having to do with intermolecular bonds).

The individuation condition requires that the members of a quasi-natural kind be differentiated along common dimensions but not in ways that answer projectible questions or *w*-projectible questions. So, for instance, samples of mercury are at different places at different times and these locations are not the consequence of laws or principles common to all of them. Their parts get scattered and assembled by agents and in ways for which no single principled explanation is forthcoming. So that third condition is

(24) If N is a quasi-natural kind, then there is a nonempty set Q_i of questions whose presupposition is satisfied by every member of N, but which are neither projectible nor w-projectible for N.

Let us call such questions *individuating questions for N*. So

(25) Where was it on 7 July 1924?

is an individuating question for samples of mercury.
   The definition of a quasi-natural kind is then:

(26) A class of objects constitutes a quasi-natural kind relative to triple $<Q_p/A_p, Q_w, Q_i>$ – in which Q_p, Q_w, and Q_i are nonempty sets of questions and A_p a nonempty set of answers matched with members of Q_p – if and only if it is the largest class of objects for which the questions in Q_p are projectible, those in Q_w are w-projectible, and those in Q_i are individuating, and that bear the members of A_p as answers to the members of Q_p with which they are matched.

   The notion of quasi-natural kind is a relative notion: no class of things is a quasi-natural kind absolutely, and a given class may be a quasi-natural kind relative to more than one set of questions. When this happens, the individual members will belong to distinct but coextensive quasi-natural kinds, like cordates and renates. They may of course also belong to distinct quasi-natural kinds that are not coextensive.
   Some questions are ruled out as potential projectible, w-projectible, or individuating questions for taxonomizing the members of some classes. For instance

(27) How much income tax did it pay in 1924?

(28) What nutrients does it require to survive?

are ruled out for the members of the class made up of samples of mercury.

Archetype of a quasi-natural kind

The archetype of a quasi-natural kind is an entity very similar to but also very different from the members of that quasi-natural kind. It is very similar to the members because it is an exact model of them relative to the projectible questions of the kind. (By exact model I mean a model that bears the same answers to the same questions.) But it is very different from them because it bears no answer at all to any of the w-projectible questions or to any of the individuating questions of the kind.
   So, for instance, the archetype of samples of mercury is an entity that is very similar to a sample of mercury: it bears the same answer as any sample of mercury to questions such as

(29) What is its boiling point? Answer: 356.6°C

(30) What is its freezing point? Answer: $-38.87°C$

(31) What is its molecular weight? Answer: 200.6

In other words, it is an exact model of any sample of mercury with regard to these questions. But it is very different from any sample of mercury when it comes to such questions as

(32) What was its temperature on 7 July 1924 at noon?

(33) Where was it on 7 July 1924?

Whereas samples of mercury bear various answers to (32) and (33) and other w-projectible and individuating questions, their archetype bears none at all. It had no temperature at all on 7 July 1924, and it was nowhere on 7 July 1924.[17] The archetype of samples of mercury has a boiling point, a melting point, a molecular weight, an index of electric conductivity, but it has no mass, no volume, no history, no location, no age. That is how it is an abstract entity: it fails to meet the presuppositions of the w-projectible questions and of the individuating questions in the same sense as the samples themselves fail to meet the presuppositions of (27) and (28).

So far I have spoken of 'the' archetype of the samples of mercury, as if there is only one, as if samples of mercury (or members of other quasi-natural kinds) have – that is, exemplify – only one archetype. That is not quite right: samples of mercury and members of other quasi-natural kinds may – and do – exemplify more than one archetype. This is so because they belong to more than one quasi-natural kind and because some of these quasi-natural kinds differ from each other by being related to different sets of projectible questions. They exemplify each of the archetypes that emerge through the projectible questions from these various quasi-natural kinds. Furthermore, since distinct samples of mercury (or members of any quasi-natural kind) probably also belong to distinct and *non-coextensive* quasi-natural kinds, distinct samples of mercury probably also exemplify distinct archetypes.

Summarizing all this, the definition of an archetype is then:

(34) R is the archetype of Q – where Q is a quasi-natural class relative to the triple $<Q_p/A_p, Q_w, Q_i>$ – if and only if R bears A_p as answers to Q_p and bears no answers at all to any of the members of Q_w or Q_i.

where we understand 'R bears A_p as answers to Q_p' to mean that R bears the members of A_p as answers to the questions in Q_p matched to them for Q.

And a statement of the Platonic Relationship Principle follows readily from this definition:

(35) If T is the archetype of the quasi-natural kind relative to $<Q_p/A_p, Q_w, Q_i>$, then the answer to any question in Q_p with reference aimed at T is the matched member of A_p with reference aimed at T.

The operation of the principle is so simple and transparent that – not surprisingly – it is hardly ever noticed. To infer the properties of an archetype from any of its examples is often trivially easy. The difficult job is to discover $<Q_p/A_p, Q_w, Q_i>$ triples relative to which individuals form revealing quasi-natural kinds.

Most interesting archetypes lack spatial or temporal locations. But their intrinsic attributes are in principle – that is, but for limits of expressive power – exhaustively describable: each archetype is characterized by a set of question–answer pairs, namely the set of projectible question–answer pairs of some quasi-natural kind, and is therefore exhaustively described – except for relational properties – by any text that encodes the information in such a set.[18] So, for instance, one of the archetypes of samples of mercury is specified by an array such as

(36) a. What is its boiling point?/356.6°C
b. What is its freezing point?/−38.87°C
c. What is its molecular weight?/200.6
and so on

and that archetype is described by any text that describes it as bearing these answers to those questions.

Since fictitious entities too are exhaustively describable, this may suggest that archetypes are but fictions. But if archetypes are fictions, they are very unlike the garden variety of fictitious entities. The latter are describable only because someone has actually described them. Archetypes are describable even if no one has described them. In fact, most will probably never be described. Our archetype of samples of mercury happens to be describable in contemporary English. It could not have been described in classical Greek. Classical Greek lacked the right nomenclature. Similar lexical shortcomings no doubt block the description of other archetypes in contemporary English. And in all likelihood archetypes exist that will never be describable in any of the languages that have or will ever be spoken by anyone. I cannot prove this, but the subjective probability is irresistible. Whether a given archetype is describable in a certain language depends on whether certain questions are expressible in that language. And some questions will never be expressible in any language that will ever be spoken by anyone.[19] Some quasi-natural kinds, and hence some archetypes, must be related to some of these questions. Even these archetypes are inherently describable. They are not ineffable. Only accidents of lexical evolution block their description. Even so, unlike garden-variety fictitious entities, they are doomed never to be described. So those archetypes at least are not garden-variety fictitious entities. Why should any of them be?

Archetypes may nevertheless seem unreal. The archetype of the samples of mercury, for instance, presumably has a molecular weight. But can anything real have a molecular weight without being made up of molecules and hence being in space and in time? And if it is in space and in time, must it not have spatio-temporal locations, and thus satisfy the presuppositions of individuating questions about where it was when? Similar worries may come up around other archetypes, including the linguistic types to which I am about to turn. They need not concern us for the present. The crucial point, for present purposes, about the archetype of a quasi-natural kind is that it is fully characterized by an array of question–answer pairs, and that it is fully described by any text that encodes the contents of such an array, and that we have ways of referring to it. We can even think of archetypes as simply such arrays. Of course, if we do this, we will have to talk about them differently. We will, for instance, have to stop saying that the archetype of samples of mercury satisfies the presuppositions of (29)–(31). No such array can. We will have to say instead that the archetype 'includes' (29)–(31).[20] I will not adopt this way of speaking because I do not see the need for it. But it should be compatible with everything that matters in the rest of the chapter. And it will be more pleasing to anyone who feels that my notion of archetype may have a role in theorizing about the world (the way virtual images or frictionless planes do for instance) but cannot denote any actual item in it.

Tokens and types

We can now understand (4). If the first clause is true, then tokens cluster into sets each of which satisfies (26), and if the second clause is true, each type exemplified by tokens corresponds to a set of questions whose answers are shared by that type and each of its tokens, that is, projectible questions. If both clauses are true, then the Platonic Relationship Principle is available to infer properties of types from properties of the tokens that exemplify them: the properties of the type are those born as answers to projectible questions by each of the exemplifying tokens.

But are the two clauses of (4) true? It is difficult to tell without knowing more about the triples $<Q_p/A_p, Q_m, Q_i>$ pertinent to each case. And the number of such cases is infinite! With the information we have so far, it is even difficult to tell whether all types that have tokens are archetypes, or whether only some are. Fortunately, we need not find out whether (4) is true to deal with our problems about linguistics, that is, with (1) and (2) of the introduction. The important issue as far as our problem is concerned is whether linguistics operates on the presumption that both clauses of (4) are true. For that to be true, by the way, it is not necessary that linguists ever express the notions of *quasi-natural kind*, or *projectible question*, or *archetype*, that is, notions that have applications beyond linguistics. But it is required that they on occasion rely either explicitly or implicitly on the Platonic Relationship Principle in a way that implicates its erotetic aspects. And there are reasons for holding that they do.

One somewhat strange but nevertheless good reason for holding this is that linguists seldom if ever mention tokens or, more precisely, habitually conflate mention of tokens with mention of types. That is easily explained if linguists are held to rely on the Platonic Relationship Principle. The questions that concern linguists when they focus on a token (and attending judgments) while concerned about its type are questions that apply indifferently to the type and to the token and whose answer is the same for both.[21] If types are what they care about and tokens are but fleeting evidence, then only pedantry could drive them to highlight the distinction.

A more obvious reason for holding that they rely on the Platonic Relationship Principle is that it is difficult to see how else any inference from types to tokens can proceed. One view is that tokens group under types simply by resemblances with respect to certain traits, and that these traits are directly imputed to their types, without the intrusion of questions. On this view mention of questions is an uncalled-for complication. I will argue later that, on the contrary, questions play a critical role – or, if not questions, at least the determinables that constitute their core. But even now we can see that this view leaves us in the dark about the kinds of resemblances that are relevant for the construction of further theories.

A further reason for holding that linguists rely on the Platonic Relationship Principle is that they conceptualize tokens in ways that make these amenable to applications of the principle, and that cannot just be an accident. Examples will establish the point.

Tokens of the English word type represented orthographically as

(37) bell

for instance, are presumed to form a quasi-natural kind relative to a set whose projectible questions/answers include at least

(38) What is its underlying phonological structure?/[bəl]

(39) How many syllables does it have?/One

(40) What are the dorsal features of its second segment?/[−back], [−high], [−low]

(41) What is its syntactic category?/Noun

(42) What is its number?/Singular

whose *w*-projectible questions include

(43) What thematic role did it express?

(44) How strongly was the vowel stressed?

(45) In what speech act did it occur?

(46) Was it being used literally?

(47) To what object, if any, did it refer?

and whose individuating questions include

(48) Where was it uttered?

(49) When was it uttered?

(50) To whom, if anyone, was it addressed?

(51) By whom was it uttered?

And the type of these tokens bears the same answers to (39)–(42) as the tokens themselves, but fails to meet the presuppositions of (43)–(51) and the rest.

Tokens of the English sentence type orthographically depicted as

(52) John's picture of himself is nice.

are presumed to form a quasi-natural kind relative to a set whose projectible questions/answers include at least

(53) What is its S-structure?/$[_S[_{NP}[_{NP}John's][_{NP}[_N picture][_{pp}of himself]]][_{VP} is nice]]$[22]

(54) What is its phonological representation?/(I omit the lengthy answer.)

(55) What is the antecedent of the reflexive?/The determiner of the subject NP

(56) What thematic roles are represented by which phrases?/(I omit the answer, again, as too lengthy and also too controversial.)

with w-projectible questions that include

(57) What object does the subject NP refer to?

(58) What is its truth value?

(59) What speech act was performed through its production?

(60) Which vowels were reduced in its production?

and so on,

with individuating questions that include

(61) Who uttered it?

(62) When was it uttered?

(63) Why was it uttered?

(64) How loudly was it uttered?

and so on.

And the type of these tokens bears the same answers to (53)–(56) as the tokens themselves, but fails to meet the presuppositions of (57)–(64) and the rest.

It may be objected that this way of viewing the relation between tokens and their types is implausible and cannot accord with linguistic practice. Spoken tokens are sounds describable in acoustic terms or articulatory gesticulations describable in physiological terms. It is as sounds or articulatory gesticulations that they affect our senses. But sounds and articulatory gesticulations have no grammatical or phonological underpinnings. Therefore, the objection goes, no token can satisfy the presuppositions of questions such as (38). Tokens themselves do not have underlying structures. That fact may be hidden in the 'bell' example because, in this case, the surface structure of the type is identical to the underlying structure. But is it plausible that a token of the word spelled 'dogs' should in any sense have an underlying structure roughly like '/dog+es/'? Similar objections will readily come to mind about some of the questions said to be projectible for the tokens of (52).

The claim that spoken tokens are sounds describable in acoustic terms, or articulatory gesticulations describable in physiological terms, and that they affect our sense organs as such is uncontroversial. They undoubtedly even form quasi-natural kinds relative to some $<Q_p/A_p, Q_m, Q_i>$ with other noises and articulatory gesticulations that have affected someone's senses, that is, quasi-natural kinds anchored to questions about acoustic and articulatory attributes with presuppositions also satisfied by grunts and burps and snorts and snores.[23] We have seen that members of quasi-natural kinds can belong to more than one natural kind. But that fact does not disqualify tokens from being topics of questions about phonological or syntactic attributes, and hence from also belonging to quasi-natural kinds relative to sets of such questions. Speech utterances are, after all, very different from other noises and articulatory gestures. Unlike other noises, they are produced by agents with phonological, syntactic, semantic, and pragmatic intentions. They embody and manifest such intentions. And they have attributes that encode such intentions. Their underlying phonological structure, the number and structure of their surface phonological segments, the category of their constituents, their thematic structure, their constituent structure, their logical form are among such attributes. Utterances are endowed with these attributes by their creators, that is, by their utterers. Competent (that is, linguistically proficient) listeners can detect them as intentionally present,[24] indeed must detect them as intentionally present in order to understand. Admittedly, only speakers and listeners who have undergone the appropriate mental development can do this. But that is because the mental states that result from such development are prerequisites for certain causal effects between intentional speech events and responsive attention events. It does not make those attributes any less real or true of tokens. It is also true that linguists often can impute and characterize such attributes only with the help of theories. But the same holds for the imputation and characterization of most attributes of any scientific interest, even temperature and acceleration. It does not entail that the attributes do not belong to the tokens.

The objection may, however, take another form. Tokens cannot have types as parts,[25] for tokens are temporal and their parts must be temporal, but types are atemporal. Syllables, it may be argued, are types. It follows that they cannot be parts of tokens and that no token therefore can satisfy the presuppositions of (39), and that furthermore no one – no matter how competent or theoretically sophisticated – will ever be able to detect a syllable in a token. Other versions of the argument may be constructed about other constituents recognized by linguistic theory.

But even in that form, the objection is mistaken. 'Syllable' is one of the terms which, like 'word' and 'sentence', are used indiscriminately to refer to either types or tokens. Syllables – the types – are archetypes of temporal segments of tokens, and as such, as archetypes, are obviously never segments of tokens themselves (though they are nontemporal segments of types). But syllables – the tokens – are temporal parts of tokens.

These facts may elude us because of certain limitations on our ability to talk about specific tokens. For instance, in replying to the question

(65) What is its first syllable?

raised about a specific token one cannot display the syllable itself, or point to it. It is gone! And so one must refer to it by seeming to mention the type it exemplifies. What one actually does is to produce another token (of a so-called quote name) that, depending on circumstances, will refer to either its own type or another token. Similarly, I could have mentioned 'John' as answer to (55) instead of the convoluted answer I did mention. Had I done so, I would then have used an expression (that is, another so-called quote name) that functions indiscriminately to mention either tokens of its own type or the type itself.[26] Such linguistic practices may be the source of confusions, but they do not indicate that tokens cannot have syllables as parts, or that no tokens of 'John' can be a part of some other token.

Two difficulties remain, however.

The first difficulty concerns types that have no tokens. Linguistic theory is not limited to types that have tokens. It is concerned with all the linguistic types, including those that will never have any tokens. It admits no essential distinction between exemplified and unexemplified types. The Platonic Relationship Principle, however, is restricted to inferences about exemplified types, and does not, by itself, account for inferences about types that have no tokens.

The second difficulty concerns the selection of projectible questions. Tokens arrange themselves into quasi-natural kinds in many different ways, that is, relative to innumerable sets of $<Q_p/A_p, Q_m, Q_i>$ triples. But only some of these arrangements yield archetypes of linguistic significance. As was already pointed out, applying the Platonic Relationship Principle is a trivial exercise. The important reasoning occurs while looking for revealing $<Q_p/A_p, Q_w, Q_i>$ triples.

To resolve these difficulties we have to consider further aspects of quasi-natural kinds. But doing so will eventually also enable us to see how (1) and (3) are related.

Types and minds

Categories

Samples of mercury are also samples of chemical substances. Chemical substances include not only mercury, but also gold, water, iron, hydrochloric acid, etc. Together these form what I shall call a category. A category is simply a set of distinct quasi-natural kinds that are all relativized to the same projectible, w-projectible, and individuating questions. They differ through their answers to projectible questions. Each is relativized to its own set. But each therefore also has its own members.

Returning to our example, the chemical substances form a category. The samples of mercury are a quasi-natural kind relative to a $<Q_p/A_p, Q_w, Q_i>$. That triple includes among its projectible questions Q_p the familiar

(66) What is its boiling point?

(67) What is its freezing point?

(68) What is its molecular weight?

and so on.

It includes among its w-projectible questions (22) and the like, and among its individuating questions (25) and the like. The samples of gold are a quasi-natural kind relative to another triple $<Q_p/A_p', Q_w, Q_i>$. That triple is identical to the previous one, except that the answers A_p' to the projectible questions are different. For samples of gold the answer to (66) is 2807°C, the answer to (67) is 1064.43°C, the answer to (68) is 197, etc. The samples of water are a quasi-natural kind relative to a third triple $<Q_p/A''_p, Q_w, Q_i>$, and that triple too is identical to the previous one except that the answers A''_p to the projectible questions (66), (67), (68), etc. are yet a third set. And the same goes for iron, hydrochloric acid, and all the other chemical substances.

Putting all this a little more precisely, the quasi-natural kinds of samples of chemical substances form a category[27] because they satisfy the following definition:

(69) A class of quasi-natural kinds forms a category relative to a triple $<Q_p, Q_w, Q_i>$ if and only if it is the largest set of quasi-natural kinds for each

of whose members the questions in Q_p are projectible, the questions in Q_w are w-projectible, and the questions in Q_i are individuating.

The notion of a category, like the notion of a quasi-natural kind, is a relativized notion. Like the notion of a quasi-natural kind again, it is relativized to triples in which questions are an essential element. The triples pertaining to both notions are in fact identical but for the fact that those which pertain to categories have no answers to projectible questions as constituents.

The notion of category turns out to be crucial in resolving the difficulties described at the end of the last section. But to appreciate this we must first consider the relationship between a category and the archetypes of its members. And there is a convenient way of describing that relationship: the archetypes are each at a specific location in a space uniquely identified with the category.

The idea involved is fairly straightforward. Each projectible question related to a category – that is, each member of Q_p in its $<Q_p, Q_w, Q_i>$ triple – represents a dimension of a space whose points are tuples of logically possible answers to these questions. I use the phrase 'logically possible answers' instead of simply 'answers' because up to now I have used 'answer' for correct answers only, and we need a broader notion, that is, a notion according to which, for instance

(70) Twenty centimeters

is an answer – though not a correct one – to

(71) What is the length of Cleopatra's nose?

whereas

(72) Three liters

is no answer at all.

So, to return to our example, the space identified with the category of chemical substances has as dimensions the projectible questions (66), (67), (68), etc. and as points the tuples made up of logically possible answers to these questions, that is, roughly speaking, actual and conceivable boiling points, melting points, molecular weights, etc. The ontological status of such tuples need not trouble us at present, though it admittedly raises vexing problems. It is a concern for the semantics of interrogatives and we must assume that they can be resolved.

The notion of a categorial space is obviously an abstraction from the notion of a Cartesian space. A Cartesian two-dimensional space has one dimension corresponding to the question

(73) What is the value of x?

and another corresponding to the question

(74) What is the value of y?

and its points are the ordered pairs of answers to (73) and (74).

The location of an archetype in a categorical space is simply the tuple-point corresponding to the answers that the archetype bears. So, in our example, the archetype of mercury is located at the point corresponding to the answers 356.6°C on the dimension of (66), −38.87°C on the dimension of (67), 200.6 on the dimension of (68), etc., the archetype of gold is located at the point corresponding to the answers 2807°C on the dimension of (66), 1064.33°C on the dimension of (67), 197 on the dimension of (68), etc., and so on for the other archetypes of chemical substances.

Seeing categories and archetypes this way enables us to characterize the difference between the scientifically significant and the scientifically uninteresting quasi-natural kinds. The scientifically significant ones are those that make up categories with spaces that are the domain of laws. The scientifically uninteresting ones (except perhaps in some purely taxonomic disciplines) are the remainder.

The following somewhat contrived example should make the point concrete. A less contrived one would require much more space.

All the objects made up of a weight swinging under the force of local gravity (that is, simple pendulums), in a region where local gravitational acceleration is 980 cm/sec^2, at the end of a relatively weightless string 50 cm long, form a quasi-natural kind relative to a triple whose projectible questions are

(75) What is the value of local gravitational acceleration?

(76) What is its length?

(77) What is its period?

with the answers to these questions respectively

(78) 980 cm/sec^2

(79) 50 cm

(80) 1.42 seconds

and whose *w*-projectible and individuating questions include

(81) What is the temperature of the weight?

(82) What holds the strands of the string together?

(83) What is the material of the weight?

(84) Where is it located?

and so on.

Furthermore, all the objects – whatever the length or the value of gravitational acceleration in their neighborhood – whose movements are constrained like the above ones, that is, all the simple pendulums, form the union of a category, namely the category relativized to the $<Q_p, Q_w, Q_i>$ triple whose set of projectible questions consists of (75), (76), and (77), and whose set of w-projectible and individuating questions includes (81) and the rest. That category is partitioned into quasi-natural kinds by the answers to (75), (76), and (77).

The categorial space of simple pendulums has as dimensions the questions (75), (76), and (77), and has as points the ordered triples of answers to these questions. Some of these points are occupied by archetypes and some are not. In that respect, the category is very much like any other arbitrary category, including those that are of no scientific interest whatsoever. What gives it scientific significance is that all the points occupied by an archetype in its categorial space obey a law, namely the law of the simple pendulum

(85) $\quad T = 2\pi \sqrt{l/g}$

that is, a law whose domain is the categorial space, which furthermore systematically selects combinations of answers to (75), (76) and (77), and which includes all the archetypes of simple pendulums among the selected positions.

Objects swinging at the end of light strings under the influence of gravity form innumerably many different quasi-natural kinds and hence enter into innumerably many different categories with each other and with other objects. Each exemplifies innumerably many different archetypes located in different categorial spaces. But they can be viewed as objects of scientific interest (that is, as simple pendulums) only in their guise as exemplifications of archetypes that conform with a law (that is, the law of the simple pendulum). This is not a peculiarity of objects swinging at the end of strings! A thing has a scientifically interesting persona, so to say, only when seen as exemplifying an archetype in a space where archetypes conform to law.

Normally, we do not interpret laws like (85) as alluding to questions, and that may explain why we don't normally think of them as associated with categories. For most expository purposes, it is more convenient to think of them as alluding to determinables – that is, to such notions as period, length, value of local gravitational acceleration – rather than to questions in which these determinables are embedded. However, laws such as (85) have peculiarities that remain obscured until we see that they also allude to questions. The most obvious of these peculiarities is that they can be exploited as means for obtaining answers to some questions (answers that may be difficult to get in any other way) from answers to other questions (that may be easier to get). Elsewhere I have called that being a 'value adder' (Bromberger, 1987b). Value adders are subject to special criteria of assessment. Another of these peculiarities is that they endow the theories from which they can be derived with instrumental merits. Finally, they affect the ranking of choices in the rational satisfaction of curiosity, that is, in the rational pursuit of answers. And, in all these respects, they are like the laws that do not implicate determinables.

However, the case of simple pendulums also illustrates an important further fact. The law of the simple pendulum partitions the space defined by (75), (76), and (77) into two sets of points: those that conform to the law (the locus) and those that do not. In other words, it defines a sort of curve in categorial space. The archetypes of simple pendulums are all located at points on that curve. But many points on the curve are not occupied by any archetype. Archetypes, as I have been using the term, always have examples. Many points on the curve do not.

The fact can be stated differently. Laws such as the law of the pendulums are supposed to be sound and complete. Soundness and completeness are notions taken from logic: a deductive system is sound and complete in a certain domain, for instance, if and only if every one of its theorems is a valid formula in that domain and every valid formula in the domain is a theorem in the system. But the notion is easily extended. The algebraic equation

$$(86) \quad x^2 + y^2 = 25$$

is a sound and complete characterization of the points on the circumference of a circle with center at the origin and radius 5, because every pair of values that satisfies (86) designates a point on the circumference, and every pair of numbers that designates a point on the circumference satisfies (86). Soundness and completeness are defined by reference to pairs of properties. They hold or fail to hold depending on whether or not the two properties are coextensive: for instance, the property of being a theorem and the property of being valid in the domain, the property of satisfying (86) and the property of designating a point on the circumference. Sense can be made of the idea that a law such as the law of the simple pendulum is sound and complete only if we can come up with an appropriate property that is expected to be coextensive with the property of being a point that conforms to the law. The property of being a point at which an archetype happens to be located is seldom an appropriate property. There is nothing particularly interesting about its extension and no plausible way of determining what it is. And imposing that property would also rule out most laws like the law of the pendulum as demonstrably unsound. That would conflict too strongly with our normal understanding.

So the view that the scientifically significant quasi-natural kinds are those that generate categorial spaces governed by laws leaves an important aspect unexplicated until the conditions on soundness and completeness of laws are clarified. The problem is an old one, and has many names. Many philosophers have assumed that it can be solved in one fell swoop through one general notion of reality that fits laws in all categorial domains at once. However, that may be a mistake. Different categorial domains may require different implementations of the notion of soundness and completeness. Their respective archetypes are, after all, abstracted along very different dimensions. In the next section, I will consider how it might be implemented in the case of linguistics.

But the view is clear enough to show the complex mixture of tasks required to discover scientifically significant quasi-natural kinds. Observation of phenomena is only the most obvious among them. Questions, answers that fit them, concepts with which to embed them into laws, expressions with which to process them, must be thought of; those that are projectible across significant numbers and varieties of things must be recognized; theories that reveal both sides of the completeness and soundness requirement must be excogitated; regularities must be spotted; canonical usages that guard against the misleading associations of the current vernacular[28] must be introduced, and so on. Since, in the performance of these tasks, conceptual and terminological creativity plays an enormous part, one might be tempted to conclude that scientists, rather than facts about the world, are responsible for the existence of categorial spaces in which laws operate. But that is hardly plausible. Surveyors label and map the territory; they sometimes divide it; but they do not create it.

More important for present purposes, the view also shows that the two difficulties left unanswered by the Platonic Relationship Principle at the end of the last section are but special versions of issues that arise in every scientific field. The first is a version of the problem of soundness and completeness. The second is a version of the problem of demarcating scientifically significant quasi-natural kinds from scientifically unimportant ones. It turns out that they can be resolved together in the case of linguistics.

Linguistics

Let us turn to soundness and completeness as it applies to linguistics. I will focus for present purposes on the study of individual languages and leave for some other occasion the study of linguistic universals.

The problem, at least as I have characterized it, arises in linguistics only if linguistics is not merely interested in types, but is interested in types that form categories, that is, views types as archetypes that are located with other types in categorial spaces. To satisfy ourselves that it is, we do not have to be convinced that linguists make explicit use of these notions but only that they analyze different types with a common set of questions. And they obviously do.

Consider for instance how they study the lexicon of a given language. They take for granted that each word in that language is open to such questions as

(87) How many syllables does it contain?

(88) What is its underlying representation?

(89) What is its surface representation?

(90) What is the onset of its first syllable?

(91) What is its argument structure?

and so on.

Different linguists guided by different theories and different conjectures rely on different questions, but whatever questions they deem linguistically significant about a word type, they will deem the question to be not only projectible across all the tokens of the word, but to be also askable (with the expectation of different answers) about every other word type.[29]

That, by itself, is still not yet enough to show that they treat words as members of categories.[30] They must also presume that there is a set of questions whose combined answers about any word type fully individuates that word type. They must presume that no two word types in English bear the same answer to, for instance, all of the questions (87)–(91) above. But most lexicographers and morphologists do presume that. A great deal of their effort, in fact, is spent on discovering such sets of questions.

In short, if I am right so far, linguists do, in practice as well as in theory, presume that word types locate themselves in categorial spaces, that is, that there is a set of dimensions, representable as questions, in which each word type will find a location, and such that each word is fully individuated by the position it occupies in that space. Let us call that space the *lexical* space of the language.

Consider now the study of the syntax of the sentence types of a given language. Linguistics here too proceeds on the presumption that there is a set of questions to which each sentence type bears an answer, and whose answers fully individuate sentence types. Typical members of such a set include:

(92) How many words does it contain?

(93) What is the matrix verb?

(94) What is the D-structure?

(95) What is the S-structure?

(96) Which phrase receives what thematic role from which predicate?

Here again, different linguists guided by different theories and different conjectures rely on different questions. But the presumption, however implemented, is tantamount to the presumption that the sentence types of a language can be located in a categorial space. Let us call that space the *sentential* space of the language.

The assumption that there is a lexical space or that there is a sentential space still do not, by themselves, raise the problem of soundness and completeness for linguistics. Three more things must be presumed by linguists.

First, linguists must presume that the laws (or rules, or constraints, to use the preferred terminology) that they try to discover will be violated by some – though not all – points in lexical space and in sentential space. In other words, they must expect that lexical theories and grammars partition lexical space and sentential space in a principled way. But they obviously expect that. This is shown by, among other things, one of the critical standards they impose on claims about such theories and grammars: such claims must not 'overgenerate', and therefore must leave some points out as violations. Of course, just leaving some points out as violations is not good enough, but that is immaterial right now.

Second, linguists must presume that the laws that they try to discover will license all the types (points) that have tokens. And they obviously do. This is shown by another critical standard that they impose on claims: such claims must not 'undergenerate', that is, must not leave out any type that has tokens deemed by speakers to be well formed.[31] Of course they can never show conclusively that a claim meets that standard, since tokens produced in the past or in the future are not available for inspection: the best they can do is to consider tokens produced at the time and accept them as evidence.[32]

Third, linguists must presume that the laws that they try to discover will also license types (points) that have no tokens. And again, they clearly do. This is not shown by their use of any particular standard, but by the fact that they refrain from using certain standards, to wit, standards which would imply that only types with tokens should be licensed. One might think that the only reason they refrain from imposing such standards is that this would make the task of linguistics impossible. The only way it could conceivably ever be accomplished, under such a standard, would be by coming up with a list of all those types. The list would be shorter than a list of the tokens themselves, but it would still be impossibly long (and utterly boring!). Not only that, but it would have to include types whose tokens have left no trace and, in the case of living languages, types whose first token has not yet been produced. Somebody may some day think of a plausible theory that enumerates all and only those types. But that is unlikely. In any case, no sane linguist is after such a theory. On the contrary, all sane linguists operate on the principle that many types will never have tokens, and that a good theory of the lexicon or the grammar does not discriminate between those that do and those that do not. And their reasons are not merely practical. They assume that the rules of language are infinitely productive or at least license an infinite number of types, and the number of types with tokens must be finite.

It follows then that linguistics not only presupposes that there are questions relative to which types exist and have a location in categorial spaces, but it also presupposes the existence of an appropriate notion of soundness and completeness.

The problem now is to decide what that notion might be. This means deciding what attribute (or attributes) all word types or sentence types of a language share, over and above the attribute of being licensed by some lexicon or grammar that licenses the types that happen to be exemplified.

One suggestion might be the attribute of being the type of a token that speakers of the language would, under conceivable circumstances, produce understandingly or hear and understand. This proposal, plausible though it may appear, is open to a number of objections. First, there are metaphysical difficulties. Since there are types that have no actual tokens, it would require that we admit in our ontologies possible tokens, that is, possible individuals, a notion fraught with obscurities and probably incoherent. Even if we disregard that objection by, for instance, indulging in possible world metaphors, the proposal is still likely to collapse. The proposed attribute becomes the attribute of being a type such that there is at least one possible world in which one of its tokens is uttered and understood by a speaker of the language (in the actual world). However, any speaker of any language could, under suitable circumstances, have ended up as a speaker of a different language. Given any speaker of English, for instance, there is at least one possible world in which that speaker grows up in China and ends up as a native speaker of Chinese, and at least one possible world in which he ends up as a speaker of German, etc. Thus pick any type of any language (actual or conceivable) and any person, there is a possible world in which (that is, conceivable circumstances under which) that person utters and understands or hears and understands a token of that type. Every type has that attribute. In fact, probably any point on any reasonable categorial space for words or sentences has it. The attribute will not do as a measure of soundness, and its virtues as a measure of completeness are uninteresting.

If we try to save the proposal by restricting the range of possible worlds to the actual one, then the attribute is simply turned into that of being a type with actual tokens. And we have already seen that no sane linguist subscribes to that notion.

Another possible suggestion starts from the assumption that the maxims of scientific induction provide rules for constructing lexicons or grammars (as the case may be) from the set of types known to have tokens, and that lexicons or grammars constructed in this way can be ranked by maxims of simplicity. A lexicon or grammar constructed that way and selected as simplest by the maxims of simplicity could, given some reasonable further assumptions, be presumed to select some superset of the set of types that have tokens. The suggestion then is that the attribute should be that of being encompassed by such a simplest lexicon or grammar. In practice, this would mean being encompassed by a lexicon or grammar built on known or presumed exemplified types.

This proposal clearly admits types that have no tokens, and has the further virtue of making linguistic theory invulnerable to contradiction by invisible facts. It assumes, however, that we have reliable theory-independent measures of simplicity for ranking lexicons and grammars; in other words, measures of simplicity that are not inextricable parts of specific lexical theories or syntactic theories. That is a very questionable assumption. More important, the attribute is utterly arbitrary as a measure of soundness and completeness unless supplemented by still further assumptions. Why maximum simplicity and certification by the rules of induction? Why not maximum complexity and certification by some rules of counter-induction? Why not expressibility in iambic pentameters? The answer, presumably, is that simplicity and induction are guides to some truths. But the proposal leaves us in the dark about the nature of those truths. It simply raises the problem of soundness and completeness in a new form.

We are left, as far as I can see, with only one further reasonable suggestion, and that is that the attribute is that of being a type generated by the lexicon or grammar (whatever the case) in a speaker's mind. That suggestion admits types that have no tokens, does not rely on an unanalyzed notion of possible tokens, and takes a stand on the nature of the truths sought by lexical and grammatical theory.

It is admittedly open to objections. With that stand on the nature of the truths sought by linguists comes the risk of increased commitment: what if no lexicon (or grammar) is represented in the speaker's mind? How do we know if any is? In other words, the proposal makes factual and not just methodological assumptions. And the factual assumption it makes involves things (minds, brains, organisms, wetware) whose archetypes (no matter how relativized) cannot be located in the categorial spaces of words and sentences. They do not belong to the subject-matter of pure generative linguistics. So the proposal puts the whole linguistic enterprise at the mercy of discoveries in other fields of investigation, and the fact that this has happened to other disciplines in the past (for instance, classical thermodynamics and chemistry were at the mercy of particle physics, astronomy was at the mercy of projectile theory) does not make it more attractive.

Even so, this suggestion offers the only plausible interpretation of soundness and completeness for theories of the lexicon and for grammars. (Or, to be more precise, the only plausible interpretation of which I am aware.) And, as we have seen, linguistic practice presupposes that some interpretation exists. Without such an interpretation, the practice is ungrounded and cannot be understood as a principled partitioning of the points in its categorial spaces.

As it stands, the proposal may not seem to impose very constraining requirements. It does not say anything about the form that theories of the lexicon or grammars must have to be sound and complete. It tells us that they must be coextensive with a mental lexical structure or with a mental grammar. But if one is, no doubt infinitely many others are as well. That leaves a large field, and linguists may decide to seek only the simplest ones in it, even though there is no prior reason to believe that mental lexicons and grammars are simple by our standards.

Even so, the proposal does imply at least two kinds of methodological consequences. The first pertains to the conceptual repertoire on which the theories can draw. Theoretical lexicons and grammars can be coextensive with mental ones only if there is a match between their respective categorial spaces, that is, only if the questions with which linguists analyze types – and that means the questions through which they abstract from tokens to types – match question-representing constituents of minds. This follows from the fact that coextensiveness is defined in terms of correspondences across such spaces. But that requires that linguists discover questions that correspond to dimensions acknowledged by mental faculties. For instance, if (87)–(96) are acceptable dimensions for theories of the lexicon and of the syntax, they must correspond to mental dimensions; for instance, dimensions in a space of intentions or perceptions in speakers' minds.

The second pertains to evidence. If the proposal is right, then linguistic behavior and linguistic judgments do not exhaust the evidence on which linguistics should or can proceed. Other phenomena currently studied – but with different concerns in mind – by neurologists, developmental psychologists, and – though that seems unlikely – artificial intelligencers, will also be pertinent. The study of natural languages becomes, in this respect at least, very different from the study of formal languages, and linguistics cannot simply confine itself to special versions of issues appropriate to such languages.

The Platonic Relationship Principle left us with two unresolved difficulties. First, how is it possible to infer anything about types that have no tokens? The answer can now be put succinctly. It is possible because such types, if linguistically significant, belong in categorial spaces with types that have tokens. We can discover the dimensions of these spaces by examining tokens, and we can partition these spaces in a principled way by reasoning about minds.

Second, how do the triples $<Q_t/A_p, Q_w, Q_i>$ to which linguistically significant archetypes (word types and sentence types) are related differ from those to which linguistically uninteresting types are related? The answer to this too can now be put very succinctly. They differ by fitting in categorial spaces that are the domain of psychological laws.

And so, (1), (2), and (3) are compatible after all and linguists who dismiss qualms about them are right in doing so.

Notes

I am grateful to Ned Block, Noam Chomsky, Morris Halle, Jim Higginbotham, Tom Kuhn, Scott Soames, Steve Stich, Linda Wetzel, and Richard Wollheim for comments on previous drafts of this chapter or for discussions of some of the issues in it. The chapter was written while I was a visiting scholar at the Center for the Study of Language and Information, Stanford University, and I am very grateful for the warm intellectual and physical hospitality of that wonderful place.

1 In this chapter, I shorten 'generative linguistics' to 'linguistics'.
2 By intrinsic properties I simply mean properties whose possession does not depend on contingent relations to concrete objects via tokens. Thus the fact that a token of the word type 'dog' was uttered by Richard Nixon does not represent an intrinsic property of the type 'dog', but the fact that it is a noun, and that it is monosyllabic, and that it can occur as the subject of a sentence does represent intrinsic properties.
3 The problem may be partly hidden by our use of such expressions as 'word', 'sentence', 'syllable' and others that refer indiscriminately to either types or tokens. Thus we speak of hearing words or sentences, though what affects our senses are tokens, not their types, metonymy notwithstanding. I will come back to this point later in the chapter.
4 Linguists on the whole restrict their attention to spoken language, and I will do the same in this chapter.

5   Viewing types as mental entities will not reconcile (1) and (2). It comes down either to the view that types can be the object of mental attitudes, which still leaves in the dark how their attributes can be inferred from attributes of tokens. Or it comes down to the view that there are mental representations and that these too have tokens and types, which simply means that a problem similar to the one raised by the juxtaposition of (1) and (2) may arise for the view that there are mental representations.

6   Some modes of inference yield information about unobserved things from information about observed ones without presupposing causal links between the two, namely inductions from observed samples of a population to other members of that population. Inductions of that sort demand that the observed and the non-observed make up a class across which projections of some properties are licensed, and that in turn demands that they share attributes which warrant these projections. It is doubtful that spatio-temporal and abstract entities can share projection warranting attributes. Offhand it would seem that they cannot.

7   This is another difference between mathematics and linguistics. Though both are concerned with abstract entities, linguistics, unlike mathematics, relies not only on empirical evidence but is also after contingent truths.

8   'English' here must be understood as a rigid designator.

9   If (1) is false then (2) will *ipso facto* fail to be true, since it presupposes (1).

10   Chomsky does not use the expression 'type'; he writes instead of, for instance, 'actual or potential speech events'. He may thus not agree with the way I have extended his argument.

11   The convention is stated in a way that imputes reality to questions over and above the reality of the locutions that express them. This, in the eyes of many people, may be suspect. I do not intend to address the issue here, though it is important. The convention can be easily rephrased to fit more puritanical ontologies.

12   Here, and elsewhere in this chapter, I am committing a sin that I have rightly condemned in other writings: the sin of disregarding that many explanations are not answers to why-questions and that many answers to why-questions are not explanations. The two notions are very loosely connected, except in philosophic literature, where they are often irresponsibly conflated. The commission of sins usually brings some pleasure. In this case, the pleasure is avoidance of circumlocution at the cost of relatively little immediate confusion.

13   Here and elsewhere I use the locution 'the answer' in a way that suggests that questions can have only one correct answer. Whether this is true or not depends on how one individuates questions and answers. I ignore these issues too for the time being for nothing presently crucial hinges on how they get resolved. If we adopt a position according to which some questions have more than one right answer, then we must rephrase some passages more carefully, but that can be done without essential distortion of what is intended, though not without more ugly circumlocutions.

14   The presumption behind this formulation that some answers do not give rise to why-questions is allowed deliberately: some of these answers represent brute, ultimate facts not amenable to explanation.

15   Except, of course, the existential presuppositions that refer to the member.

16   Subject to the above qualification about (21).

17   I don't mean, of course, that no appropriate or informative reply can be offered to someone who raises one of these questions about the archetype. A reply which

points out that the archetype is not a thing that has a temperature at any time or locations, for instance, would be appropriate and informative. What I mean is that no 'direct' answer will do, no reply that gives a temperature or location for the archetype on 7 July 1924.

18 Complicated issues loom behind this claim. Demonstrably there exist non-denumerably many question–answer pairs. The claim therefore assumes that sets of non-denumerably many questions play no role in the arrangement of things into quasi-natural kinds or in the emergence of archetypes. But that is a topic for another day.

19 For a sketch of an argument see Bromberger, 1987. Unfortunately, in the course of publication, some sentences were dropped and an incoherent quotation system was imposed on it. However the passages pertinent to this discussion should still be understandable.

20 To what do the questions and answers in such a set refer, since – on the picture now proposed – they cannot refer to archetypes? They need not refer to anything. Think of the question and answer as replaced by whatever semantic values correspond to the nonreferring part of a full question–answer pair. Or think of the question–answer pair as containing only the sense/character of some deictic instead of an actual reference. Here and elsewhere I have used 'question' to refer to the sorts of things that are the contents of interrogative sentences in their guise as devices for expressing questions – and I have also assumed that these contents can have constituents that refer. Such a use implies many promises. Since I believe that the semantics of interrogative expressions will some day be explained, I feel fairly confident that these promises can be kept, though not today.

21 They too, in effect, rely on the Related Questions Convention, (14).

22 I know that this answer is controversial. That in itself is not without interest. It shows that perceptual recognition of attributes is not sufficient for theoretical – that is, non-perceptual – understanding. Theory is also required, as I discuss below. That holds for perceptual recognition of the properties of nonlinguistic events as well.

23 It may be helpful to compare utterances here with inscriptions. Inscriptions too exemplify simultaneously a number of different types, that is, orthographic types, calligraphic or font types, geometric types, sample of substance types, etc.

24 For instance, in the standard American dialect tokens of the words spelled 'sense' and 'cents' are produced so as to be acoustically almost indistinguishable. However the stop (*t*) between the nasal (*n*) and the continuant (*s*) in tokens of 'sense', unlike in tokens of 'cents', is not put there intentionally by speakers but is there as an effect of tongue inertia. The stop is thus acoustically present and can be heard even by American hearers. But it is not linguistically present, that is, it is either not detected by these hearers at all or detected as unintentional.

25 For a brilliant discussion of this objection and issues surrounding it, see Wetzel (1984, chap. 3). The view imputed to me there is a previous version of the one in this chapter.

26 Matters are further confounded by the fact that this discussion is in writing. I count on the reader to enact the above passages as a spoken exchange taking place on a specific occasion, at a specific time, and under circumstances that disambiguate between use and mention.

27 The union of the quasi-natural kinds in a category may itself be a further quasi-natural kind. All the samples of substances, for instance, probably form a

quasi-natural kind relative to some triple or other, though not a triple defining any of the members. Nothing in the definition of category in the text rules this out. In other contexts this becomes important.

28   Scientists must use language but may be hampered by what is available in their vocabulary. At any given time, that vocabulary will include words that belong to the designated nomenclature of a science, that is, words that have been introduced in the language with the explicit proviso that their extension must constitute a quasi-natural kind or a category, a proviso whose implementation is subject to deliberate, and publicly acknowledged, revision or modification (I don't mean, of course, that the proviso is stated using 'quasi-natural kind', 'category', etc., but that such terms are explicitly introduced in canonical texts under conventions that have the effect of attaching such provisos). That part of the vocabulary is apt to be marked and to be controllable. But other words will not have been explicitly introduced in the language at all. They will belong to the generally used, naturally acquired lexicon. And these words can be a source of difficulty. English and other languages, for instance, contain so-called natural kind terms. Those words do not have extensions that make up quasi-natural kinds or categories, in spite of the label now attached to them. Or at least there is no evidence that they do. Mere knowledge of their semantic and syntactic features, in any case, will not be enough to determine whether they do, since terms whose extension are quasi-natural kinds or categories are not likely to form, by themselves, a grammatically natural class. (If they did – if so-called natural kind terms formed a grammatically relevant category – knowledge of a language would include more knowledge of the world than anyone has!) Scientists cannot rely on such words to mention their subject-matter. Thus, to perform their task, to be able to refer to quasi-natural kinds and to categories, scientists must produce and maintain control over their terminology.

29   This claim is open to an obvious objection. There are questions such as, for instance:

(97) What is the onset of its third syllable?

or

(98) What is its gender?

that, at first glance at least, can be asked about some words but not about all. Question (97) can be asked about words that contain three or more syllables, but, it may seem, not about shorter ones; (98) cannot be asked of English prepositions. Such questions obviously occur in linguistics. That objection can be met in a number of ways. One way would be to admit the claim is an oversimplification, and to modify it so that linguists regard all word types as forming not one single category, but as forming a relatively small number of categories. Another way would be to deny the objection and to point out that we can and do adjust to our theoretical needs the distinction between bearing an answer and violating a presupposition. Thus for some theoretical purposes 'none' is significant as an answer to (97) and for others it is not, just as 'zero' is an answer to 'How many people live permanently at the North Pole?' but is not an answer to 'How many numbers live permanently at the North Pole?' A third way would be to include in our scheme hypothetical questions, for instance,

(99) If it has a third syllable, what is its onset?

A fourth way would be to recognize that I have given a very sketchy account so far, and that a fuller one would incorporate erotetic structures in which some answers to some questions license further questions, while others do not. I don't want to choose here among these options because none of them is warranted for all the cases, though one at least should be warranted for each case. In short, the objection is one that calls for technical refinements rather than a change of outlook.

30   To be more precise, I should have written 'to show that they treat words as archetypes of quasi-natural kinds that are members of categories'!

31   Utterances deemed to be ill-formed by speakers are irrelevant. They belong with grunts and snorts and other noises that may be acoustically and phonetically similar to linguistic tokens. They do not execute linguistic intentions, or execute them with only partial success.

32   In actual practice only parts of the language are treated as relevant to any actual proposal. Most of the language is left out of consideration altogether. This probably shows the idea of a single lexical space and a single sentential space for any language is an oversimplification. The complication called for will not affect the main points of this chapter.

References

Bromberger, Sylvain 1987a: What we don't know when we don't know why. In Nicholas Rescher (ed.), *Scientific Inquiry in Philosophical Perspective*, Lanham, Md.: University Press of America.

1987b: Rational ignorance. In L.M. Vaina (ed.), *Matters of Intelligence*, Dordrecht: Reidel, 333–52.

Chomsky, Noam 1985: *Knowledge of Language: Its Nature, Origin, and Use*. New York: Praeger.

Wetzel, Linda 1984: On numbers. Unpublished Ph.D. dissertation. MIT, Cambridge, Mass.

5

How Not to Become Confused about Linguistics

Alexander George

I

Confusion ensues if one does not distinguish the following five notions:

(1) grammar;
(2) psychogrammar;
(3) physiogrammar;
(4) algorithm;
(5) physioalgorithm.

A few remarks about each in turn.[1]

A speaker's *grammar* (1) is a formal entity that mechanically generates syntactic structures and assigns them representations at a number of levels, in the current theory at the two distinguished levels of PF (Phonological Form) and LF (Logical Form). Ever since the birth of generative linguistics in the 1950s, disagreements over the structure of the grammar have arisen. What cannot be disputed is that the grammar is a mathematical object, hence abstract and not located in space or time. Linguists, in seeking to characterize a speaker's grammar, are identifying the structure of a particular mathematical entity.

Which one? The grammar of a speaker is the object of that speaker's knowledge.[2] That is, the grammar is known by the speaker and constitutes the information about his or her language that the speaker has. This claim about grammars raises no special mystery about how a person can have a psychological attitude towards an abstract entity. Just as '3' might answer the question 'Which number is X thinking of?', so 'G' (the name of some particular grammar) might answer the question 'Which grammar does X know?'

A speaker's knowledge of the grammar, the speaker's *psychogrammar* (2), is a mental condition on a par with the state of *thinking of the number 3*. States of mind (like other states) can, of course, be picked out by descriptions that contain terms referring to abstract entities. For this reason, in seeking to discern the structure of a mathematical object (the grammar G such that X knows G), linguists are engaged in an empirical inquiry.

Study of a speaker's grammar, however, must be distinguished from study of that speaker's psychogrammar. Whether or not one considers the psychogrammar to be an abstract object, it is distinct from the abstract object that is the speaker's grammar. The grammar is what is known by the speaker, whereas the psychogrammar is, loosely, the knowing of it. The psychogrammar characterizes features of a speaker's mind in virtue of which the speaker knows those facts about his or her language that are determined by the grammar. Conceptually, there is a world of difference between these two notions though, as we shall see, there is also substantial confusion.

A speaker's psychogrammar, the mental state of knowing a grammar, may be cited in explanations of an open range of facts about the speaker's thoughts and actions. The range is open for the familiar reason that an agent's knowledge serves as a general resource[3] to be tapped during deliberations about what to think and how to act.

It is often claimed that being in such a mental state involves mentally representing the grammar. This claim is compatible with the grammar being silent as to the nature of these mental representations. Indeed, the grammar is not itself a characterization of a system of mental representation; it is the object of a speaker's knowledge, not a description of how that object is represented by the speaker (if it is). We might come to be able to articulate the object of a speaker's knowledge, the grammar, without thereby being able to say how that object is represented by the speaker. The grammar is what is represented, not what is doing the representing.[4]

The foregoing is agnostic with respect to which particular stripe of materialism is correct; it is even agnostic about whether any brand of materialism is true. Many believe that there is a definite material state of a speaker, the *physiogrammar* (3), which is in principle characterizable in physiological, and eventually physical, terms and which physically realizes the speaker's knowledge of his or her grammar; the physiogrammar underlies the speaker's psychogrammar. If we accept the analysis of psychogrammar in terms of mental representations, then we shall say that we are able to represent mentally the grammar in virtue of being in some definite, though as yet unknown, physical state.

We just noted that one might be able to characterize the information a speaker, *qua* speaker, has at his or her disposal, without being able to say how that information is mentally represented (again, if it is). Additionally, we might discover how the information is mentally represented without being able to describe the physical state that underlies these representations. Articulation of a speaker's grammar leaves open articulation of the corresponding psychogrammar, which in turn leaves open articulation of the corresponding physiogrammar.

If explanations of human thought and action that proceed by attributing attitudes like knowledge (a subspecies of belief) are *causal*, then it follows that a speaker's psychogrammar, his or her knowledge of a grammar, enters the causal nexus.[5] If we assume that the relation between a speaker's psychogrammar and the physical state underlying it, the physiogrammar, is identity, then it follows that the physiogrammar will also be part of the causal chain terminating in linguistic activity.[6] Grammars, however, are not causally effective. This is not because (or only because) they are mathematical entities. It is due, rather (or also), to a grammar's being *what* is known by a speaker.[7] Imagine I scream whenever I think of Ronald Reagan. There is no reason to believe that reference to Ronald Reagan will have to be made in a causal explanation of my screams. (Imagine I scream when I think of someone who, as it happens, does not exist.) Similarly, the object of our knowledge need not be referred to in causal explanations of our use of language; this use will be causally consequent upon the psychological state of knowing the grammar, that is, upon the psychogrammar.

So long as we restrict ourselves to the study of (1)–(3), we must recognize that there will be lacunae in our explanations of human action, of linguistic actions in particular. This is the inevitable fate of any account that explains events through attribution of propositional attitudes to agents. An explanation that does not go beyond imputing beliefs, say, to an agent leaves unaccounted *how* those beliefs were applied in the particular case at hand. In order to bridge this gap, it must specify the other factors (e.g., relevant attitudes, mediating mechanisms) that determine the path from the agent's beliefs to his or her actions. For example, Y leaps out of the room as a spider crawls into view and we say in explanation that Y believes spiders are poisonous. Now this account cannot be complete because there is no fixed route from Y's belief to his or her actions. Y could well have had that belief and not leapt from the room (he or she could have wanted to be poisoned). Indeed, all Y's attitudes (beliefs, desires, fears, etc.) could have been just as they were compatible with Y not batting an eyelid upon catching sight of the spider.[8] In a sense, all explanations that proceed by attributing beliefs to an agent are enthymematic, since a person's beliefs can be put to use in boundlessly many different ways. (This is related to the fact that there is no satisfying dispositional analysis of belief.) The same holds true for other attitudes. In a fuller account, one would describe those mechanisms that mediate between an agent's attitudes and actions, mechanisms that draw on the information available to an agent and apply it to particular cases.

In the case of verbal actions, we want to describe the mechanisms that link the knowledge speakers have about their language to their use of language. In particular, researchers are seeking to understand the mechanisms which are involved in the perception of linguistic input and the production of linguistic output, and which, it is thought, tap the information made available to speakers through their knowledge of a grammar. As the term 'mechanism' suggests, there is some consensus that the mental processes that drive speech perception and production operate, in large part, mechanically according to *algorithms* (4), undoubtedly complex ones. The study of these algorithms is a healthy area of research in psycholinguistics. The goal, to repeat, is an understanding of the flow chart that details the mental processing that takes place when speakers perceive or produce linguistic utterances.[9]

These algorithms, like grammars, are mathematical objects. Again, this does not mean that the task of their description is non-empirical. It is no less empirical than, say, the task of characterizing the function that describes the orbit of the earth about the sun. Algorithms and grammars, however, are fundamentally distinct entities. The latter are the objects of knowledge of competent speakers; they do not characterize how speakers use their knowledge. The former do describe the recipes that the perception and production mechanisms follow, recipes that will somehow tap the information speakers have about their language, as captured by the grammar.

The confusion is not difficult to fall into because the output of the perception algorithm, for example, is often assumed to be the very syntactic, phonological, and semantic representations of the input that are assigned to it by the grammar; that is, on one view of the role of a parser, it computes the same function in extension as does the grammar. It is easy to assume that the grammar is itself the algorithm employed to parse linguistic inputs. This is incorrect. The grammar is the object of knowledge of speakers, whereas the parsing algorithm describes the processes of linguistic perception (processes that we think employ this knowledge). An analogy might help. In characterizing the method a chess player uses to determine whether a configuration of chess pieces on the board is a legal position, we are not characterizing what the player knows about the rules of chess, although the method will undoubtedly tap what is known and (if correct) will output verdicts that are consequences of what is known.

Unlike grammars, processing algorithms are not objects of knowledge of the speaker; there is no notion of 'psychoalgorithm' on the above list. One reason why processing algorithms are not taken to be known is that doing so would launch us on a regress. For how then would *this* knowledge get applied? Through the mediation of yet further algorithms, also known? If these processing and production algorithms are to span the gap between knowledge and its applications, then they cannot themselves be the objects of knowledge.[10]

This does not mean that the algorithms cannot make use of representations individuated by semantic or intentional properties. It could be that any entity capable of following an algorithm for linguistic perception must be ascribable certain representational contents, without it following that the algorithm itself is the content of any representation. Recall, however, that, while a speaker's grammar is not itself a system of representations, it is often taken to be represented mentally by the speaker.

Though not themselves represented (i.e., not the content of any representation), algorithms that govern the processing of linguistic material must obviously be instantiated somehow in the organism following those algorithms.

A question arises as to the physiological implementation of the algorithms. An answer is supplied insofar as we can describe the corresponding *physioalgorithms* (5), that is, insofar as we can say how the algorithms are physically realized in the material body in question.

A final remark: (1)–(5) are all entities in the objective (which is not to say spatio-temporal) world and have been deemed fit topics for rational investigation. Each of them must be distinguished from the theories we formulate to describe and explain their nature. These theories are linguistic objects and as such are abstract entities. Though both the theory of grammar and grammar are abstract objects, we must take as much care in distinguishing between them as we do in distinguishing between a theory of the human heart and the muscle that is the object of the theory.

II

I would now like to apply these distinctions and remarks to a number of recent discussions of the nature and status of linguistics. This should show how error and confusion follow from their neglect and should also, in the process, clarify their content.

These confusions are not restricted to those who find something peculiar about current linguistics. They creep into the discussions of even those who have developed and defended modern linguistics.[11] Noam Chomsky, for example, though the main architect of this entire conception, occasionally lapses into a confused, or at least confusing, mode of presentation. A few examples: Chomsky writes that 'Any interesting generative grammar will be dealing, for the most part, with *mental processes* that are beyond the level of actual or even potential consciousness' (1965, p. 8; my italics). More recently, he has described a grammar as a device that 'assigns to each expression a structure, which we may take to be a set of representations, one on each linguistic level, where a linguistic level is a particular system of *mental representation*' (1986, p. 46; my italics).[12] It should be clear, however, that a generative grammar is not about a speaker's 'mental processes,' nor does it characterize his or her 'system of mental representation', it is, rather, *what* is known by the speaker. If anything deals with a speaker's mental representations or processes, it will be, respectively, the theory of the speaker's psychogrammar (the theory characterizing the mental state of knowing the grammar) and the theory of the algorithms employed by speakers in language use.

Some of Chomsky's writings are replete with such confusing statements. Here is one, chosen almost at random: 'It seems,' he writes, 'that the mind carries out precise computational operations, using mental representations of a specific form, to arrive at precise conclusions about factual matters of no little complexity, without conscious thought or deliberation.' Chomsky then goes on: 'The principles that determine the nature of the mental representations and the operations that apply to them form a central part of our biologically determined nature. They constitute the human language faculty,' or universal grammar.[13]

Now universal grammar offers a parametrized characterization of a family of formal entities, namely, those languages learnable in the normal way by human beings. It does not describe the mental operations that speakers perform on mental representations in analyzing the form and meaning of an expression. Universal grammar is what every child knows, it is not the collection of principles governing how that knowledge is put to use, nor the system of mental representation that makes this information available to the child (if any does).

Chomsky has written that I-language 'is an element of [a speaker's] mind, namely, an element abstracted under the relational analysis of the steady state of the language faculty.' According to this analysis, 'we analyze knowledge of language as a relation R (H,L) between person H and a particular language L, thus abstracting L as a topic for inquiry' (1987, pp. 181, 179). But the I-language, or grammar, is *not* 'an element of [a speaker's] mind.' If it were, then on the 'relational analysis' knowledge of language would be a relation between a person and an element of his or her own mind, a peculiar position. Grammar characterizes the object of knowledge of a speaker, the object our knowledge of which is indeed a component of our minds. I-language, however, is no more contained in the speaker's mind than is Manhattan contained in mine when I happen to think about it, or than is the sentence 'Everyone has a mother' contained in the minds of all who know it to be true.

Chomsky and Jerrold Katz have insisted that there are no arguments against linguists adopting the 'realist position' according to which 'a dag [descriptively adequate grammar] actually describes the speech mechanisms at work . . .' (1974, p. 360).[14] Neither the grammar nor the psychogrammar, however, describes 'the speech mechanisms'; rather, these mechanisms are characterized, at different levels, by processing algorithms and the physioalgorithms that materially realize them.

And according to Jerry Fodor, 'It is nomologically necessary that the internal representation of the grammar (or, equivalently for these purposes, the internally represented grammar) is causally implicated in communication exchange between speakers and hearers in so far as these exchanges are mediated by their use of the language that they share' (1985, p. 149). In his parenthetical aside, Fodor slides from a correct (given the assumption about the causal nature of explanations adverting to beliefs) to an incorrect remark. An 'internally represented grammar' is no less a grammar and hence does not enter the causal stream leading to language use, unlike its 'internal representation'. The two following quotations illustrate a similar error: ' . . . grammars function in the mental processes of speaker/hearers,' 'the production/perception of speech [is] causally mediated by the grammar that the speaker/hearer learns' (pp. 150, 152).

These errors fall into two broad categories: (a) confusion between the grammar (what is represented) and the psycho- or physiogrammar (respectively, the mental state of knowing the grammar and the realizing physical state) and (b) confusion between the grammar and the speech processing algorithms (or the theory of), and perhaps even the physioalgorithms (or the theory of).

Corresponding to each type of error, we can find *façons de parler* which have become common in discussions in and about linguistics and which have facilitated, if not caused, its commission. For example, the term 'grammar' is often used with what Chomsky has called a 'systematic ambiguity' (1986, p. 29), denoting in some contexts what I have called 'psychogrammar' (and hence 'physiogrammar,' depending on one's assumptions), and denoting in others what I have called 'grammar' (or perhaps the linguistic theory whose subject is the grammar). This looseness can reinforce the idea that, when talking about a speaker's grammar, one is really talking about a feature of the speaker's mind or brain. That is, it can reinforce errors of kind (a).

The flip side of this ambiguity arises with the expression 'knowledge of language'. This shares the ambiguity often encountered in discussions of a person's beliefs, which can be read as concerned either with the propositions believed by that person or with the psychological states that constitute his or her believing them.[15] Similarly, 'knowledge of language' can be used to refer to that body of truths that someone knows when he or she knows a language or (as I have done throughout) to the corresponding psychological state.[16] Since linguists are typically said to be studying a speaker's knowledge of language, this ambiguity makes it easy to suppose that their topic is the speaker's mental state of knowing the language and that the grammar describes a system of mental representations. And now again, errors of kind (a) are just around the corner.

A different kind of ambiguity contributing to confusions of kind (b) arises with 'to generate' and its cognates. Sometimes these terms are used to describe the relation between the rules of a formal system and the result of their application, and sometimes to describe the activity of a speaker during speech perception or production.[17] It is likely that this looseness encourages the idea that linguists study how speakers actually use their linguistic knowledge, and thus that the grammar is really the parser that speakers employ in analyzing speech.

These confusions have infected the philosophical literature on linguistics and have yielded commentary based on outright error. For example, Anthony Kenny has criticized Chomsky for being philosophically 'confused and incoherent' (1984, p. 145). Yet his own discussion displays unclarity about the position he is attacking. '[W]hat Chomsky in fact studies,' Kenny writes, 'are relations between different abilities: in particular the ability to render the value of certain functions (e.g. linguistic transformations) for given arguments.' '[I]n performing intellectual tasks – including the comparatively modest ones of pronouncing a word or constructing a sentence – there are many sub-tasks that we perform without conscious advertence. When we ask what rules and principles we employ in performing these tasks, we are asking what sub-abilities we are exercising when we exercise the ability to use language' (p. 146).

All this seems to involve confusion of kind (b). Neither the theory of grammar nor of knowledge of grammar should be taken to be about the abilities speakers have in virtue of which they can use their language. These abilities, their components, and their interactions, will be given an abstract characterization by the theory of the algorithms of linguistic processing (algorithms that access our grammatical knowledge), while the theory of physioalgorithms will explain how these algorithms are physically realized in human speakers. So, though study of grammar will be relevant (indeed crucial) to understanding the nature of human linguistic ability, the theory of grammar is not itself concerned with those abilities. The grammar shows what competent speakers know, namely, which structural descriptions are assigned to which linguistic expressions; the grammar, however, does not reveal the methods speakers employ, which 'sub-abilities' they exercise, in determining those assignments.

Kenny is by no means the only one who discusses linguistics without having a clear grasp of the work or assumptions involved. In a recent popular discussion of some of these issues, John Searle spoke of 'the formal rules of grammar which people follow when they speak a language,' and he went on to attribute to modern linguistics the view that 'people follow rules of syntax when they talk' (1984, pp. 45, 48). This is another instance of what should by now be a very familiar error, namely, thinking that the rules of grammar are the algorithms that describe what people do when they perceive or produce speech. Searle compounds the confusion by attributing to Chomsky the view that 'there must be an entire complex set of rules of universal grammar in the brain' (p. 51), an apparently incoherent view (of type (a)), since grammar, an abstract entity, is not spatio-temporally locatable.

As a final example, consider Michael Devitt and Kim Sterelny's discussion (1987) of the psychological reality of grammars. They ask how one could determine whether a particular grammar offers a correct characterization of a speaker's competence, the mental state of knowing a grammar.[18] They reply that the kind of evidence relevant is of 'the behavioural sort needed to throw light . . . on the processes by which the speaker understands and produces sentences' (p. 143).[19] They believe that 'So little is known of the computational mechanisms of the mind that we have no idea whether G is a candidate for psychological explanation.' In order to know *that*, they claim, we would have to know whether 'the transformational processes it implicated were within the computational ambit of the mind' (pp. 145–6). Here we have an example of a confusion between psychogrammar and algorithms, between the state of knowing the grammar and those effective means used in the processing and production of speech. Devitt and Sterelny move from the hypothesis that a grammar characterizes that state to the conclusion that it characterizes the mental processes underlying the use of language. Not only is the hypothesis incorrect, but the inference is as well.[20]

III

The above examples give a sense of both the nature of the confusions and their prevalence. It is worth pursuing the topic, however, and asking why these errors are being made. Since the distinctions drawn above do not, after all, require great sophistication to grasp, we might sensibly inquire whether, in addition to the misleading ambiguities already noted, there are deeper pressures that lead to their neglect.

In fact, for each of the two kinds of error, (a) and (b), we can find an assumption that facilitates its commission. Recall that, according to the first confusion, grammars are located in the minds or brains of speakers and are thus fit links in the causal chain leading to linguistic behavior. On the conception I have urged, however, a grammar is not itself causally implicated in the production or perception of speech. It seems a plausible speculation that this conception has been resisted on the ground that it would turn linguistics into a non-empirical discipline, basically, a branch of mathematics. Indeed, some have already drawn just this conclusion.[21] In order to secure the empirical nature of the linguistic enterprise in the face of such arguments, one might be tempted to claim that the grammar really is part of the empirical world, more precisely, part of the brains of normal speakers. The implicit thought is that by thrusting grammar into the causal fray, one can place inquiry into a speaker's grammar on an equal footing with other investigations of the natural world.

As indicated above, however, this is not the correct response to this worry. It is instead properly addressed by pointing out that research into the identity of an abstract entity can be empirical.[22] Entities can be referred to in many different ways. In particular, mathematical objects (e.g., 35) can be given contingent descriptions, ones that only contingently pick out their denotations (e.g., 'the number of Oxford colleges'). For this reason, given such a description, an empirical inquiry will be required in order to discover which mathematical entity is denoted. Similarly, that physical objects can be given descriptions in a mentalistic vocabulary is compatible with research into their identity falling squarely within psychology. Just as an inquiry into the identity of Z's favorite planet is not plausibly considered part of planetary astronomy, so an inquiry into the identity of Z's grammar is not plausibly considered part of mathematics. It is a contingent fact that a speaker knows the grammar he or she does; consequently, identification of that grammar, an abstract object, is a fully empirical inquiry.

The second kind of error, a confusion between grammars and the algorithms that describe the processes facilitating linguistic perception and production, appears also to be explicable as the product of a worry fostered by another, again incorrect, assumption. The worry in this case is that, on the above conception, research into a speaker's grammar could not be psychological. The assumption, essentially, is that cognitive psychology proper is concerned with mental *processes*. Given this assumption, it is clear why those who believe, or want, linguistics to be a branch of psychology are moved to view grammars as descriptive of what speakers actually do when they produce or interpret speech.

This assumption appears to be widespread among linguists, psychologists, and philosophers. Joan Bresnan, for example, has claimed that unless one defines mappings from 'distinct grammatical rules and units into distinct processing operations and informational units . . . the grammar could not be said to represent the knowledge of the language user in any psychologically interesting sense' (Bresnan, Halle, and Miller (eds), 1978, p. 3).[23] Walter Kintsch and other psychologists have complained that the above conception of the subject-matter of linguistics 'permits the linguist to deal with convenient abstractions, uninhibited by psychological reality, and it provides the psychologist with the facetious argument that linguistic theories have nothing to do with processes anyway. As long as linguistic theory is strictly a competence theory, it is of no interest to the psychologist' (1974, chap. 1).[24]

To see how this assumption about the subject-matter of cognitive psychology is put to use in philosophical reflection on linguistics, consider Scott Soames's essay (1985, pp. 204–26).[25] According to him, theories in cognitive psychology 'attempt to explain a subject's intellectual capacities by positing internal computational routines that are causally responsible for his abilities' (p. 210). Consequently, if semantic theories 'are to be internally represented, they must accomplish some task that speakers of a language are capable of performing,' in particular they must characterize 'the process of comprehending a sentence' (pp. 216, 217). Given this assumption, it is hardly surprising that Soames concludes that 'truth conditional semantics are not psychological theories ... [because] they do not specify or make predictions about cognitive structures and processes' (p. 223).[26] Soames, then, aligns himself with Bresnan and Kintsch and those who believe that identifying a speaker's grammar could not be part of psychological research unless that grammar described the mental processing that speakers perform in using language.

At this point we could distinguish several positions. The first is the one just outlined: grammars are not psychologically significant unless they characterize the process of linguistic understanding. The second position demands only that grammars be explicitly represented in some internal system of mental representation that is causally effective during language use.[27] The third position does not require that the grammar be explicitly represented in order to be psychologically significant; it demands only that the information contained in the grammar be realized in a particular state that is causally influential in the operation of some processes responsible for the perception or production of speech.[28] The final and weakest position holds that identifying a speaker's grammar is already part of the psychological enterprise just in virtue of delineating the object of the speaker's knowledge; no further claim need be made about processing mechanisms, about the mental state of knowing the grammar, about the brain state that realizes this mental state, or about the causal impact these states have.

The first position outlined, that of Bresnan, Kintsch, Soames, and many others, appears to me unmotivated and blind to most of what is actually taken for psychology. Amounting to little more than a proprietary use of the term 'psychological,' it is the result of a process fetishism that distorts the nature of what typically passes for psychological research. This research is by no means solely concerned to study scientifically human mental processes or the underlying mechanisms that make them possible. It has a broader concern, namely, the phenomenon of mind, which includes of course mental processes, but is not exhausted by them. Psychology, in addition, encompasses the study of what minded creatures believe (about themselves, about the world around them, about abstract structures, etc.), when they acquire these beliefs, in what order, what the contribution of the environment is, what principles govern change of belief, and so on; and the same holds for fear, desire, and other attitudes basic to mental life. Of course, we will also want to know how what is believed is represented in the mind (if indeed it is) and which operations are performed on these representations, but none of these interests impugn the psychological nature of an inquiry into the objects of these beliefs. On the contrary, it is hard to see how we could realistically pursue an investigation into how the mind represents what is believed in complete ignorance of what is believed.[29]

Consider, for example, the computational theory of vision, as presented by David Marr (1982).[30] This active research project is directed to answering many questions, including these: 'What kind of information does the human visual system represent, what kind of computations does it perform to obtain this information, and why? How does it represent this information and how are the computations performed and with what algorithms? . . . How are these specific representations implemented in neural machinery?' (1982, p. 99). Note that one of the tasks Marr and his colleagues set themselves is the discovery of the information used by the human visual system. Marr writes that: 'The question to ask is, What assumptions are reasonable to make – that we unconsciously employ – when we interpret silhouettes . . . as three-dimensional shapes?' (p. 219).[31] Whether these assumptions are *explicitly* represented, and, if not, how they are, are open questions, but note that one cannot even raise these issues in a serious way without first having articulated what these assumptions are. This task is on a par with the project of describing what a speaker knows about his or her language, information which may or may not be explicitly represented, but whose representation it is thought enters somehow into the actual processing of speech. If the first task can be reckoned part of cognitive psychology, then so can the second.

Thus mechanism mania should be rejected. Seeking the structure of what is known by a creature is an essential part of cognitive psychology. It follows that Soames's argument should also be rejected, as it depends on arbitrarily restricting the adjective 'psychological' to theories concerned with mental processes. That grammars or semantic theories 'do not specify or make predictions about cognitive structures and processes' does not mean that research into their nature is not psychological. Once we recognize this, we shall be less tempted to make the grammar into something it is not by viewing it as an account of what speakers do when they perceive or produce speech, thereby committing error (b).

I do not want to enter into an extended discussion of the merits of the three remaining positions on what is properly psychological. Personally, I do not find any but the fourth and weakest position at all plausible. The second and third could only appeal to closet process fetishists. While they do not demand that a grammar characterize the speech processing mechanisms, both assume that, unless the grammar is in some way connected to these mechanisms, research into its nature is not part of psychological inquiry. Again, there seems little motivation for this position. When we learn what a creature knows, we learn a fact that is no more or less psychological (in any ordinary sense of 'psychological') than facts about, say, the period or circumstances in which this knowledge was acquired (a major concern of developmental psychology). It is undeniable that we come to understand a creature (its psyche) better as we discover what it knows, believes, wants, fears, etc. The first three positions simply appropriate the term 'psychology' for the study of a restricted subset of mental life, namely, that associated in some close fashion to mental processes, now arbitrarily designated as privileged objects of psychological research.[32] I conclude therefore that of the four views the last one deserves to be taken most seriously.

I am not, however, urging that it should be taken seriously, for I am skeptical about the value of debates on disciplinary boundaries; there is little reason to suppose that these divisions carve nature at its joints rather than institutions.

More serious would be the suggestion that the grammars known by speakers are not real and that investigating their identities cannot be part of ordinary empirical inquiry until a tighter connection is established between them and the processing mechanisms underlying speech.[33] This position, however, flies in the face of actual linguistic practice, in which theories are carefully elaborated, tested, falsified, revised, and retested; in which consensus among practitioners on a substantial framework has been attained; in which there is considerable agreement on the major accomplishments and problems in the field; and so on. It would take a very compelling argument to show that this practice is somehow illusory or irrelevant. No such argument has been offered to date, I believe, and in its absence we should feel free to consider investigation of the grammars known by speakers a respectable empirical enterprise, part of psychology in fact – or, if this makes one nervous, part of a 'different' science: linguistics.

Once these false assumptions are identified, they can be more easily resisted, as can the errors, (a) and (b), they bring in their wake. This not only enhances conceptual clarity, but also makes irrelevant a couple of common reservations about linguistics. The first is a doubt about attribution of tacit knowledge of anything like present-day grammars, on the ground that the psychological experiments designed to test this attribution have not yielded the anticipated results.

These experiments actually tested what has come to be called the Derivational Theory of Complexity, according to which the amount of mental processing involved in understanding a string should vary with the number of transformations needed to derive it in the grammar tacit knowledge of which is attributed to the speaker. The Derivational Theory of Complexity, however, was misconceived from the start, born from the confusion between grammar and algorithm. This is not to say that the experiments spawned by the

Derivational Theory of Complexity have taught us nothing about the mental processes underlying the perception and production of speech, only that these results are not the sought-after sticks with which to beat linguistics, an enterprise concerned to characterize what speakers know, not how they apply that knowledge.

The second worry is that linguistics has too much truck with a substantial notion of mental representation, a notion on which many would hesitate to hang an entire program of inquiry. This criticism does not, like the first, question the empirical adequacy of the enterprise, but rather the intelligibility of what are assumed to be its most basic assumptions.

This worry too can be turned back if we remember to distinguish between a grammar and the corresponding psychogrammar. We will then see that linguistics, the systematic investigation of what speakers know *qua* speakers, does not depend on any specific substantive position on the nature of the psychological state that constitutes the speaker's knowledge of grammar. Linguistics does not rely, in particular, on any theses, philosophical or other, about the nature or even the cogency of such notions as *mental representation, semantic content, language of thought*, and the like.[34] There is, in short, a certain autonomy of linguistics.

Notes

1 The following is much influenced by the work of James Higginbotham, in particular 'Is grammar psychological?' (1983) and 'The autonomy of syntax and semantics' (1987).

2 This paper is couched in terms of 'knowledge' and its cognates. This should not be construed as an endorsement of the widely held view that knowledge is the cognitive attitude speakers have towards their grammars. Nothing in this paper depends on that claim.

I shall assume, without further discussion, that speakers do bear some cognitive relation toward their grammars. For a discussion illustrating how difficult it is to draw a principled distinction between states of so-called tacit knowledge and 'ordinary' attitude states, see Martin Davies's 'Tacit knowledge and subdoxastic states,' this volume.

3 The term is Higginbotham's (1987, p. 128).

4 Christopher Peacocke, in section 4 of 'When is a grammar psychologically real?' this volume, provides examples, some drawn from actual psychological research, of different ways in which the same information can be represented.

5 For a defense of the claim that belief-desire explanations of actions are causal, see Donald Davidson, 1985.

6 A speaker's psychogrammar could be identical to the corresponding physiogrammar without it following that there is only one way to characterize the relevant entity or state in the context of explanation. Temperature might be identical to mean molecular energy, although an account of the relevant features of reality employing 'temperature talk' might differ substantially from one using 'mean molecular energy talk'. If a certain kind of materialism is true, then psychogrammar and physiogrammar are one and the same; nevertheless, the relevant entity or state can

be referred to in an explanatory context using language drawn from substantially different vocabularies. Sometimes this point is put by saying that the descriptions are on different levels (see, e.g., Chomsky, 1983, p. 23); sometimes by saying that the characterizations, or the explanations in which they are embedded, follow different constitutive principles (see essays 11, 12, and 13 in Davidson, 1985; p. 239, for example).

7 The last two parenthetical additions may be unjustified. I remarked above in passing that psychogrammars, candidate components of causal explanations, might be abstract entities as well. For an examination and partial defense of the thesis that mathematical objects can enter into causal explanations, see Mark Steiner, 1975, ch. 4, especially sections I and II.

8 It seems that the phenomenon of weakness of the will just consists in people not acting in the manner most rational in the light of all their beliefs and desires. See Donald Davidson, 'How is weakness of the will possible?' (1985). Additionally, impairments to Y's memory, motor mechanisms, nervous system, etc. might also prevent Y from acting as he or she did. My point here is merely that beliefs and desires do not entail action.

9 Note that there is no claim that these processes *exhaust* what is involved in what we loosely call 'understanding'. There is no reason to suppose that that everyday activity could be analyzed in terms of just one set of notions or principles. The claim, rather, is that some algorithmic processing is a necessary component of the full-blown activity of linguistic understanding.

10 Perhaps for this reason, one should find Chomsky's talk of 'performance competence' unfortunate. (See, e.g., Chomsky, 1980, p. 59.) The term is appropriate in suggesting that one must distinguish between normal and abnormal functioning of the mechanisms involved in a speaker's linguistic performance. It is misleading insofar as it suggests that the principles involved are objects of a speaker's knowledge.

11 There is confusion and there is confusion. Some doctrines are so deeply confused that nothing is salvageable, any further reflections on them being a waste of time. I do not believe there are any grounds for thinking that linguistics is in that state. It is comparable, rather, to the calculus before the nineteenth century: an area of active and fruitful research with a real subject-matter, whose foundations it took some time to clarify. As Quine has quipped, 'It is a commonplace predicament to be unable to formulate a task until half done with it' (1979, p. 235).

12 Elsewhere, Chomsky is careful to distinguish between a grammar and a speaker's knowledge of, or representation of, that grammar: 'a generative grammar, represented in the mind, determines the set of well-formed sentences' (1986, p. 126); 'the fundamental concepts are *grammar* and *knowing a grammar*' (1986); 'The grammar, in whatever form its principles are represented in the mind and brain, simply characterizes the properties of sentences, much as the principles of arithmetic determine the properties of numbers' (1986, p. 222); 'a language [is] a generative procedure that assigns structural descriptions to linguistic expressions, knowledge of language being the internal representation of such a procedure in the brain' (1988a, p. 4). It would be hard to interpret these and other passages if Chomsky simply understood 'grammar' to be a speaker's mental representation of the grammar. This suggests that he accepts the distinction between rules and their mental representations, between the rules that we know and our knowing of them. Nevertheless, as indicated in the text and as the reader will find in perusing

Chomsky's writings, he frequently asserts that the linguist is uncovering the nature of mental representations and of the rules that operate on them. (Contrast, for example, 'the rules of grammar are mentally represented' with 'the grammar generates mental representations', 1980, pp. 129, 143.)

13 Chomsky, 1988b, p. 131. And another: 'The principles of universal grammar,' he writes, 'are part of the fixed structure of the mind/brain, and it may be assumed that such mechanisms operate virtually instantaneously. To the extent that sentence analysis relies on these principles, understanding should be virtually as fast as identification of vocabulary items' (pp. 73–4). See also pp. 85, 90–1, 98, 136, and 185, to cite just a few passages that could easily lead readers astray. In fairness to Chomsky, it should be mentioned that this book is largely a transcription of lectures he delivered 'live' in Managua, Nicaragua. Also, for something of a clarification, still at odds with the view presented here, see pp. 93–4.

14 Here again the lapse is only temporary. Later they write: 'We postulate certain properties of the brain, e.g. that it must contain some neural mechanism that stores the information in the grammar, on the grounds that properties of linguistic behavior can be explained by assuming them to be causal consequences of brain mechanisms with access to such information' (1974, p. 365).

15 Ruth Marcus put her finger on the ambiguity when she complained that 'A difficulty with discussions of epistemological attitudes is the equivocation engendered by shuttling between describing beliefs *as* psychological states or features of psychological states, and describing beliefs as objects of believing' (1983, p. 322 n. 1).

16 Chomsky, it seems to me, often moves between these two senses. For example, on the one hand he writes that 'knowledge [of English] is in part shared among us and represented somehow in our minds' – here knowledge is what is known – while, on the other, he calls knowledge of grammar one of several interacting 'cognitive systems', 'now analyzed in terms of a certain structure of rules, principles and representations in the mind' – and now knowledge is a psychological state (1980, pp. 50, 90, 91).

17 For instance, Jerome Bruner writes of 'the grammatical rules of the language by which the aspirant speaker was enabled to generate well-formed utterances and none that were ill-formed' (1983, pp. 32–3). And according to Chomsky, 'a person who knows language L has a specific method for interpreting arbitrary expressions'; such a person 'has acquired a generative procedure' for that language (1987, pp. 181, 180). (But see in this connection, n. 5, p. 181.) These passages lend themselves to incorrect interpretations. If we are not to go astray, we must understand 'generate,' etc. as referring to the formal relation defined by the grammar and not to psychological processes that speakers undergo.

18 Though, to their credit, they find it a confusion to think that the grammar does offer such a characterization; see their section 8.2.

19 Note also the peculiar, but common, assumption that we know *a priori* which kind of data (here, 'the behavioural sort') is relevant to which conjectures. In fact, such questions cannot be intelligently considered in a theoretical vacuum; for example, it is only in the context of a very elaborate background theory that meter readings in Florida could be evidence relevant to hypotheses about the atmosphere on Neptune.

20 It would be a mistake to think that Gareth Evans's account of tacit knowledge of a theory of meaning falls foul of the same confusion. According to Evans, a speaker

tacitly knows such a theory just in case that speaker has a particular set of dispositions, 'one corresponding to each of the expressions for which the theory provides a distinct axiom' (1985, p. 238). Martin Davies (1987) has characterized Evans's proposal in the following way:

The requirement on semantic theories – a crude version of the *Mirror Constraint* – is that the derivational structure in a semantic theory should match the causal explanatory structure in actual speakers. The account of tacit knowledge is this. We attribute to an individual speaker tacit knowledge of a particular semantic theory on condition that the theory meet the Mirror Constraint with respect to that speaker. (1987, p. 447)

Davies goes on to argue that a refinement of this account (the precise nature of which is irrelevant here) indeed yields a correct picture.

It would be an error to think that on an account like that of Evans and Davies, the grammar is viewed as descriptive of the system of causal states through which speakers pass during linguistic performance; nor is it claimed on this view that the grammar somehow enters into the causal nexus. Rather, such a position is making a claim about a speaker's physiogrammar, in particular, about the structure of the material state of a speaker that constitutes his or her tacit knowledge of a grammar or of a semantic theory. The claim is that there is an isomorphism between the structure of the states comprising the physiogrammar and the axiomatic structure of the object of knowledge.

The trouble with the view, rather, is that it seems motivated by dubious assumptions about what constitutes appropriate evidence for attributions of tacit knowledge. (For another possible motivation, equally questionable in my view, see the discussion below of Joan Bresnan's position, which Evans's resembles.) An underlying assumption is that ascription of tacit knowledge of one grammar over another to a speaker S can be justified only by facts about S's behavioral abilities. This *(behavioral) evidential individualism*, most persistently advanced by W.V. Quine, is central to much recent philosophical reflection on language (George 1986a, ch. 4), though one that cannot be reconciled with the practice of modern linguists. For a nearby instance, see Michael Dummett's 'Language and communication,' in which he claims that 'it is by a speaker's linguistic and non-linguistic behaviour that we must judge whether or not some given theory of meaning, of the Fregean type, can be taken as governing that speaker's idiolect' (this volume, p. 203).

Davies grants that 'there is no point in imposing restrictions on the class of admissible evidence. Given a proper constitutive account of what tacit knowledge is, any evidence for or against the empirical hypothesis that such a condition obtains in a speaker is relevant to the attribution of tacit knowledge.' It is especially peculiar, then, that Davies should find it at all interesting or significant 'to meet Quine's challenge on something like its own terms, by citing evidence which concerns the very speaker to whom the attribution is being made' (1987, p. 442). Given the evidential individualism behind 'Quine's challenge,' there is no reason why someone who takes off from actual research into natural languages need meet it.

Elsewhere, I have argued that there is more in common between Quine and Chomsky than is usually thought and that the central source of disagreement between the two is that the first holds, while the second rejects, that explanations in linguistics limp because a claim about which grammar a speaker tacitly knows 'is not a claim that can be reduced to, or whose full content is given by, claims about a speaker's dispositions to attest to the well-formedness of given strings or, indeed, any claims about a speaker's behavioral dispositions' (George, 1986b, p. 495). See also George, 1987, esp. pp. 162–4. Since for Quine the proof of explanatory strictures is in their eating, we must wait and see what is yielded by his approach to language use and acquisition. If nothing is (as seems to be the case), then, Quine might himself urge, so much the worse for those particular restrictions and whatever philosophical consequences were drawn from them. These indeterminacy generating strictures are for Quine nothing more than 'traits of the science of our day' which 'might well change as science advances' (1979, p. 244). The indeterminacy thesis itself, then, might be abandoned on account of the future (or even present) course of science. Indeed, any other conclusion would ill accord with Quine's insistence that his is not a philosophy prior to the scientific enterprise. For further discussion, see George, 1986b.

Hilary Putnam (in his 'Model theory and the "factuality" of semantics,' this volume) contends that I overemphasize the empirical nature of the dispute between Quine and Chomsky. But since he there discusses *Fodor's* view of 'broad content,' it is hard to evaluate his charge. In fact, it is questionable whether Chomsky believes linguistics is, or will be, committed to the intelligibility of 'broad content' and related notions; he stresses (again with Quine) that 'there is no reason to suppose that the concepts of general psychology will be those of ordinary usage, just as the concepts of physics, or of the subbranch of psychology called "linguistics", typically are not' (Chomsky, 1988a, p. 20).

21 Thus, according to F.R. Palmer, Chomsky's notion of 'competence is some kind of idealised system without any clear empirical basis' (1981, p. 8). And David D. Clarke writes that the recursive rules of a grammar 'are best viewed as instrumentalist rather than realist descriptions of the source of grammaticality' (1983, p. 114).

Jerrold Katz (1981) has argued at great length that linguists should not be offended by the suggestion that their theories cannot be interpreted realistically or as dealing with the empirical world. (Page references that follow are to his 'An outline of Platonist grammar' printed in Katz (ed.), 1985). This is only something to be disturbed by if one accepts the empirical interpretation of linguistics that he now believes is thoroughly mistaken.

Katz's position seems to me to be based partly on a misunderstanding, partly on an incorrect assumption. He argues that conflicts can arise within what he calls 'conceptualist' linguistics because it is torn between the different tasks of characterizing natural languages and of describing the system of mental representations used by speakers: 'Conceptualists have to construct grammars as theories of the *knowledge* an ideal speaker has of the language, whereas Platonists construct grammars as theories of the *language* that such knowledge is knowledge of. . . . Because the mental medium in which human knowledge is internally represented can materially influence the character of the representation, there can be a significant divergence between what a theory of such an internal representation says and what is true of the language' (p. 195–6). Katz here falls prey to the same confusion as do many others concerning the object of inquiry of modern linguistics. There is a sense in which this object can be called a speaker's 'knowledge of language,' but not the sense in which this is the system of mental representations that the speaker uses to represent what is known. Linguists are investigating what speakers know, and what they know is a grammar, *not* the system of representations by which that grammar is made available to them. (Compare: what I see is a tree, *not* my own representation of the tree.)

Katz denies 'that linguistic theory is a psychological theory of the competence underlying human language learning' (p. 182). Now linguists should agree with him here, if he means only that linguistics is not concerned with the internal mental representations of speakers. But Katz slides from the view that linguistics is not about those internal representations to the view that linguistics is not psychological. He seems to assume that the nature of the objects one is investigating determines the nature of one's investigation. On his view, apparently, if one is seeking to describe mental representations, then one is doing psychology, whereas if one is seeking to describe abstract objects, then one is doing mathematics. This assumption, however, must clearly be rejected (for, among other reasons, those given in the text). In identifying abstract objects, one can be engaged in an empirical inquiry; one, furthermore, that is most naturally construed as psychological. This assumption and the confusion illustrated in the previous paragraph run throughout Katz's discussion.

To summarize: while linguists study just those objects that Katz thinks they should be studying (though which he believes, incorrectly as the result of confusion, they are not studying), nothing follows from this concerning the psychological or empirical nature of the enterprise (unless one makes, with Katz, a false assumption).

22 This point is emphasized in Higginbotham, 1983, p. 171.
23 Note also that though there is a sense in which the grammar does, as Bresnan claims, 'represent the knowledge of the language user,' it is not the case that it makes claims about how the user represents what is known; rather, the grammar is, simply, what is known. (See the discussion on p. 96 of the ambiguity of 'knowledge of language'.)
24 Also cited, with discussion, in Chomsky, 1980, pp. 202–5.
25 In addition to the unwarranted assumption to be discussed in the text, other errors creep into Soames's presentation. For example, he writes that it is part of the 'received view among generative grammarians' that 'the rules and representations that make up linguists' grammars are psychologically real mechanisms which are causally responsible for (some significant portion of) the linguistic behaviour of competent speakers' (1985, p. 205). This is our old error (a) again. Grammars, to repeat, are not 'causally responsible' for language use, unlike, perhaps, the mental state of knowing the grammar.
26 Soames is certainly not the only philosopher to adopt this assumption about psychological reality. Searle, for example, writes that: 'What is psychologically relevant about the brain is the fact that it contains psychological processes and that it has a neurophysiology that causes and realises these processes' (1984, p. 50). See also the discussion of psychological reality by Devitt and Sterelny who find relevant only those facts about 'the processes by which the speaker understands and produces sentences' (quoted 1987, p. 97).

As noted earlier, Chomsky's remarks sometimes suggest a conception of semantic theories that is psychological in this sense, for example, when he writes that 'most of the theory of meaning . . . is a theory of representations in the mind – mental representations and the computational systems that form and modify these representations' (1988b, p. 191).

27   It seems that Soames does not recognize this as a distinct position. As just noted, he writes that if semantic theories 'are to be internally represented, they must accomplish some task that speakers of a language are capable of performing,' and thereby rules out the possibility of a semantic theory which is internally represented and there to be 'accessed' by computational routines, but which is not itself a theory of those mental processes.

28   This seems to be Christopher Peacocke's view; see his 'When is a grammar psychologically real?' (this volume) and Peacocke, 1986. It is from this position that Peacocke argues (in the latter article) against Soames's conclusion that semantic theories cannot be part of psychological explanations.

29   I find this accords with James Higginbotham's conclusion that 'Even if there is a medium through which the speaker thinks about meaning, our first access to that medium must be through the direct characterization of the knowledge that translation into it makes available' ('Knowledge of reference,' this volume, p. 159).

30   In understanding Marr's theory, I have benefited from Gabriel Segal (1987). The quotations from Marr are also cited in his paper.

31   Examples of such assumptions are 'the visible world can be regarded as being composed of smooth surfaces having reflectance functions whose spatial structure may be elaborate' (p. 44); 'if direction of motion is ever discontinuous at more than one point – along a line, for example – then an object boundary is present' (p. 51).

32   Thus I disagree with Peacocke's claim that 'All [psychological reality of a grammar] requires is that the parser draw somehow or other on the information stated in the rules of the grammar,' that 'for a rule of a grammar to be psychologically real for a given subject is for it to specify the information drawn upon by the relevant mechanisms or algorithms in that subject' ('When is a grammar psychologically real?,' this volume, pp. 118, 114.) Peacocke and others seem to assume that mental algorithmic processing is a first-class psychological phenomenon, providing a touchstone for psychological existence. But on the basis of which analysis of the notion *psychological* is this assumption made? And what is its justification?

33   This appears to be a vestige of behaviorism that cognitive psychology has still not shed, namely, the idea that theoretical constructs can only be vindicated through a tight link with the behavior of speakers – the cognitive turn having weakened this to 'with the mechanisms speakers employ to perceive and produce linguistic behavior'.

34   There are other ways in which falling prey to error (a) can lead one to views that really are independent of the viability of the linguistic enterprise. Consider, for example, someone who believes, reasonably enough, that, were there no humans, then human minds, brains, and their components, would not exist. If this person now also believes (confusedly) that grammars are elements of the human mind/brain, then he or she will conclude that, were there no humans, grammars would not exist. Indeed, this seems to be just Chomsky's view: 'language has no objective existence apart from its mental representation' (1972, p. 169); '. . . grammar does not have an independent existence apart from the functions of the human mind, but they are in fact precisely systems of principles that the human mind is capable of constructing, given the primary linguistic data' (1982, p. 16).

Yet, grammars are mathematical objects and, according to the folk theory of most working mathematicians, these objects do not depend for their existence and properties on such contingent facts as whether a particular species of animal is still walking the earth. Chomsky's views about linguistics, which do involve confusion (a), lead him to adopt a kind of constructivism as regards (some) mathematical entities. He suggests, in fact, that: 'One could perhaps take the intuitionist view of mathematics as being not unlike the linguistic view of grammar' (1982, p. 16).

What is objectionable in all this is not so much the particular position on mathematical existence at which Chomsky arrives (though for some it would certainly be objection enough). It is, rather, the idea that linguistics is in some way committed to a contentious view, or indeed to any view, in the philosophy of mathematics. In fact, linguistics is not so committed, but only seems to be due to confusion between grammar and psychogrammar. (Note that even if grammars *were* elements of the mind, because all mathematical entities were, there would still be a distinction to be drawn between grammar and psychogrammar: the former is the object of knowledge, the latter the knowledge of that object, though both would now be (different) elements of the mind.)

Along similar lines, Chomsky writes elsewhere: 'Knowing everything about the mind/brain, a Platonist would argue, we still have no basis for determining the truths of arithmetic or set theory, but there is not the slightest reason to suppose that there are truths of language that would still escape our grasp' (1986, p. 33). Here everything hinges on how one takes the expression 'truths of language'. If we understand it as denoting the truths about the identity of grammars speakers can and do know, or the truths about the mental and the physical states in virtue of which they have and acquire this knowledge, then Chomsky is correct; for these truths are a subset of all truths 'about the mind/brain'. If, however, the expression is understood to mean the truths about all languages and grammars, in the sense in which these terms are used in model theory or automata theory, then obviously Chomsky is wrong. Again, we risk error and confusion if we do not distinguish between the language that is known (one abstract structure among many) and the psychological state of knowing that language.

References

Bresnan, Joan, Halle, M. and Miller, G. (eds) 1978: *Linguistic Theory and Psychological Reality*. Cambridge, Mass.: MIT Press.

Bruner, Jerome 1983: The social context of language acquisition. In Roy Harris (ed.), *Approaches to Language*. London: Pergamon Press.

Chomsky, Noam 1965: *Aspects of the Theory of Syntax*. Cambridge, Mass.: MIT Press.

1972: *Language and Mind*, enlarged edn. New York: Harcourt Brace Jovanovich.

1980: *Rules and Representations*. New York: Columbia University Press.

1982: *The Generative Enterprise: A Discussion with R. Huybregts and H. van Riemsdijk*. Dordrecht: Foris.

1986: *Knowledge of Language: Its Nature, Origin, and Use*. New York: Praeger.

1987: Replies to Alexander George and Michael Brody. *Mind and Language*, 2 (2).

1988a: Language and interpretation: philosophical reflection and empirical inquiry. Ms. Cambridge, Mass.: MIT. (Forthcoming in University of Pittsburgh Series on the Philosophy of Science.)

1988b: *Language and Problems of Knowledge: The Managua Lectures*. Cambridge, Mass.: MIT Press.

Chomsky, Noam and Katz, Jerrold 1974: What the linguist is talking about. *The Journal of Philosophy*, 71 (12).

Clarke, David D. 1983: *Language and Action: A Structural Mode of Behaviour*. London: Pergamon Press.

Davidson, Donald 1985: Actions, reasons, causes. In Donald Davidson, *Essays on Actions and Events*. Oxford University Press.

Davies, Martin 1987: Tacit knowledge and semantic theory: can a five per cent difference matter? *Mind*, October.

Devitt, Michael and Sterelny, Kim 1987: *Language and Reality*. Oxford University Press.

Evans, Gareth: 1985: *Collected Papers*. Oxford University Press.

Fodor, Jerry 1985: Some notes on what linguistics is about. In Jerrold Katz (ed.), *The Philosophy of Linguistics*. Oxford University Press.

George, Alexander 1986a: Must the language of knowledge be used in explaining knowledge of language? Unpublished Ph.D. dissertation. Cambridge, Mass.: Harvard University.

　1986b: Whence and whither the debate between Quine and Chomsky? *The Journal of Philosophy*, September.

　1987: Review of Noam Chomsky's *Knowledge of Language*. *Mind and Language*, 2 (2), summer.

Higginbotham, James 1983: Is grammar psychological? In Leigh S. Cauman *et al.* (eds), *How Many Questions? Essays in Honor of Sidney Morgenbesser*. Hackett Publishing Co.

　1987: The autonomy of syntax and semantics. In Jay L. Garfield (ed.), *Modularity in Knowledge Representation and Natural-Language Understanding*, Cambridge, Mass.: MIT Press.

Katz, Jerrold J. 1981: *Language and Other Abstract Objects*. Totowa: Rowman and Littlefield.

　(ed.) 1985: *The Philosophy of Linguistics*. Oxford University Press.

Kenny, Anthony 1984: *The Legacy of Wittgenstein*. Oxford: Basil Blackwell.

Kintsch, W. *et al.* 1974: *The Representation of Meaning in Memory*. London: John Wiley and Sons.

Marcus, Ruth 1983: Rationality and believing the impossible. *The Journal of Philosophy*, 80 (6).

Marr, David 1982: *Vision*. San Francisco, Calif.: W.H. Freeman and Co.

Palmer, F.R. 1981: *Semantics*, 2nd edn. Cambridge University Press.

Peacocke, Christopher 1986: Explanation in computational psychology: language, perception and level 1.5. *Mind and Language*, 1 (2), summer.

Quine, W.V. 1979: The scope and language of science. In Quine, *The Ways of Paradox and Other Essays*. Cambridge, Mass.: Harvard University Press.

 Searle, John 1984: *Minds, Brains and Science*. London: British Broadcasting Corporation.

Segal, Gabriel 1987: Seeing what is not there. Ms. Dept of Philosophy, University of Madison at Wisconsin, forthcoming in *The Philosophical Review*.

Soames, Scott 1985: Semantics and psychology. In Jerrold Katz (ed.), *The Philosophy of Linguistics*. Oxford University Press.

Steiner, Mark 1975: *Mathematical Knowledge*. New York: Cornell University Press.

6

When is a Grammar Psychologically Real?

Christopher Peacocke

What is it for a grammar to be psychologically real? This question poses one of the most fundamental conceptual issues raised by Chomsky's great contributions to the study of language. The question is one which has to be addressed by any theorist who agrees with Chomsky that the standpoint of generative grammar 'is that of individual psychology' (1986, p. 3). In this paper, I will be recommending a particular answer to the question, and considering some of its consequences. Chomsky has remarked (1987, pp. 182–3), surely truly, that it is sometimes a mistake to address conceptual questions without waiting for further theoretical and empirical investigation involving the concepts in question. While our understanding is obviously very incomplete, I think our grasp of what is distinctive of computational and psychological explanation has improved sufficiently to allow us to make some progress with this particular conceptual issue about psychological reality.

Drawing on information

In earlier discussions (Peacocke, 1986), I distinguished a level of description of a computational mechanism which lies between Marr's first and second levels.[1] Marr's first level states which function is computed (and why); his second level identifies the algorithm which computes it; and his third level describes the hardware realization of the algorithm (Marr, 1982, pp. 24ff). The intermediate level of description I claimed to find I labelled 'level 1.5': it identifies the information drawn upon by an algorithm. There will surely be many other levels between Marr's first and second, and these further levels may well need to be classified along more than one dimension. But it is this level of information drawn upon which I want to exploit in the present paper. We can start with an example.

Consider a subject's ability to pronounce words he sees written on a sheet in front of him. We can fix on a given function described at Marr's first level, a function from inscription-types – words, say – to sequences of phonemes. One can conceive of three quite different bodies of information which might be drawn upon by the algorithm which computes this function. There might (a) be a listing which specifies for each complete inscription-type the corresponding sequence of phonemes. This would be analogous to what psychologists call 'the lexical route' for reading aloud. There might (b) be an algorithm which draws upon information about the pronunciation of sublexical syllables, and computes the sequence of phonemes for the whole word from information about phonemes corresponding to its parts. A third possibility (c) is that there is an algorithm which draws on information about the pronunciation of a proper subset of the given class of whole words, and extrapolates from their pronunciation via a similarity relation to the pronunciation of the remainder. Under this third possibility, no information about syllable/phoneme correspondences need be used.

These characterizations of the information drawn upon are not descriptions at Marr's level 2: they do not specify the particular algorithm employed. Consider, for instance, the description just given of case (b), in which information about the pronunciation of individual syllables is used. In other examples falling under case (b), different algorithms may compute the pronunciation of the whole from its parts. One algorithm may compute the sequence of phonemes by proceeding through the word from left to right; another may proceed from right to left; a third might make the assignments by proceeding through some deeper tree-structure assigned to the word by a syntactic or semantic theory, and then re-ordering the phonetic representation to obtain the pronunciation of the surface word. For present purposes, it is not to the point that one of these algorithms is empirically more plausible than the rest. What matters is that each algorithm is consistent with the fact that the information drawn upon concerns the pronunciation of individual syllables.

These characterizations of the information drawn upon are not at Marr's level 1, either. The same function (the 'function-in-extension') from inscription-types to sequences of phonemes may be computed in cases (a)–(c). In effect, a characterization at the intermediate level 1.5 collects together an equivalence class of algorithms, namely, all those drawing on the same body of information. The pattern of one–many relations between Marr's levels is preserved when we insert level 1.5. One and the same function may be computed by drawing on different bodies of information. One and the same body of information may be drawn upon by different algorithms.

Some phenomena are properly explained by facts stated at level 1.5. Explanations of such phenomena at lower levels are less general and unnecessary. We can continue with the case of the inscriptions as an example. Suppose that the syllable *ad* in a word always receives a certain pronunciation. It could be that the explanation of this fact is that the mechanism draws upon the information that that very syllable is so pronounced. This is an empirical, contingent claim. It will not be true of a subject who falls under cases (a) or (c) above; but suppose it is true. The identity of the particular algorithm which draws upon the information that *ad* has a certain pronunciation is not then crucial for the explanation of the general fact about this subject that he

pronounces any word of the form — ad — as something of the form
. . .**æd** . . . . The explanation which cites that piece of information as drawn
upon is correct whatever the detailed algorithm which draws upon it. This
explanation is also of greater generality than anything which mentions a specific
algorithm. These points are not artefacts of selecting as the fact to be explained
a general truth about the pronunciation of all words of the form — ad —. They
apply equally if the fact to be explained is the pronunciation of a particular
sequence of graphemes. Under the conditions of the example, such a particular
fact can be explained by the information concerning the pronunciation of individual graphemes which is drawn upon, together with information about the
significance for pronunciation of concatenation. To make these points is not to
denigrate Marr's level 2, which is obviously of great importance. The force of
these points is rather this: the fact that a proposed explanation neither mentions
nor requires a unique algorithm need not detract from its explanatory power.

Explanation by facts stated at level 1.5 is a form of causal explanation. Facts
about the meaning, syntactic structure, and phonetic form of expressions are
causally explained by facts about the information drawn upon by algorithms or
mechanisms in the language-user. No doubt we would not say, in the above
example, that a mechanism is drawing on information that the syllable 'ad' is
pronounced a certain way unless words containing it have certain pronunciation
properties. But the words could have those pronunciation properties without
that information being drawn upon. There is no obstacle here to the
explanation being causal.

A subtler complaint would be that in speaking of an informational state which
is the common cause of (say) the common feature of the way in which all words
of the form — ad — are pronounced, we are simply *reading back* into the
common cause a content which summarizes its effect. And if this is all we are
doing, how can the informational property of the cause be explanatory, rather
than a mere overlay? This is a good objection to a view which is not mine. Such
reading back of content is never by itself sufficient for a cause to be a state with
an informational content. Even in the humble example of the pronunciation of
'ad', we can agree that such reading-back is insufficient. No state is the relevant
informational state that 'ad' is pronounced **æd** unless it has certain relations to
the ground of the ability to perceive an inscription as an 'ad'. For more
complex contents, such as the content that 'man' is true of an object just in case
it is a man, the required relations will be complex and multiple. They will
concern the state's connections with the subject's possession of the concept
man, with the ground of his ability to recognize the word 'man', and with his
general grasp of predication. It is a fascinating and difficult question what the
nature of the required connections is. But for present purposes, the mere
existence of such requirements is enough to show that the sufficiency claim on
which the objector is relying is false. The existence of these required
connections is also enough to show that no state which can exist without them
can be identified with an informational state in the present sense (as opposed to
realizing an informational state).[2]

Psychological reality of grammars for individual languages

It is this notion of explanation at level 1.5 which I propose to use in saying what it is for a grammar to be psychologically real. In the paper mentioned above, I argued that explanation at level 1.5 can be found in many areas of psychology; but in fact in the case of language I considered only semantic theories in any detail. Here I aim to extend the argument to grammars generally. It will be convenient to consider first grammars for particular languages. Further below, I will use the results of the discussion of that case in addressing the question of what it is for a universal grammar to be psychologically real.

Let us say, then, for a first approximation, that a *grammar* for a language L is a theory which for each sentence *s* of L entails

(i)   a theorem giving the D-structure of *s*
(ii) a theorem giving the S-structure of *s*
(iii) a theorem giving the phonetic form of *s*, and
(iv) a theorem giving the meaning of *s*.

The meaning may be given by a Fregean Thought, a structured proposition, or whatever your favoured theory of content suggests. 'D-structure' and 'S-structure' are used in the senses of current Chomskyan grammatical theory. Grammars as written in linguistics are not usually written out as formal theories with axioms and inference rules, but there is a natural correspondence between the grammars as written there and formalized theories. Actually more than one formal theory naturally corresponds to a grammar as written in linguistics. For now, we can concentrate on one particularly salient kind of correspondence. Where a standardly written grammar has, say, the primitive rule 'S→NP VP', the corresponding theory in question will have the axiom

$$\forall A \forall B((A \text{ is an NP \& } B \text{ is a VP}) \rightarrow A^\wedge B \text{ is an S});$$

and so forth. It will, for our purposes, be important that a formal theory be identified with its axioms and proper inference rules (if any), rather than with its set of theorems.

The proposal I wish to advance is, intuitively, that for a rule of a grammar to be psychologically real for a given subject is for it to specify the information drawn upon by the relevant mechanisms or algorithms in that subject. That is, the claim of psychological reality for a rule of grammar is a claim at level 1.5. So for VP→V NP to be psychologically real is for the subject's syntactic mechanisms or algorithms to draw on the information that a V followed by an NP is a VP. For the phonological rule 'Aspirate a segment which is [−VOICED, − CONTINUANT]' to be psychologically real is for the relevant mechanisms or algorithms to draw on the information that segments which are [−VOICED, − CONTINUANT] are aspirated; and so forth.

The general 'criterion for reality' for grammars of particular languages is as follows. Suppose we have rules $R_1 \ldots R_n$ of a grammar G, rules which state that

$p_1 \ldots p_n$ respectively. Then, to a first approximation, for $R_1 \ldots R_n$ in G to be psychologically real for a subject is for this to be true:

Take any statement q of grammar which is derivable in G from rules $R_1 \ldots R_n$: then not merely is it true that q, but the fact that q holds for the subject's language has a corresponding explanation at level 1.5 by some algorithm or mechanism in the subject, an algorithm or mechanism which draws upon the information that p_1, upon the information that $p_2 \ldots$ and upon the information that p_n.

I call this the *Informational Criterion* for psychological reality. So, for instance, consider a simple phrase structure grammar, and the linguistic fact that in *John hit the boy*, *the boy* has the phrase marker [$_{NP}$[$_{DET}$*the*][$_N$*boy*]]. If the simple phrase structure grammar is psychologically real according to the Informational Criterion, the phrase is assigned this structure because some mechanism or algorithm draws on these several pieces of information: that a determiner followed by a noun is a noun phrase; that *the* is a determiner; and that *boy* is a noun.

A grammar as written in linguistics does not fix a unique algorithm used to compute grammatical properties. It is one of the attractions of the Informational Criterion that this fact will not prevent a psychologically real grammar from being explanatory. In this respect, explanations which cite grammatical rules are like any other explanation at level 1.5 which proceeds by citing the information drawn upon.

As displayed, the Informational Criterion is only a first approximation for several reasons. One reason is that the Criterion is of course not meant to apply when q has the same content as one of the R_i (nothing explains itself). Another reason is that in the case of semantic theories in particular, we may wish to restrict the relevant derivations of q to be considered to those with a certain canonical form (such as canonical proofs of T-sentences in truth-theories). These and other necessary qualifications are interesting and important, but are matters of detail from the standpoint of our present topic.

I have taken the case of several rules $R_1 \ldots R_n$ first, because normally possession of the information stated in a rule is explanatory of particular phenomena only in the presence of several other informational states. But we can, derivatively by existential quantification upon the Informational Criterion, say what it is for a single rule of a grammar of a particular language to be psychologically real for a subject. Such a rule R_1 is psychologically real for the subject if there is some grammar G containing R_1 and some (possibly) other rules $R_2 \ldots R_n$ such that $R_1 \ldots R_n$ in G is psychologically real for that subject.

We can move a step beyond these first approximations by refining the Informational Criterion as follows. I said that there are other formal theories than those so far mentioned which equally correspond to a linguist's grammar containing the rule S→NP VP. These other theories contain the proper rule of inference

$$\frac{a \text{ is an NP} \qquad b \text{ is a VP}}{a^\wedge b \text{ is an S.}} \quad (T)$$

A grammar containing this rule can also be psychologically real. When it is, we can say that some mechanism or algorithm in the subject *uses the transition-type* expressed by the rule (T) above. The concept of using a certain transition-type is, like the concept of drawing on information, a causal notion. When some mechanism or algorithm uses the transition-type expressed by (T), it is in a state with this causal power: that of causing the organism, if it is in a suitable pair of states with informational contents of the forms *a is an NP* and *b is a VP*, to move into a state with an informational content of the form *a^b is an S*. Correlatively, the Informational Criterion can be expanded to take account of such rules of inference. Suppose we have a grammar G with axioms $A_1 \ldots A_n$ stating that $p_1 \ldots p_n$ respectively and proper rules of inference $T_1 \ldots T_j$. Then for these axioms and inference rules to be psychologically real for an individual is for this to be true:

> Take any statement q of grammar which is derivable in G from $A_1 \ldots A_n$ by means of $T_1 \ldots T_j$: then the fact that q holds for the subject's language has an explanation at level 1.5 by some mechanism or algorithm which draws upon the information that $p_1, \ldots$, and the information that p_n, and does so by using the transition-types expressed by $T_1 \ldots T_j$.

Is everything which is involved in the psychological reality of a grammar already captured at Marr's level 1? After all, the functions that can be specified at level 1 are not confined to those which merely give properties of whole sentences. They also include that function which maps any sentence of a language L onto a 4-tuple whose elements are respectively the sentence's D-structure, its S-structure, its phonetic form, and its meaning. Suppose we have a grammar G which assigns to each sentence of L a unique D-structure, S-structure, phonetic form and meaning. We can then speak of the function *corresponding to* the grammar G, *viz.* the function which maps any sentence of L to precisely the 4-tuple of properties assigned to it by G. Does the psychological reality of G for an individual amount to any more than the correctness of its corresponding function?

It is important to appreciate that this question goes beyond the challenge Quine (1972) raised for Chomskyan grammatical theory. Quine queried the significance of the distinction between grammars which count the same classes of sentences as well-formed. The correctness of the function corresponding to a grammar goes beyond this, since it requires that one rather than another analysis of any well-formed sentence be correct. The first two components of the 4-tuple to which the function maps a sentence make such commitments; and the other two components could be formulated so that they concern the subsentential level too. So the issue we are raising is whether a level of analysis which is already much finer-grained than Quine's does not already capture all the distinctions in grammatical theory which are psychologically real.

I maintain that the psychological reality of a grammar does amount to more than the correctness of its corresponding function. In moving from the theory to its corresponding function, we obliterate distinctions that correspond to psychologically real differences, differences at a level above that of Marr's level 2. Take the simple case of a language with only finitely many sentences, which nevertheless have apparent structure. One grammar G1 for it may be a standard grammar in which the syntactic properties of a particular sentence are derivable from general principles applying to any expressions of the appropriate types. The other grammar G2 may, in its syntactic part, simply consist of a finite list of axioms, each one giving outright the D-structure and S-structure of a single sentence. G1 and G2 may, consistently with this description, have the *same* corresponding function. But if G1 is psychologically real for an individual, then the mechanisms or algorithms in him will draw on (say) the information that a V followed by an NP is a VP. No such information will be drawn upon by the mechanisms assigning a syntactic analysis to a given sentence in an individual for whom G2 is the correct grammar. For this second individual, there is no one state of syntactic information whose content is drawn upon in the assignment of a syntactic analysis to two distinct sentences of his language. This need not, incidentally, make the syntactic analysis explanatorily idle for the second individual. The syntactic analysis may be used by the mechanisms which assign phonetic and semantic properties to the sentences.

The Informational Criterion aims to elucidate the relation holding between a grammar and a person when the grammar is psychologically real for the person's language. We may, with theoretical advances, revise our beliefs about which grammar stands in that relation to the language of a given individual; but that does not undermine the account of what it is for an arbitrary grammar to be psychologically real for an individual. Similarly, the criteria for psychological reality employed by the working practitioner in psycholinguistics may take into account all sorts of further constraints which emerge from empirical investigation. These constraints may relate to particular rules, to their form and content, and no doubt to much else about human cognition that we do not currently understand. So the present position is in complete accord with Chomsky when he writes: 'There are innumerable ways in which [one grammar may accord better with the evidence than another] . . . and we cannot offer strict "criteria" to determine such a choice anymore than we can anywhere in rational inquiry' (1986, p. 250). For ease of introduction, I also used in this first statement of the Informational Criterion some current Chomskyan grammatical concepts in the characterization of what a grammar, taken as a theory, is. These concepts too may be replaced on further investigation – in a stricter, less readable formulation of the present position, we would use variables and quantify over the concepts employed by an arbitrary grammatical theory. The Informational Criterion is, then, not in conflict with the more specific, and we hope constantly improving, criteria for psychological reality used by the practitioner of psycholinguistics. The Informational Criterion rather aims to make explicit what state of affairs all his evidence is evidence *for*.

It is also important to be scrupulous right from the start about the distinction between a rule, considered as a sentence-type or token with a given significance, and what it states. The Informational Criterion does *not* say that a grammar is psychologically real for a subject only if there are rules written out as sentences in a natural language or in Mentalese in the subject and causally explaining the linguistic phenomena in question. For a psychologically real grammar with proper axioms which say that $p_1 \ldots p_n$, the Informational Criterion requires such causal influence only of states with the contents $p_1 \ldots p_n$. These states may, for anything we have said so far, be nonlinguistic. We touch briefly on this crux below. It is of course open for a theorist to mount an argument that only a language of thought will be capable of delivering all we require of the informational states which must exist if a grammar is to be psychologically real according to the Informational Criterion. The present point is just that this argument has to be additional: it goes beyond what the Criterion says. For the case of proper rules of inference such as (T) in a psychologically real grammar, the Informational Criterion does not require them to be written out in a language of thought even if the states with the contents of its premises and conclusions are cast in a language of thought. Indeed it is an application of a familiar point to note that the Criterion requires them not to be so written out, on pain of Lewis Carroll-like regresses. Finally amongst these initial observations, I note that the Informational Criterion does not require a grammar to function directly as a parser for its rules to be psychologically real. All it requires is that the parser draw somehow or other on the information stated in the rules of the grammar.

There is a significant ambiguity in the Criterion. Is it for any given rules $R_1 \ldots R_n$ the *same* set of states with contents $p_1 \ldots p_n$ which for any q explain in the way specified in the Criterion? Or can it be a set of different states with those given contents $p_1 \ldots p_n$ for different qs as *explananda*? The range of cases we need to consider here is this: the case in which it is the same set of states for each q; the case in which the sets of states may be different but are causally related in such a way as to ensure that their contents are the same; and the case in which the sets of states are causally independent. Pre-theoretically we do indeed talk of the same information, about meaning or syntax, for instance, being drawn upon both in the production and the perception of language. But our question is whether the psychological reality of a grammar requires merely states with the same content, or requires causally related states, or requires identically the same states.

Consider two states, $I(pc)$ and $I(pd)$, which have the same informational content, and whose informational content is drawn upon respectively in the perception and the production of sentences. It is more problematic than may at first appear to suppose that these states are causally independent of one another. It is one and the same language, with its given set of meanings for sentences, in which it is the function of the states $I(pc)$ and $I(pd)$ to allow the subject to participate, now as perceiver, now as producer. Suppose evidence accumulates for the subject that the deliverances of the state $I(pc)$ involved in perception are incorrect and the informational state is altered. Does this eventually involve or result in a similar alteration or replacement of the informational state $I(pd)$ involved in production, or not? If it does, then either $I(pc)$ and $I(pd)$ are identical, or they are causally linked in some way which ensures that their informational contents do not continue to diverge. So in this case we do not have two causally independent states. When the states are causally independent, there is no corresponding alteration, and we have a strange phenomenon. The alleged informational state $I(pd)$ is not, even in the long run, sensitive to evidence that its content is incorrect. In this case I would question whether it is right to say that the state has the same informational content as the state $I(pc)$ which was appropriately sensitive.[3] We seem instead to have a case in which certain states happen to simulate part of the causal role of states with informational content which underlie linguistic ability, but do not have the full sensitivity required of such states.

It is worth noting that the Informational Criterion is neutral on the degree of modularity of the language faculty. Suppose there were virtually no informational encapsulation, so that almost any information available to the organism could, for example, affect the meaning a sentence is perceived to have. It could still be true of this organism that a particular grammar is psychologically real for it in the sense of the Informational Criterion. This is not just an epistemic possibility; it is a metaphysical possibility. It follows that if the Informational Criterion is correct, then modularity is not the real essence of psychological reality for grammars.

Though this paper is about language, it is worth noting that the Informational Criterion has analogues in other domains. We can take the case of music. There is considerable evidence that experienced listeners to Western music have internalized a 'richly structured system of knowledge concerning the use of tones and chords' (Krumhansl 1985, p. 377), an internalization which occurs whether or not the listener has had any training in music theory.[4] Part of this system concerns the hierarchy of tonal stabilities in Western tonal music. In this hierarchy, the tonic is the most stable, followed jointly by the third and fifth, followed in turn by the other diatonic tones; less stable still are the chromatic notes. What is it to have internalized this hierarchy? It is implausible that internalization requires a particular unique perceptual algorithm to operate: it seems that many different algorithms would be consistent with internalization of the hierarchy. Music is also a domain in which it is maximally untempting to say that some explicit statement of the hierarchy must be written out in a language of thought. I suggest that for the hierarchy to be internalized is for it to specify the information drawn upon by the algorithms or mechanisms operative in the perception of Western tonal music. The structural parallel with language also prompts questions about music which are the analogues of our most recent concerns about language. Is the same information about tonal music drawn upon in both perception and in vocal production? Is there a single informational state whose content is drawn upon?

Christopher Peacocke

Rival accounts

The Informational Criterion is in competition with at least two other kinds of claim. There are claims that say, for one reason or another, that it is a mistake to try to give a criterion for psychological reality in advance of empirical investigation; and there are claims that offer different criteria for psychological reality. A claim of the first sort might be defended by using an analogy given by Chomsky for a rather different purpose (1986, pp. 256–7). The analogy is that it would be unreasonable to demand of nineteenth-century chemists, as a condition of the legitimacy of their use of the notion of valence, that they give subatomic criteria for an element's having valence two, say. Why should we demand more, it may be said, of present-day grammarians?

Naturally, I dispute the analogy. I do agree that in both the case of grammars and the case of valence, the realization needs or needed empirical investigation. But in such examples, three things are in question: there is what is to be realized; there is the realization *relation*; and there is the realization itself. The nineteenth-century chemists knew the system of combinability and reactions whose realization was in question; equally we have some idea, though much less detailed, of what a grammar for a particular language is like. But the nineteenth-century chemists also knew what relation of realization was in question. That is why, when subatomic theory was developed, there was no question but that it gave a suitable set of realizations for the system of relations captured in the valence theory. The present chapter aims to discuss the nature of the realization *relation* for grammars. That we are not so clear about its nature is suggested by the fact that it is a nontrivial claim, given any detailed description of a person's psychological structures and processing mechanisms implicated in his linguistic abilities, which grammar is psychologically real for him. Indeed it is an issue at what level a realization would have to be located. So it is not true to describe the goal of the present chapter as trying (no doubt mistakenly on this objector's conception) to supply for grammar what subatomic theory did for the theory of valences. It is rather trying to elucidate a relation whose nature is relatively clear in the chemical case but not in the linguistic case. The need for clarification results from the additional levels of description and explanation present in the linguistic and other psychological cases.

One of the Informational Criterion's competitors as a test which is statable in advance of empirical investigation is the claim that a principle of a grammar is psychologically real if it corresponds to a 'determinate complex of neural mechanisms' (Chomsky, 1986, pp. 39–40).[5] This criterion I would argue to be necessary, as things actually are, but not sufficient. The problem is that determinate complexes of neural mechanisms are a dime a dozen, and this allows such complexes to be found even for principles of grammatical theories which are partially incorrect. This can be illustrated by reference to an example I developed in a previous paper (Peacocke, 1986, pp. 103–4). There I took a simple language which the subject subpersonally parses by means of an Augmented Transition Network. The parsing yields a labelled tree, which in turn activates a tree-structure of distinctive types of pointers. These pointers point to nodes which correspond to Fregean modes of presentation, or to whatever else you favor as entities to function as constituents of the structured meaning of the perceived sentence. In such a device, what subpersonally realizes the subject's possession of the information that a predicate, say, has a particular meaning is the associative link between a pointer of a given type and a node which can legitimately be labelled with a Fregean mode of presentation (or whatever). Such a subject's understanding of his or her sentences is structured, even if his or her language contains only finitely many sentences. The subject possesses and draws upon information about the sense of the predicate in coming to understand sentences containing it. But now consider what is intuitively an incorrect meaning theory for this subject's language, one which treats some of the sentences containing that predicate as unstructured; that is, it treats these sentences as idioms. Does an axiom of such a theory, for instance the axiom ' "Marie est jolie" means that Marie is pretty' correspond to a determinate complex of neural mechanisms in such an example? It certainly could. The determinate complex is one which has as components both what realizes the associative link between a pointer-type and a node corresponding to a mode of presentation of Marie, and that which realizes such a link between another type and a node labelled with the sense of 'is pretty'. Intuitively, this determinate complex ought not to count, because it does not correspond to the fundamental informationally significant boundaries: it is composed of two informationally significant complexes. This kind of example suggests that one who appeals to determinate neural complexes in elucidating the psychological reality of grammars will need to rely after all at some point on informational notions which he aimed to replace.

Suppose, for example, that the supporter of this rival, neural, criterion responded to the immediately preceding example by saying that in it, the 'determinate complex of neural mechanisms' is composed of more than one such determinate subcomplex, and that his criterion is meant to apply only to complexes not so composed. But this theorist is aiming to use a non-informational criterion of such non-compositionality. As a result, he then faces the converse problem. In a case of genuinely unstructured understanding of a finite set of sentences, there might be common neural components underlying the understanding of different sentences but which nevertheless do not realize the possession of informational states about the subsentential semantics of those sentences. Our rival theorist would then have trouble in trying to account for the understanding being *un*structured: for we can develop the example so that application of the revised criterion requiring non-compositionality of the 'determinate neural complexes' could bar this as an unstructured case.[6] It seems that if we neglect informational notions, a criterion of 'determinate neural complexes' will slice either too thickly or too finely.

The Informational Criterion is also in competition with an intermediate proposal. The intermediate proposal is that a grammar for a particular human language is psychologically real if it is a suitable instance of the universal form of grammars for all possible human languages – where it is an empirical matter to determine what this universal form is. This intermediate proposal plausibly states a truth, as things actually are, about the conditions under which a grammar is psychologically real; once again, we have something which as a criterion for the working psycholinguist is not to be disputed. But it does not answer the constitutive question of what it *is* for a grammar to be psychologically real, because it does not capture all the possible cases in which that notion applies. Suppose we were to encounter a child who, as a result of some genetic accident or other, had learned a language which is not of the form common to other human languages. This fact about the child should not make false the statement that one grammar for his language rather than another is the one which is psychologically real for him. The Informational Criterion allows, as it should, for such counterfactual possibilities.

Are grammars and PDP models incompatible?

Now let us return to rules and what they state. We need to apply a three-fold classification in this area:

(i) something may be explained by an explicit rule R written out in and used by a mechanism or algorithm;
(ii) something may be explained by a state with the same content as the rule R;
(iii) something may behave in the actual world and in nearby counterfactual situations in a way which *fits* rule R.

The characterization of case (ii) need not involve commitment to an ontology of contents: to describe the category, we just need a relation having-the-same-content-as ('fused' if need be) between the rule and the state. I will touch on case (iii) further below.

   We have in effect already noted that a processor whose operations realize a mechanism's use of a certain transition-type will be an example of case (ii) while not being a case of kind (i). But even when we set aside such transition-mediators, something can still fall under case (ii) without falling under case (i). The case most recently mentioned, of the ATN and pointer system, is an example of this. But it may be helpful to develop the point with another example, provided by the early McClelland and Rumelhart model (1981) of interactive context effects in the perception of written letters. This model has many features which would now be rejected; but it still allows us to make a conceptual point. In the model, there are feature-detectors for line segments; in fact there is a set of such detectors for each letter-position in a four-letter word. There are also detectors for whole letters and whole words. McClelland and Rumelhart's diagram shows some of the excitatory ($\longrightarrow$) and inhibitory ($\longrightarrow\bullet$) links between units corresponding to 'hypotheses' about the inscription presented to the system. In virtue of its various excitatory and inhibitory links, a

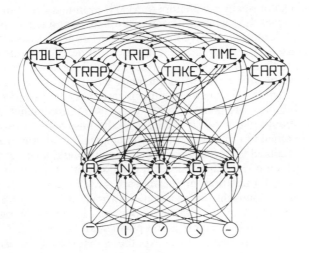

mechanism correctly described by this model is in states with certain informational contents. The presence of a given pattern including an excitatory link from the node labelled 'A' to the node labelled 'ABLE' may, for instance, realize the system's possession of the information that 'A' is the first letter of 'ABLE'. Other links realize the system's possession of information about the occurrence or non-occurrence of line segments in particular letters. These informational states can have the same content as those of a device with hypotheses explicitly written out in a language of thought. We can imagine someone who infers from the patterns in the output of such a Rumelhart–McClelland device that it must contain written-out hypotheses about the components of letters and words. We can imagine this person arguing that the device must be making inferences about the degree of confirmation of such hypotheses given the degrees of confirmation of other such hypotheses. In arguing this, the hypothetical person would be making a mistake. But there would be no mistake in saying that information about the components of words and letters is being drawn upon.[7] As far as I know, Chomsky has never cited evidence that bears differentially and immediately upon the hypothesis that there is any representational system akin to a language of thought. If the Informational Criterion is the correct criterion for psychological reality, he is not under any immediate obligation to do so. If that Criterion is correct, then the psychological reality of a rule in a grammar requires only explanation of kind (ii).

Some PDP theorists overdraw the contrast between what they call rule-based systems and their own theories (McClelland and Rumelhart, 1986, vol. 1, pp. 24–5, 43). The contrast would be vivid if those who have offered systems of rules as explanatory of human abilities were always committed to the rules' explanatory role being as in (i) above. But I have argued that a grammarian does not need to do so to retain explanatory power. If grammars are put forward as explanatory at level 1.5, it would need additional argument beyond simply fulfilment of the criterion of psychological reality itself to establish that they cannot be realized in a PDP model. Of course some PDP models will have corresponding to them formal theories which do not look anything like even the formalized versions of the grammars currently written in linguistics. Disputes about whether anything like linguists' current grammars are psychologically real are certainly genuine. My point is rather that general arguments in favour of PDP models should not be taken to foreclose the possibility of explanation of linguistic phenomena by an interesting psychologically real grammar.

If the Informational Criterion is correct, we can defend some of Chomsky's formulations which might otherwise seem overcommitted, given the evidential basis he cites. The formulations in question are those in which he implies that a grammar gives not only the information drawn upon, but also a particular computational mechanism for drawing upon it. He writes in passing of a subject's 'using the mode of computation postulated' (1986, p. 256). Later, he represents himself as entertaining 'the hypothesis that the mechanisms of mind permit something akin to deduction as part of their computational character' (p. 270). How is this consistent with my claim that Chomsky has not committed himself to a language of thought? The Informational Criterion allows us to answer this question as follows.

If a grammar is psychologically real by the test of the Informational Criterion, then there will indeed be the possibility for us, the theorists, of making certain deductions from the information drawn upon by the mechanism in question. We can thereby move to conclusions about the output of the mechanism. To exploit this possibility we have to ensure that in drawing conclusions from the informational content of states in the organism, we use only inferential principles which suitably correspond to the means of drawing on that content which are available to the organism itself. Given the derivability of certain propositions in a theory meeting this condition, we can make inferences to claims true of any organism which draws on the given information in the specified ways. We can do so regardless of the finer-grained algorithm it uses to draw upon the information and regardless of the medium in which the algorithm is realized. (In employing such a theory, we would be operating with a fragment of a theory which in an earlier work I called a *content-correlate* of a level 1.5 explanatory structure (1986, p. 109).) Chomsky's own illustrations of reasoning from the (parametrized) principles of grammar in *Knowledge of Language* to establish the D-structure, S-structure, and meaning of particular sentences of English are examples of such reasoning. But it does not follow from the soundness of such reasoning that in the computational mechanism itself there are sentence-analogues stating the parametrized principles, and processes operating on them of deduction in a language. We would need further evidence about the particular algorithms at Marr's level 2 and the nature of their realization before we could legitimately draw any such conclusion. If we acknowledge that the intermediate level 1.5 is essential to formulating the genuine sense in which a good grammar *is* psychologically real, the otherwise seemingly problematic passages in Chomsky are coherent and legitimate without any postulation of a language of thought.

Psychological reality for universal grammar

Now we can turn to the question of what it is for a universal grammar to be psychologically real. Chomsky is as clear as possible that theories of universal grammar are to be taken as explanatory theories. 'Universal grammar attempts to formulate the principles that enter into the operation of the language faculty . . . [it] provides a genuine explanation of observed phenomena (1988, pp. 61–2). I suggest that

> for a proposed principle of universal grammar to be psychologically real is for it to give a specifically linguistic content drawn upon, or a specifically linguistic transition-type used, in the individual's acquisition of a psychologically real grammar for a particular language.

We can call the displayed claim the *Criterion of Informationally-Determined Acquisition*. This Criterion relies in two ways on the discussion in the preceding sections of this chapter. It uses the notion of drawing upon information; and it is intended that this Criterion rely upon the Informational Criterion for psychological reality of a grammar for a particular language. As in that earlier case, the Criterion of Informationally-Determined Acquisition is intended to give a constitutive account of what it is for a universal grammar to be psychologically real. There are no restrictions in advance on the sources of evidence that may be relevant to whether a given proposed principle of universal grammar is psychologically real in the sense of the Criterion.

The requirement of the Criterion that the principle give a 'specifically linguistic' content is not redundant. It is essential to capturing what Chomsky has meant by his claim that there is a psychologically real universal grammar. For many years now, Hilary Putnam has argued that the states which lead to the internalization of grammatical rules are not specifically linguistic.[8] Presumably this does not commit him to saying that there are no informational states leading to the acquisition of grammatical rules. It commits him only to the view that any such states are not restricted to language in their subject-matter. I mention this not to endorse or deny Putnam's view, but to emphasize that it is a substantive claim that the informational states leading to the acquisition of particular rules have as their content principles which are reasonably describable as principles of universal grammar. Only the informational states with specifically linguistic contents, if such there be, are the psychologically real principles of universal grammar.

There are two ways in which the Criterion of Informationally-Determined Acquisition can be met. In each of these two ways, a state with a certain content constrains the acquisition of grammars of particular languages. But the type of content is different in the two cases. In the first case, the content is a first-order content which is not about grammatical rules or other informational states. This first case includes the hypothetical example of a child who is in an initial state with a content given by this alternation:

(D) [∀A∀B((A is an NP and B is a VP)→A^B is an S) v
       ∀A∀B((A is an NP and B is a VP)→B^A is an S)].

We can imagine that after exposure to a small sample of positive evidence from simple sentences, this hypothetical child moves into a state with the informational content of just one of the two clauses of this alternation. This is one way in which a parameter could be set in the present informational framework.

The other way in which the Criterion of Informationally-Determined Acquisition can be met is by the child being in a state with a content which is not first-order. If we say that a first-order content is one which is not about any informational state, then all the following states have first-order contents: possession of the information that 'white' means *white*; possession of a Marr–Nishihara 3D model-description for the shape stereotypically associated with the concept *bird*;[9] and possession of the information given in (D). We can then say that a *second-order* content is about informational states with first-order contents. We would expect informational states with second-order contents to be of particular interest to those studying developmental aspects of cognition. It should surely be a goal of developmental psychology to identify the second-order information, if any, on which the child draws in building new informational states. The content of the new informational state may, for instance, be drawn upon by perceptual mechanisms. The new informational state may be to the effect that *chairs* may take a certain range of shapes, or that *persons* may. Some of the states investigated by researchers in Artificial Intelligence also have contents with this second-order status. The theory of self-modifying production systems is one example. Such a system may be in a state with a content which specifies, given information about the recent environment, what new, more discriminating condition–action pair is to be added to those it already possesses. If we regard the condition–action pairs as informational states ('in such-and-such conditions, so-and-so action is to be performed'), this makes the content of the modifying state second order.[10]

The type of second-order content of an informational state which concerns us here is that whose members specify the information drawn upon when a subject is constructing new, psychologically real grammatical rules. When Chomsky says that the child knows in advance of experience that the rules of a language will be structure-dependent, he is attributing a state with a second-order content (1988, p. 45). Within the class of informational states with second-order contents, we can, as before, also distinguish those with an outright propositional content from those which mediate transitions, and so have their content given by a transition-type. This latter is the status of one of the informational states in Berwick and Weinberg's model of acquisition (1984, pp. 206ff). The device envisaged there is in a state which, given the information available when a parse of a presented sentence is blocked using the device's current rules, causes the construction of a new rule. The new rule is determined by the given information and by the condition that it has to have as its consequence in the triggering context either the switching of items in the first and second buffer cells, or the insertion of a lexical item or trace into the first buffer, and allows an existent rule to apply after its application. Since what is newly constructed is an informational state with a first-order content, the state just described is characterized in content-involving terms by a second-order transition-type.

If the Criterion of Informationally-Determined Acquisition is correct, then we must acknowledge that conceptually the fundamental notion here is person-relative: it is that of a universal grammar *for a given subject*. This is what leaves room for the conceptual possibility we touched on earlier, that of a genetically radically altered subject whose universal grammar is different from that of the rest of us.

If both of the Informational Criterion and the Criterion of Informationally-Determined Acquisition are correct, then we are committed to drawing two distinctions.

First, there will be a distinction between a principle being universally true of possible human languages (genetic alteration aside), and that principle being psychologically real in the initial state of a subject prior to language acquisition. Even universal truth is not sufficient for psychological reality. The truth might be universal because it is a consequence of other principles which are psychologically real in the initial state, taken together with other facts about the human language-processing device; or it may be a consequence of other facts alone. The Berwick–Weinberg explanation of the holding of the Subjacency principle in the modified Marcus parser itself suggests a way in which this possibility might obtain (1984, ch. 5). Subjacency restricts the ways in which transformations may move a phrase. In Berwick and Weinberg's theory, Subjacency is explained as a consequence of certain properties of the finite control table of the parser. There are limitations on the kind of conditions that can be formulated in that table, and these limitations ensure that Subjacency will not be violated. When Subjacency is explained entirely derivatively in this way, it need not be a principle specifying information drawn upon when the child learns new grammatical rules.

The example also bears on our classification of cases (i)–(iii) earlier. If the Berwick–Weinberg account is correct even as an account of a possible language-acquisition device, then we have a model of how it might be possible that human languages *fit* a certain constraint though no rule stating that constraint, nor any state with the same content as such a rule, enters the causal explanation of why this fit obtains.

Second, when a principle *is* psychologically real in the initial state, it does not follow that in the acquired state that principle (or some parametrization of it) is psychologically real. Again, it is on the present conception a substantive, empirical claim that it is so. Consider Chomsky's Projection Principle, which states that lexical structure is represented categorially at every syntactic level; and let us suppose that it is, for a given individual, psychologically real in the initial state in the sense of the Criterion of Informationally-Determined Acquisition. We would then expect the psychologically real grammar of that individual's acquired state to respect the Projection Principle. But this could well fall short of some (possibly parametrized) Projection Principle being psychologically real in the acquired state. Indeed it is redundant for the device to possess the information that in the acquired language, lexical structure is represented categorially at every syntactic level. All that is required is that the lexical structure *be* so represented, and not necessarily that there exist a state with the parametrized informational content that it is so. The same point could be made for Chomsky's Principle of Full Interpretation.

If these two distinctions are correct, there would then be a double *non sequitur* in arguing from the universal truth of certain principles about possible human languages to parametrizations of those principles being psychologically real in humans' acquired states. From such a premiss, one cannot without further assumptions move to the psychological reality of those principles; nor can one move from the psychological reality of those principles to the psychological reality of parametrizations of those principles. To establish the psychological reality of a proposed principle of universal grammar, we need evidence which bears more specifically on the content of the informational states operative in language acquisition – a requirement which should be all the more congenial to any grammarian whose standpoint, like Chomsky's, is that of individual psychology.

Notes

Versions of this chapter were presented in 1987 to the Interdisciplinary Seminar in Cognitive Science at the University of Maryland and to a conference on Philosophy and Computation at King's College London. I thank Christopher Cherniak, Martin Davies (once again), Norbert Hornstein, and Kim Sterelny for comments.

1   See also the comments on this paper by J. Higginbotham, S. Schiffer, and S. Soames, and my replies, *Mind and Language*, 1 (1986), 388–402.

2   When applied to the case of informational states with a content about the semantics of the subject's language, these considerations provide another way of arriving at M. Davies's conclusion that '*mere* causal structure does *not* justify articulation in a semantic theory' (1987, p. 448). See also his example of the nutrients (pp. 451–2). This prompts the general question of the relation between the conception of drawing on information defended above and Davies's conception of tacit knowledge. The issue merits extended discussion. Here I confine myself to recording this belief: there are plausible ways of elucidating the informational conception, and plausible ways of elaborating and extending Davies's notion to other domains, under which the two approaches can be shown to be equivalent.

3 Of course an immediate inclination to say something by uttering a particular sentence can persist in the presence of a newly acquired overruling belief that what one intends to say has to be said by uttering a different sentence. When we make this distinction, my point concerns beliefs, not the immediate inclinations.

4 The parallel between these internalized musical structures and grammars of natural language is noted in Krumhansl and Keil, 1982.

5 Chomsky is here considering a more limited proposal; the criticisms of the text above should not be taken as applying to any view he has defended.

6 The example could be set up as a neural analogue of Davies's nutrient example (1987, pp. 451–2).

7 For an expression of a similar attitude, see P. Smolensky's excellent paper (1986).
   Perhaps it is metaphysically necessary and *a priori* that an upper-case 'A' contains a horizontal bar. This does not undermine the possibility of a psychological explanation which says that a device draws on the information that it is so. As always, it is an *empirical* issue what information is drawn upon by a perceptual mechanism. It is equally necessary and *a priori* that, for instance, for the Rumelhart–McClelland style of capitals, both an A and an S contain an upper left-hand corner shaped thus: ⌐. But in the Rumelhart–McClelland model, no such information is drawn upon.

8 For a representative statement, see Putnam (1980), and subsequent exchanges in the same volume.

9 See Marr (1982) on 3D model-descriptions.

10 There is more on the significance of self-modifying production systems for the psychology of acquisition in D. Klahr, 1984.

References

Berwick, R. and Weinberg, A. 1984: *The Grammatical Basis of Linguistic Performance: Language Use and Acquisition*. Cambridge, Mass.: MIT Press.

Chomsky, Noam 1986: *Knowledge of Language: Its Nature, Origin, and Use*. New York: Praeger.

1987: Replies to Alexander George and Michael Brody. *Mind and Language*, 2 (2), 178–97.

1988: *Language and Problems of Knowledge: The Managua Lectures*. Cambridge, Mass.: MIT Press.

Davies, M. 1987: Tacit knowledge and semantic theory: can a five per cent difference matter? *Mind*, 441–62.

Klahr, D. 1984: Transition processes in quantitative development. In R. Sternberg (ed.), *Mechanisms of Cognitive Development*. New York: Freeman.

Krumhansl, Carol 1985: Perceiving tonal structure in music. *American Scientist*, 73, July–August, 371–8.

Krumhansl, Carol and Keil, F. 1982: Acquisition of the hierarchy of tonal functions in music. *Memory and Cognition*, 10, 243–51.

McClelland, J. and Rumelhart, D. 1981: An interactive activation model of context effects in letter perception: part 1. An account of basic findings. *Psychological Review*, 88, 375–407.

McClelland, J. and Rumelhart, D. (eds) 1986: *Parallel Distributed Processing*, vol. 1. Cambridge, Mass.: MIT Press.

Marr, David 1982: *Vision*. San Francisco, Calif.: Freeman.
Peacocke, Christopher 1986: Explanation in computational psychology: language, perception and level 1.5. *Mind and Language*, 1, 101–23.
Putnam, Hilary 1980: What is innate and why: comments on the debate. In M. Piatelli-Palmarini (ed.), *Language and Learning: The Debate Between Jean Piaget and Noam Chomsky*. London: Routledge.
Quine, W.V. 1972: Methodological reflections on current linguistic theory. In D. Davidson and G. Harman (eds), *Semantics of Natural Language*. Dordrecht: Reidel.
Smolensky, P. 1986: Neural and conceptual interpretation of PDP models. In J. McClelland, D. Rumelhart and the PDP Group (eds), *Parallel Distributed Processing*, vol. 2. Cambridge, Mass.: MIT Press.

Acknowledgement

The figure on p. 123 is from: J. McClelland and D. Rumelhart. An interactive activation model of context effects in letter perception: part 1. An account of basic findings. *Psychological Review*, 88, p. 380. Copyright 1981 by the American Psychological Association. Reprinted by permission of the publisher and author.

7

Tacit Knowledge and Subdoxastic States

Martin Davies

Introduction: two questions about tacit knowledge

Fundamental to Chomsky's work in both linguistics and philosophy are these two claims. First, ordinary speakers of natural languages tacitly know a grammar – a set of rules or principles – for their language. Second, the acquisition of this attained grammar by an infant speaker depends upon a massive innate endowment; namely, innate knowledge of universal grammar. This paper is about just the first of these claims; indeed, about just one aspect of that first claim.

Over the years, various terms have been used to elaborate the tacit knowledge claim. What the speaker tacitly knows is equated with the speaker's *competence* (Chomsky, 1965, p. 8; cf. Chomsky, 1980a, p. 39); and, in a further attempt to fend off what are argued to be irrelevant objections from terminologically fussy philosophers, the expression '*cognize*' is sometimes deployed. Thus, ordinary speakers know – in the familiar everyday sense – and also cognize facts about, for example, what various complete sentences mean. In addition, they cognize, even if they do not know in the ordinary sense, the facts from which those first facts follow (Chomsky, 1976, pp. 164–5; Chomsky, 1980a, pp. 69–70).

We might think of the first facts as stated by some of the theorems of a systematic theory. Then, the basic idea would be this. Ordinary speakers know and cognize the facts stated by these theorems. They also cognize – even if they do not know in the ordinary sense – the facts stated by the axioms from which the theorems are derived.

If we think of the issue in these terms, then it is easy to raise the first of two major questions that confront any friend of tacit knowledge. There will always be distinct sets of axioms from which we can derive the same theorems about, say, the meanings of whole sentences: extensionally equivalent sets of axioms. So, how can it make empirical sense to suppose that an ordinary speaker stands in any psychological relation to one set of axioms, rather than to an alternative extensionally equivalent set?

This is essentially *Quine's challenge* (Quine, 1972) to Chomsky's notion of tacit knowledge. A similar challenge about alternative axiomatisations arises when we consider theorems assigning more complex properties to sentences. I would aim to meet challenges of this form by construing tacit knowledge as a certain kind of causal-explanatory structure underlying – explanatorily antecedent to – the pieces of knowledge that a speaker has about whole sentences. (See Evans, 1981; Davies, 1986; 1987; forthcoming.) The basic idea is that tacit knowledge of a particular systematic theory is constituted by a causal-explanatory structure in the speaker which mirrors the derivational structure in the theory. Where there is, in the theory, a common factor – for example, a common axiom – used in the derivations of several theorems, there should be, in the speaker, a causal common factor implicated in the explanations of the several corresponding pieces of knowledge about whole sentences.

Of course, not just any kind of causal common factor constitutes a state of tacit knowledge. Intuitively, we require that, if a state is to have semantic, as well as causal, properties, then its causal consequences should be sensitive to its semantic content. There are various ways of building this requirement of content sensitivity into an analytical account of tacit knowledge. For example, elsewhere (Davies, 1987), I have made use of the condition that, in order to constitute a state of tacit knowledge, a causal common factor should also be a locus of systematic revision – keeping the speaker's various beliefs about whole sentences in step with each other. The account of psychological reality for a grammar which Peacocke offers in his contribution to the present volume makes crucial use of the idea that the causal common factor should be a state of information that is drawn upon (see also Peacocke, 1986). This account is very much in the same spirit as the constitutive account of tacit knowledge that I would favour. (Indeed, under plausible assumptions about the notion of the information content of a state, the two accounts turn out to be equivalent.)

However exactly the details go, an account of tacit knowledge along these lines enables the theorist to meet Quine's challenge. For there can certainly be empirical evidence in favour of attributing to a speaker one underlying causal structure rather than another; and, as Chomsky often stresses (e.g. 1986, p. 250; 1987, p. 184), there is no *a priori* limit to the kinds of evidence that might be relevant.

No doubt, this construal of tacit knowledge will fail to apply to many cases in which 'we can know more than we can tell' (Polanyi, 1967, p. 4). For example, if the proposal is to seem plausible at all, then the notion of tacit knowledge under scrutiny must be distinguished from what Lycan (1986) calls 'tacit belief'. Tacit beliefs are, roughly, the as yet undrawn consequences of what might be called, in contrast, 'explicit beliefs'. The construal in terms of a structure of causal-explanatory states is intended to be faithful to the fact that tacit knowledge, in Chomsky's sense, lies causally upstream, rather than downstream, of ordinary beliefs.

Dennett (1983) draws a distinction that is analogous to Lycan's; but he makes the contrast in terms of explicit versus implicit representation of information. He then constrasts both explicit and implicit representation with 'merely tacit knowhow' which is 'built into the system in some fashion that does not require it to be represented . . . in the system' (1983, p. 218), and goes on to categorize tacit knowledge in Chomsky's sense as a species of explicit representation, rather than merely tacit knowhow (pp. 218–19). Whether or not Dennett is right about Chomsky's commitments, the construal of tacit knowledge in terms of causal-explanatory structure is intended to group some cases of tacit knowhow together with certain cases of explicit representation of information; for cases of both kinds can exhibit the requisite pattern of causal common factors.

Supposing, then, that attributions of tacit knowledge are respectably empirical, and have a legitimate and specifiable role in psychological theory, we can turn to the second major question that confronts the friend of tacit knowledge.

This second question concerns the best way of describing the psychological relation between a person – a thinker, a speaker – and the axioms or rules of the person's internalised grammar. States of tacit knowledge are states that have semantic contents and figure in causal explanations. But are they like or unlike the more familiar psychological states which have those two properties; namely, propositional attitude states – beliefs, desires, intentions, hopes, wishes, and the rest?

It is this second question that is addressed in what follows. I begin with Chomsky's own answer.

1 Chomsky's answer; and three intuitive differences

Chomsky's answer to our question about tacit knowledge and propositional attitudes is not a simple one. There are several threads to be discerned.

One line of thought (Chomsky, 1976, p. 163) leads to the idea that one 'might refer to the postulated cognitive structure as a "system of beliefs" ':

Since the language has no objective existence apart from its mental representation, we need not distinguish between 'system of beliefs' and 'knowledge', in this case. (1972, p. 169)

Another line culminates in the clear claim (1980a, p. 93) that 'we do not "believe" rules of grammar or other cognitive systems'. Chomsky attributes this claim to Fisher (1974), who stresses the distinction between knowledge *of* a rule and knowledge *about* a rule. And Chomsky (1986, p. 266) himself insists on the distinction between a speaker's knowing a rule R and knowing 'that R holds, obtains, is a rule of his language'.

Each of these threads deserves careful attention. But one dominant and recurrent component of Chomsky's position is the doctrine that what is cognized or tacitly known is something from which ordinary beliefs follow. The picture is of a complex cognitive structure, some parts of which happen to surface in consciousness as ordinary beliefs. Chomsky often suggests (e.g. 1986, p. 269) that the difference in point of accessibility to consciousness is all there is to the distinction between ordinary states of knowledge and belief, on the one hand, and states of tacit knowledge or mere cognizing, on the other. And he argues that the distinction between those states which are conscious and those which are not is of little significance. Thus, for example (1976, pp. 163, 165):

> It may be expected that conscious beliefs will form a scattered and probably uninteresting subpart of the full cognitive structure. . . . For psychology, the important notion will be 'cognize', not 'know'.

Thus, according to this dominant thread in the Chomskyan fabric, first, states of merely tacit knowledge differ from ordinary attitude states just in being inaccessible to consciousness, and second, the difference is of no theoretical importance.

Stich (1980) disputes both these claims. First, he argues that states of tacit knowledge are not only inaccessible to consciousness; they are also not inferentially integrated with beliefs. Then, second, he urges that this distinction between our beliefs and other psychological states does have theoretical significance. The latter states, which 'play a role in the proximate causal history of beliefs, though they are not beliefs themselves' Stich labels *subdoxastic* states (Stich, 1978, p. 499).

Chomsky himself finds Stich's suggestion problematic (Chomsky, 1980b, p. 57). For states of tacit knowledge certainly do combine with each other to yield consequences, which might be described as inferential consequences; and some of these consequences are ordinary beliefs. That is a crucial part of Chomsky's picture of a complex structure of states of cognizing. So we cannot say straightforwardly that states of tacit knowledge are inferentially isolated from beliefs.

But, despite this problem, it is very plausible that there is something right in the thought that inferential integration is a feature of beliefs that is not shared by states of mere cognizing. Certainly, this is a second intuitive difference which demands examination.

In a recent presentation, Chomsky says this (1986, p. 269):

> It has been argued that it is wrong, or even 'outrageous', to say that a person knows the rules of grammar, even in the sense of tacit or implicit knowledge. As a general statement, this cannot be correct. We do not hesitate to say that John knows, whereas Pierre does not know, that verbs cannot be separated from their objects by adverbs or that stops are aspirated except after /s/ – *assuming, of course, that we know the meaning of the terms used in these ascriptions of knowledge.* (my italics)

This passage alludes to one of several putative sources of philosphical hesitation about attributions of tacit knowledge; namely, that we have reservations about attributing knowledge in cases where we do not ourselves grasp the terms used in the attribution.

Chomsky rejects this putative source of hesitation (1986, pp. 266–7), on the grounds that it has nothing especially to do with knowledge about language – let alone any special connection with tacit knowledge. For anyone making a claim about anything needs to know the meanings of the terms employed; otherwise he does not know what he is claiming.

Chomsky is surely right that this putative source of philosophical hesitation is spurious. But there is a rather similar point that is, in contrast, highly relevant. The question to focus on is not whether the person making the attribution needs to understand the terms used in the attribution; that is, needs to grasp the concepts involved in the contents of the states that are being attributed. Rather, the salient question is whether the person to whom the state is being attributed needs to grasp those concepts.

It is a familiar point (particularly stressed by neo-Fregeans, but not only by them) that no one can have a belief with a particular content – or entertain a thought with a particular content – without grasping the constituent concepts of that content; and Lycan extends this familiar point to cover his notion of tacit belief (1986, p. 78). But, if ordinary speakers are to be credited with tacit knowledge of linguistic rules, principles, or generalisations, then there can be no corresponding requirement relating to the contents of tacit knowledge states. For most ordinary speakers have no grasp at all upon the concepts of linguistic theory.

The requirement of conceptualisation by the thinking, speaking, person marks a third intuitive difference between ordinary propositional attitude states and states of merely tacit knowledge.

We need to explore in detail these three apparent differences between ordinary propositional attitude states and other cognitive psychological states, such as states of tacit knowledge of linguistic rules. The three intuitive differences add up to a *prima facie* case for a principled distinction between attitude states – particularly belief states – and subdoxastic states. And the aim of the current exploration is to discover whether a considered case for such a distinction can be made out. Such an exploration must presume upon some *prima facie* examples of subdoxastic states; but it must not begin by begging questions about how much falls within or without the domain of the commonsense scheme of attitude attribution and rational explanation.

The constitutive accounts of tacit knowledge that I mentioned in my Introduction (Davies, 1986; 1987; Evans, 1981; Peacocke, 1986, this volume) are all developed using the case of systematic semantic theories (in fact, theories of truth conditions) as a central example. This has the expository advantage that the derivational structure of such theories is very familiar. But the choice of example may give the impression that these accounts simply take for granted something that ought to be left as a matter for further argument; namely, that states of an ordinary speaker which contain information about the semantic properties of words and constructions belong on the subdoxastic side of any principled divide.

This would, however, be a misleading impression. For all these accounts have the feature that their requirements for tacit knowledge could be met by an ordinary piece of conscious knowledge or a belief, provided that it served as a causal common factor in the right way. What these accounts really provide are conditions for *at least* tacit knowledge. Under certain empirical conditions, they license attribution, to an ordinary, unreflective speaker, of tacit knowledge of semantic rules. But it does not follow from such attributions that, if there is a principled distinction between attitude states and subdoxastic states, then knowledge of semantic rules or generalisations falls on the side of the subdoxastic – that is, of the *merely* tacit. These accounts of tacit knowledge are not guilty of begging delicate questions. Nor do they render redundant the present exploration of the differences between beliefs and subdoxastic states.

2　Accessibility to consciousness

It is an appealing idea that, if there is a principled distinction between the domain of attitudes and the domain of mere information processing, then accessibility to consciousness should mark the boundary. But the waters surrounding the notion of accessibility to consciousness can be muddied easily enough. It may be that, once the notion of consciousness is better understood, it can be employed as a basis for the distinction. But what I shall argue in this section is that the pre-theoretical and undifferentiated notion of consciousness cannot bear the required weight. To that extent, Chomsky's scepticism about the importance of any distinction between conscious knowledge and tacit knowledge will be vindicated.

There are at least three reasons why it is unwise to rest the weight of a principled distinction upon the contrast between accessibility and inaccessibility to consciousness.

The first reason is simply that we do make use of – or at least psychoanalysts make use of – the notion of an unconscious belief. But these states are intuitively quite unlike the cognitive psychological states which we would take as *prima facie* examples of subdoxasticity. So, inaccessibility to consciousness had better not be a sufficient condition for a state to be subdoxastic.

It is certainly legitimate to respond to this example by noting that it is possible to protect the claim that states in a certain class are beliefs, even in the face of the fact that the states cannot be brought to conscious awareness. For the claim can be protected in the context of a psychological theory which postulates a mechanism blocking access to beliefs in the particular class (cf. Stich, 1978, p. 505). But that protective strategy must itself be constrained, on pain of a spurious defence of the claim that the *prima facie* examples of subdoxastic states are themselves beliefs. And it is difficult to escape the conviction that the required constraint will be furnished by some independent foundation for the distinction between beliefs and subdoxastic states.

The second reason is that there are features of the inferential web of beliefs of which we are typically unconscious. Fodor gives as an example (1983, p. 85) our unconscious 'acquiescence in the rule of *modus ponens*'.

The idea behind the example is this. A thinker can systematically perform inferences which are, in fact, instances of *modus ponens*, can offer the premises of each such inference as reasons for accepting the conclusion, and can perform the inferences as a result of a single inferential disposition, without being able to frame the rule in its generality. The inferential rule is, in this sense, something of which the ordinary unreflective thinker is not conscious; in this respect, it is like a linguistic rule. But, for all that, our commitment to the rule of *modus ponens* is intuitively quite unlike the *prima facie* examples of subdoxastic states.

To this second reason for doubting that the notion of accessibility to consciousness can bear the weight of a principled distinction, there is a very natural response. For within information-processing psychology there is a distinction drawn between content bearing, or representational, states on the one hand, and processes, or computations, over such states on the other. And this distinction is in many ways analogous to the distinction in logic between a formula and a rule of inference.

The natural response to the example of *modus ponens* would then be this. The distinction between beliefs and subdoxastic states is, in the first instance, a distinction between belief states – over which inferences are performed – and other representational states – over which other computations are performed. Inaccessibility to consciousness is, in the first instance, to be taken as a mark of the subdoxastic for representational states. *Modus ponens* is a rule of inference, so our acquiescence in it can be thought of as the presence of a computational processor – what Peacocke (this volume, p. 122) calls a transition mediator – rather than of a representational state. Consequently, the inaccessibility to consciousness of that inferential rule does not threaten its credentials as a feature of the web of beliefs.

The distinction on which this response depends is important. But the response does not constitute an effective defence of the claim that the notion of accessibility to consciousness can bear some theoretical weight. For, if inaccessibility to consciousness is only a mark of the subdoxastic in the case of representational states, then it follows that the inaccessibility to consciousness of linguistic rules is itself not directly relevant. For there is no reason to suppose that, in an information-processing model, an internalised linguistic rule must appear as a representational state rather than as a computational processor. The response thus undermines the significance of accessibility to consciousness still further.

Someone might seek to defend the theoretical significance of accessibility to consciousness, by pointing out that *if* accessibility to consciousness at least provides a clear distinction between beliefs and other representational states, then it also furnishes a derivative distinction between genuinely mental rules of inference and the computational processes of mere information processing.

For, given the initial distinction, it will be easy enough to classify a rule or process according as its domain is a class of beliefs, on the one hand, or a class containing subdoxastic representational states, on the other.

But, of course, the significance of this conditional claim depends upon whether accessibility to consciousness does provide for a clear and principled distinction among representational states. And the third reason why it is unwise to rest the weight of a principled distinction upon the undifferentiated notion of accessibility to consciousness concerns representational states directly.

This third reason is that there is a sense in which accessibility to consciousness is intuitively compatible with the classification of a state as subdoxastic; for there is more to conscious experience than propositional attitudes. Suppose, for example, that low-level representational states – *prima facie* examples of subdoxastic states – surfaced in conscious awareness, as distinctive itches or tickles, perhaps. That empirical difference from our actual situation would obviously not be enough to make those states into beliefs.

The idea behind this third challenge to the significance of accessibility to consciousness as such is that there might be an aspect of conscious experience whose cognitive psychological underpinning is the occurrence of a representational state, but which does not make a difference to what the experiencer would believe, taking the experience at face value. We can suppose that a certain aspect of the phenomenological character of an experience might depend systematically upon the semantic content of the underlying representational state. That goes no way towards making that aspect of the experience into a candidate for belief. (On sensational properties of experience, see Peacocke, 1983; Sterelny, 1987.)

Someone might reply to this challenge as follows. We might allow that, in the imagined cases, the representational state is accessible to consciousness. But, even so, the content of the state is not accessible to consciousness; and it is this that matters for a principled distinction between beliefs and subdoxastic states.

But this reply does not amount to a case for the load-bearing potential of the undifferentiated notion of accessibility to consciousness. What it amounts to is a suggestion for refining the undifferentiated notion into a notion of accessibility of content to consciousness. As we have just seen, this accessibility of content would need to be sharply distinguished from the mere systematic reflection of content in aspects of experience. It would also need to be distinguished from the kind of case where a person has beliefs about the contents of his or her own representational states. The fact that a theorist of vision, for example, may have beliefs about the representational states implicated in the information processing that is going on within her or him does not render those states any less subdoxastic.

The intuitive basis for the distinction between accessibility of content and the possibility of beliefs about the content of a state might be this. If the content of a state is accessible to consciousness, in the required sense, then to be in that state is *ipso facto* to have the content available for report. (Cf. Fodor, 1983, p. 56: ' . . . if we take the criterion of accessibility to be the availability for explicit report of the information that these representations encode'.) This condition is not met merely by the possibility of a belief about the content.

But the idea of actual verbal report seems inessential to this intuitive idea. What is more fundamental than availability for report is availability for thought. Consequently, what the suggestion for refining the undifferentiated notion of accessibility to consciousness ultimately provides is this. A representational state is subdoxastic if being in that state is not *ipso facto* to have the content of the state available as a content of thought, that is, of propositional attitudes. Arguably, this captures something of our idea of a belief as a conscious state. But – however compelling it may be – it cannot serve at this point as the basis for a principled distinction between subdoxastic states and attitude states. The third challenge to the significance of accessibility to consciousness as such remains unanswered.

For these three reasons, we should not presume upon the undifferentiated notion of accessibility to consciousness to ground a principled distinction between beliefs and subdoxastic states. If we set aside accessibility to consciousness, then two intuitive differences between beliefs and *prima facie* examples of subdoxastic states remain. One concerns inferential integration; the other concerns conceptualisation.

In section 1, I remarked that the suggestion that subdoxastic states are not inferentially integrated with beliefs is plausible, despite the problem that Chomsky notes. It is time to explore the difference between inferential integration and isolation in more detail.

3   Inferential isolation and the modularity of mind

The idea of the inferential integration of beliefs can be illustrated this way. A belief state is 'at the service of many distinct projects' (Evans, 1981, p. 337). The belief that these things before me are items of furry, purple footwear can combine with another belief – say, the belief that the only items of furry, purple footwear around here are Granny's slippers – and lead inferentially to a new belief – that these are Granny's slippers. That latter belief might, in its turn, combine with a desire – to pour champagne into Granny's slippers – to provide a reason for action. The original belief could also combine with quite different beliefs – say, that furry, purple things are liable to keep the cat amused – to yield different inferential consequences, and to contribute towards reasons for quite different actions.

In the familiar image, beliefs form a web, with inferential and evidential links. And part of what is involved in that image is that a new belief – that Granny has just entered wearing her slippers – may lead inferentially to the adjustment of previously held beliefs – those furry, purple things are not, after all, items of footwear.

Beliefs combine to yield inferential consequences; and beliefs are adjusted to avoid inconsistency. These are two aspects of the inferential integration of beliefs. But there is something else involved in the idea of a belief being at the service of many projects, but which is not immediately revealed by the image of a web of beliefs. For one belief can combine with many different desires to provide reasons for many different actions. This third property of beliefs is a striking feature of the domain of attitudes; and it is this feature that most directly blocks the reduction of statements about beliefs to statements about dispositions to behaviour (cf. Evans, 1981, p. 337).

Cognitive psychological states which are *prima facie* examples of subdoxastic states seem to lack these three properties of beliefs. For example, states of tacit knowledge of syntactic rules or principles, or the states implicated in early visual processing, do not directly combine with desires to provide reasons for action. It is only the distant consequences of those states that contribute to such reasons. These states thus seem to lack the third property of beliefs.

There is no intellectual discomfort over holding a belief which is incompatible with what is merely tacitly known (cf. Stich, 1980, p. 39). So states of tacit knowledge seem to lack the second property of beliefs; or rather, they lack that property relative to ordinary beliefs.

As Chomsky points out (1980b, p. 57), states of tacit knowledge do yield ordinary beliefs as (inferential) consequences. So we cannot say straightforwardly that subdoxastic states lack the first property of beliefs. But there is still a clear sense in which tacit knowledge states are inferentially isolated from the web of beliefs. This isolation has two aspects.

The first aspect is that *prima facie* examples of subdoxastic states do not combine inferentially with beliefs to yield further beliefs, even when their semantic content is closely related to the contents of the beliefs. For example, our identification of spoken words involves, at an early state, the registration of information about acoustic properties such as voice onset times. So a person who hears a word beginning with an unvoiced consonant will subdoxastically register the information that the voice onset time is, say, 25 milliseconds. Such a person might, for whatever inscrutable reason, have the belief that if the next syllable he hears has a voice onset time of 25 milliseconds, then it is time to prepare his lecture. But merely hearing the unvoiced consonant as such will not be enough to provide the person with a reason for starting his preparation.

The idea behind this example is that, if a thinker has two beliefs – one of the form *that if P then Q* and the other of the form *that P* – then the thinker will often draw the conclusion *that Q*. But if the two premises for *modus ponens* are divided – one the content of a belief and the other the content of a subdoxastic state – then the thinker typically does not come to believe the conclusion.

The second aspect of the inferential isolation of subdoxastic states is this. Ordinary beliefs usually – or at least often – do not combine with subdoxastic states to yield further subdoxastic states. Rather, the procedures that operate over states which are *prima facie* examples of subdoxastic states are to a considerable extent unaffected by what the person in question believes.

It is surely in virtue of this family of differences between the web of beliefs and *prima facie* examples of subdoxastic states that plausibility attaches to

Stich's suggestion about inferential integration versus isolation, despite the problem that Chomsky notices.

Stich offers a picture of our mental and cognitive lives in which (1980, p. 39):

> Our mental apparatus is divided into a number of distinct components. Among these is a store of beliefs that are well integrated inferentially and generally accessible to consciousness.

Similarly: 'beliefs form a consciously accessible, inferentially integrated cognitive subsystem', while 'Subdoxastic states occur in a variety of separate, special purpose cognitive subsystems' (1978, pp. 507–8). This is a picture of the mind as modular; and, as such, it is welcomed by Chomsky (1980b, p. 57).

However, there are several different notions of modularity employed in psychological theory, and the proposal for a principled distinction between beliefs and subdoxastic states to be considered next concerns the specific idea of modularity elaborated by Fodor (1983). Before stating the proposal, I give some brief reminders about Fodor's thesis.

The major bifurcation within Fodor's schematic architecture of the mind is between the central cognitive system and input systems. An input system is an information-processing system which ultimately delivers information to the central cognitive system whose primary business, in turn, is the fixation of belief. In this model, the central cognitive system seems to correspond to the domain of propositional attitudes. Indeed, Fodor credits the central system with typical properties of the domain of the attitudes; in particular, with the property of evidential holism or isotropy (1983, p. 105).

Fodor's major thesis is that input systems are modules. This amounts, *inter alia*, to the claim that input systems are informationally encapsulated and domain specific, have their operation fast and mandatory and their interlevels relatively inaccessible to the central system, and exhibit a characteristic pace and sequencing of development and characteristic patterns of breakdown. For Fodor's modularity is defined in terms of these and other marks (1983, pp. 47–101).

The official definition of informational encapsulation is this. A system within an organism is informationally encapsulated if the information available to the system is considerably less than the totality of information represented in the organism (Fodor, 1983, p. 69). Informational encapsulation is 'what I take to be perhaps the most important aspect of modularity' (p. 37), and 'the essence of . . . modularity' (p. 71).

Given Stich's picture and Fodor's thesis, it is tempting to propose that the scientific psychological category of modularity is what underlies the philo-sophical category of the subdoxastic. Several factors combine to reinforce this temptation. First, the apparent correspondence, in Fodor's model, between the central cognitive system and the domain of propositional attitudes suggestively leaves input systems corresponding to the domain (or domains) of subdoxastic states. Second, our *prima facie* examples of subdoxastic states are, indeed, states of Fodorian input system: 'the perceptual systems *plus language*' (Fodor, 1983, p. 44). Third, the property of informational encapsulation – which is the essence of modularity – is very reminiscent of one aspect of the inferential isolation of subdoxastic states. Fourth, Fodor himself explicitly suggests (p. 86) that it is the states of modules that exhibit the pair of features that Stich takes as characteristic of subdoxastic states.

This tempting proposal – that modularity is what underlies the subdoxastic domain – could be elaborated as a bolder or as a more cautious claim. In its boldest form, the proposal would be that modularity is the real essence of the subdoxastic. This would involve three substantial requirements upon modularity. First, the notion of modularity and its accompanying taxonomy should pull their weight in psychological theory. Second, the theory of modularity should furnish an explanation as to why the intuitive characteristics of subdoxastic states go together, to the extent that they do. Third, the taxonomy should permit a principled classification of cases whose status is left indeterminate by the intuitive marks of the subdoxastic. The real essence proposal would also involve a controversial commitment to the possibility of fools' subdoxasticity: a commitment to refuse to classify a state as subdoxastic if it is not a state of a module, even if it exhibits all the philosophical characteristics of the subdoxastic domain.

A more cautious claim can retain much of the interest and appeal of the boldest form of the proposal, without the controversial commitment. According to the form of the proposal to be considered in the next section, modularity pulls its weight in psychological theory, explains – as things are – the co-occurrence of the intuitive marks of subdoxastic states, and assists in the classification of difficult borderline cases.

4 Assessing the proposal: explanation and classification

This is not the place for a general evaluation of the explanatory credentials of Fodor's modularity thesis. I shall assess the proposal that modularity is what underlies the subdoxastic domain in terms of just two criteria. First, what are the prospects for a satisfying explanation, in terms of modularity, of the intuitive marks of subdoxastic states? Second, what are the prospects for using the notion of modularity to plot a boundary through border territory? In fact, I shall restrict the application of the first criterion to the explanation of the inferential isolation of subdoxastic states.

What kind of account of the inferential isolation of subdoxastic states can be extracted from Fodor's modularity thesis, if we take subdoxastic states to be states of input systems? Recall that this isolation has two aspects. One aspect is that beliefs do not combine with subdoxastic states to yield further subdoxastic states. This aspect, let us agree, is to be explained in terms of the informational encapsulation of modules. After all, the similarity between informational encapsulation and this aspect of inferential isolation was one of the factors that originally made the proposal tempting.

The other aspect of inferential isolation is that subdoxastic states do not combine with beliefs to yield further beliefs. This is not explained simply by informational encapsulation. The mark of modularity which is most closely related to this aspect of inferential isolation is, rather, the relative inaccessibility to the central system of the interlevels of a module (Fodor, 1983, pp. 55–60).

Our example of this aspect of the inferential isolation of subdoxastic states from beliefs concerned the early stages of identification of spoken words. A person may hear a word beginning with an unvoiced consonant, and register the information that the voice onset time is, say, 25 milliseconds; and may also believe that if the next syllable has a voice onset time of 25 milliseconds, then it is time to prepare his lecture. But merely hearing the unvoiced consonant will not be enough for the person to draw the consequence that it is time to prepare his lecture.

Is this aspect of inferential isolation well explained by the relative inaccessibility to the central system of a module's interlevels? There are reasons to think not. (The reasons are closely related to arguments towards the end of section 2, concerning the third challenge to the significance of accessibility to consciousness.)

The interlevel that is relevant to our example is one at which acoustic analysis is complete, but phonetic analysis is not. This interlevel is inaccessible to the central system in quite a strong sense. For there are pairs of sounds which differ acoustically just as much as a pair comprising a voiced and an unvoiced consonant, yet which are heard as indistinguishable. Differences in voice onset time, as such, are not phenomenologically accessible. But this does not account for the inferential isolation of states which register such differences.

One reason (cf. Fodor, 1983, pp. 59–60) is that even phenomenologically inaccessible differences can affect reaction times, and can be the basis for a conditioned response. So we need a further explanation as to why such differences do not bring about systematic changes in the web of beliefs.

A further reason for doubting that this notion of inaccessibility can do the required explanatory work here is that there can be interlevels of input systems which are phenomenologically accessible – in the sense that information at this level is reflected in the character of experience – but which still do not interact inferentially with the web of beliefs.

An alternative explanation seems to be required for this aspect of the inferential isolation of subdoxastic states from beliefs. There is a kind of ancillary explanation that is certainly available to the friend of modularity. It begins from the idea of an information-processing system with its own proprietary code or format. According to this idea, the code of the central processing system is the language of thought. (See Fodor, 1987, pp. 135–54, for a recent statement.) A domain specific input system will have its own proprietary code; or rather, it will have a series of codes in use at its various interlevels. Given this, a representational state at an intermediate level of analysis does not combine inferentially with beliefs, simply because it is not in the code or format over which the inferential processors of the central system operate.

However, although this kind of explanation is available, it is not clear that there is any very close connection between the idea of a proprietary code, and the several marks of Fodorian modularity. So, the availability of this ancillary explanation does not count towards a positive assessment of the proposal.

Let us turn to the second criterion for assessing the proposal. In the case of our knowledge of language, it is plausible that our knowledge of syntactic rules or principles will be classified on the side of the subdoxastic. And it is plausible that our knowledge of pragmatic principles belongs in the domain of propositional attitudes. The difficult borderline case is provided by semantic rules. (For some inconclusive arguments about the status of semantic rules, see Evans, 1981; Campbell, 1982.)

What are the prospects for using the notion of modularity to plot a boundary through this border territory? Clearly this is an empirical issue, heavily dependent upon the results of work in experimental psycholinguistics. But the prospects are not enhanced by the fact that modularity is defined in terms of a large class of characteristic features. For different characteristic features of modules suggest different ways of locating the interface between input systems and the central system.

We can see this kind of conflict at work in the case of vision. On the one hand, consider informational encapsulation. Sometimes it seems *prima facie* that a psychological process does draw upon the wealth of background information available in the central cognitive system. In these circumstances we can still defend the claim that there is a modular process operating. We argue that the locus of interaction is not the process within the module, but rather the output of the module. That is to say, we draw the boundary of the modular input system earlier in the total process. The less processing that is assigned to the input system itself, the easier it is to maintain that the input system is informationally encapsulated.

It is not surprising, then, that in his discussion of informational encapsulation Fodor says this about the visual input system (1983, p. 74):

> There is a great deal of evidence for context effects upon certain aspects of visual object recognition. But such evidence counts for nothing in the present discussion unless there is independent reason to believe that these aspects of object recognition are part of visual input analysis. Perhaps the input system for vision specifies the stimulus only in terms of 'primal sketches' . . .

Since the primal sketch is a very early state of visual processing in Marr's model, this suggestion for drawing the boundary of the input system will leave a great deal of what might reasonably be called visual processing to be performed by the central system.

On the other hand, while the interlevels of a module are supposed to be relatively inaccessible to the central system, the outputs of a module are supposed to be 'phenomenologically salient' (p. 87).

> It seems to me that we want a notion of perceptual process that makes the deliverances of perception available as the premises of conscious decisions and inferences . . .

This sits very happily with the picture of the input systems as presenting to the thinking subject candidates for belief. Given this picture, we are to see context effects as just one aspect of the intelligent process of assessing a candidate for belief in the light of background knowledge, before going forward in judgment.

It is in this spirit that Fodor says (p. 94):

> various candidates [for the output of the visual processor] . . . must . . . be rejected on the grounds of phenomenological inaccessibility. I am thinking of such representations as Marr's 'primal', '2.5D', and '3D' sketch. . . . Such representations . . . would seem to be too shallow. If we accept them as defining visual processor outputs, we shall have to say that even object recognition is not, strictly speaking, a phenomenon of visual perception, since, at these levels of representations, only certain geometric properties are specified. But, surely, from the point of view of phenomenological accessibility, perception is above all the recognition of objects and events.

Here, in the interests of defending the phenomenological salience of a module's outputs, we find that very much more processing is being assigned to the input system.

These conflicting pressures upon the boundaries of modularity are generated by the competing claims of informational encapsulation of processing and phenomenological salience of output. The net result is that Marr's 2.5D sketch and 3D sketch are left as borderline cases. This does nothing to enhance the prospects for using the taxonomy generated by the modularity thesis to settle the classification of difficult borderline cases as belonging to the domain of the subdoxastic or the domain of the attitudes.

In the case of language processing, there is a similar indeterminacy created by the different characteristic features of modularity. On the one hand, the condition of informational encapsulation suggests that a great deal of what might reasonably be called language processing is not, in fact, performed by the language system at all. The detection of irony is evidently not an encapsulated process (Fodor, 1983, p. 88); that is hardly controversial. But Fodor suggests, more radically, that the task of the language system might just be to classify a presented token as being of a certain syntactic type, and perhaps to assign it a logical form (p. 89).

In short, if you are looking for an interesting property of utterances that might be computed by rigidly encapsulated systems – indeed, a property that might even be computed by largely bottom-to-top processors – then the type-identity of the utterance, together, perhaps, with its logical form would seem to be a natural candidate.

This assigns comparatively little work to the language system.

On the other hand, the output of the language input system is supposed to be phenomenologically salient. And as Fodor points out, when you hear someone's utterance in a language that you understand, you quite literally cannot help hearing what the speaker said: 'and it is what is *said* that one can't help hearing, not just what is *uttered*' (p. 55). If the output of an input system is supposed to be phenomenologically salient, then it is not merely syntax and logical form that is computed by the language system, but also content or message.

In the case of visual processing, the conflicting pressures on the boundaries of modularity leave indeterminate the status of every component of visual object recognition after the primal sketch. Similarly, in the case of language processing, those same conflicting pressures leave indeterminate the status of every component of utterance comprehension after the assignment of logical form. In particular, the status of systematic semantic processing is left indeterminate by all this.

As things stand, then, the proposal that modularity is what underlies the subdoxastic does not measure up to the second criterion of assessment: the prospects are not good for using modularity to plot a boundary through philosophical border territory. It might seem that the way forward is to relieve the conflict of pressures by allowing the boundaries of modularity to be dictated by considerations of informational encapsulation, setting aside the requirement of phenomenological salience (cf. Fodor, 1983, p. 136, n. 31). But, there would be a price to be paid for that relief. For the requirement of phenomenological salience of the output of modules – of the interface between input systems and the central system – is very closely related to the ideas that the business of the central system is the fixation of belief, and that the central system corresponds to the domain of propositional attitudes. To give up that requirement, and with it those ideas, is to give up a good deal of what made the proposal tempting in the first place. Indeed, it seems inevitable that, if the boundaries of modularity are dictated solely in terms of informational encapsulation, then very much more will be assigned to the central system than belongs in the domain of the propositional attitudes.

We cannot give a positive assessment to the proposal that Fodorian modularity is what underlies the subdoxastic domain. The failure of the proposal does not, of course, count against the significance of the difference that inspired it – the difference between inferential integration and isolation. But I shall not pursue the question whether it is possible to rest the weight of a principled distinction between beliefs and subdoxastic states directly upon that difference. Instead, I shall sketch a proposal drawing upon the third intuitive difference between beliefs and *prima facie* examples of subdoxastic states; namely, that beliefs have their semantic contents conceptualised by the person whose beliefs they are, while this is not so for the contents of subdoxastic states.

5 Conceptualisation and the Generality Constraint

Strawson (1959, p. 99) says that 'the idea of a predicate is correlative with that of a *range* of distinguishable individuals of which the predicate can be significantly, though not necessarily truly, affirmed'. This truth about predicates has its echo in the domain of thought. For a thinker to have the concept of *being F*, the thinker must know what it is for an object to be *F* – that is, what it is for an arbitrary object to be *F*. And, taken together with the idea that having a belief – or in general, entertaining a thought – involves deploying concepts, this echo of the truth about predication has an important consequence.

To believe that *a is F* – or even to entertain the thought that *a is F* – a thinker must have the concept of *being F*. If a thinker has that concept, then the thinker knows what it is for an arbitrary object to be *F*. So, if a thinker believes that *a is F* and is able to think about the object *b*, then the thinker is able to entertain the thought that *b is F*. In particular, if a thinker can be credited with the thought that *a is F* and the thought that *b is G*, then the thinker has the conceptual resources for also entertaining the thought that *a is G* and the thought that *b is F*. Thus, one consequence of the conceptualisation of the contents of propositional attitude states is that the domain of thought contents available to a thinker exhibits a kind of closure property. Thoughts are essentially structured; they have constituents that can be recombined in further thoughts.

Evans (1982, pp. 100–5; cf. 1981, p. 338) connects the idea of conceptualisation with what he calls the *Generality Constraint* upon the contents of attitude states (1982, p. 104):

> If a subject can be credited with the thought that *a is F*, then he must have the conceptual resources for entertaining the thought that *a is G*, for every property of being *G* of which he has a conception.
> We thus see the thought that *a is F* as lying at the intersection of two series of thoughts: on the one hand, the series of thoughts that *a is F*, that *b is F*, that *c is F* . . . and, on the other hand, the series of thoughts that *a is F*, that *a is G*, that *a is H*.

The proposal to be considered now is that the Generality Constraint – or rather, the extension of the constraint to cover more than just subject-predicate thoughts – can provide for a principled distinction between the domain of propositional attitudes and the subdoxastic domain. Indeed, Evans himself makes the suggestion that the Generality Constraint marks a distinction between the contents of propositional attitude states and the contents of states involved in 'the information-processing that takes place in our brains' (1982, p. 104, n. 22; cf. Davies, 1986, pp. 143–6).

The basic point here is that the following possibility is open. A thinker may be able to entertain the thought that *a is F*, and may be in a subdoxastic state which has the content that *b is G*. Yet it may be that the thinker cannot entertain the thought that *a is G* – because he lacks the concept of *being G*; and it may be that there is no actual or possible subdoxastic state whose content is that *a is G*, because the system which processes the information that *b is G* simply does not contain information about the object *a*. This basic point illustrates the way in which the total domain of attitude states and subdoxastic states taken together can easily infringe the Generality Constraint.

It does not follow from the basic point that, if we simply focus on a single information-processing system, then we shall find actual infringements of the Generality Constraint. On the contrary, it is possible to imagine systems whose states are *prima facie* examples of subdoxastic states, but for which the following is true. If there are actual or potential states of the system which have the contents that *a is F* and that *b is G*, then there are further actual or potential states of the system which have the contents that *a is G* and that *b is F*. So, given this possibility, does the Generality Constraint fail, after all, to capture any important difference between attitude states and subdoxastic states?

The answer to this question depends upon the way in which the Generality Constraint is supposed to ground the distinction between the two domains. Suppose that it is claimed simply that the contents of attitude states exhibit the closure property, while the contents of subdoxastic states fail to exhibit that property. Then the kind of example just imagined would show that claim to be false. But the claim on behalf of the Generality Constraint does not have to be quite so simple.

In the imagined system, the contents of the states do, in fact, meet the closure condition. But still, the assignment of contents to those states does not depend upon that fact. The states' having those contents is one thing; their meeting the closure condition is another. In contrast, the assignment of a semantic content to an attitude state is immediately answerable to the Generality Constraint. To believe that *a is F* is *ipso facto* to exercise mastery of the concept of *being F*; and that piece of concept mastery can be exercised by the thinker in thoughts about other objects. Meeting the closure condition is an essential, rather than a contingent, feature of the contents of attitude states.

What emerges from the proposal is that a principled distinction between attitude states and subdoxastic states is to be grounded in a distinction between two notions of content (cf. Woodfield, 1986). The Generality Constraint is partly constitutive of the notion of conceptualised content, which is applicable to attitude states. But it is only accidentally related to the notion of content applicable to subdoxastic states.

This emergent idea keeps us close to the third of the original intuitive differences between beliefs and *prima facie* examples of subdoxastic states. The Generality Constraint can simply be viewed as making explicit part of what is involved in mastery of concepts or conceptualisation.

However, since those intuitive differences were introduced in section 1, we have acknowledged (in section 2) a distinction between, on the one hand, representational states and, on the other hand, computational processes or procedures that are performed over those states. One consequence of this refinement is that the present proposal for a principled distinction between belief states and subdoxastic states will not immediately confirm our intuitive judgment that tacit knowledge of syntactic rules falls on the side of subdoxasticity.

The distinction between conceptualised and unconceptualised semantic content yields, in the first instance, a distinction amongst representational states. In this respect, it is similar to the putative distinction in terms of accessibility to consciousness. Indeed, the idea of a distinction based upon the accessibility or inaccessibility of the content of a representational state might be regarded as an attempt in the direction of the present proposal.

But knowledge of syntactic rules might be realised by the presence of a computational processor, rather than by the presence of a collection of representational states over which processes are performed. So the fact that the semantic contents of certain states of (at least) tacit knowledge are not conceptualised by the person in question is not decisive in assigning that knowledge to one side of a binary divide rather than the other.

The classification of some pieces of (at least) tacit knowledge is a derivative matter. It answers to the prior classification of the representational states which serve as inputs and outputs of the processors which realise the tacit knowledge. In the case of tacit knowledge of linguistic rules and principles, the prior classification turns directly upon the question whether the descriptions of sentences by which the sentences are brought within the scope of the linguistic generalisations are descriptions that are conceptualised by the person in question. No doubt, this derivative classification will still result in many pieces of linguistic knowledge being assigned to the subdoxastic side of the divide.

The corresponding question about the rule of *modus ponens*, for example, is whether the descriptions of the world which serve as premises for inferences falling under the rule are themselves conceptualised by the person in question. Since the answer to this question is affirmative, a thinker's knowledge of that rule will be classified derivatively as belonging in the domain of attitude states rather than in the domain of subdoxastic states. It is in the former domain, rather than the latter, that the rule operates.

Speculative conclusion

The proposal that we have just considered is relatively philosophical and *a prioristic* in character. The earlier – ultimately unsatisfactory – proposal that modularity is what underlies the subdoxastic domain is, in contrast, based on empirical psychological theory. It is natural to speculate as to whether there is an alternative to Fodor's schematic architecture of the mind, which would cohere more or less happily with the philosophical distinction in terms of conceptualisation.

Fodor's characterisation of 'the perceptual systems *plus language*' (1983, p. 44) as input systems has struck many readers as odd; for knowledge of language is used in production as well as in comprehension. There are only relatively few aspects of language processing – computing phonetic descriptions from acoustic descriptions, for example – which are specific to linguistic input processes. So, if the choice is between knowledge of language being embodied in a module – that is, an input system – and being part of the central system, then – it seems – we should say that knowledge of language belongs in the central system (cf. Chomsky, 1986, p.14, n.10).

Now, this sits ill with the picture of the central system as engaged in the business of belief fixation, with candidates for belief being furnished by input systems. But perhaps we have to forsake that picture anyway. For that picture coheres with some of the marks of modularity, but not with others. In particular, it coheres with the phenomenological salience of the outputs of modules; but considerations of informational encapsulation – the essence of modularity – conspire to set the boundaries of modularity far nearer the sensory surfaces.

Suppose that we accept the apparent consequences of those more essential considerations. Then there is a new picture which can be sketched using materials that we have been obliged to use in earlier stages of this exploration. The new picture retains a division between informationally encapsulated modules and a central system; but the central system is engaged in more business than the fixation of belief.

Some of the representational states of the central system are attitude states, and some are not. As a philosopher would put it: some of the states of the central system have their contents conceptualised by the person in question, and some do not. A scientific psychological account will (partially) reconstruct this distinction as a difference between representational states in the language of thought, and states in other codes or formats. (As we noticed in section 4, this difference is not essentially connected with Fodorian modularity.)

In this new picture, there are many different kinds of processes operating in the central system. There are ordinary inferential processes – such as *modus ponens* – which have sentences in the language of thought as both their inputs and their outputs. These processes link the representational states whose code is the language of thought into an integrated inferential web. There are other processes which effect transitions between formulae in one code and formulae in some other code. Some of these have as their input code, or as their output code, the language of thought. Some processes may be bidirectional.

There could be a processor which effects or constrains transitions back and forth between, say, representational states in a proprietary code for describing the syntactic properties of English sentences and representational states in the language of thought. The presence of such a processor could realise tacit knowledge of a particular set of linguistic rules, principles, or generalisations.

In this way, according to the new picture, tacit knowledge of linguistic rules could be realised in the central system. The rules would not have to be explicitly represented in any representational state of the system. Still less would knowledge of the rules be realised in a state of the same kind as an attitude state. Nor would linguistic rules be indistinguishable, on this account, from ordinary rules of inference; for they are differentiated by their characteristic input and output domains.

Such promise makes the picture initially attractive. Needless to say, its philosophical and empirical credentials will not be corroborated here.

Note

Versions of this material were given as talks at the University of Sussex, the CNRS seminar 'Philosophie de l'esprit' in Paris, the University of New England, the Australian National University, and the University of Bradford. I am particularly grateful to Christopher Peacocke and Kim Sterelny for their comments.

References

Campbell, J. 1982: Knowledge and understanding. *Philosophical Quarterly*, 32, 17–34.
Chomsky, N. 1965: *Aspects of Theory of Syntax*. MIT Press.
    1972: *Language and Mind*. Harcourt Brace Jovanovich.
    1976: *Reflections on Language*. Fontana/Collins.
    1980a: *Rules and Representations*. Blackwell.
    1980b: Rules and representations (with Open Peer Commentary and Author's Response). *Behavioral and Brain Sciences*, 3, 1–61.
    1986: *Knowledge of Language: Its Nature, Origin, and Use*. Praeger.
    1987: Replies to Alexander George and Michael Brody. *Mind and Language*, 2, 178–97.
Davies, M. 1986: Tacit knowledge, and the structure of thought and language. In C. Travis (ed.), *Meaning and Interpretation*. Blackwell, 127–58.
    1987: Tacit knowledge and semantic theory: Can a five per cent difference matter? *Mind*, 96, 441–62.
    forthcoming: *Tacit Knowledge*. Blackwell.
Dennett, D.C. 1983: Styles of mental representation. *Proceedings of the Aristotelian Society*, 83, 213–26.
Evans G. 1981: Semantic theory and tacit knowledge. In S. Holtzman and C. Leich (eds), *Wittgenstein: To Follow a Rule*. Routledge and Kegan Paul; reprinted in *Collected Papers*. Oxford University Press, 1985, 322–42.
    1982: *The Varieties of Reference*. Oxford University Press.
Fisher, J. 1974: Knowledge of rules. *Review of Metaphysics*, 28, 237–60.
Fodor, J. 1983: *The Modularity of Mind*. MIT Press.
    1987: *Psychosemantics*. MIT Press.
Lycan, W.G. 1986: Tacit belief. In R. Bogdan (ed.), *Belief: Form, Content and Function*. Oxford University Press, 61–82.

Peacocke, C. 1983: *Sense and Content*. Oxford University Press.

   1986: Explanation in computational psychology: Language, perception and level 1.5. *Mind and Language*, 1, 101–23.

Polanyi, M. 1967: *The Tacit Dimension*. Routledge and Kegan Paul.

Quine, W.V.O. 1972: Methodological reflections on current linguistic theory. In D. Davidson and G. Harman (eds.), *Semantics of Natural Language*. Reidel, 442–54.

Sterelny, K. 1987: Review of Peacocke, *Sense and Content*. *Philosophical Review*, 96, 581–5.

Stich, S. 1978: Beliefs and subdoxastic states. *Philosophy of Science*, 45, 499–518.

   1980: What every speaker cognizes. *Behavioral and Brain Sciences*, 3, 39–40.

Strawson, P.F. 1959: *Individuals*. Methuen.

Woodfield, A. 1986: Two categories of content. *Mind and Language*, 1, 319–54.

8

Knowledge of Reference

James Higginbotham

In this chapter I will develop some themes in a conception of semantic theory as the theory of our tacit knowledge of reference and truth. In saying that the theory of reference and truth is a *semantic* theory, I endorse the thesis that understanding a natural language involves a conception of an expression's having a reference or a truth value, over and above conditions on its form and use. In saying that the theory is a theory of tacit knowledge, I am assuming that there will be explanations of a speaker's behaviour that involve such knowledge. These explanations will impute complex tacit attitudes to the speaker, of which his or her behaviour is a rational outcome. Explanations of this kind are associated above all with Chomsky's work over the years. Finally, in saying that the speaker's complex attitudes involve reference and truth, I am sticking with the idea that just these notions are the fundamental ones for semantics. In particular, the notions of reference and truth are not taken to be derived from a more primitive association of meaning with fact, as in the view of Russell in his logical atomism phase, or as more recently revived by Barwise and others. Each of these three assumptions is open to question and discussion; here, however, I will be more interested in using them to sort out some dominant considerations in the philosophy of language than in their explicit defense, or their specific consequences for contemporary linguistic theory.

1 Partial knowledge

Semantics as the theory of knowledge of reference and truth might be contrasted with semantics as comprising just the theory of reference (in the sense of Quine, thus including truth as a special case; I will continue to use this terminology below). Let us call semantics in the latter sense a *pure* theory of reference. A pure theory of reference might be a theory for a person at a time, for an idiolect, or for a society. It will be articulated in a language (say mine, or the reader's), and it gives at least part of what Dummett (1986) calls a 'schematic representation' of the abilities of the person or persons that it is about. However, it is not assumed that they know it, tacitly or otherwise.

Suppose that the objects of the pure theory of reference are idiolects. Then as one goes through the process that we call 'learning a language,' or as one changes linguistically otherwise, idiolects succeed one another, according to principles we would hope to discover. The language of a person who is in the midst of learning, or who, although a mature speaker, is in part ignorant or idiosyncratic (as we all in fact are), could be taken as in some respects only partly interpreted, and in other respects fully interpreted, but deviating from the languages of other persons.

Fully interpreted but deviant speech is widely attested. Bowerman (1982) documents the use by children of resultative complements that overgeneralize the patterns available to adults. A resultative that is acceptable for both adult and child is (1), where the direct object of the verb is the subject of the adjectival complement:

(1) I wiped the table clean

The meaning of (1) is that I wiped the table, with the result that it became clean. It is easy to imagine circumstances in which I could wipe the table, with the result that it became dirty. However, the resultative complement is not licensed:

(2) I wiped the table dirty

The sentence (2), although interpretable as a resultative, is somehow 'strange.' Children learning English, according to Bowerman's research, are not so inhibited as we are. She collected examples like (3):

(3) I pulled it unstapled

meaning that I pulled on the document, with the result that it became unstapled. The child has a language in which (3) is permitted, with resultative meaning. That language, although it is not ours, is fully intepreted with respect to (3) and similar sentences.

Partially interpreted idiolects will arise when the learner cannot distinguish the different roles that two expressions play in the adult language. Pinker (1988) reports work showing that American children at a certain stage of development typically know that selling involves transfer of property, without knowing that it involves monetary compensation. Thus, they do not discriminate between A's selling something to B and A's giving something to B. Ignorance of this kind persists even into adulthood. To cite an example due to Hilary Putnam, if I have heard about elms and beeches (both are some kind of deciduous tree), but know about them only that they are different kinds of tree, my lexical entries for 'elm' and 'beech' do not discriminate their reference. Assuming, as we are, that semantics is the theory of *reference*, we might expect that my language, or the language of the child who cannot discriminate all of the features of the word 'sell', is only partly interpreted. In both cases there is not enough information available to the speaker to fix the reference of terms.

As we ordinarily think of reference, however, this seems wrong. Our words do refer to certain things, or at least are held to refer to them, even when our knowledge of reference is incomplete. Moreover, it appears that incomplete understanding does not even prevent attribution of the same *concept* to the ignorant as to the learned.[1] As we learn, we seem to come to know, or to know more fully, what things we refer to and through what concepts we refer to them. If this appearance is correct, then we should not view the language of the learner or of the ignorant as only partly interpreted, but rather as having an interpretation that is only partially grasped.

The language that is incompletely understood therefore seems to be fully interpreted. Cases of partial interpretation surely exist; for instance, if a person mistakenly thought about some nonsense word that it actually had a meaning (only it was not known what) utterances using that word could be viewed as only partially interpreted. These cases are conspicuously unlike normal partial knowledge of meaning.

Such considerations seem to argue that it is the language of a community that should be regarded as the locus for the pure theory of reference; for how can it be meaningful to say that one 'partially grasps' one's *own* idiolect? I might, of course, have only partial knowledge or a mistaken opinion about how I myself use a word or construction, but there is nothing about my own use of 'elm' and 'beech' that I do not know. Taking another horn of the dilemma, one might retain the thesis that idiolects rather than community languages are fundamental, but use the phenomenon of the partial understanding of reference as grounds for doubting that the theory of reference is the right form for semantic theory in the first place.

Actually, neither of these counsels is warranted by the facts. We can still assume in linguistic theory that the object of study is the idiolect, or language of a person at a time. References to community languages, or to dialects of languages, if they are needed at all, are in any case references to derivative things, characterized loosely in terms of the overlapping idiolects of members of groups whose individuals are in frequent serious communication with each other. However, that the notion of a community language is at best a derivative one does not show that the facts constitutive of a person's idiolect are indifferent to the natures of the persons with whom she interacts. What we need to recognize is that one can indeed have partial knowledge of one's own idiolect, and we need to adjust semantic theory accordingly.[2] I believe that the right way to do this is to abandon the idea that the pure theory of reference for an idiolect is the appropriate form for a theory of understanding. The theory of understanding should be taken as the theory of what is known about reference.

Some difference between a pure theory of reference and a theory that brings in the speaker's cognitive relation to reference may be illustrated by considering the following objection to the pure theory, due to Gilbert Harman. In Harman (1974) (responding to an argument of Lewis (1972), which I consider more fully below) it is observed that just as we can know how to translate between two languages without knowing the meaning of the expressions in either, so we can have knowledge of truth conditions without having knowledge of meaning. Indeed, Harman writes (p. 6):

> there is a sense in which we can know the truth conditions of an English sentence without knowing the first thing about the meaning of the English sentence.

The first-time reader of Carroll's *Through the Looking Glass* knows, at a certain point in the story, (4):

(4) 'All mimsy were the borogoves' is true if and only if all mimsy were the borogoves

However, Harman continues:

> in knowing this we would not know the first thing about the meaning of the sentence, 'All mimsy were the borogoves.'

To his example, Harman envisages the response that the metalanguage in which truth conditions are to be stated is to be taken as completely understood. He goes on to argue that the distinction between translational and truth-theoretic semantics then threatens to lapse. I want to dwell on the example, resuming only afterwards the question of truth theory versus translation.

All of us, in learning our first languages as children, and in our linguistic maturity, are frequently in the condition of the first-time reader of *Through the Looking Glass*: we are able to use words, sentences, and phrases in the absence of a complete understanding of them. When we do use them, we are held to the same standards of truth and falsehood as those who do have complete understanding of them. In part, we can be held to those standards only because we do not wholly lack understanding. In the case of (4), for example, we know, even before it is explained to us what 'mimsy' and 'borogove' mean (actually, the latter is not fully explained), that the sentence is a stylistic inversion of a sentence that attributes a certain property, expressed by the adjective 'mimsy', to certain things. So we know that the sentence has, except for the unknown words in it, the interpretation of 'The plates were all broken.' The word 'mimsy' could not mean *tree*, and 'borogove' could not mean *run*. The context in which the words have appeared, together with the already known meaning of the other lexical items, the structure of the sentence, and the principles for interpretation of sentences with that structure, have told us that much.

Because we have a lot of information about 'All mimsy were the borogoves', it can be misleading to declare that 'we do not know the first thing' about it. In fact, we know almost everything about it – all that is lacking is the interpretation of 'mimsy' and 'borogoves'. If so, we should not respond to Harman's point by restricting the metalanguage to terms that are fully understood, but rather by allowing a theory that includes partial understanding.

More precisely, the semantic theorist should assume that the first-time reader of *Through the Looking Glass* knows (4), knows 'mimsy' is an adjective (and therefore true of x if and only if x is mimsy), but does not know what that word means, or even have a conjecture about it. In the special case where one's theory is about oneself, one will employ a metalanguage that is only partially understood. There is no paradox in that.

I have argued that statements of truth conditions such as (4) give only partial knowledge of meaning. Other 'disquotational' statements about the extensions of words have the same property. If I merely know that 'red' is an ordinary adjective, I know that it is true of the red things (whatever they are) and nothing else. Adding parameters for possible worlds or counterfactual situations changes nothing. A number of researchers understand the expression 'the truth conditions of S' in terms of the spectrum of truth values that S takes on in various possible worlds, or the *intension* of S, in a technical sense of that term. But I can know what the truth conditions of S are, so understood, without knowing the meaning of S. Likewise, even before 'mimsy' is explained to me, I know that it is true of a possible object x in a possible world w if and only if x is mimsy-in-w.[3]

Allowing for partial knowledge of meaning, is the truth conditional view of semantics distinct from the translational? If it is assumed from the beginning that semantics must involve truth conditions, or at any rate some idiom for directly stating meaning, then the question answers itself, for it becomes sufficient to observe that a theory of translation is formally distinct from a semantic theory, so understood.[4] I will continue, however, to press Harman's original question, whether a truth-conditional theory imparts information that a translational theory does not.

Knowledge of translation can be partial too. In fact, there are two cases of partial translation to be distinguished. In one case, we partially interpret a language by translating it into a language that we partly understand; in the other, we are able to construct only a partial translation into a language that we fully understand. Harman's thesis was that there is no difference between what you know about a language when you can give a theory of reference for it in a language that you fully understand and what you know about it when you can translate it into a language that you fully understand. I have not questioned this thesis, but on the contrary have extended it, by taking in the case where one has only a partial theory of reference. I will assume further that what one learns from such a theory is matched by what one learns from a partial translation, in either of the two senses just given. If this is correct, then David Lewis's argument (1972) against semantics in the style of translation into semantic representations (which Lewis illustrated with respect to certain proposals by Jerrold Katz), seems to lose its force. Lewis pointed out that we could know how to translate between English and the representational vocabulary without knowing the meaning of the English. And, he remarked, 'Translation into Latin might serve as well.' So we could, and so it might. It does not follow that by giving a translation we do not explain meaning. We do explain it, and give ourselves an understanding of it, to the extent that we understand the language into which English is translated.

The situation changes, however, if we think of the statements of a theory of meaning as representing what the speaker tacitly knows. In this case, we imagine the learner as *framing hypotheses* about reference, finding them *confirmed* in subsequent speech, *rejecting* them in the face of counterevidence, and so forth. Then we might as well imagine the learner as trying to translate the language into the medium through which thinking about reference or meaning occurs (the language of thought, in the sense defended in Fodor (1975)). It is not credible that Latin, or any other natural language, is the medium used by the learner in thinking about meaning (although it may well be that certain features of some natural languages are characteristic of that medium). So translation into Latin would definitely not do. However, there is no appreciable difference, or only a pedantic difference, between characterizing a person's state of understanding with respect to a language L by saying what that person, whether learner or mature speaker, knows about the meanings of expressions in L, and characterizing it by stating a possibly partial translation of L into the medium in which that person represents meaning. For the learner of a first language that medium is by definition completely understood (if 'understanding' is appropriate in a case where misunderstanding is impossible). Hence, only the second of the two kinds of partial understanding via translation obtains.

Or rather, there would be no difference between these approaches if we had any prior purchase on the medium; but we do not. Hence, Lewis's point against translation into semantic representations still holds. Katz's Semantic Markers, or other more recent alternatives, are just formalisms awaiting interpretation. *We* could interpret these formalisms by translating them back into English (or some other language that we understand), and it would be by no means required that the translation of the translation of x be x. In general, we would expect something that clarifies the meaning of x: in might go 'bachelor', and out might come 'unmarried man'. But that method of interpretation is not available to the learner, and so does not help us characterize what the learner knows. Moreover, for English words that are not decomposed in the medium, and for syntactically complex expressions, the whole route through translation is superfluous, and nothing has been gained. We will have been told that a person who learns the meaning of 'red' learns that it is to be translated into his or her representational medium as something that has the meaning of the word 'red'; that a person who learns the meaning of 'Johnny runs' learns it is to be translated into something that has the meaning of 'Johnny runs', and so forth. That is not progress.

A number of authors have seen the very idea of tacit knowledge of meaning as threatened by a vicious circle, on the ground that it presupposes a language of thought. I don't think that the charge of circularity is justified, but I have argued here that it is not possible (in fact, it is absurd) to attempt to state the content of tacit knowledge via translation into this language. However, it is a reasonable objective to attempt to get at the language of thought by trying to construct a theory of tacit knowledge, both the knowledge that the mature speaker has, and the knowledge that the learner brings to the task of acquiring a language.

Reviewing the discussion to this point, I envisage an account according to which persons acquire their idiolects by constructing theories of reference (or theories of meaning, in which the theory of reference plays a crucial part). The learner and the mature speaker will in general have only partial knowledge of their idiolects, for that will explain the difference between a partly interpreted idiom and a fully interpreted idiom whose interpretation is unavailable. The speaker's knowledge must be directly stated by the theorist, and cannot be presented through some hypothetical translation. Even if there is a medium through which the speaker thinks about meaning, our first access to that medium must be through the direct characterization of the knowledge that translation into it makes available to the speaker.

The view just outlined implies that knowing the 'disquotational' facts about words and sentences, facts such as (4), is not knowing very much. In the next section, I will take up some more specifically linguistic questions, afterwards returning to some of the issues that this view raises.

2 Interactions with syntax

Semantics connects forms with meanings: but the theory of meaning and the theory of form do not proceed along separate tracks. Information about each can provide evidence for the other. This is already illustrated in (4) above, where the syntactic frame, and our knowledge of the meanings of some of the words within it, gave information about the meanings of the others. Natural generalizations, together with observations and studies of children, have even led to the proposal that much of language learning proceeds from correlations between syntax and semantics, information about each feeding conclusions about the other in a 'bootstrapping' fashion (see especially Pinker (1984)). Obviously, a psychological theory that proceeds in this mentalistic way, accepting the picture of the learner of a first language as extrapolating conditions on form and meaning from the ambient speech, used as evidence, is involved with a conception of semantics as a theory of what persons know about meaning.

Our tacit knowledge of meaning somehow pairs forms with meanings, or, as I have been assuming, yields statements about reference and truth that have syntactic and semantic premises. The problem for research is then a problem in two unknowns, one for form, the other for the nature of the principles that connect forms to their interpretations. Tradeoffs are possible: adjustments toward greater complexity of form can lead to simplification of the semantics, and inversely a complex semantics can accept simplified inputs on the formal side. I want here to locate what I see as one of Chomsky's major contributions to the adjustment question.

A major philosophical issue to which the problem of adjusting form and meaning is pertinent is that of explaining what is sometimes called the *autonomy* of meaning. Our expressions have autonomous meaning, in that they mean what they do independently of what we may intend to communicate, and independently of the intentions of any particular speakers. The autonomy of meaning is thus a phenomenon, exemplified by Wittgenstein's question whether you can say, 'It's cold here' and mean, 'It's warm here,' or whether you can say, 'Abracadabra!' and mean, 'Close the door!' I want to understand it as a *mere* phenomenon, which any adequate grounding of the notion of meaning must nevertheless explain.

Chomsky's own explanation of the phenomenon is essentially Cartesian. As we learn language, a 'mechanism' is set up in us, associating thoughts with linguistic forms. This mechanism will resemble those that others set up, but it is not constrained to be identical to theirs; in fact, it commonly isn't. With the mechanism in place, things mean what they mean, willy-nilly. Fodor (1983, p. 55), as I understand him, supports this explanation, adding evidence from the 'mandatoriness' of our interpretation of heard sounds. The persistence of linguistic illusion, and the possibility that with maturity change in the linguistic system may be rare or impossible in critical respects, further buttress the Cartesian view, and show the range of the phenomenon.

There are two major attempts of which I am aware to account for the autonomy of meaning in a non-Cartesian way. These are illustrated, respectively, in Davidson (1986), and in Dummett (1986), commenting on Davidson. The first of these, roughly speaking, advances the idea that the autonomy of meaning results from our knowledge of how we will be understood; such an idea may be put in the service of a broad program that would ground meaning in the beliefs and communicative intentions of speakers. The second, due to Dummett, sees the autonomy of meaning as supporting the view that languages are social practices, and as indicating that the choice of the idiolect as the fundamental object of study is fundamentally flawed. I will return to these views. First, I will consider Chomsky's general approach to the interactions of syntax and semantics.

A famous example, which Chomsky considered at length (1965), is the near-minimal pair of sentences (5)–(6):

(5) John is eager to please

(6) John is easy to please

It is obvious that 'John' is the 'understood subject' of 'please' in (5), and the 'understood object' of 'please' in (6). Chomsky's point was that simple diagrams or bracketings would fail to reveal this difference. Hence, linguistic theory must avail itself of other expressive means than those that the bracketings provide.

Chomsky's specific proposals, both early and late, have featured the idea that understood elements are sometimes or always literally present in 'remoter' syntactic structures than those that may be associated, on prosodic or syntactic grounds, with the heard string. These remoter structures, or linguistic levels, are assumed in current work to include *S-Structure*, a level at which, suppressing certain details, (5) is represented as in (7), and (6) is represented as in (8):

(7) John is eager [*e* to please]

(8) John is easy [*e* to please *e*]

where the elements *e* are 'empty categories,' or formatives without a phonetic form, taking 'John' as antecedent as shown, and the subject of transitive 'please' in (8) is another empty category, roughly meaning 'one', as in 'John is easy for one to please.'[5]

Alternatives to the above proposal are possible (as usual), and it is specifically possible to do much of what is done with multiple linguistic levels within a single level, containing a lot of extra annotations within phrase structure diagrams, or trees. Nevertheless, it is not doubted that the information represented either in the connections between levels of representation or in the phrase structures is part of what must be available if an adequate theory is to be achieved. In this respect, Chomsky's argument that linguistic description must go beyond what he described in 1955 (reprinted as Chomsky (1975)) as the 'level of phrase structure' still stands.

Now, Chomsky made the point that, although (6) is, in virtue of having the form shown in (8), allowed to mean that it is easy for one to please John, nothing so far prevents its *also* having the meaning that it is easy for John to please one. That meaning, in fact, would be obtained by hooking things up as in (9):

(9) John is easy [*e* to please *e*]

However, some structural condition prevents this.

It was an early observation in generative grammar (and in fact was observed in more traditional sources as well) that there were structural conditions on the relations of pronouns to their antecedents, pronominal anaphora, as it is called. These conditions, for example, make it impossible for (10) to mean (11):

(10) He saw John in the mirror

(11) John saw himself in the mirror

Furthermore, the structural conditions can up to a point be simply stated. Let the *scope* of an element in a tree structure be the least subtree to which it belongs (scope is so characterized in the standard formalized languages).[6] In simple sentences, given the division into subject and predicate, predicates are within the scope of subjects, but subjects are not within the scope of arguments of predicates. The generalization that suggests itself is (12):

(12) Nothing can have an antecedent within its own scope

(A defense of the above as a general condition on anaphora is found in Higginbotham (1983).) Evidently, (10) would violate the condition (12), if 'John' were antecedent of 'he'; but taking 'John' as antecedent of 'himself' in (11) does not violate it.

The structural condition (12) obviously transcends anything that might be called a condition on *use* (except in the extreme sense in which one might try to turn even the meaning of an ordinary word into a condition on use). That an element cannot seek its antecedent within its own scope is part of the *sense* of the configurations that constitute the syntax of English. It is this fact that justifies the linguist's assumption that the relation of antecedence among the elements of configurations is a part of syntactic reality, every bit as much as words and phrases, and their classes and subclasses. Similarly, as Chomsky has argued, it is part of the sense of the configurations of English that the understood element meaning 'one' cannot occur as the object of a verb; that thesis explains the non-ambiguity of (6).[7]

Among the lessons I deem Chomsky to have taught me, then, is the lesson that grammatical configurations carry autonomous meaning. I want now to consider the issue that this poses for the attempt to ground the autonomy of meaning in a non-Cartesian way.

The autonomy of meaning seems to consist in there being facts about meaning that present themselves to the speaker as objective. If appearances are not deceiving, then the link between meaning and intention goes without saying: I cannot say, 'It's warm here' and mean, or intend to convey, that it's cold here, because my words don't mean that. Inversely, it appears that what my words mean cannot be derived from my communicative intentions, because the meanings of my words exercise *constraints* on my intentions.

However, the constraints on my intentions need not come from meanings; as Davidson has suggested, they might come from my knowledge of how I will be interpreted. For example, knowing as I do that I will not be taken as intending to convey that John saw himself by saying 'He saw John,' I cannot say 'He saw John' intending to be so taken. The facts of nature constrain my intentions generally, and so the facts about other people can constrain my intentions in endeavoring to communicate.

As Dummett points out, it is not obvious how to extend Davidson's account to non-communicative situations: to soliloquy, for example. It seems that the thoughts a speaker's words express, in or out of communication, should be seen as reflecting a communicative system of some sort, showing the persistence of associations derived through bygone and unremembered transactions with others.

The constraints on meaning must be of a general character; that is, they must apply to whole classes of sentences. The need for system is particularly apparent when we consider that certain types of sentences are forbidden from certain types of meanings. In terms of the generalization governing pronouns and their antecedents, it is systematically true that no utterance of mine with N in the scope of a pronoun will be taken as intending to convey a meaning with N as the antecedent of that pronoun. How does such a system come to be followed?

We must distinguish between the case where a certain type of expression is to be paired with a certain type of meaning and the case where a certain type of expression can *never* be paired with a certain type of meaning. The pairing of expressions with what they are permitted to mean might be extrapolated from hearing those expressions in contexts where it is manifest what meanings they are to carry. But the extrapolation is far greater if one is to know, from not happening to have heard an expression paired with a certain meaning, that it *cannot* have that meaning. Sometimes the potential meanings of a sentence exclude each other, in the sense that evidence that one is permitted is simultaneously evidence that the other is excluded. But such is not the case with (10). The fact that it can mean that some person or other saw John in the mirror does not exclude its also being able to carry the meaning that John saw himself in the mirror; and of course many sentences, such as 'John saw his mother in the mirror', are ambiguous in just the way (10) would then be. The problem of seeing how a system incorporating (12) comes to be in place is far from trivial.

The considerations that I have been rehearsing are known in developmental psycholinguistics as the problem of the *absence of negative evidence*.[8] Classically, it first appeared in syntax, where it was observed that children are seldom corrected for saying things such as Bowerman's (3), that are not grammatical in adult speech. The question is how they come to 'unlearn' their childhood grammars. The problem of the absence of negative evidence has been less visible in semantics, no doubt partly because of the difficulties in experimentation, but also because the logical independence of the meaning attached to a sentence from the meaning excluded from it has not always been as obvious as it is in the case of pronominal cross-reference. (Recent research on children's acquisition of anaphora, in which the absence of negative evidence plays a crucial role, includes Manzini and Wexler (1987), and de Villiers and Roeper (1987).)

Returning to the general issue, it seems that if the autonomy of meaning is to be accounted for along the lines that Davidson has suggested, then we will have to suppose that a speaker's beliefs about how he or she will be taken will have a general, systematic, and relatively inflexible character, and we will have to face complex issues of learning if these systems come to be in place despite the comparative absence of negative evidence. Add to these points the observation that the system itself makes reference to aspects of linguistic structure (scope or Reinhart's c-command) that are not transparently available in potential utterances. The question then arises how the speaker's intentions, or beliefs about how she will be understood, can make reference to matters that she does not appear to know or have learned anything about.

We have stumbled across a certain objection to the power of Davidson's suggestion to explain the autonomy of meaning, an objection that has in some quarters long been urged against the conception of tacit knowledge itself.

Following Wright (1986, pp. 219 ff), I will call it the *objection from technicality*.

The objection from technicality, in its strongest form, holds that it is folly to seek to explain rational linguistic behavior in terms of guidance by principles of which speakers are unaware. In the present case, it is raised in a somewhat weaker form (I shall not discuss the stronger form here): can we regard speakers as having tacit intentions, or tacit beliefs about the beliefs that others will have about what they intend? My belief that I will not be taken as having intended (11) by saying (10) is to be rationalized on the assumption that my interlocutor will not understand a person as intending for a pronoun to have an antecedent within its own scope. If that rationalization is correct, then we can, as Davidson says, see the autonomy of meaning presenting itself to us as a fact. But the rationalization itself is not consciously available to us.

At this point, it seems that Davidson's view is at best marginally different from the Cartesian. The strength of the objection from technicality to the picture of meaning in language as stemming from communicative intentions, a picture which Davidson at least partly endorses for explaining the autonomy of meaning, and which has been central to Grice's approach, depends on how intentions are conceived as related to other states of mind, and to potential awareness. The objection may have force. But it does not have any *special* force against Chomsky's Cartesian view, since other accounts of the autonomy of meaning are liable to it as well. I turn now, more briefly, to Dummett's view.

Dummett (1986) suggests that the phenomenon that I have labelled the autonomy of meaning is going to be visible in language, provided that language is viewed as a social practice. The intentions that participants in a practice can have are constrained by the rules that govern it. The nature of social practices raises questions I won't consider here. Sometimes it seems they are thought of as congeries of *regularities*, or statistical correlations among behaviors that one could discover or describe pre-theoretically. But the regularities of linguistic behavior do not seem to be of this nature. In any case, Dummett's view invites the question of how our capacity to *participate* in the social practice of language is to be explained, a question that Chomsky has characteristically raised in similar connections. Unless this question can be answered without appealing to the background that Chomsky assumes, I think we must regard the case against the Cartesian picture of the autonomy of meaning as not proven.[9]

In concluding this section, I will briefly consider the objection from technicality with respect to a Cartesian view of the autonomy of meaning, for it raises a point that I think linguistic theory must contend with. The concepts of theoretical linguistics are removed from the most ordinary explicit knowledge. But they cannot be regarded as recent historical products if they are to figure in tacit knowledge. Persons such as myself at the age of 6, or forgotten men and women of 20,000 years ago, must have had them. How plausible is it that they did?

I would conjecture that it is in fact quite plausible, and at least as plausible as the assumption that I at the age of 6, or those long-ago persons, had combinatorial powers of the sort needed for the apprehension of numbers.

Whether or not this conjecture is correct, I would stress that the situation with respect to syntax and semantics seems to be very different from that of phonology, vision, or any other purely perceptual or motor capacity. In the latter cases, just because of the close links of our faculties with perception and action, the objection from technicality has no force whatever. When we listen, we hear words, and when we look, we look at objects. The mechanisms that map from sensory input to what we hear or see are as alien to us as any other parts of our bodies, and obey whatever laws they obey. If it turns out, as it seems to, that the eye sees edges of objects in part by solving differential equations, it does not matter that most people have no idea of differential equations, or even that the very concept was a recent historical creation. The case is rather different with syntax and semantics, since these must enter into thoughtful activities of all kinds. To use Chomsky's terminology of modules, syntax and semantics must represent modules of understanding, not just of perception, or perception and speech.[10]

I conclude that the objection from technicality does raise a substantive issue for syntactic and semantic theory, inasmuch as these theories, viewed as theories of tacit knowledge, cannot depend on an idealization of our capacities so extensive as to outstrip what is potentially available to us in thought. But then it seems to me that the objection is turned aside in virtue of the properties of syntax and semantics, as we now understand them.

I began this section by outlining the view that conditions on form and meaning interact both to drive learning and to set theoretical issues for semantics, especially those issues that involve a sentence not having a meaning that it would be reasonable to ascribe to it. Assuming that the autonomy of meaning was a phenomenon to be accounted for, I have argued that neither an explanation in terms of social practices nor an explanation in terms of intentions and beliefs of individuals about one another can abstract from the question how individuals come to participate in the practices, or have the required beliefs and intentions. The kind of view of what makes their participation possible I have associated with Chomsky, and have called Cartesian inasmuch as it takes the power to associate thoughts with words largely for granted. It may be regarded as promissory and tentative; but it is not clear what could replace it. My examples have concerned the meanings of whole sentences, or linguistic structures. In the next section, I will consider some questions that have to do instead with lexical meaning, returning to the question of the basis clauses of the theory of reference.

3 Meanings of words

In section 1, I assumed without argument that a person who did not know what 'red' means, but knew that it was an ordinary adjective (that is, not a syncategorematic adjective like 'fake', or a dyadic adjective like 'fond'), would know that 'red' refers to red things, and similarly that a person who knew how the sentence 'all mimsy were the borogoves' was made up, or knew its composition up to the meanings of certain lexical items, would know the disquotational statement (4) giving its truth conditions; and so on for like cases. My assumption is explicitly denied in Dummett (1974) (see especially pp. 106 ff), and it seems to me that its denial has often played a role in furtherance of the idea that disquotational facts about truth and reference are non-trivial.[11] The issue is not a simple one, especially when we reflect with Dummett that a person who does not know what 'the earth moves' means will know, by my lights, that it means that the earth moves. I think that the air of paradox apparent here can be dispelled. First, however, I want to consider a certain consequence of my assumption, and compare it with the conclusions in Dummett (1974), to which much of what I have to say may be seen as a response.

Let us say that a person who knows what the predicates, singular terms, connectives, and other expression-types of a sentence are, and how they are combined to make that sentence, knows its *logical skeleton*. Then it is possible for a person to know the logical skeleton of a sentence without knowing the meanings of any of the words that it contains, including the logical words, if any. Such a person would, by my assumption, know the disquotational statement giving its truth conditions, or its meaning, without knowing anything of great significance about its meaning. If that person were in the same state of knowledge with respect to every other sentence of a language, then he might give a theory of truth for the language, without understanding a single sentence of it.

I think that the possibility just sketched is genuine. If it is, then what more must be supplied to get at the meanings of sentences? Evidently, a lexicon, since that is just what was missing. The lexicon, however, cannot be only disquotationally presented or, more precisely, we cannot assume that a disquotational presentation of the lexicon represents all the knowledge that we possess about the words used in presenting it.

If this is correct, then from a starting-point that denies one of the premises of Dummett (1974, p. 102), we have come close to one of his central conclusions in that article, namely that a theory of meaning should be, in his terminology, 'full-blooded' rather than 'modest'. In a full-blooded theory in Dummett's sense, one seeks to explain the primitive concepts of a language; in a modest theory, one is content with an interpretation adequate to understanding for an interpreter already possessing the concepts used in presenting it. Dummett argues from the premiss that a person who knows only the logical skeleton of a sentence does not know the disquotational statement of its meaning or truth conditions to the conclusion that our knowledge of meaning cannot consist in the knowledge given by a modest theory of meaning, whose power is limited to the deducibility of such statements. I have argued that, precisely because knowledge of the logical skeleton *is* sufficient for knowledge of these statements, and such knowledge is therefore possible without understanding, a modest theory is inadequate.

Suppose, then, that further information is added to the modest theory.

Elsewhere, I have argued that such information must include, besides the logical skeleton of a word, a description or, as I called it, an *elucidation* of critical aspects of its meaning.[12] The verb 'cut', for example, should include in its elucidation that cutting a thing involves disrupting its material integrity, or 'affecting' the object in a way that satisfies the requirement of appearance in the English middle construction, as in (13):

(13) The fish cuts easily

(Compare, 'the fish pats easily', which is bizarre.) Somewhat more conjectur- ally, we might suppose that the elucidation of 'wipe' in which wiping x involves *removing material from the surface of x* is responsible for the acceptability of (1), and the unacceptability of (2), and that the child's failure to appreciate the close link of resultative predicates to the character of the verb governing the object is responsible for the overgeneralization of this construction.[13]

However specific examples may go in theoretical linguistics or in experimental psychological studies, there is evidence that a modest theory of meaning would be a mistaken ideal. I want now to observe that Dummett's sense of a theory's being 'full-blooded' is stronger than the view I have just suggested. Suppose we articulate lexical knowledge by means of a non-modest theory; that is, one that probes into the meanings of words, and especially those aspects of their meaning that interact with linguistic structures, such as the English middles and resultatives. Such a theory, although not modest, is *purely propositional*; that is, it conceives of the speaker as knowing a set of more or less complicated statements about conditions on truth and reference. However, for any purely propositional theory, we can imagine knowing that theory without understanding the language: just assume that only the logical skeleton of the clauses of the theory is known to the speaker. As I understand Dummett, he would infer from this consequence that a theory of meaning cannot be satisfactory unless it relates knowledge of meaning to practical activities that involve use of the language.

For two positive empirical reasons, and one negative one, I doubt that the consequence that I have attributed to Dummett is one that should lead us to believe we are on the wrong track. The negative reason is that the most useful descriptions of sophisticated linguistic activity that show understanding of an expression are those that presuppose propositional knowledge of the meanings of other expressions. For instance, the activity that shows that the child has come to understand the difference between 'sell' and 'give' would typically assume the child's understanding of the words for the transferred property, goods or money, and what could be done with them. Of the positive reasons, one is implicit in my discussion above of where elucidations of meaning are in practice required, namely for those aspects of the lexicon that have visible linguistic effects (Higginbotham, 1986a). The second positive reason is that the speed with which the lexicon is in fact acquired suggests that our grasp of the meaning of a word does not depend on our having engaged in the gamut of linguistic activities involving it.[14]

In closing this section, I will turn back to a residual difference between Dummett's view that the statements of a modest theory of meaning – for instance, the statement that 'red' refers to the red things – carry much information, although information that is not available to someone who does not know what 'red' means, and the view that I have taken here, that they carry, even for the mature speaker who does know what 'red' means, only the information that the word is an ordinary one-place predicate.

Dummett's view uses the distinction between knowing the proposition that a sentence expresses, and knowing that the proposition it expresses (whatever it is) is a true one. Of course, there is such a distinction; but the question is whether it is responsible for the differing assessments we may be inclined to give of the information carried to us by (14):

(14) 'red' refers to the red things

On one assessment, it is trivial. A person to whom 'red' was a novel word, but who knew the elementary combinatorial semantics of English, would know by knowing (14) only the logical skeleton of assertions, 'This is red', not what they meant. On the other assessment, it is consequential, but involves a presupposition necessary to knowing what information it in fact encodes.

If I know the logical skeleton of 'This is red', then I know more than that the statement 'This is red' is true if and only if 'This is red' expresses a truth, for I know some of its implications, for example. Hence Dummett's distinction is too coarse-grained, since it seems that a person should be credited with more knowledge than Dummett allows, even if she does not know what proposition is expressed by 'This is red'. However, Dummett's terminology is easily extended to this case. The person ignorant or in doubt about the meaning of 'red' will be said to know by knowing the logical skeleton of 'This is red' what *kind* of proposition it expresses, even if she doesn't know which one of that kind it is.

But the whole apparatus of propositions is of doubtful necessity here. One can account for the further information that its apprehension may give a person in terms of background information with which it combines to yield a genuine advance in knowledge.[15] In conclusion, I will take note of two subsidiary points.

The first point concerns the nature of (14) as a sentence of my (or the reader's) language. Because the reference of a sign is relative to an assumed background system that is not mentioned in (14) itself, that statement is of an indexical character. The parameter of indexicality need not be a *language*, in any technical sense of that term. Supposing for the sake of simplicity, however, that the background is so restricted, the near-trivial character of the indexical statement follows from the fact that the language to which the reference of 'red' is relative is the very language in which it is asserted, or otherwise put up for consideration.

A question does arise whether, on the assumptions I have made, it is possible to represent reference as inscrutable in the sense of Quine; that is, whether one can represent the possibility of there being many languages each of which is as attributable to me as any other, and at least one of which it would not be wrong to attribute to me. Perhaps reference is not inscrutable, but the possibility of its inscrutability, and in particular the possibility of its inscrutability with respect to the predicate 'red', ought to be expressible. Moreover, inscrutability should be statable as a possibility even for one's own case.

The inscrutability of the reference of 'red' becomes the statement that in some language L that it is appropriate for me to attribute to myself, if 'refers' is taken as 'refers in L', then (14) is false. That statement is compatible with its being the case (as it is) that in any language that it is appropriate for me to attribute to myself, (14) is true as a sentence of that language. Self-ascribed inscrutability is not, then, inconsistent with the view I have sketched.[16]

My second point concerns the near-triviality of disquotational statements about meaning, statements that would include, '"red" is used to say of things that they are red', or Dummett's example, '"the earth moves" means that the earth moves.' On the view that intensional contexts, such as 'say of things that —', or 'means that—' involve both use and mention of the expressions that they embed, these statements too emerge as near-trivial, requiring at most knowledge of their logical skeletons, which I am assuming confers the ability to use them.[17] A person who says '*s* means that *p*' speaks truly just in case the embedded clause means something appropriately similar in meaning to *s*. Everything is similar in meaning to itself, and so '"the earth moves" means that the earth moves' is true, and so 'the earth moves' means that the earth moves. We need not, on this view, say that there is any proposition that is imperfectly grasped by a person who does not know what 'the earth moves' means, or that there is something more to the statement that 'red' is used to say of things that they are red than that 'red' is a one-place predicate.

However, the argument just given shows at best that the *ordinary* expressions 'means that' and 'says of things that', understood as I have indicated, cannot be used to give disquotational facts of consequence for linguistic theory. There could be other predicates, for which all of the statements of the disquotational paradigm were true, that presupposed more than these seem to do for knowledge of them. Philosophers often use such predicates in statements of definition such as

'water' means *a potable colorless liquid found in lakes and streams*

and, disquotationally,

'water' means *water*

In fact, I have fallen in with this practice above in writing, in effect:

'wiping *x*' means *removing material from the surface of x*

The italics in these statements serve as a reminder that we are not talking merely of the reference of the words in question. Those statements that are not merely disquotations are hypotheses about meaning, either about what the concepts expressed by 'water' and 'wiping' are, or about what speakers put in their lexical entries for these words, their elucidations of them in the sense used above. But even the disquotational statement is to be understood as non-trivial, and distinct in particular from the merely formal truth that 'water' means whatever it means.

Bringing this usage back to sentences, we might distinguish a more demanding notion of meaning, for which '"the earth moves" means that the earth moves' is not known unless the meanings of the significant parts 'the earth' and 'moves' are known. Even on the less demanding notion of meaning, the statement that 'the earth moves' means that the earth moves and the statement that 'the earth moves' means whatever it means are far from being equivalent. A person who knows only that 'the earth moves' is a sentence knows the latter, but not the former. The difference between the two conceptions of meaning is that on the less demanding conception a person working his way into our language need not know the particular bit of it that involves the noun 'earth' and the verb 'moves' to know that 'the earth moves' means that the earth moves; whereas on the more demanding conception precisely this knowledge is required.

There cannot, of course, be any *a priori* objection to the introduction of the more demanding conception of meaning. However, the articulation of linguistic theory using only the more demanding conception would miss something about our knowledge of language, namely our capacity to use words that we only partly understand. As a normal speaker of the English language, I can speak of leveraged buyouts, having only the dimmest conception of what they are, and so I know (using the less demanding conception of meaning) that 'X carried off a leveraged buyout of Y' means that X carried off a leveraged buyout of Y. I am in an intermediate state of knowledge, somewhere between the state of the person who cannot use English, but knows that 'leveraged buyout' is a relational nominal, and someone who knows in detail about leveraged buyouts. The less demanding conception of meaning is suitable to expressing what I know in this state.

The views that I have advanced here concerning partial knowledge of meaning, and the reciprocal interaction of knowledge of form and knowledge of meaning, have involved the thesis that disquotational statements carry their own proper information to a person capable of using the language in which they are expressed. Some at least, and perhaps all of these, can be expressed on Dummett's kind of view, provided that it is supplemented with a mechanism for saying that a person may know what sort of proposition a sentence expresses without knowing fully what it is. And in either case, as I have remarked, we should conclude that a 'full-blooded' theory is needed to explain the meanings of words, and the relations of those meanings to their syntactic distribution. But if I am right to conclude that the notion of propositions is not needed to characterize a full-blooded theory, then it will be possible to keep within a strictly referential account of semantics.

4 Cartesian semantics

The subject of tacit knowledge, long a controversial one, is one that should receive continued investigation, because it marks a distinctive turn in reflection on the relations of language and thought. One reason for being dissatisfied with the notion of tacit knowledge is that it appears to renege on the prospect of getting at the nature of thought and rationality by inquiring into the nature of language. If language is made available to us only because we can think, and therefore form hypotheses about meaning, then the very power has been presupposed that linguistic investigation was intended to clarify. Responding to this dissatisfaction, Chomsky has repeatedly defended his view that linguistic theory is a theory of competence or tacit knowledge by arguing that the study of language has made progress on the assumption that the learner is pictured as constructing a theory, of which the mature speaker is in possession. Typically, therefore, he has thrown back the challenge to his Cartesian assumptions by observing that no alternative to those assumptions presents itself as a serious option for inquiry.

Chomsky has often expressed skepticism about the setting and goals of semantics as I have presented them here, not because he is skeptical of the powers of a theory of reference to serve for a theory of meaning, but because he is skeptical of a theory of conditions on meaning, in a sense conceptually distinct from that of conditions on form. I have not followed him in this, and I think that the arguments that he has been wont to use in support of his skepticism are unpersuasive. But I do believe that his rebuttal to challenge is as effective in semantics as in syntax. In closing, I would like to remark a singular respect in which the kind of view that Chomsky has proposed ought to be seen as a continuation in current philosophy of a type of inquiry that we can recognize from a number of historical and contemporary sources.

The inquiry I have in mind can be roughly characterized in the following way. Given that we have the schemes that we have for thinking about the world, including the people in it, we endeavor to isolate our contribution to those schemes by distinguishing what is peculiar to us humans from what comes as a matter of course, assuming minimal standards of rationality. We succeed in this endeavor to the degree that we can picture a space of possible rational beings, among whom the rational beings that we can become are a small subset. In syntactic theory along Chomsky's lines, we have made progress when we can isolate features of our first language that clearly need not belong to all possible languages, even when the constraints imposed by our bodies and the conditions under which we use language are taken into account. Semantic theory may be conceived similarly, although here the problem of constructing a space of possible systems can be much harder. Among the areas where progress has been made, I would include systems of lexical semantics (including logical constants), and principles of compositionality of meaning.[18] These systems and principles are tacitly known to native speakers, and in part responsible for their acquisition of human first languages.

However successful they may be or become, semantic theories conceived as I have described do not tell us how thought or rationality are possible, or how the attribution of thought is exhaustively to be grounded in physical phenomena. But these theories do mark us off to ourselves as the peculiar thinkers that we are. By showing how linguistic theory can figure in the general enterprise of clarifying the categories of mind, Chomsky has guaranteed that the study of language will never be the same.[19]

Notes

1 The first point was stressed in Kripke (1972, 1980). For detailed discussion of examples bearing on the second, see especially Burge (1986) and references cited there.

2 I am indebted here to discussion with Tyler Burge and Alexander George. For a defense of the idiolectal conception against objections stemming from the intentions of speakers to adjust themselves to their communities, see George (1989).

3 For related points, see Lycan, 1979.

4 See Davidson, 1973, reprinted in Davidson, 1984, p. 129.

5 The view just sketched was developed by Chomsky over a number of years, and is still undergoing modifications and extensions of many sorts. Chomsky, 1981, chapter 2 contains motivating arguments, as well as much detailed exposition.

6 In the linguistics literature this notion is often called *c-command*, following the nomenclature of Tanya Reinhart, who first demonstrated its significance for generative grammar. Certain refinements are possible, which will be omitted here; see Reinhart, 1983. Similar notions were employed earlier. See Lasnik, 1976 and references cited there.

7 For example, the sentence 'Who to see is unclear' has only the meaning, 'It is unclear who one ought to see,' and never the meaning, 'It is unclear who ought to see one.'

8 See for example Pinker (1984), pp. 28ff.

9 A contemporary 'anti-Fregean' trend in semantic theory, well articulated in Wettstein, 1988, self-consciously advances a conception of language as a social practice, in which words and sentences have a reference, but any conception like that of Fregean sense or linguistic meaning is abandoned. Here also, it seems to me, the question for which grasp of sense might be advanced as a potential answer, goes unnoticed.

10 I have argued for this view further in Higginbotham, 1987.

11 See, for instance, Loewer, 1982, p. 307; Lycan, 1984, pp. 28ff; Wright, 1986, p. 220.

12 Higginbotham, 1986a, and especially section 1.

13 I am indebted here to discussion with Steven Pinker. In syntactic theory one speaks of the resultative's being 'selected' by the main verb. Notice that the selection appears to be governed only by the verb, and not also by its object; thus 'wipe x clean' is preferred to 'wipe x dirty', independently of x.

14 Literature on the speed of acquisition of words, even in the absence of much syntactic cuing, goes back a number of years; again see Pinker (1984) and references cited there.

15 For example, if Maria, a monolingual speaker of German, should obtain an English grammar book in German, and therein read (i), she would come to know about English just what I myself know by knowing (14):

(i) 'red' bedeutet (auf Englisch) die roten dinge

If she seems thereby to learn more, that is because she already knows more about the German word 'rot' than the mere statement (ii) records:

(ii) 'rot' bedeutet die roten dinge

(Thanks to Friedericke Moltmann for screening the German.)

16 The above view of inscrutability may be attributable to Quine, See Quine, 1986, p. 367.

17 A version of a double-valued view of at least certain intensional contexts, which goes back a ways, is explained more fully in Higginbotham, 1986a.

18 At this point, I think, neglect of semantics proper, as opposed to elaborate structural proposals for remote levels of syntax, has sometimes made it harder than it need have been to isolate the principles in question.

19 Material based on this article was presented at Brandeis University, at Wolfson College, Oxford, at a colloquium of the C.R.E.A., Paris, France, and at the conference *Gli Stili della Argomentazione*, Fondazione San Carlo, Modena, Italy. I am grateful to a number of persons in these places for discussion and criticism, and to Alexander George for help as editor, colleague, and friend.

References

Bowerman, M. 1982: Starting to talk worse: clues to language acquisition from children's late errors. In S. Strauss (ed.), *U-Shaped Behavioral Growth*. New York: Academic Press.

Burge, T. 1986: Intellectual norms and foundations of mind. *Journal of Philosophy*, 83 (12), 697–720.

Chomsky, N. 1965: *Aspects of the Theory of Syntax*. Cambridge, Mass.: MIT Press.

1975: *The Logical Structure of Linguistic Theory*. Chicago: University of Chicago Press.

1981: *Lectures on Government and Binding*. Dordrecht: Foris.

Davidson, D. 1973: Radical interpretation. *Dialectica*, 27, 313–28. Repr. in Davidson 1984.

1984: *Inquiries Into Truth and Interpretation*. Oxford: Clarendon Press.

1986: A nice derangement of epitaphs. In E. LePore (ed.), *Truth and Interpretation: Perspectives on the Philosophy of Donald Davidson*. Oxford: Basil Blackwell, 433–46.

Dummett, M. 1974: What is a theory of meaning? In S. Guttenplan (ed.), *Mind and Language*. Oxford University Press, 97–138.

1986: A nice derangement of epitaphs: some comments on Davidson and Hacking. In E. LePore (ed.), *Truth and Interpretation: Perspectives on the Philosophy of Donald Davidson*. Oxford: Basil Blackwell, 459–76.

Fodor, J. 1975: *The Language of Thought*. New York: Crowell.

1983: *The Modularity of Mind*. Cambridge, Mass.: MIT Press.

George, A. 1989: Whose language is it anyway? Some remarks on idiolects. Forthcoming in *The Philosophical Quarterly*.

Harman, G. 1974: Meaning and semantics. In M.K. Munitz, and P.K. Unger (eds), *Semantics and Philosophy*. New York: New York University Press, 1–16.

Higginbotham, J. 1983: Logical form, binding, and nominals. *Linguistic Inquiry*, 14 (3), 395–420.

1986a: Elucidations of meaning. *Linguistics and Philosophy*, forthcoming.

1986b: Linguistic theory and Davidson's program in semantics. In E. LePore (ed.), *Truth and Interpretation: Perspectives on the Philosophy of Donald Davidson*. Oxford: Basil Blackwell, 29–48.

1987: The autonomy of syntax and semantics. In J. Garfield (ed.), *Modularity in Knowledge Representation and Natural Language Understanding*. Cambridge, Mass.: MIT Press, 119–31.

Kripke, S. 1972, 1980: *Naming and Necessity*. Cambridge, Mass.: Harvard University Press.

Lasnik, H. 1976: Remarks on coreference. *Linguistic Analysis*, 2, 1–32.

Lewis, D. 1972: General semantics. In D. Davidson, and G. Harman (eds), *Semantics of Natural Language*. Dordrecht: Reidel, 169–218.

Loewer, B. 1982: The role of 'conceptual role semantics'. *Notre Dame Journal of Formal Logic*, 23 (2), 305–15.

Lycan, W. 1979: Semantic competence and funny functors. *The Monist*, 62 (2), 209–22.

1984: *Logical Form in Natural Language*. Cambridge, Mass.: MIT Press.

Manzini, M.-R. and Wexler, K. 1987: Parameters, binding theory, and learnability. *Linguistic Inquiry*, 18 (3), 413–44.

Pinker, S. 1984: *Language Learnability and Language Development*. Cambridge, Mass.: Harvard University Press.

1988, forthcoming: *Learnability and Cognition: The Acquisition of Argument Structure*.

Quine, W. 1986: Reply to Nozick. In L. Hahn and P. Schilpp (eds), *The Philosophy of W.V. Quine*. La Salle, Ill.: Open Court, 364–7.

Reinhart, T. 1983: *Anaphora and Semantic Interpretation*. London: Croom Helm.

Villiers, J. de and Roeper, T. 1987: Ordered parameters. Ms., University of Massachusetts, Amherst.

Wettstein, H. 1988: Cognitive significance without cognitive content. *Mind*, 97 (385), 1–28.

Wright, C. 1986: Theories of meaning and speaker's knowledge. In Wright, *Realism, Meaning and Truth*. Oxford: Basil Blackwell, 204–38.

9

Wherein is Language Social?

Tyler Burge

In this paper I will develop two limited senses in which the study of language, specifically semantics, is the study of a partly social phenomenon. These senses are compatible with the idea that the study of language is a part of individual psychology. I will argue for this standpoint from some obvious facts about human interaction together with elements from a view, which I have supported elsewhere, that the semantics of a language is partly dependent on relations between individual speakers and their physical environments. Most of what I say about language will apply to individual psychology. I begin by discussing two background senses in which language is social.

Language is social in that interaction with other persons is psychologically necessary to learn language. Some philosophers have made the further claim that there is some conceptually necessary relation between learning or having a language and being in a community. I do not accept this view. I assume only that it is a psychologically important fact that we cannot learn language alone.

Language is social in another sense. There is a rough, commonsensical set of languages – English, German, and so on – and dialects of these languages, that are in some vague sense shared by social groups. Of course, problems attend taking commonsense languages to be objects of systematic study. The normal divisions among languages correspond to no significant linguistic distinctions.

But this issue is really quite complex. In studying language or dialect in a systematic way, we commonly do not specify who uses the construction at issue, and we commonly assume that there is common ground among a large number of speakers – even though we are studying matters that are not species-wide. In historical studies, for example, we must abstract from individual usage in order to get any generality at all. We simply do not know enough about the quirks of individual usage to make an interesting subject-matter: one must study such things as the history of a word, understood more or less in the commonsensical, trans-individual way. In semantics, one provides theories of reference or meaning in natural language again in nearly total disregard of individual variations, even for phenomena that are by no means universal or species-wide.

These facts of theoretical usage suggest that there is some theoretical point to taking dialects or other linguistic units as abstractions from some sorts of social patterns. Perhaps the abstractions warrant thinking of individual variation as an interference to be accounted for after the primary theorizing is done. I think that there is something to this point of view. Nothing that I will say contradicts it. But the point of view is limited. It cannot provide anything like a complete picture.

One source of limitation derives from the wide variation among any group of individuals on numerous non-universal aspects of language use. People do not share exactly the same vocabulary, for example. People often use words in idiosyncratic ways that exempt them from evaluation by any socially accepted standard. Such quirks motivate the bromide that one should not invoke majority usage 'imperialistically' to fit individual variations into a standardized mold. These two points alone make it likely that no two people speak the same 'version' of any natural language or dialect.

There is a general reason for variation among individuals' language use. Languages depend on the experiences, usage, and psychological structures of individuals. Variation in individuals' word meaning, for example, is the natural result of the close relation between meaning and belief. Although the precise character of this relation is controversial and although intuitively meaning does not vary as freely as belief, some variation in meaning with individual belief is inevitable. The interplay between meaning and belief is a special case of the interplay between actual languages and psychology – about which similar points regarding individual variation could be made. It is therefore plausible that in studying language one must study the languages of individuals, idiolects.

These considerations suggest aiming for a science of universal aspects of language and for a study of non-universal aspects of language, both of which are tailored to the usage and psychology of individual speakers. I accept this much. Some have drawn the further inference that such a program's method of kind-individuation is independent of any considerations of social interaction among individuals. I will argue that this inference is unsound.

The inference just cited may be suggested by Chomsky's methodology for studying syntax. Actually, Chomsky is more cautious. What he is firm about is that there is a study of *universal grammar* which can be investigated independently of the diversity among individuals, and that linguistics (at least the sort of linguistics he pursues) – both universal and individual – is a part of individual psychology.[1] I shall argue that social factors may enter in complex ways into individual psychology and the semantics of idiolects.

Unlike many philosophers, I do not find Chomsky's methodology misguided. His views that linguistic structures are real, that some of them are universal, and that they are mental structures seem to me substantially more plausible than alternatives.[2] Arguments that we may speak merely in accidental accord with the structures postulated in linguistics, or that there is no scientific way to investigate universality of syntax, or that generative linguistics has no direct place in psychology, seem to me unconvincing and indicative of mistaken methodology. I shall not review these arguments.

The study of universal grammar is informed by certain simplifying idealizations. The idealization most relevant to this discussion attempts to cut through the variation and 'noise' associated with usage in a community. The linguist considers an idealized 'speech community' that is 'uniform' – internally consistent in its linguistic practice (cf. n. 1). Without denying that individuals are members of a community, and without denying that they could develop into mature language-users only because they are, the idealization attempts to study an individual in complete abstraction from the actual presence of others. Any given individual is taken as a representative having universal linguistic abilities or cognitive structures. The assumption is that underlying the variation among individuals, there is a common initial linguistic capacity that is specific enough to have certain definite structural features and that is capable of further linguistic development in certain delimited and specifiable ways. Variations in individual grammar are taken to be results of a fixing of parameters from a set of delimited alternatives.

For present purposes, I accept this idealization regarding universal grammar. It has received substantial support through its fruitful application both in pure linguistics and in developmental psycho-linguistics. (I will conjecture about a qualification on the idealization as applied to individual syntax later; cf. n. 4.) I believe that the methodology accompanying this idealization has some application to universal and individual aspects of semantics. But here the situation is, I think, more complex. In particular, I think that relations to others do affect the individuation of some semantical kinds. To consider the role of social elements in semantics, I want to start further back.

In recent years I have argued that the natures of many of our thoughts are individuated *non-individualistically*. I shall have to presuppose these arguments. But according to their common conclusion, the individuation of many thoughts, of intentional kinds, depends on the nature of the environment with which we interact. What information we process – for example, what perceptions we have – is dependent on the properties in the empirical world that members of our species normally interact with when they are having perceptual experiences. What empirical concepts we think with are fixed partly through relations to the kinds of things we think about.[3]

It is easy to confuse this view with another more obvious one. It is obvious that if we did not interact with the empirical or social worlds, we would not have the thoughts we do. Our thoughts and perceptions are causally dependent on the environment. My view concerns not merely causation; it concerns individuation.

Distinguishing the point about individuation from the point about causation is easiest to do by putting the point about individuation in terms of supervenience. Our thoughts do not supervene on the nature and history of our bodies, considered in isolation from the environment, in the following sense: It is in principle possible for one to have had different thoughts from one's actual thoughts, even though one's body had the same molecular history, specified in isolation from its relations to a broader physical environment. The same chemical effects on our bodies might have been induced by different antecedent conditions (perhaps, but not necessarily, including different causal laws). The point about individuation is not only that actual thoughts (like actual chemical effects) depend on the actual nature of the environment. Even if the effects had been chemically the same, it is possible in some cases for the thoughts, the information about the environment carried in our mental states, to have been different – if the environmental antecedents of those effects had been relevantly different. The kind of thought that one thinks is not supervenient on the physical make-up of one's body, specified in isolation from its relations to the environment. Thought kinds are individuated in a way that depends on relations one bears to kinds in one's physical environment. On this view individual psychology itself is not purely individualistic.

The failure of supervenience in no ways casts doubt on investigations of neural or biological realizations of mental structures. The failure of supervenience requires only that the identity of certain mental structures be dependent on relations between the individual and the environment. The identity of a heart depends on its function in the whole body – on its relations to parts of the body outside the heart. In a crudely analogous way, the identities of some mental kinds depend on those kinds' relations to entities beyond the individual's body. They depend on cognitive function, on obtaining information, in an environment in something like the way the kind *heart* depends for its individuation on the function of the heart in the body that contains it.

The failure of supervenience also does not entail that an individual psychology that takes its kinds not to be supervenient on an individual's body must study – or make theoretical reference to – the relations between individual and environment that are presupposed in the individuation of its kinds. It is open to psychology to take such kinds as primitive, leaving their presupposed individuation conditions to some other science or to philosophy. I believe this often to be the right course.

The arguments for anti-individualistic individuation of mental kinds can be extended in relatively obvious ways to show that much of semantics is not purely individualistic.[4]

The claim that semantics is non-individualistic is not merely a claim that the *referents* of an individual's words could in principle vary even though the history of the individual's body, considered in isolation from the environment, were held constant.[5] The claim is more comprehensive. The empirical referents of an individual's word are obviously not themselves part of the individual's psychology, or point of view. Thoughts are the individual's perspective on the world. And meanings or senses are, very roughly speaking, a speaker's way of expressing such perspective in language. They are what an individual understands and thinks in the use of his words. My thesis is that even (many of) those aspects of semantics that would be reflected in meaning or sense, and that would be represented in an individual's thought processes, in his psychology, are non-individualistically individuated. What a word means, even in an individual's idiolect, can depend on environmental factors, beyond an individual's body, considered as a molecular structure.

I think it plausible that some meanings of words are universal to the species in that if a person has the requisite perceptual experience and acquires language normally, the person will have words with those meanings. A likely source of such universality is perceptual experience itself. It appears that early vision is language-independent and constant for the species. Because of the evolution of our species, we are fashioned in such a way that perceptual experience will automatically trigger the application of perceptual notions associated with innate dispositions. Linguistic expressions for such perceptual notions as edge, surface, shadow, under, curved, physical object, and so on, are likely to be tied to elementary, universal perceptual experience, or to innate states fixed by species-ancestors' perceptual interactions with the world.

Many such notions can be shown to be non-individualistically individuated. It is possible to construct hypothetical cases in which the optical laws of the world are different, and the interactions of one's species with elements of the world are different, so that different perceptual notions, carrying different perceptual information, are innate or universally acquired. But in these same cases, one can coherently conceive an individual whose bodily history is molecularly identical to one whose perceptual notions are like ours. (The optical differences need not prevent, in certain special cases, a given individual from being affected in the same chemical way by different causal antecedents in the empirical world.) So the perceptual content or information of his experience is different – he has different perceptions – even though his body is, individualistically specified, the same. In such a case, it is clear that the meanings or senses of his words for objective, perceptual properties will also be different.[6]

Thus the view that certain concepts and meanings are non-individualistically individuated is compatible with those concepts and meanings being innate. The effect of the environment in determining psychological kinds may occur in the evolution of the species as well as in the experiential history of the individual.

Whether or not they are universal, virtually all concepts and meanings that are applied to public objects or events that we know about empirically are non-individualistically individuated. Such meanings attributed by semantics, and such concepts attributed by individual psychology, are non-individualistic to the core.

So far I have stated an anti-individualistic view of psychology and semantics that is entirely independent of social considerations. The failure of individualism derives, at this stage, purely from relations between the individual and the empirically known physical world. Now I want to use considerations that underlie this non-social anti-individualism to show how social elements enter the individuation of linguistic and psychological kinds. In a sense I will derive principles underlying social anti-individualistic thought experiments (see Burge, 1979) from obvious facts, together with some of the principles underlying non-social anti-individualistic thought experiments.

As a means of setting background, I begin with Chomsky's suggestion for incorporating social elements into semantics. Responding to Putnam's 'division of linguistic labor', he writes:[7]

> In the language of a given individual, many words are semantically indeterminate in a special sense: The person will defer to 'experts' to sharpen or fix their reference. . . . In the lexicon of this person's language, the entries [for the relevant words] will be specified to the extent of his or her knowledge, with an indication that details are to be filled in by others, an idea that can be made precise in various ways but without going beyond the study of the system of knowledge of language of a particular individual. Other social aspects of language can be regarded in a like manner – although this is not to deny the possibility or value of other kinds of study of language that incorporate social structure and interaction.

Chomsky's proposal is certainly part of a correct account of the individual's reliance on others. I do not want to dispute the cases that he specifically discusses. I think, however, that the proposal cannot provide a complete account. My first concern is that it might be read to imply that in all relevant cases, the reference of an individual's own word is semantically indeterminate: determinateness only appears in the idiolects of the 'experts'. (I am not sure whether Chomsky intends the proposal in this way.) Sometimes the reference of a relevant term is incomplete or vague. But sometimes, even in cases where the individual's substantive *knowledge in explicating* features of the referent is vague, incomplete, or riddled with false belief, the reference is as determinate as anyone else's. The reference of an individual's word is not always dependent on what the individual knows or can specify about the referent. When the individual defers to others, it is not in all cases to sharpen or fix the reference, but to sharpen the individual's explicative knowledge of a referent that is already fixed. Our and the individual's own attitudes toward the specification of the reference often makes this clear (see n. 5).

For present purposes, brief reflection on various natural kind terms that we use without expert knowledge should make the point intuitive. One might use 'feldspar', 'tiger', 'helium', 'water', 'oak', or 'spider', with definite referents even though one cannot oneself use one's background knowledge to distinguish the referent from all possible counterfeits. Knowledge obtained from better-informed people – they need not be experts – often tells one more about the standard kinds we all refer to with these words. It does not *in general* change the referents of our words. (This is not to deny that sometimes experts' terms have different, more technical meaning than lay usage of the same word forms.) The referents of such kind terms is simply not fixed entirely by the individual's background knowledge. Individuals often recognize this about their own terms. Although this point could be supported through numerous cases, and through more general considerations, I think that it is fairly evident on reflection. I shall assume it in what follows.

Even granted this qualification, Chomsky's proposal will not provide a complete account of the individual's own language – or even of the individual's knowledge of his or her idiolect. For in some cases, an individual's explicational ability not only does not suffice to fix the referent of the individual's word; it does not exhaust the meaning expressed by a word in the individual's idiolect.

I distinguish between a lexical item and the explication of its meaning that articulates what the individual would give, under some reflection, as his understanding of the word. Call the former 'the word' and the latter 'the entry for the word'. I also distinguish between the concept associated with the word and the concept(s) associated with the entry. Call the former 'the concept' and the latter 'the conceptual explication'. Finally, I distinguish between a type of meaning associated with the word, 'translational meaning', and the meaning associated with its entry, 'explicational meaning'. For our purposes, the explicational meaning is the semantical analog of the conceptual explication. The translational meaning of a word can be articulated through exact translation and sometimes through such trivial thoughts as *my word 'tiger' applies to tigers*, but need not be exhaustively expressible in other terms in an idiolect.

A traditional view in semantics is that a word's explicational meaning and its translational meaning are, for purposes of characterizing the individual's idiolect, always interchangeable; and that the individual's conceptual explication always completely exhausts his or her concept. This view is incorrect. It is incorrect because of the role that the referent plays in individuating the concept and translational meaning, and because of the role that non-explicational abilities play in the individual's application of the word and concept. Accounting for a person's lexical entry or conceptual explication is relevant to determining the nature of a person's meaning or concept. But the two enterprises are not the same. I will try to give some sense for why this is so.

Let us begin by concentrating on the large class of nouns and verbs that apply to everyday, empirically discernible objects, stuffs, properties, and events. I have in mind words like 'tiger', 'water', 'mud', 'stone', 'tree', 'bread', 'knife', 'chair', 'edge', 'shadow', 'baby', 'walk', 'fight', and so on. Except for tense, these words are not and do not contain indexicals in any ordinary sense. Given only that their meaning in the language is fixed, their applications or referents are fixed. They do not depend for their applications on particular contexts of use; nor do they shift their applications systematically with context or with the referential intentions of speakers. Without contextual explication or relativization, we can trivially, but correctly, state their ranges of applications: 'tiger' applies to tigers; 'walk' applies to instances of walking; and so on. Contrast: 'then' applies to then. This latter explication requires a particular context to do its job, a particular, context-dependent application of 'then' to a salient time. The constancy of application of non-indexical words, within particular idiolects, is a feature of their meaning and of the way that they are understood by their users.

Although the reference of these words is not all there is to their semantics, their reference places a constraint on their meaning, or on what concept they express. In particular, any such word w has a different meaning (or expresses a different concept) from a given word w' if their constant referents, or ranges of application, are different. That is part of what it is to be a non-indexical word of this type.[8]

The individual's explicational beliefs about the referents of such words, his conceptual explications, do not always fix such words' referents, even in his idiolect. So, by the considerations of the previous paragraph, they do not always fix such words' meanings or concepts in the individual's idiolect.

The point that explicational beliefs do not always fix reference is substantiated not only through the examples that have dominated the theory of reference for the last forty years (see n. 5). It is also supported by considering the dialectic by which we arrive at conceptual explications, or lexical entries.

Sometimes such explications are meant to produce approximate synonymies (as in the explication of 'knife'). Other times, not ('tiger', 'water'). In the cases we are discussing, applications of the words are backed by and learned through perceptual experience. Perceptually fixed examples typically determine the application of the word before conceptual explications do.[9]

Conceptual explications are typically inferences from these perceptual experiences, or general epithets derived from the remarks of others, or both. In attempting to articulate one's conception of one's concept, one's conceptual explication, one naturally alternates between thinking of examples and refining one's conceptual explication in order to accord with examples that one recognizes as legitimate. It is crucial here to note that the legitimacy of examples does not in general derive from one's attempts at conceptual explication. Although sometimes examples are shown to be legitimate or illegitimate by reference to such explications, the normal order – in the class of words that we are discussing – is the other way around. The examples, first arrived at through perception, tend to be the touchstone for evaluating attempts at conceptual explication.

Consider the sort of dialectic in which people try to arrive at an explication of the meanings of their words. First attempts are usually seen to be mistaken. Reflection on examples leads to improvements. The altered characterizations improve on one's characterization of a referent that is assumed to have been fixed. (They are not normally mere sharpenings of reference, or changes in the meanings of one's word.) They are equally improvements in one's conceptual understanding of one's own concept or meaning.

Such dialectic typically adds to one's knowledge. Suppose I explicate my word 'chair' in a way that requires that chairs have legs, and then come to realize that beach chairs, or deck-chairs bolted to a wall, or ski-lift chairs, are counterexamples. Or suppose that I learn more about how to discriminate water from other (possible or actual) colorless, tasteless, potable liquids. In such cases, I learn something about chairs or water that I did not know before. In these cases it is simply not true that the reference of my words 'chair' and 'water' must change. Although it is true that my conception – my explication – changes, it remains possible for me to observe (with univocal use of 'chair'): 'I used to think chairs had to have legs, but now know that chairs need not have legs.' It remains possible for me to have thoughts about water as water, knowing that there might be other liquids that I could not, by means other than use of my concept *water*, discriminate from it. Thus there is a sense in which the concept, and the translational meaning of the word in the idiolect, remain the same despite the changed discriminating ability, or change in explication.

Of course, my ability to come up with better explications by considering examples with which I am already familiar indicates that I have more to go on than my initial explications suggest. Perhaps I have 'tacitly cognized' more than what I give as my reflective explication, before I arrive consciously at a better explication.

I think that this view is right. But it would be a mistake to infer that I always already know the correct explication in some suppressed way. It would be an even more serious mistake to infer that our tacit conceptual explications exhaust our concepts. There are several reasons why these moves are unsound.

In the first place, the dialectic involves genuine reasoning – using materials at hand to form a better conception. Granting that we have the materials in our mental repertoires to form a better conception does not amount to granting that we have already put them together. Reflection on the examples seems to play a role in doing this. When I give a mistaken explication of 'chair', I may have failed to hold empirical information in my memory, or failed to put together things that I knew separately. I may have failed to believe at the time of the explication that there were legless chairs, even though I had experience and even perhaps knowledge from which I could have derived this belief. Thus the sort of unconscious or tacit cognition that is involved is not just an unconscious analog of having reflective knowledge of the proposition formed by linking the concept and the improved conceptual explication. Attribution of tacit cognition entails only that the mental structures for deriving the recognition of examples are in place and will (ideally) lead to such recognition, when examples are presented.

In the second place, there is substantial evidence that some of the 'underlying' materials are stored in our perceptual capacities and are not, properly speaking, conceptualized (see n. 9). We are often able to project our concept (e.g. *chair*) to new cases never before considered. Often this projection seems to be based on perceptual capacities that are modular and preconceptual. Thus the 'materials' that are put together and worked up into conceptual explications through the process of dialectic sometimes do not, before reflection begins, appear to be the right sort to count as criterial knowledge, even unconscious criterial knowledge.

In the third place, even the perceptual abilities need not suffice to discriminate instances of the concept from every possible look-alike – from look-alikes that might have been normal in other environments, and which in that case might have determined other concepts; but which play no role in the formation of concepts in the speaker's actual environment. The explicated concepts are determined to be what they are by the actual nature of objects and events that we can perceptually discriminate from other relevantly similar things in the same environment. Thus even our perceptual abilities and our conceptual explications combined need not provide necessary and sufficient conditions for the correct application of our concepts in all possible environments in which the concepts have a definite application. They therefore need not fully exhaust the content of our concepts.

There is a more general reason why our explicational abilities, including our unconscious ones, do not in general and necessarily suffice to exhaust the concepts that they serve to explicate. One's cognitive relation to the examples that played an initial role in fixing one's concept is perceptual. That relation inherits the fallibility of perceptual experience. Since the concepts under discussion are not merely given by conceptual explications, but are partly fixed through examples in the environment, their conceptual explications must correctly describe the examples. Conceptual explications (and dictionary entries) are not normally true by logic and stipulation. They are true because they capture examples that are fixed partly through perceptual experience. But our cognitive relations to the examples are fallible. So the conceptual explications and dictionary entries that sum up our current discriminative abilities are fallible. The things that we perceive and that fix our concepts may not be just as we see and characterize them. Yet they may be genuine instances of the concepts. And we are subject to misidentifying other things that fit our perceptual schemas and conceptual explications as instances of our concepts, when they are not. So those schemas and explications do not necessarily exhaust the concepts or meanings that they explicate.[10]

Our commitment to getting the examples right is part of our understanding of the relevant class of words and concepts. This commitment is illustrated in, indeed explains, many cases of our *standing corrected* by others in our attempts to explicate our own words and concepts. Such correction, by oneself or by others, is common in the course of the dialectic. One sees oneself as having made a mistake about the meaning of one's own word, in one's explication of one's own concept.

Some philosophers have characterized all cases of standing corrected as pliant shifts of communicative strategy. According to this view, I previously used 'chair' in my idiolect with a meaning that did in fact exclude legless chairs. But on encountering resistance from others, I tacitly shift my meaning so as to surmount practical obstacles to communication or fellowship that would result from maintaining an idiosyncratic usage.[11]

I agree, of course, that such practically motivated changes occur. But they cannot explain all cases of our standing corrected. For such correction is often – I would say, typically – founded on substantive, empirical matters about which there are cognitive rights and wrongs. We make mistakes, sometimes empirically correctable mistakes, that others catch, and that bear on the proper explication of the meaning of words in our idiolects. In such cases we come to understand our idiolects better.

Others are sometimes better placed than we are to judge the fit between our proposed lexical entries, or our conceptual explications, and the examples to which our words or concepts apply. Thus we may correctly see others as sometimes understanding our own idiolects better than we do. When we defer to someone else's linguistic authority, it is partly because the other person has superior empirical insight, insight that bears on the proper characterization of examples to which our words or concepts apply. The reason for their insight is not that they have made a study of us. It is also not that they are foisting some foreign, socially authorized standard on us. It is that they understand their idiolects better than we understand ours, and they have a right to assume that our idiolects are in relevant respects similar, or the same.

The justification of this assumption, also fallible, has two main sources. One is the publicity of the examples and our shared perceptual and inferential equipment. Given that we have been exposed to substantially similar knives, chairs, water, trees, mud, walkings, and fightings, and have heard these associated with the same words, it is to be expected that we project from actual examples in similar ways. Although our kind-forming abilities may differ in some instances, it is reasonable to expect that they will typically be the same, especially with concepts that apply to entities of common perceptual experience. Normally we will be committed to the legitimacy of the same examples, and will be committed to characterizing those examples, correctly. Given that the examples are public, no one has privileged authority about their characteristics.

A second source of the assumption that others can correct one's explications is that a person's access to the examples – to the applications that help fix the relevant concept – is partly or fully through others. Words are initially acquired from others, who are already applying those words to cases. Word acquisition occurs in conjunction with acquisition of information, information from testimony, or communication with others, about those cases.

Of course, until the learner develops some minimal amount of background knowledge and likeness of application, he or she cannot be said to have acquired the word in the predecessor's sense, or with the predecessor's range of applications. But as we have seen in the preceding paragraphs, possession of an infallible explication is not required – because it is not possible.

The dependence on others for access to examples grows as one's linguistic and cognitive resources widen. In some cases we depend heavily on the perceptual experience of others (as with 'tiger', 'penguin' and 'rain', for those of us in California). In other cases we depend on theoretical background knowledge ('gene', 'cancer') or on more ordinary expertise ('arthritis', 'carburetor'). In many such cases, we intentionally take over the applications that others have made. We rely on their experience to supplement our own. And we accept corrections of our explications from them because they have better access to the examples which partly determine the nature of our concepts. Although the function of explication varies significantly in these various cases, the main points of the argument for social dependence apply equally, indeed even more obviously, to terms that are less closely associated with direct perception.

Since fixing examples – or more broadly, referents – that partly determine an individual's concept or translational meaning is sometimes dependent on the activity of others with whom he interacts, the individuation of an individual's concepts or translational meanings is sometimes dependent on his interaction with others. Even where the individual has epistemic access to the examples independently of others (for example, where he perceives instances directly), others may have superior knowledge of the examples. They may therefore have superior insight into the proper explication of the individual's words and concepts: they may have put together relevant cognitive materials in a way that provides standards for understanding the individual's words and concepts. In such cases, the individual's deference may be cognitively appropriate.

The cases in which the individual does and does not have independent access to the examples might seem to be significantly different. The former case might be seen as showing only that others may know more about the explication of the individual's meanings and concepts than he does, and that it is easier to understand an individual's idiolect by studying idiolects and attitudes of others. One might still insist, relative to this case, that the materials for determining the individual's concepts or meanings do not involve the individual's relations to others.

Though I need not contest this point for the sake of present argument, I doubt that it is correct. It is metaphysically possible for an individual to learn his idiolect in isolation from a community. But it is no accident, and not merely a consequence of a convenient practical strategy, that one obtains insight into an idiolect by considering the usage and attitudes of others. In learning words, individuals normally look to others to help set standards for determining the range of legitimate examples and the sort of background information used in explicating a word or concept. I believe that this is a psychological necessity for human beings.

The second case, where the individual has had limited relevant access to the examples independently of others, provides independent ground for thinking that individuation of an individual's concepts or meanings is sometimes dependent on the social interactions that the individual engages in. If others had provided access to a different range of examples, compatible with one's minimal background information, one would have had different meanings or concepts.

Let me summarize the argument that an individual's idiolect and concepts cannot be fully understood apart from considering the language and concepts of others with whom he interacts. Numerous empirically applicable words are non-indexical. Non-indexical words must have different translational meanings, and express different concepts, if their referents are different. Our explicational abilities, and indeed all our cognitive mastery, regarding the referents of such words and concepts do not necessarily fix the referents. Nor therefore (by the first premise) do they necessarily fix the translational meanings or concepts associated with the words. To be correct, our lexical entries and conceptual explications are subject to correction or confirmation by empirical consideration of the referents. Since such empirical consideration is fallible, our cognitive relations to the referents are fallible. Others are often in a better position to arrive at a correct articulation of our word or concept, because they are in a better position to determine relevant empirical features of the referents. This, for two reasons: the referents are public, so no one has privileged authority regarding their properties; and we are frequently dependent on others for linking our words to the referents and for access to the referents. Since the referents play a necessary role in individuating the person's concept or translational meaning, individuation of an individual's concepts or translational meanings may depend on the activity of others on whom the individual is dependent for acquisition of and access to the referents. If the others by acting differently had put one in touch with different referents, compatibly with one's minimum explicational abilities, one would have had different concepts or translational meanings.[12] Although I have argued only that this conclusion derives from obvious facts of social interaction, I have conjectured that it derives from psychological necessities for human beings.

The argument does not depend on assuming that people ever share the same concepts or translational meanings.[13] However, the argument makes it plausible that people in a community do often share concepts and translational meanings, despite differences in their beliefs about the world, and even differences in their explications of the relevant terms. Most empirically applicable concepts are fixed by three factors: by actual referents encountered through experience – one's own, one's fellows', or one's species ancestors', or indirectly through theory; by some rudimentary conceptualization of the examples – learned or innately possessed by virtually everyone who comes in contact with the terms; and by perceptual information, inferential capacities, and kind-forming abilities, that may be pre-conceptual. The referents are often shared, because of similarity of experience and because of intentional reliance on others for examples. So the concepts and translational meanings associated with many words will be shared. Shared idiolectal meanings and shared concepts derive from a shared empirical world and shared cognitive goals and procedures in coming to know that world.[14]

Traditional philosophy tended to ignore the first and third factors in concept determination, and to expand the second into the requirement of necessary and sufficient conditions that 'define' the meaning or concept and that must be believed if one is to have the relevant concept at all. The dissolution of this picture makes possible an appreciation of the dependence of the individuation of our empirical concepts on direct or indirect perceptual relations to our empirical environment.

Drawing on these ideas, together with obvious facts about social interaction, I have tried to show that idiolects are social in two senses. First, in many cases we must, on cognitive grounds, defer to others in the explication of our words. Second, the individuation of our concepts and meanings is sometimes dependent on the activity of others from whom we learn our words and on whom we depend for access to the referents of our words. The second sense grounds the view that individual psychology and the study of the semantics of idiolects are not wholly independent of assumptions of interaction among individuals.

Notes

1 Chomsky, 1986, p. 18. Chomsky recognizes the possibility of 'other kinds of study of language that incorporate social structure and interaction'. Chomsky's methodology for studying language goes back to *Aspects of the Theory of Syntax*, 1965.

2 This view hinges not only on intuitive linguistic data but on studies of development, learning, psychological simplicity, language deficit, psychological processing, and so on. See e.g. Chomsky 1981, ch. 1.

3 'Non-individualistic' in this context does not entail 'social'. The environment can be either physical surroundings or social surroundings. I begin with physical surroundings alone.

  The arguments against individualism that I shall be presupposing may be found in Burge, 1979; 1982; 1986(a), (b) and (c). Different arguments bring out different environmental interdependencies.

4 Are syntactical elements and structures individualistically individuated? This question is close to the issue regarding the autonomy of syntax. But one should not identify the two questions. The discussions of the autonomy of syntax concern whether some non-syntactical parameter must be mentioned in stating syntactical generalizations. Our question concerns not the parameters mentioned in stating rules of syntax, but the individuation of the syntactical elements. Syntax could be non-individualistic and yet be autonomous (see the preceding paragraph in the text). Evidence has been suggesting that syntax is much more nearly autonomous than common sense might have realized. My reasons for thinking that individual psychology is non-individualistic in its individuation of some thought kinds have nothing directly to do with syntax. They derive purely from considerations that, within the study of language, would be counted semantic. What is at issue then is whether because of some functional relation to semantics, some syntactical kinds are non-individualistically individuated.

  I think it arguable that much of syntax is individualistically individuated, or at least no less individualistically individuated than ordinary neural or biological kinds are. But it seems likely that lexical items are individuated in a content-sensitive way. Words or morphemes with the same phonetic and structural-syntactic properties are distinguished because of etymological or other semantical differences. Even if it turned out that every such lexical difference were accompanied by other syntactic or phonological differences, it would seem plausible that the latter differences were dependent on the former. So it seems plausible that the lexical differences do not supervene (in our specified sense) on other syntactic or phonological differences.

  Although most philosophers write as if only word types are ambiguous, it is clear that word tokens are often ambiguous. It is arguable that *only* word tokens, never word types, are ambiguous. I do not find this view plausible: words with different but etymologically and semantically related senses are individuated as the same word type. But the view is a useful antidote to habits in thé philosophy of language. In any case, word individuation appears to be semantically dependent.

  Assuming this to be true, and assuming that semantics is non-individualistic, it follows that what it is to be a given word sometimes depends (in the way that what it is to be a given meaning or concept depends) on relations between the individual and the objective, empirical world. *Whether* this is true about lexical items, and how far it might extend beyond the individuation of lexical items, is a question I leave open here. The answer will not very much affect the practice of generative grammar, since environmental relations need not be mentioned in syntax. But it will affect our understanding of the place of syntax in our wider theorizing about the world.

Similar issues might be raised about some universal syntactic categories (animate, agent, etc.). And as James Higginbotham has pointed out to me, analogous questions may be raised about the relation between phonology and ordinary perception. Ordinary perceptual kinds are not individualistically individuated (see n. 6). It may be that this fact should affect our understanding of perception studies in phonology.

5 This view, though not trivial, is a consequence of a view that is widely accepted. It is a consequence of the work of Donnellan and Kripke, and indeed Wittgenstein, on reference. I will not defend it here. But I will develop a reason for its inevitability below. Numerous examples indicate that an individual's proper names, kind terms, demonstratives, and various other parts of speech have definite referents even though the individual could not, by other means, discriminate the referent from other possible or actual entities that might have been in an appropriate relation to the individual's words – other entities that might have been the referent even though the individual's body could have remained molecularly the same. See Kripke, 1980; Donnellan, 1972; Hilary Putnam, 1975; and numerous other works.

6 See Marr, 1982 for a very explicit statement of the non-individualistic methodology. For a more general review of the point that anti-individualistic individuation is implicit in all scientific theories of perception, see Stillings, 1987. For the cited philosophical arguments, see Burge 1986(a) and (b). The former article discusses Marr's theory. For perception, the point is really pretty obvious even apart from philosophical argument: perceptual states are individuated by reference to physical properties that bear appropriate relations to the subjects' states or those of his species-ancestors.

Although Chomsky does not discuss non-individualistic features of the visual system, he clearly makes a place for psychological states that have a different genesis and different conditions for individuation from those psychological states that constitute the structures of universal grammar. He counts such states part of the 'conceptual system', and uses vision as a prime example (see Chomsky, 1980).

7 Chomsky, 1986, p. 18. The relevant articles by Hilary Putnam are 1975(a) and (b).

8 The ontology of meanings or concepts is unimportant for these purposes. But I assume the standard view that the meaning or concept should not be identified with the word – since different words could express the same meaning or concept, and the same word can express different meanings or concepts. I assume also that the meaning or concept should not be identified with the referent, since a meaning or concept is a way of speaking or thinking about the referent. Of course, sometimes words express meanings or concepts that have no referent. And meanings or concepts normally have vague boundaries of application.

The point about non-indexicality can be established on purely linguistic grounds. I discuss the non-indexicality of the relevant words in more detail in Burge, 1982.

9 This point is now common not only in the philosophical literature (see Putnam, 1975(a) and (b) and Burge, 1982), but also in the psychological literature. Cf. Eleanor Rosch and Barbara Lloyd, 1978; Edward Smith and Douglas Medin, 1981. For excellent philosophical discussion of this literature, with criticism of some of its excesses, see Bernard Kobes (1986, ch. 6).

10 I have discussed other problems with exhaustive conceptual explications (1982; 1986c).

11   See Donald Davidson, 1987.

12   I think that this argument admits of an important extension. The argument derives non-individualistic variation in an individual's meanings or concepts from variation in empirical referents to which the community provides access. But the variation need not occur in the referents. It may depend on the nature of our cognitive access through the community to the examples. The variation may occur in the way the referents are approached in the community. Thus it may be that the referents are held fixed, but the community's cognitive access to them may vary in such a way as to vary the concept, without varying the effect on the individual's body or rudimentary explicational abilities. This extension is, I think, a corollary of the Fregean observation that referents (or examples) do not determine meanings or concepts. Since my purpose has been to establish a minimal sense in which language is social, I shall not illustrate or develop this extension here.

13   This is also true of the argument in Burge 1979. The conclusion can rest on the mere assumption that the referents of the concepts in the actual and counterfactual communities are different. (Loar (1988) seems mistakenly and crucially to assume the contrary in his critical discussion of 'Individualism and the mental'.) For all that, I know of no persuasive reason for thinking that in every relevant case the person in the actual community cannot share his concept or meaning (e.g. *arthritis*) with his fellows.

14   So it appears that there is an element of meaning that can remain constant and common across individuals, despite the interdependence of meaning and belief noted at the outset. It is notable that this constancy in no way depends on the assumption of a distinction between sentences that are *true* purely by virtue of their meaning and sentences that depend for their truth on the way the subject-matter is. (Like Quine, I find this distinction empty.) See Burge 1986(c). Belief in the relevant element of meaning does not even depend on invocation of a distinction between criterial or linguistic truths and other sorts of truths (although like Chomsky and unlike Quine, I think that this latter distinction, commonly conflated with the previous one, is clearly defensible).

     Another point about the semantics of word meaning bears emphasizing. There is a relevant semantical distinction between cases in which the individual has sufficient materials in his conceptual repertoire to construct a given lexical entry, maximally faithful to the range of applications or examples that he recognizes as legitimate, and cases in which the individual's dependence on others is such that his repertoire allows only entries that are less full than those of others. In the latter cases, it is *not true*, on my view, that the 'communal' entry is the 'correct' entry within the person's idiolect. I take it that lexical entries sum up an idealized conceptual understanding. If the person lacks resources to arrive at some given entry, the entry is not a part of his idiolect.

     But it does not *follow* from this difference that the person does not have the same concept, or the same translational meaning, that others have. To think this would be to confuse concept and conceptual explication, or translational meaning and explicational understanding. In not sharing this explication with others, the person will not fully share an understanding of the word (or the conception of the concept) with others. But lexical entries (conceptual explications) do not determine the translational meaning (concepts); they may even be mistaken, and only contingently related to it. The person still has his or her perceptual abilities for picking out referents, and the relevant referents may still be partly fixed by the person's reliance on others. Thus as far as present considerations go, the person's concept may be shared with others even though his or her conceptual explication or lexical entry may differ.

References

Burge, Tyler 1979: Individualism and the mental. *Midwest Studies*. 4, 73–121.
1982: Other bodies. In A. Woodfield (ed.), *Thought and Object*. Oxford University Press.
1986a: Individualism and psychology. *The Philosophical Review*, 125, 3–45.
1986b: Cartesian error and the objectivity of perception. In P. Pettit and J. McDowell (eds). *Subject, Thought and Context*. Oxford University Press.
1986c: Intellectual norms and foundations of mind. *The Journal of Philosophy*, 83, 697–720.
Chomsky, Noam 1965: *Aspects of the Theory of Syntax*. Cambridge, Mass.: MIT Press.
1980: *Rules and Representations*. Oxford: Basil Blackwell.
1981: *Lectures on Government and Binding*. Dordrect: Foris.
1986: *Knowledge of Language: Its Nature, Origin, and Use*. New York: Praeger.
Davidson, Donald 1987: Knowing one's own mind. *Proceedings and Addresses of the American Philosophical Association*, 60.
Donnellan, Keith 1972: Proper names and identifying descriptions. In D. Davidson and G. Harman (eds), *Semantics of Natural Languages*. Dordrecht: Reidel.
Kripke, Saul 1980: *Naming and Necessity*. Cambridge, Mass.: Harvard University Press.
Kobes, Bernard 1986: Individualism and the cognitive sciences. Unpublished dissertation. University of California at Los Angeles.
Loar, Brian 1988: Social content and psychological content in Robert Grimm and Daniel Merrill (eds), *Contents of Thought*. Tucson: University of Arizona Press.
Marr, David 1982: *Vision*. San Francisco: W.H. Freeman and Co.
Putnam, Hilary 1975a: Is semantics possible? Repr. in *Philosophical Papers*, vol. 2, Cambridge University Press.
1975b: The meaning of 'meaning'. Repr. in *Philosophical Papers*, vol. 2, Cambridge University Press.
Rosch, Eleanor and Lloyd, Barbara 1978: *Cognition and Categorization*. Erlbaum.
Smith, Edward and Medin, Douglas 1981: *Categories and Concepts*. Cambridge, Mass.: Harvard University Press.
Stillings, Neil 1987: Modularity and naturalism in theories of vision. In J.L. Garfield (ed.), *Modularity in Knowledge Representation and Natural-Language Understanding*. Cambridge, Mass.: MIT Press.

10

Language and Communication

Michael Dummett

Language, it is natural to say, has two principal functions: that of an instrument of communication, and that of a vehicle of thought. We are therefore impelled to ask which of the two is primary. Is it because language is an instrument of communication that it can also serve as a vehicle of thought? Or is it, conversely, because it is a vehicle of thought, and can therefore express thoughts, that it can be used by one person to communicate his thoughts to others?

A view that might claim to represent common sense is that the primary function of language is to be used as an instrument of communication, and that, when so used, it operates as a code for thought. On this view, it is only because we happen to lack a faculty for directly transmitting thoughts from mind to mind that we are compelled to encode them in sounds or marks on paper. If we had the faculty, therefore, we should have no need of language. But the corollary conflicts with common sense: namely that language is not a vehicle of thought at all. Common sense exclaims against this that surely we often think in words: but the advocate of the code theory of language, if he has his wits about him, will reply that we never do any such thing, indeed, that the very notion is unintelligible. Rather, words, spoken aloud or rehearsed in the imagination, often *accompany* our thoughts, but in no way embody them. For, if we should not need language but for the need to communicate our thoughts, we must be capable of having *naked* thoughts (to vary the metaphor once again) – thoughts devoid of linguistic or other representational clothing: thoughts may represent the world, but, to have thoughts, we need nothing that represents *them*. Thus thoughts do not *need* a representation, although, for purposes of communication, they may be verbally represented; and from this it follows that a thought cannot exist – cannot be present to the mind – merely through some verbal or other symbolic representation, which is what it would be for the representation to be the vehicle or embodiment of the thought. The whole substance of the code theory of language is that the speaker encodes his thought as a sentence and the hearer decodes the sentence as that thought: but, if language could be the vehicle of thought, the hearer would not need to decode the utterance nor the speaker to have encoded the thought in the first place. Either no thoughts have vehicles or all thoughts must have them.

What we call 'thinking in words' is, then, according to the code theory of language, one of two things. It may be thinking *about* how to express our thoughts in words, as with someone rehearsing a speech or lecture or writing a book or article. On this view, we should resist the illusion that the thought is not fully formed until it is articulated in words: it need no more be so than it is for the translator who is considering how to express in a sentence of one language the thought expressed in one of another language.

More usually, the code theorist maintains, the relation of the words to the thought is that of the sound to the written letters. Someone who is fluent in reading a given script, say Roman script, cannot see a written or printed word, for instance a name at a railway station, without mentally attaching a pronunciation to it. If it belongs to a language of whose pronunciation he is uncertain, he may have no confidence that he is mentally pronouncing it correctly; but he is as unable to read it dissociated from any phonetic value as he is unable to see it as one illiterate in that script would do (or as he himself would see a word in a script of which he was ignorant). Likewise, according to the code theorist, we are so overwhelmingly accustomed to speech in our mother-tongue, or sometimes in other languages, that, except in moments of emergency, we are unable to entertain thoughts in the forefront of our minds without putting them into words: and so we fall victims to the illusion that the words embody the thought, whereas they merely adorn it. But, he urges, try repeatedly going over, aloud or silently, some familiar words – a well-known quotation or an often-used formula – not abstractedly, but with attention. However hard you try to fasten your attention on the words, you will keep having, in the background or, as it were, skimming between the words, wisps of thought, which you could without difficulty express: and ask yourself whether these background thoughts are also in words. Surely you will agree that they are naked thoughts, he says: the whole conception of thinking 'in' words is spurious. An amusing example occurred in a novel I recently read, in which a character remarked that she was interested to note, while she was thinking through some question, that she did so entirely verbally, thus confirming her long-held opinion that all our thinking is in words: her interlocutor failed to ask her whether her thought, 'I am thinking in words', was itself in words.

The question was one which exercised Wittgenstein, as illustrated by the following quotation from the *Philosophical Investigations*, in which I thought it best to replace the word 'pen' by 'pencil'.

> Speak the line, 'Yes, the pencil is blunt: oh, well, it will do', first thinking it; then without thought; and then just think the thought without the words. (I, 330.)

Wittgenstein goes on to describe a case in which someone would naturally be described as having had just that thought without words; but remarks that 'what constitutes thought here is not some process which has to accompany the words if they are not to be spoken without thought'. His idea is surely that, if it were, it would not be difficult to obey the instruction, 'Just think the thought without the words', whereas it needs a quite special kind of background to make sense of saying of someone that he had such a thought, but not in words. We could say – although Wittgenstein himself does not expressly say this – that thought needs a vehicle of some kind, although this may not consist of words, but of something quite different like actions.

The difficulty of obeying the instruction to think the thought without the words is, however, due, in part, to the ambiguity of the term 'thinking'. When Wittgenstein speaks of someone's uttering the sentence, 'The pencil is blunt', thinking it, he does not mean his doing what would ordinarily be described as thinking that the pencil is blunt: there may be no pencil around, or, if there is, it may be quite evidently sharp. Wittgenstein means, rather, that he utters the sentence aware of what the words mean. In Frege's terminology, he grasps the thought expressed by the sentence, without necessarily judging it to be true; or, rather, since no definite thought will be expressed in the absence of any salient pencil, he attends to the meanings of the words, considered independently of any occasion of utterance. Now suppose someone were to say to me, 'Think that the pencil is blunt', or, 'Think the thought that the pencil is blunt', without raising the question whether I am to think in words or without them: even if it is obvious which pencil is being referred to, what am I to do? If 'think' is to be taken in its most usual sense, as in contexts like, 'I suddenly thought that this would be my last chance of getting a meal that night', then it means 'judge' rather than merely 'grasp', and I might answer, 'I cannot have thoughts to order: the pencil just isn't blunt at all.' If, on the other hand, 'think' is being used to mean 'entertain the thought', with no implication that it is to be taken as true, then again I am in difficulties, this time because I cannot help but have obeyed the command as soon as it was given: for just understanding the command involved grasping the thought that the pencil was blunt.

It is plain that having a thought is something of a quite different kind from uttering a sentence: it is not merely in a different medium, as it were, but of a different character. A policeman shows me a photograph, and asks, 'Have you ever seen this man?': I study the photograph, perhaps trying and failing to evoke a feeling of familiarity, perhaps running through in my mind the facial appearance of a range of slight acquaintances, decide I have never seen the man, and answer, 'No.' In the context of the question, the word 'No' expresses the thought, 'I have never seen this man.' I may have had that thought just before answering, or my answer may have been the first embodiment of my thought. In neither case, however, would it be natural to say that I thought, 'No': only that I thought, 'I have never seen him.' For all that, the thought came to me with no greater articulation than the one-word answer. This is because the content of a thought is much *more* determined by context than that of an utterance. If, for example, I am walking out of my house, the coming to mind of a single personal name, or of an image of the person's face, may constitute my having the thought, 'I've left the book I promised So-and-so behind.' Thoughts, when not framed in sentences, are not framed in some mental language private to the thinker: they are, rather, embodied in (inner or outer) *reactions* which, in the whole context, are intelligible only as embodying those thoughts. We give verbal reports of such thoughts, at the time or later: asked by my companion, 'Why are you turning back?' I will say, 'I've left So-and-so's book behind'; recounting my day hours afterwards, I may say, 'Just as I was leaving the house, I thought, "I've left So-and-so's book behind".' Such a report may be called an *interpretation*: it is not read off from an inner tape recorder, but is, as it were, *ascribed* to oneself on the basis of the remembered stimuli and reactions to them. This ponderous terminology, of interpretation and ascription, is not intended to suggest that there is anything dubious about a report of this kind. On the contrary, although my inner reactions, or the inner stimuli that prompted them, may have been hidden from view, anyone who knew what they were, and knew enough about my background, would put the same interpretation on them.

This fact is sufficient to show that, when someone reports his unverbalised or unarticulated thoughts, he is not recalling some inner utterance in a language of the mind: on a few occasions, he may contradict an interpretation suggested by another in favour of a different one, but he cannot intelligibly lay claim to a thought that fails to make sense of his actions and reactions. It is for this reason that the code conception of language is untenable. For language to be a code for thought, thoughts have to be like sentences, and have constituents analogous to words, and the thought-constituents must be matched to the words by some process of association. A word will then evoke the associated thought-constituent in the mind of the hearer, and, for one who wishes to communicate his thought, its constituents will evoke the corresponding words. But this fantasy will not serve as an account of our understanding of language, because there is no such thing as a thought-constituent's coming to mind, independently of any word or symbol that expresses it. To suppose that such a mental event can occur is to have an altogether primitive picture of the character of thinking.

The point is obscured when the term 'thought' is used in Frege's way: for Fregean thoughts indeed have constituents, and, for a sentence to *express* such a thought, there must be a certain match between its composition and that of the thought. For instance, no one could have the thought that Venus has an elliptical orbit without possessing the concept of an ellipse; and, in accordance with Gareth Evans's 'Generality Constraint' (1982, pp. 100–5) this requires that he be able to think of other things as elliptical. Moreover, to grasp a thought involves an apprehension of its complexity: one could not think that the orbit of Venus is an ellipse without being aware that one could judge other shapes to be or not to be ellipses. What does not, in general, have an analogous structure is the *thinking* of the thought – the inner or outer process that, against the necessary background, constitutes having that thought. This is why Frege rightly held that thoughts, in his sense, and their component concepts or senses, are not contents of the mind, as a mental image is: a mental content, as here understood, must be something whose presence does not depend upon there being any particular background.

Were the code theory of language tenable, it would be easy to explain how the words and sentences of a language have the meanings that they do; but it would still be necessary to give a philosophical explanation of what a thought is. For a thought does not resemble a mental image or a sensation: it has the distinctive feature of being, or at least of being capable of being, true or false, and thus relating to reality external to the mind. The same may, of course, be said of a mental image, in so far as it is apprehended as an image *of* a particular thing, and even of a sensation, in so far as it is taken as engendered by some non-mental object or event. A mental image or sensation, considered as such, does not, however, *have* to be so apprehended: it can exist simply as a constituent of inner experience, unintegrated with an awareness of external reality. For this reason, it is highly plausible that what renders an image the image of a certain object is nothing intrinsic to it as an image, but a concomitant *thought* to the effect that it represents that object, and similarly for sensations: hence, if this is right, thought remains unique in its representative character. This representative character requires philosophical explanation. Mental images and sensations are sufficiently explained when a description has been given of what it is like to have them: but a description of what it is like to have a thought, were it possible to give such a thing, would be quite inadequate as a philosophical account of thoughts, since it could not encompass what makes them capable of possessing a truth-value.

The failure of the code theory of language leaves us without an explanation of what it is for an expression of a language to have a meaning. But, if that cannot be explained in terms of a coding of thoughts into sentences by means of an association between words and thought-constituents, it must be explained in such a way as to make manifest how sentences serve to express thoughts, without taking as given a prior understanding of what a thought is. Just such an explanation was in effect essayed by Frege. He insisted that the important thing was the thought, not the sentence; he claimed that the existence of the thought did not depend upon its being grasped or expressed by any rational being; and he also claimed that there might exist beings who could grasp the very same thoughts as we do without needing to conceive them as clothed in language. But his semantic theory made no appeal to an antecedent conception of thoughts: the theory itself sought to explain what it is for a sentence to express a thought without invoking any conception, given in advance, of the thought that it expresses.

That is why Frege is rightly regarded as the grandfather of analytical philosophy, whose distinctive methodology, until quite recently, was to approach the philosophy of thought via the philosophy of language. From such a standpoint, the most important feature of language is that it serves as a vehicle of thought. It is not necessary, in order to adopt this standpoint, to deny that unverbalised thought is in principle possible, nor even to deny, as Frege did, that it is in practice possible for human beings. It is not necessary, either, to deny that thought is possible for creatures who have no language in which to express it. It is necessary only to believe that thought, by its nature, cannot occur without a vehicle, and that language is the vehicle whose operation is the most perspicuous and hence the most amenable to a systematic philosophical account. This is so for two reasons. First, the ascription to a subject of his having a given thought at a particular time can be justified only by the presence of an often extensive background to the occurrence of whatever served as the vehicle of the thought. In the ideal case when the vehicle is a fully explicit verbal expression of the thought, however, the only background to which appeal is needed is the existence of the language and the subject's knowledge of it – an immensely complex but structured phenomenon, relatively isolable from other circumstances. And, secondly, a fully explicit verbal expression is the only vehicle whose structure must reflect the structure of the thought.

From this standpoint, to analyse linguistic meaning along Gricean lines is to pursue an altogether misconceived strategy. When the utterance is an assertoric one, Strawson's version of such an analysis is given in terms of the hearer's recognition of the speaker's intention to communicate that he has a certain belief. McDowell's emendation, that what the speaker wishes to communicate is a piece of information, which may be about anything, rather than only about his own doxastic condition, is undoubtedly an improvement, for language is certainly used primarily as contributing to our transactions with the world, rather than as conveying to one another how it is with us in our thinking parts (McDowell, 1980, pp. 117–39). It is essential to our most basic acquisition of the practice of using a language that we learn to act on what others tell us; only as a more sophisticated by-product do we learn to use their utterances as revealing their beliefs, and, even then, *their* intention is still typically to inform us that what they say is so rather than to allow us a glimpse of their private convictions. Were it otherwise, it would be, as it were, an afterthought that we could, by making an unintended use of them, gain information from the assertions of others; and we should accept those assertions as true only on occasions on which we had particular reason to trust the speaker's veracity, rather than, as now, whenever we have no particular reason to doubt it.

McDowell's formulation and Strawson's both suffer, however, from an awkwardness in generalising them to utterances of all kinds, rather than merely assertoric ones: more importantly, both go astray by in effect helping themselves to the specific content of the utterance instead of explaining what confers that content upon it. Their formulations, in their ungeneralised forms, are candidates for being characterisations of *assertions*, as opposed to questions, requests, and so on: they purport to explain what it is to make an assertion with a certain content, given that we already grasp the notion of something's having that content. That is to say, they aim to characterise asserting that something is the case, on the assumption that we already know what it is to have the information that it is the case (McDowell), or to ascribe to someone a belief that it is the case (Strawson). However, being informed that such-and-such is so and believing that such-and-such is so both obviously involve having the *thought* that such-and-such is so: and thus this strategy of explanation takes as already given the conception of the thought expressed by a sentence, and, at most, explains what it is to assert that that thought is true.

The Gricean line of explanation is hence essentially no more than a sophisticated version of the code conception of language. To understand an assertoric utterance, I must understand two things: that it *is* assertoric, that is, serves to voice an assertion; and what, specifically, it is used to assert. Any explanation of linguistic meaning must, among other things, explain what features of such an utterance enable a hearer to recognise these two aspects of its significance. An explanation of what constitutes a grasp of the concept of being informed that something is so, or of that of believing that something is so, is certainly called for; but let us suppose that such an explanation is to hand. Assume, now, that I, as hearer, do grasp these concepts, and, further, that I am able to recognise the utterance in question as assertoric. What matters, much more than *how* I recognise this – what feature of the utterance indicates to me that this is its character – is what it is for me to take it, rightly or wrongly, as assertoric. Given that I have the general concept of information or of belief, this is at least arguably explicable in the manner of Grice, as amended by McDowell or otherwise. On any account of language, there remains to be explained which features of the utterance convey to me what, specifically, is being asserted: the content of the assertion or, in Frege's terminology, the thought asserted to be true. This formulation, however, makes it appear that we already have a clear conception of what it is for me to grasp the thought, and are concerned only to explain how I identify it as that which the sentence expresses; but, when the philosophy of language is treated as supplying the only route to a philosophical account of thinking, the formulation is misleading. Rather, we need to explain what it is for me to grasp what thought is being asserted in such a manner as thereby to explain what it is for me to grasp that thought at all. By contrast, the Grice/Strawson/McDowell theory assumes that, by some conventional means, I am able to recognise which thought it is that the utterance serves to assert as true; but, in assuming this, it takes my ability to grasp this thought as given antecedently to my recognising it to be that which is asserted. It thus treats the sentence as *encoding* the thought, rather than as *expressing* it.

The fundamental point made by Frege (1923, p. 36) and slightly earlier by Wittgenstein (1921, 4.027, 4.03) that language enables us to grasp *new* thoughts, is often sneered at by those too impatient to stop to reflect upon it. In Chomsky's writings it reappears, heavily emphasised, both in the form that we are able to understand new *sentences*, and more importantly, in the form stated by Frege.[1] If it was merely that we could understand a new way of conveying a familiar thought, a language could be simply a code for thoughts. According to the appropriate version of the code conception of language, we can grasp a large range of thoughts, independently of their formulation in language, and can apprehend relations between them by means of which they may be located in logical space: sentences then serve to pick them out by their co-ordinates in this space, enabling us to identify the thoughts so conveyed; and a certain redundancy in the co-ordinate system allows distinct sentences to convey the same thought. This picture of language depends upon taking our grasp of the thoughts that can be conveyed by language as antecedent to our understanding of the language: it is therefore exposed as false by the fact that such an understanding suffices to enable us to grasp quite new thoughts when they are expressed in that language. There is a fundamental difference between expressing a thought and using some conventional means to identify it. Given an invalid argument, the phrase 'the weakest additional assumption needed to render the argument valid' picks out a unique thought; but it does not *express* that thought, since it is possible to understand the phrase without knowing which thought it picks out. A sentence expressing the thought, on the other hand, cannot be understood without knowing what thought it expresses. It is an essential feature of anything properly called a 'language' that its phrases and sentences genuinely *express* their meanings. That is the difference between a language and a code; and that is why the mastery of a language enables a speaker to grasp new thoughts expressed in it.

The Grice/Strawson/McDowell theory may, then, conceivably be on the right track to an explanation of a restricted facet of linguistic meaning, namely the assertoric force attached to certain utterances, as contrasted with the interrogative, optative, imperatival or other type of force attached to others. Here it is unimportant that the overt indicators of the force attached are, in most languages, unreliable and insufficient in number: what matter are the distinctions that a hearer needs to draw if he is to have understood what has been said. Someone who mistakes a request for a question is not in error merely about the *point* of the utterance, that is, about why the speaker said what he did: he is mistaken about what it was that was said. But a theory of the Gricean type is powerless to explain any other aspect of meaning. For that, an approach along Fregean lines is required: one, namely, that, by explaining what, in general, the specific content of a sentence is, and by displaying the contributions made by particular words to determining the content of sentences that contain them, shows what it is for a sentence to express a thought, and, thereby, what thoughts are.

So far, then, the contest between the view that the primary function of language is that of an instrument of communication and the view that it is that of a vehicle of thought appears to be going decisively in favour of the latter. This was the contest staged by Strawson in his celebrated inaugural lecture 'Meaning and Truth', in which he dubbed proponents of the former view 'communication-intention theorists' and proponents of the latter 'theorists of formal semantics' (repr. 1971, pp. 170–89). If the foregoing argument has been right, communication-intention theories, that is, Gricean theories, at best contribute to that part of a theory of meaning which, in Fregean terms, constitutes the theory of force.

What, then, is needed in order to give an account of that ingredient in meaning called by Frege 'sense'? From the dichotomy drawn by Strawson, it would appear that it can only be what he terms 'formal semantics', that is to say, a theory of sense along Fregean lines, built, like his, on a theory of reference as a basis. If so, does it follow that the primary function of language is to be a vehicle of thought, and that it is the contingent fact that many people happen to know the same language that enables us to put it to a secondary use as an instrument of communication? This is Chomsky's conclusion (1975, p. 71). Of course, the 'contingent fact' is an essential feature of the way in which we all in practice acquire language: but, from the present standpoint, it is contingent in that it does not follow from the essence of language as language.

On the face of it, a theory of sense of Frege's kind supports such a conclusion. Frege insisted that thoughts and the senses that are constituents of them are equally accessible to all, and hence fully communicable: but, for all that, in an account, of the type he envisaged, of what grasping the senses of expressions of a language comprises, no reference is made to the existence of more than one speaker of the language. On such a theory, for every expression of the language possessing a genuine unity, one who understands the language grasps a particular condition for something to be its referent, that referent consisting of an object or a function according to the logical type of the expression. Attaching a given sense to an expression is thus, on this account, personal to the individual speaker. In so far as he wishes to use the language to communicate with others, he will, of course, be concerned to attach the *right* sense to the expression, that is, the sense which it bears in the language; but his attaching a particular sense to it, rightly or wrongly, does not depend upon anything but his own cognitive state, and it does not appear that, for this, he need so much as have any conception of there being other speakers of the language. This fact is vividly illustrated by Frege's remarks in 'Der Gedanke' about the understanding that two speakers may have of a personal name, in Frege's example the name 'Dr Gustav Lauben'. Leo Peter knows Dr Lauben as a medical doctor who lives in a certain house; Herbert Garner knows, of Dr Lauben, the date and place of his birth, but not where he lives now or anything else about him. Frege comments that 'So far as the proper name "Dr Gustav Lauben" is concerned, Herbert Garner and Leo Peter do not speak the same language; for, although they in fact use this name to signify the same man, they do not know that they do so' (1918, p. 65).

Something very similar holds good of Davidson's account of the matter (1984a, pp. 125–39; 1984b, pp. 141–54). In his earlier writings, he emphasised the existence of the whole linguistic community as bearing upon the way in which a theory of meaning for a language might be arrived at, and upon the criterion for its being an acceptable theory: but the theory itself was a body of knowledge that might be possessed by a single individual, his possession of which would enable him to speak the language. In his later work, he has gone a great deal further, taking the primary notion to be that of an idiolect – the language of some individual at a particular time – or refining this notion still further so as to make it relative to a hearer as well as to a speaker: the language that, at a particular time, A uses when he is speaking to B (1986, pp. 433–46). It is plain from Frege's observations in 'Der Gedanke' that he, too, conceives of a language as an idiolect. He does not take Davidson's step of relativising the language to both speaker and hearer, since he is less concerned with the language that the subject *uses* as with that which he *understands* (and the manner in which he understands it); the subject is thus considered more in the role of hearer than of speaker. Frege's conception is that a sentence uttered by another will convey to a hearer a thought, and that which thought it conveys will depend upon the senses the hearer attaches to the words, and thus upon the hearer's language. Which thought a speaker intends to convey by a sentence that he utters will doubtless likewise depend largely upon the speaker's language; but this is not the focus of Frege's attention. In any case, the language of speaker or hearer is not conceived of as such a language as German, but as that individual's idiolect: it is to the expressions of such an idiolect, or at least of a language that might be someone's idiolect, that a theory specifying senses and referents should be taken as applying.

Chomsky embraces with great warmth the conclusion that Strawson, by his endorsement of the communication-intention theory, had sought to defeat, namely that language is primarily a vehicle of thought, and only secondarily an instrument of communication (Chomsky, 1975, pp. 61–2, 69). He cites instances of the many cases in which we employ language with no direct, and sometimes no remote, communicative purpose. These, of course, prove nothing: they serve merely to underline the problem. It is agreed, on both hands, that language serves both purposes: it is easy to cite examples in which it serves the one and other examples in which it serves the other. There is no question, therefore, of its being like the game of bridge. It would be senseless to say that someone, having learned the game of bridge by playing it with others, was now in a position to go off and play it by himself: there is no such thing as playing bridge on one's own. We know in advance, by contrast, that, having learned a language by learning to converse with others, one can then use it in silent, spoken or, so to speak, written soliloquy: the question at issue is whether it is because it can be used to communicate with others that it can also be used as a vehicle of one's own thought, or whether, conversely, it is because two people are able to use the same language as a vehicle of thought that they are also able to use it to communicate with one another.

The most direct strategy for answering this question is to enquire whether either ability can be explained in terms of the other. It seems, at first sight, that it is straightforward to explain our capacity to communicate by means of language if we assume an ability to use it as a vehicle of thought: given that, for each of two individuals, a sentence of the language expresses the same thought, either of them must be able to communicate that thought to the other by uttering that sentence. At second glance, however, it is not at all so clear, at least in the context of theories of meaning for those individuals' idiolects running roughly along the lines of a Fregean theory of sense and reference.

In order for the speaker successfully to communicate with the hearer, the hearer must understand him as he intended to be understood. The explication that is proposed for the notion of the way in which the speaker intends to be understood is that his idiolect can be correctly characterised by a certain theory of meaning: the hearer will then understand him as he intended if the hearer's idiolect – or at least the idiolect attributed by the hearer to the speaker – is characterised by the same theory of meaning. The status of such a theory of meaning is open to dispute. At one extreme, it may be taken as merely a theory propounded from the outside, playing no actual role in the mechanism that governs either speaker's or hearer's linguistic behaviour. At the other extreme, that represented by Chomsky, the speaker's knowledge of his language is identified with his knowledge of such a theory. Since the speaker obviously has no explicit knowledge of more than a few fragments of such a theory, this must be classed as unconscious knowledge; and, if anyone objects to the notion of unconscious knowledge, he is to be pacified by the replacement of the word 'knowledge' by 'cognition'. This is not offered as the outcome of conceptual analysis, but as an empirical scientific hypothesis, specifically a psychological hypothesis. It is guarded from attack as embodying a mythological conception of an immaterial psychic mechanism by the identification of psychology as neurophysiology on an abstract level: the theory of meaning is an abstract description of a structure within the brain. Since a subject cannot be expected to have even an abstract awareness of much that goes on within his brain, it is unsurprising that his knowledge of the theory should be unconscious.

On the face of it, this account is open to the criticisms that Frege and Husserl brought against psychologism: meaning becomes private and hence no longer in principle communicable. This is to say that faith is required if we are to believe that we communicate with one another. The hearer must presuppose that he is interpreting the speaker as the speaker intends: but the speaker's intention and the hearer's interpretation are, at best, constituted by inner states of each respectively, not accessible to themselves, let alone to the other. Frege insisted on the communicability of thoughts, as contrasted with the contents of consciousness: thoughts are not contents of consciousness, but, being common to all, are objective extra-mental entities existing independently of our grasping or expressing them. Notoriously, this doctrine fails to explain how thoughts can be communicated by language. It is not enough that the senses should themselves be objective: their attachment to the words whose senses they are must likewise be objective, or at least objectively ascertainable, and that is something that cannot be independent of us.

If communication is not to rest on faith, it is necessary to maintain that any misunderstanding can come to light. The hearer may indeed be construing the speaker's words in accordance with the wrong theory of meaning; if so, there must be something that the speaker is liable to say or do, in virtue of the way he intends what he says to be understood, that would demonstrate to the hearer that his understanding of the speaker has up to now been incorrect. But it is not enough to make such a claim: it must be made out. We are here taking it that a theory of meaning for an idiolect of the 'formal semantic' type will conform to the Fregean prototype in issuing in an assignment, to every possible utterance of any (assertoric) sentence of the language, of the condition for that utterance to be true. What has, therefore, first to be done, in making out the claim, is to explain in detail the consequences such a theory has for what a speaker may say and do. It naturally cannot be demanded of such an explanation that it should enable us to predict what any given speaker will say, let alone what he will do, in response to the utterances of others; but, since it is by a speaker's linguistic and non-linguistic behaviour that we must judge whether or not some given theory of meaning, of the Fregean type, can be taken as governing that speaker's idiolect, it must be possible to state the basis of such a judgement. Consequently, the explanation will lay down the principles that determine what behaviour on the part of a speaker is consistent with a given theory of meaning for his idiolect: in other words, it will exhibit the connection between the theory of meaning for a language and the actual use of that language.

It is precisely the lack of any such connecting explanation that makes theories of meaning constructed after the Fregean prototype so unsatisfying and so hard to evaluate. Davidson, for instance, has emphasised that, in proposing a truth-theory of the kind he has advocated as the proper form for a theory of meaning, he is turning a Tarskian truth-definition on its head (1984c, p. 173). He is not, like Tarski, defining the property of being true, taking the meanings of the sentences as antecedently explained without appeal to the notion of truth: rather, he is taking as given an understanding of what it is for a statement to be true, and explaining the meanings of words and sentences of the language by laying down when utterances made by means of them are true. It follows that someone can derive the meanings of those words and sentences from the truth-theory only if he grasps, at least implicitly, whatever Davidson is presupposing him to grasp concerning the notion of truth. What he must grasp is, precisely, the manner in which the truth-conditions of utterances of a sentence go to determine its use: that is, when it is appropriate to utter it, and what are the consequences, for speaker and hearers, of such an utterance. We are disposed to overlook the need for such a connecting explanation because we do, of course, have an implicit grasp of the notion of truth: but a philosophical elucidation demands that it be made explicit.

That there is something to be made explicit is evident from the fact that the result of replacing the word 'true' as it occurs in the truth-theory by some arbitrarily invented word would yield nothing with any pretensions to being a theory of meaning: but it is far easier to see that there is something that needs to be made explicit than to make it so. Davidson, we may say, commits the opposite error to that made by the classical theories of truth such as the correspondence theory. To know what proposition a sentence expresses is to know what it means: hence, by asking after the condition for any given *proposition* to be true, rather than for the truth of an utterance of a given sentence, those theories in effect assumed that meanings could be assigned to the sentences of a language in advance of determining the conditions for them to be true. Once such an assumption is made, all hope of arriving at a genuinely explanatory account is lost, because the notions of meaning and truth can only be elucidated together, as part of a single theory. Davidson, on the other hand, assumes that he can take the notion of truth as already understood, and explain that of meaning in terms of it: and this condemns his explanation of meaning to be as sterile as was that of the notion of truth in the classical theories.

Supplying an explanation connecting the theory of meaning for an idiolect with the linguistic behaviour of the subject would only be the first step in making out the claim that, on an account of language given in such terms, communication does not need to rest on faith. Whatever the exact status of such a theory of meaning, two such theories will need to be invoked in explaining the process of communication: that governing the speaker's idiolect and that attributed to the speaker by the hearer. The claim is that any divergence between the two theories in the truth-conditions they assign to any sentence must be capable of being revealed by something said or done by speaker or hearer. The second step in establishing this claim would therefore have to be a demonstration, by appeal to the connecting explanation, that a divergence in the assignment of truth-conditions would always result in a divergence in linguistic or associated behaviour, potential if not actual.

It is a long way from being evident that such a demonstration would be possible. It would clearly be possible if the condition for the truth of every utterance were such that we could be credited with an ability, in particular favourable circumstances, to recognise whether the condition obtained or not: but it is obvious that is far from being so. To this it may be said that those (including Davidson) who accept the thesis of the indeterminacy of translation would not maintain the possibility of any such demonstration: use, for them, does not uniquely determine meaning. Then why not simply conclude that, for them, communication does rest on faith, or else is only to a limited degree possible? Precisely because they further contend that, to the extent that use leaves meaning undetermined, there is no fact of the matter concerning what someone means: there would therefore be no substance to a faith conceived as underlying communication, nothing, in other words, that would be left uncommunicated. If so, the original notion of meaning, regarded as captured by a theory of meaning, was unnecessarily refined, and may be coarsened. Theories of meaning will stand to others in an equivalence relation, holding between any two theories just in case they cannot be distinguished by anything a speaker says or does: and the expressions of two idiolects may be held to have the same coarse meaning just in case those idiolects are governed by two equivalent theories. A characterisation of coarse meaning will be given, not by a single theory of meaning, but by an equivalence class of such theories. Coarse meaning will both determine and be determined by use: fine meaning, on the other hand, may, for present purposes (or for all), be disregarded, since there is no fact of the matter whether it attaches to an utterance or not.

The word 'meaning' is used in a sense relevant to the present enquiry if, under it, there is a genuine difference between someone's attaching one meaning to an expression and his attaching another, so that successful communication depends upon the correct apprehension of meaning in this sense. But, on reflection, it becomes unclear that it is of any importance to us whether or not it would be possible to demonstrate that use determines meaning, in such a sense of 'meaning'. If it would not, then communication certainly depends upon an irreducible residue of faith. But, even if we had such a demonstration, it would remain that truth-conditional theories of meaning for idiolects are not autonomous. That is to say, the criterion for whether a given theory of meaning governed a speaker's idiolect would be whether, in the course of linguistic interchange, he always spoke and responded in a manner consistent with it; and this would apply whether or not his mastery of his idiolect were supposed to consist in his having 'internalised' the appropriate theory of meaning. But, if that is so, it seems that the possibility of using language to communicate with others cannot, even in principle, be a contingent feature of having a language: for ascribing an idiolect to a subject would appear to have no substance save in virtue of his use of it to communicate with others.

A possible reply to this would be that the behaviour, linguistic and non-linguistic, by means of which we might judge how a speaker intended his utterances to be understood, that is, on the account under consideration, what his idiolect was, is merely *evidence* for the hypothesis that he has internalised a certain theory of meaning and that the representation of that theory in configurations of his brain issues in such behaviour. Does such a reply rebut the argument?

Our question was whether an account according to which the primary function of language was as a vehicle of thought could explain how it can also be used as an instrument of communication. Any such explanation must consider what constitutes successful communication, in order then to show how an understanding of language as a vehicle of thought is a sufficient basis for it. Successful communication takes place when the hearer understands the speaker as the speaker intended. What, then, constitutes a subject's understanding the sentences of a language in a particular way? Is it what he says and does, or would say and do, when engaged in linguistic interchange? Or is it, rather, his having internalised a certain theory of meaning for that language? If it is the internalisation, then indeed his behaviour when he takes part in linguistic interchange can at best be strong but fallible evidence for the internalised theory. In that case, however, the hearer's presumption that he has understood the speaker can never be definitively refuted or confirmed: he can only have evidence that he has done so, which falls short of being conclusive. So regarded, communication does rest ultimately on faith – faith that one has hit on the very theory of meaning that one's interlocutor has internalised.

The only escape from the absurdity of this conclusion is to treat the supposedly internalised theory of meaning, not as constitutive of the speaker's attaching the meanings that he does to his words, but, indeed, as an empirical hypothesis to explain what enables him to use the language to express those meanings. It then becomes irrelevant to the philosophical task of explaining what it is so to use them, that is, what it is to attach a certain range of meanings to the words and sentences of the language. There is now no obstacle to taking a speaker's understanding the language in a particular way as consisting in his being disposed to say certain things in certain circumstances and to respond in certain ways to the utterances of others; and, in this case, whether two participants in a linguistic exchange understand one another will either already be manifest from what they say and do or, at worst, could be made manifest if the exchange were continued in one or another way. But now the internalised theory of meaning has fallen out of the picture (the philosophical picture, though not the scientific one): no attempt is now being made to explain the possibility of using language for communication on the basis of an existing understanding of it as a vehicle of thought.

When the theory of meaning for a speaker's idiolect is not conceived as internalised by him or as the content of a piece of knowledge of any kind that he possesses, the matter stands differently. In this case, the theory of meaning is intended merely as a systematisation of the understanding which he manifests in his use of the language. As was argued above, it can in fact be at best a truncation of such a systematic description, needing to be supplemented by an explanation which links the truth-conditions which the theory ascribes to (certain types of) utterances with the linguistic and related behaviour by means of which he manifests his understanding. The question now naturally arises whether the detour through truth-conditions was not superfluous. If a complete account of what it is for the words and sentences of a language to have (in the mouth of a given speaker) the meanings that they do requires a specification of how truth-conditions determine use, and if the only criterion for whether such an account is correct lies in its agreement with the use actually made of them, should we not obtain a simpler account by describing that use directly, without invoking the notion of a statement's being true or being false (independently of whether it is or can be recognised as such)?

That was certainly Wiggenstein's idea. In his later work, he treated the notion of truth as essentially a shallow concept, wholly explicable in Ramsey's way by appeal to the schematic principle that, for each statement 'A', 'It is true that A' is equivalent to 'A'.[2] The meaning of a statement or form of statement is therefore not to be explained by stating the condition for it to *be* true, but by describing its use. He understood a description of the use of a statement to consist in saying: under what conditions we should be disposed to make it; to what criteria we should appeal to decide whether it was true and hence to be accepted; what might subsequently compel us to withdraw it; what anyone commits himself to by making it or by accepting it as true when another makes it; what consequences, if any, follow from someone's making it; what we take to be the point of making it on a given occasion; what we take to be the point of having such a form of words in the language – just those things (except the last) by means of which one speaker may judge whether he is understanding another as he intends. The occurrences of the word 'true' in the phrases 'decide that it is true' and 'accept it as true' are not here supposed to be understood in terms of any more substantial notion of a statement's being true than that yielded by Ramsey's equivalence. Accepting or rejecting a statement made by another, checking whether it was warranted, and evaluating circumstances as warranting or as not warranting an assertion made at once or subsequently – all these are activities which demand to be described in any full account of the practice of using language: they are all components of that practice. A statement's satisfying the condition for it to *be* true, on the other hand, is certainly not in itself a feature of its use. The question at issue is whether there is nevertheless a need to appeal to it in a characterisation of linguistic practice. Wittgenstein's view was clearly that there is not, but, as things stand, neither that view nor its contrary can be more than an *opinion*: without a detailed account of how linguistic practice may be exhibited as depending on or derivable from the truth-conditions of sentences of the language, it is impossible to decide the question with assurance.

There are two components of Wittgenstein's view: his hostility to systematic theories and preference for piecemeal descriptions; and his rejection of the centrality to an account of meaning of the notion of truth – that is, of a statement's being true, independently of its being accepted or being recognisable as true – in favour of a direct description of use. The second does not depend on the first. Providing piecemeal descriptions admittedly makes it far easier to give the appearance of dispensing with the notion of truth; but, by the same token, it cannot be established that the notion is genuinely dispensable until it has been shown how a comprehensive and hence necessarily systematic account can be constructed without it. Systematisation is not motivated solely by a passion for order: like the axiomatic presentation of a mathematical theory, it serves to make a clear separation of the concepts and principles assumed from those explained or derived. A piecemeal description of the use of a particular expression or form of sentence will inevitably presuppose an understanding of much of the rest of the language: only a systematic theory can reveal on what basis it is possible to explain in general what linguistic meaning is and how our understanding of sentences depends upon our understanding of the words composing them and of the constructions they employ. By his refusal to contemplate even an outline of a systematic theory, Wittgenstein left it uncertain whether his strategy of describing linguistic practice without appeal to the notion of truth could or could not be successfully executed.

The same holds good of his strategy for philosophical enquiry. He wished to replace the philosophical study of phenomena by a study of the kind of statement we make about phenomena. But such a study, if it is to yield illumination, cannot accept whatever is normally or frequently said as immune to criticism: statements do not in general acquire authority from the frequency with which they are made. We need, rather, to distinguish what is merely customarily said from what the principles governing our use of language and determinative of the meanings of our utterances require or entitle us to say. To draw such a distinction, it is not enough merely to confine oneself to describing what may be observed to happen, or of assembling reminders of what everyone knows, as Wittgenstein claimed that a philosopher should do: the distinction does not draw itself, but requires some theoretical apparatus. The very methodology that Wittgenstein employed rested on general ideas concerning meaning that could be vindicated only by an outline of the very thing that he repudiated, namely a systematic account of how a whole language functions; and so, to borrow a phrase of his, his entire philosophy hangs in the air.

Thus his rejection of a general theory is not only not a consequence of his dismissal of the notion of truth as a deep one essential to a grasp of the notion of meaning, but is an obstacle to evaluating that dismissal. But his negative attitude to the notion of truth should also be distinguished from his positive insistence on use as the determinant of meaning. Even if the negative view is wrong, a theory yielding specifications of the truth-conditions of sentences of a language can be at most a part of an explanation of their having the meanings that they have; whether it is even such a part depends upon whether it is possible to supplement it with a description of the uses of sentences as determined by their truth-conditions.

Does it follow that language has to be considered as essentially an instrument of communication – not indeed because it is a code for thought, nor because meaning can be explained in terms of the intention to induce belief, but because, without reference to the communicative use of language, an assignment of truth-conditions is without substance? Such a conclusion would be natural; but, as thus stated, it would be unwarranted. My argument has been that a truth-theory is without substance if it is not linked to an account of the way in which language is used: the link between truth-conditions and use must be such as to display the manner in which the use of any particular sentence is determined by the condition for the truth of any utterance of it. But that does not show that the use of the language must be a use in communication. It could in principle be a use by a speaker who employs his language (perhaps always aloud) only for the expression of his own thoughts, resolves, judgements and uncertainties; and a passage from the *Philosophical Investigations* suggests that Wittgenstein himself accepted this as a possibility:

> A human being can encourage himself, give himself orders, obey, blame and punish himself; he can ask himself a question and answer it. So we could imagine human beings who spoke only in monologue; who accompanied their activities by talking to themselves. – An explorer who watched them and listened to their talk might succeed in translating their language into ours. (This would enable him to predict these people's actions correctly, for he also hears them making resolutions and decisions.) (I, 243)

This passage immediately precedes Wittgenstein's attack on the conception of a private language, in the sense of one that another person cannot understand. It intimates that Wittgenstein has no objection to the conception of a language which, as a matter of contingent fact, only one person actually does understand – or, at least, that he has, in this context, no concern with that conception. It does so by means of the fantasy of a language in fact understood by many people, but not used by them for communicating with each other. The explorer would find it much harder to hit on the scheme for translating the language of any one of these people if his language did not coincide with that used by the others; but the coincidence of their languages makes no difference in principle. None of them holds himself responsible to the way the others speak; if his way of using certain words diverges from that of others, he will not know it and would be unaffected by the knowledge if he had it: the language of each is therefore in principle private to himself. One might ask how the people in this fantasy acquired their knowledge of the language, but one is plainly not intended to do so: Chomsky, who attributes so much of our linguistic ability to innate dispositions, would surely not cavil at the thought of people born with a complete knowledge of a specific language, considered only as a theoretical possibility. A language that is used for communication can also be used by each for speaking to himself: why, then, should there not be a language that is only used in the latter way?

Such people could, of course, form a society of only the most primitive type. They could have no money, and only the most casual form of barter; they could make no concerted plans, hold no councils, elect no leaders; they could give no undertakings and engage in no contracts; they could ask no questions, impart no information, issue no warnings and no threats, utter no endearments and make no declarations of love or friendship: and all the while, each would be capable of the most sophisticated solitary thoughts, reasoning and plans.

Reflection on the details of this fantasy quickly shows its utter absurdity: but absurdity does not imply logical impossibility. The idea of some human beings using language only in soliloquy indeed conflicts with fundamental features of human life and human nature, and with our mode of acquiring language; but it should not be treated as a self-contradictory supposition, since the difference between the use of language in soliloquy and in dialogue is not great enough to deprive a language so used of the character of meaningful language. But if the supposition is at least logically possible, Chomsky's claim, as against Strawson, that the primary function of language is as a vehicle of thought, and not as an instrument of communication, would appear after all to be vindicated. Is that, in the end, to be our conclusion? No. Our conclusion should be, rather, that our original question, which of these two is the primary function of language, was misconceived; and that both of the contestants in Strawson's heroic struggle are in error.

Could we not save the thesis that language is primarily an instrument of communication by regarding the people in Wittgenstein's fantasy as communicating with *themselves*? Is not someone writing in his private diary communicating with his future self? If so, is not someone soliloquising communicating with his present self? Chomsky very reasonably objects to such a description on the score that it stretches the notion of communication so far as to obliterate the distinction between the use of language in converse with another and its employment by someone talking to himself: the whole question which of the two reveals the essence of language is then rendered nugatory (1975, p. 71).

Chomsky's objection is wholly just if the description is meant as a defence of the thesis that the primary function of language is as an instrument of communication. Nevertheless, taken in itself, and not as a plea in defence of that thesis, the description has considerable point. The use of language for self-addressed utterances, whether silent or aloud, is an imitation of its use in linguistic interchange, and involves nothing essentially different. We are inclined to exaggerate the contrast between them because we tend to conceive of soliloquy solely as the audible aspect of a thought-process, whereas, when we think about dialogue, we attend to the very various things that can be done by means of verbal utterances. But the things that someone does when he is addressing only himself are just as various as those done by someone addressing another. He does not merely frame propositions and acknowledge some of them as correct: he asks himself questions, draws conclusions, forms resolves, makes plans, reproaches himself, exhorts himself, ridicules himself; treats himself, in other words, much as he would an interlocutor.

It is indeed true that to describe someone as communicating with himself is to obliterate the whole distinction between using language as an instrument of communication and as a vehicle of thought: but the fact that such a description is not merely possible, but has a point, shows that the opposition between the two functions of language is a shallow one. The true opposition is between language as representation and language as activity: and it is operating as an activity in soliloquy as much as it is in dialogue.

Philosophy of language takes its origin from a wonder at the power of language to possess a significance so greatly transcending the surface reality. Two people are talking together: that is to say, each in turn utters sounds of a certain kind. But we know that what is happening reaches far beyond the sounds that are all that is evident to gross observation: they are narrating events, asking questions, propounding hypotheses, advancing grounds and objections, and so forth. How is it that, by merely making certain sounds, they can do these complicated things? More exactly, what is it to do those things? These are the questions philosophy of language seeks ultimately to answer: and, when the stage is set in this way, a particular strategy for answering them presents itself with overwhelming naturalness. Namely, the preliminary answer must be that the participants in the conversation are speaking a language that they both understand: so the understanding of a language is the notion that has to be explained; it is the explanation of this notion that will resolve our perplexity. When the matter is viewed in this way, the understanding of a language is seen as something that each of the two speakers has in his head: it is what he has in his head that makes the sounds he utters the bearers of meanings, and enables him to construe those uttered by the other as bearers of meanings. Communication is possible between two individuals, according to this picture, when they have the same thing in their heads: the business of the philosophy of language is to say what it is that they have in their heads that makes their utterances meaningful. The standard answer is that what they have in their heads is a theory of meaning, usually construed as a theory determining the truth-conditions of sentences of the language. From all this it is apparent why the primary notion must be that of an idiolect, and why the key to an account of meaning is what Strawson called 'formal semantics'.

It is this picture that prompts us to conceive of the significance of language – what makes a language a language – as residing in its capacity to represent reality: a sentence says how things are if it is true, and to understand the sentence is to grasp how things are if it is true. This natural disposition was what was attacked by Wittgenstein, who saw much deeper into the nature of language than either of Strawson's two embattled armies, when he wrote that we have to 'make a radical break with the idea that language always functions in one way, always serves the same purpose: to convey thoughts – whether these thoughts are about houses, pains, good and evil, or whatever' (I, 304), and that 'we are so accustomed to communication through language, in conversation, that it seems to us as if the whole point of communication lay in someone else's grasping the sense of my words, which is something mental, and, so to speak, absorbing it into his own mind. If he then does something further with it as well, that no longer belongs to the immediate purpose of language' (I, 363). Our disposition to think in the manner Wittgenstein is satirising is reinforced by the Fregean heritage. It was observed above that if one asks, as Frege did, what distinguishes thoughts from mental contents such as images, the answer must be that they present themselves as assessable as true or false. It is then overwhelmingly natural to regard language, by means of which thoughts are expressed, in the same light. Of course, this cannot be a simple misconception: the representative power of language is both genuine and central. The illusion is threefold: in thinking, first, that this representative power can be isolated from all the other features of language; secondly, that those other features can be explained in terms of it, or left to take care of themselves without explanation; and, thirdly, that the representative power consists in the speaker's being in the correct interior states. If this were the true account, communication would indeed rest on faith. Since it obviously cannot rest on faith, there must be an adequate outward manifestation of understanding, consisting in a complex interplay between linguistic exchange and related actions. It is this interplay which a genuine account of linguistic meaning has to make explicit, a task which 'formal semantics', in the sense of truth-conditional theories of meaning, unjustifiably shirks.

It is also this interplay towards which I intended to gesture by speaking of language as activity. What was meant was not the banal point that to utter a sentence is to do something, just as to comb one's hair is to do something. It was, rather, this: that the significance of an utterance lies in the difference that it potentially makes to what subsequently happens.

Even for an account of the role played by language in the transmisison of information – in enabling us to build up our picture of the world – a specification of the conditions for the truth of our sentences is wholly inadequate, even if it is genuinely needed and even if it can avoid triviality, both of which there are strong grounds to doubt: for since the condition for the truth of any but a very limited range of statements is not one which, in the most favourable situation, we can simply observe to obtain, such a specification will leave largely unexplained what is to be treated as a sufficient ground for accepting a statement of each given type. Until the task shirked by theories of meaning, as these are conceived by the 'formal semanticists', is carried out, we are simply not equipped to form any opinion about whether the appeal to the notion of truth provides an essential first step towards a description of the activity of using language, whether it is a harmless but unnecessary detour, or whether it is a useless and confusing blind alley.

Notes

1 See in particular Chomsky 1988, pp. 170 and 184.
2 The most explicit statement occurs in the unhappy appendix on Gödel; Wittgenstein, *Remarks on the Foundations of Mathematics*, section 1, Appendix I.

References

Chomsky, Noam 1988: *Language and Problems of Knowledge*. Cambridge, Mass.
    1975: *Reflections on Language*. New York: Pantheon.
Davidson, Donald 1984a: Radical interpretation. In Davidson, *Inquiries into Truth and Interpretation*. Oxford University Press.
    1984b: Belief and the basis of meaning. In Davidson, *Inquiries into Truth and Interpretation*. Oxford University Press.
    1984c: Reply to Foster. In Davidson, *Inquiries into Truth and Interpretation*. Oxford University Press.
    1986: A nice derangement of epitaphs. In E. Lepore (ed.), *Truth and Interpetation*. Oxford: Basil Blackwell.
Evans, Gareth 1982: *The Varieties of Reference*. Oxford University Press.
Frege, G. 1918: Der Gedanke.
    1923: Gedankengefuge.
McDowell, John 1980: Meaning, communication and knowledge. In Zak van Straaten (ed.), *Philosophical Subjects*, Oxford University Press.
Strawson, P. 1971: *Logico-Linguistic Papers*. London: Methuen.
Wittgenstein, L. 1921: *Tractatus Logico-Philosophicus*. Trans. D. Pears and B.F. McGuinness, London and New York: Routledge & Kegan Paul.
    1978 (3rd edn). Ed. G.H. von Wright, Rush Rhees and G.E.M. Anscombe. *Remarks on the Foundations of Mathematics*. Oxford: Basil Blackwell.
    1973 (3rd edn). Trs G.E.M. Anscombe. *Philosophical Investigations*. Oxford: Basil Blackwell.

11

Model Theory and the 'Factuality' of Semantics

Hilary Putnam

Although I first met Noam Chomsky over forty years ago, we really became friends in 1957, when he spent a year at Princeton University where I was teaching. I remember the excitement of learning about 'transformations' for the first time, and the long discussions we had about semantics (we were often joined by Paul Benacerraf and Paul Ziff), as well as about the sad state of the world (which has not gotten any less sad in the last thirty years). Noam is, of course, a major philosopher as well as a great linguist, and he has often discussed philosophical issues, especially the ones surrounding Quine's thesis of the indeterminacy of translation. It is a great pleasure to contribute to his *Festschrift* and to wish him the traditional Jewish 'hundert un zwanzig yohr' (may you live to be a hundred and twenty – the age Moses reached in the Bible).

In the present essay I hope to clarify the nature and purpose of my model-theoretic argument against realism. This may seem a far cry from anything Noam Chomsky has written about; but a connecting link to his work is provided by Noam's well-known criticism of Quine's attack on the factuality of semantical claims.[1] This link should not really occasion surprise; Quine himself has often linked the issues of indeterminacy of translation and ontological relativity, and the latter issue is directly connected with the model-theoretic argument.

The model-theoretic argument

I set out my model-theoretic argument in four publications,[2] beginning with my Address to the American Philosophical Association in 1976, and related issues continue to occupy my attention even today.[3] For the sake of readers who may not be familiar with it, I shall give a brief summary. The argument assumes that we have somehow succeeded in formalizing our language.[4] A function which assigns extensions to the individual constants and to the predicate and function symbols of the language is called a *reference relation*. Such a function might assign Aristotle to the individual constant '*a*', the class of cats to the predicate '*C(x)*', the class of ordered pairs $\{<x,y>|x$ is a parent of $y\}$ to the predicate '*P(x,y)*', etc. Tarski showed how such a reference relation can be extended by an inductive definition to complex predicates (i.e. formulas with free variables), so that we can say, for instance, that under the reference relation just described the one-place predicate '$(\exists x)(C(x). P(x,y))$' has as its extension the class of just those y such that y is the offspring of a cat. Once this is done, one can also define the set of 'true' sentences of the given language (that is, the set of sentences that would be true if that reference relation were used to interpret the language): a sentence S is true, assuming a reference relation, just in case the predicate '$x=x.S$' refers to at least one thing.

The traditional metaphysical realist picture of language is the following: the metaphysical realist pictures the world as a totality of language-independent things, a totality which is fixed once and for all, and, at least in the case of an ideal language, one (and only one) reference relation connecting our words with that totality is supposed to be singled out by the very way we understand our language. This description is meant to capture two features of traditional metaphysical realism: its insistence on a unique *correspondence* (to a fixed, mind-independent Reality) as the basis of truth and falsity, and its insistence that there is just One True Theory of the fixed mind-independent Reality. If we insist that our formalization of the language must be a formalization within classical two-valued logic, then we will have the third great feature of the traditional metaphysical realist picture: its commitment to bivalence.

Now, suppose that a theory I contains all (and only) those statements that we would accept in the ideal limit of rational inquiry (scientific or otherwise). Metaphysical realists – as opposed to pragmatists like Peirce – do not agree that such a theory would necessarily be *true*. According to metaphysical realists, the world could be such that the theory we were most justified in accepting would not really be true in the realist sense. (We might all be Brains in a Vat.) Rational acceptability – even in the ideal limit – is one thing, and truth is another. In this sense, the metaphysical realist views truth as radically non-epistemic.

Although metaphysical realism separates truth and rational acceptability (even idealized rational acceptability) in this way, the metaphysical realist does *expect* rationally acceptable statements to be consistent with one another in the long run. He admits that it is logically possible that we will have to live with a number of empirically equivalent systems of the world, or theories which equally well satisfy all our operational and theoretical constraints even as scientific inquiry continues indefinitely, but he does not really expect this to happen. In short, he expects scientific inquiry to converge to *one* ideal theory. (In this respect, he agrees with Peirce.)

A 'model-theoretic argument against realism', in my sense, begins by showing – that one can show this is, today, an undisputed result of modern logic – that if there is such a thing as 'an ideal theory', then that theory can never implicitly define its own intended reference relation. In fact, there are always many different reference relations that make I true, if I is a consistent theory which postulates the existence of more than one object. Moreover, if I contains non-observational terms (no matter how the line between the observational and the non-observational may be drawn), then there are reference relations that assign the correct extensions to the observation terms and wildly incorrect extensions to the non-observation terms and *still* make I come out true, as long as I does not actually imply a false observation sentence. As I put it in 'Models and reality', one can always find a reference relation that satisfies our observational constraints and also satisfies such theoretical constraints[5] as simplicity, elegance, subjective plausibility, etc., under which such a theory I comes out true.

The problem this poses for the realist is the following: if *all* his realism requires is that there be *a* reference relation (a 'correspondence') between items in the language (individual constants, function and predicate symbols) and items in the language-independent world which satisfies all our operational and theoretical constraints, then the model-theoretic results just described *show* that such a relation exists. But such reference relations are *not* unique (so the correspondence between words and the world is not 'singled out' in the sense of being singled out *uniquely*). Moreover, if there should be more than one 'ideal theory' (if there should be alternative equally rationally acceptable 'systems of the world') – and realists, as we said, regard this as a logical possibility, although an unlikely one – then there would be 'correspondences' making *each* of them true (so the idea that there is just *one* True Theory of the World would have to be given up). Finally, every ideal theory in the sense described above is guaranteed to possess a 'correspondence to the world' – a reference relation satisfying all our operational and theoretical constraints under which it comes out *true*. So the idea that even an epistemically ideal theory could in reality be false makes no sense, if truth and falsity are identified with truth and falsity under reference assignments which satisfy our operational and theoretical constraints.

The upshot is this: if the realist wants to be a *metaphysical* realist – if he wants to hold on to the picture of the reference relation as (i) unique; (ii) associated with a unique True Theory (note that there are two sorts of uniqueness involved in metaphysical realism – uniqueness of the True Theory and uniqueness of the reference relation); and (iii) radically non-epistemic (in the sense that even an ideal theory can be false under the reference relation), then he must insist that it is something *other* than operational and theoretical constraints that singles out the right reference relation. But this, I argued, is an incoherent idea.

Incoherence and inconsistency

Notice that I said 'incoherent' not inconsistent. What is consistent or not is a matter of pure logic; what is coherent, or intelligible, or makes sense to us, and what is incoherent, or unintelligible, or empty, is not something to be determined by logic but by philosophical argument. Suppose it were the case, as a matter of contingent fact, that the number of elementary particles of a certain kind, say 'gluons', in an arbitrary token of a word always equalled the number of particles of another kind, say 'chromons', in every one of the things the word referred to. If this were so, then each token of the word 'cat' would have just as many gluons as there were chromons in each cat; each token of 'house' would have just as many gluons as there were chromons in each house, etc. In such a world, there would be a simple physicalistically definable relation between tokens of terms[6] and the extensions of those tokens:

For any token T of a term, T refers to x just in case the number of chromons in x is equal to the number of gluons in T.

However, if there were no *explanation* of how we use the words to refer which involved this fact, if this fact were just a weird coincidence, then the fact that there was such a simple physicalistic definition of the extension of the reference relation would shed no light at all on the way in which the reference relation is singled out. It would only add to the mystery.

Why is this? It is because we simply would not be able to understand how such a relation connects with the activity of *denoting*. Now, the model-theoretic argument shows that for any physicalistic relation you like (satisfying the operational and theoretical constraints) there is another which does just as well. If someone says, 'Well, one of these is just *intrinsically* identical with reference; it is the *essence* of reference that, say, a term *T* refers to whatever has the same number of chromons as that token of *T* has gluons' we would not be able to say 'you are inconsistent', for the speaker would not have contradicted himself; but we would feel that we had received nothing but scholastic-sounding noises as an answer to our puzzlement.

Explanation and reference

Up to this point the problem does not look very serious. The example I used to illustrate our problem seems to point the way to a solution (and, indeed, this was the way I myself thought of the situation for some years, before I decided to 'go public' with the model-theoretic argument.) If the incoherence or unintelligibility of the suggestion that the physicalistic relation described above just happens to be the reference relation 'by the very nature of reference itself' arises from the fact that the behavior we call 'denoting' is not *explained* (in the possible world we imagined) by the fact that the thing denoted has just as many 'chromons' as the token denoting it has 'gluons', then surely the alternative is not to give up the search for a physicalistic theory of the reference relation, but rather to look for a physicalistic relation which has *explanatory value*. If there is a relation between our tokens and the things they refer to whose presence *explains* the way we behave with those tokens, our observable actions and their observable results, then the suggestion that we identify that relation with the relation of reference would make good scientific sense. And is this not precisely the program of semantic physicalism: to discover just such a physicalistic relation?

I will illustrate the obstacle to such a solution using the familiar nomological-deductive model of explanation, but it is easy to show that the suggestions that have been made for improving the nomological-deductive model, namely to add pragmatic constraints to the requirements for an explanation, and to weaken the requirement that the *explicandum* actually be *deducible* from the *explicans*, desirable as they may be on other grounds, would not affect the difficulty I am about to explain. [In the nomological-deductive model, the premises in a complete and correct explanation are required to consist of laws and initial conditions; the statements which constitute the premises are all required to be true; the laws are required to be nomological (physically necessary truths) and not merely accidentally true; and the conclusion (the statement of the fact explained) is required to follow deductively from the premises.[7]]

In fact, there is more than one difficulty with the suggestion that the existence of an *explanation* of certain facts from the supposition that *R* is the correct reference relation is what singles out *R* as 'the' reference relation for the language. One difficulty – the one I stressed in my first papers on the model theoretic argument – is that this requirement uses the notion of *truth*. Our problem, remember, was to explain how a particular reference relation – and that means, also, a particular extension for the notion of truth – gets attached to our words. To say that what does the attaching is the fact that certain sentences (even if they are sentences in the metalanguage[8] and not in the object language) are *true* (and that certain additional conditions are met), is flagrantly circular. The problem, of course, is that what the semantic physicalist is trying to do is reduce intentional notions to physicalist ones, and this program requires that he not employ any intentional notions in the reduction. But *explanation* is a flagrantly intentional notion.[9]

As I mentioned, there is more than one difficulty with using the notion of explanation to counter the model-theoretic argument. Here is the second difficulty – one to which considerably less attention has been paid in the literature.[10] Suppose we have fixed which sentences (in both the object language and the metalanguage) are true. In *Reason, Truth and History*[11] I showed that even if we do this in *every possible world* (as opposed to just fixing the set of sentences which are true in the actual world), still the *reference* of individual constants, predicate symbols and function symbols is far from being fixed. Even if the referent of some terms (the observation terms) is taken to be fixed (by the 'operational constraints'), all the other objects in the universe can be permuted as you will, and the permutation will generate a new reference relation which has the strange property that a sentence will keep its truth value (in all possible worlds) *in spite of* the change in the reference relation. I illustrated the idea (1981, pp. 33–5) in the following way: I defined properties I called 'cat*' and 'mat*' in such a way that (i) in the actual world the things which are cats* are cherries and the things which are mats* are trees; and (ii) *in every possible world*, the two sentences 'A cat is on a mat' and 'a cat* is on a mat*' have the same truth value. A consequence of this is that if instead of considering the two sentences just mentioned, we consider just the one sentence 'A cat is on a mat' and allow its interpretation to change by first using the standard reference relation and then a non-standard relation which assigns the set of cats* as extension to 'cat' (in every possible world) and the set of mats* as extension to 'mat' (in every possible world), the truth value of 'A cat is on a mat' will not change – it will be the same as before *in every possible world*. This illustrates the way in which two different reference relations may assign not just the same extension, but the same *intension* to a sentence. The model-theoretic argument in the Appendix to *Reason, Truth and History* shows that this technique can be extended to the totality of the sentences of a language.

A way of seeing what is happening here is to notice that while the sentence 'A cat is on a mat' would receive a different translation into a fixed language if we changed the reference relation in the way described, the new translation would be *logically equivalent to the old one*. Indeed, the two sentences 'A cat is on a mat' and 'A cat* is on a mat*' are such a pair of 'translations'.

Now, any sentence which is logically equivalent to a nomological sentence is also nomological. Also, the property of truth and the relation of logical consequence are preserved under logical equivalence. In short, *nomological deductive explanations are preserved under changes of interpretation of the kind just described*. What follows? Simply this: any observable event that can be *explained* (in the sense of the nomological deductive model of explanation) from the fact that the relation R holds between certain tokens and the things those tokens bear R to can also be explained (in the sense of the deductive nomological model) from the fact that those tokens bear R^* to whatever they bear R^* to, where R and R^* are related as in the model-theoretic argument of the Appendix of *Reason, Truth and History*. In short, the suggestion fails even apart from the problem of circularity.

In presenting this second difficulty, however, I have made essential use of the assumption that the requirements on an explanation are those of the deductive nomological model. What happens if we impose pragmatic constraints – plausibility, preservation of past doctrine, simplicity – as additional requirements on a good explanation?

At this point we run into the first difficulty again. What is expressed by the 'simpler', 'more plausible', etc., sentences in the metalanguage depends on what the *real* reference relation for the metalanguage is; and our problem, for the metalanguage as much as for the object language, was how we supposed this could be singled out. Remember, we are not addressing a practical problem of translation. It is not that we can suppose that we possess a metalanguage whose reference relation has somehow already been fixed, and the problem is to determine the best *translation* of the object language into the part of the metalanguage that corresponds to it. The problem is rather (to speak the language that metaphysical realists often use nowadays) how a reference relation is fixed 'from the point of view of the universe'. Simplicity, plausibility, preservation of past doctrine, make sense from the point of view of the universe only *if* the metalanguage has a singled out reference relation from the point of view of the universe. Appeal to these notions to explain *how* a reference relation is singled out 'from the point of view of the universe' is flagrant anthropomorphism.

And this, indeed, is why I spoke of 'incoherence'. If the universe is supposed to be informed by Platonic Ideas, which attach something intentional to every particular, or if in some other way we manage to inhabit a world view quite other than the world view of modern physical science, then we may not see anything incoherent in the idea that what is outside of our minds somehow *interprets our languages for us*. But the modern physicalist should not ascribe powers to nature for which his own image of nature has no room.

Reference and causal connection

A variant of the idea that 'explanation' is what fixes reference is the idea (put forward vigorously by Michael Devitt (1981) as well as by a host of others) that 'reference is causal connection'. Since causal connection is supposed by these philosophers to be a language-independent relation between events in the world, it might seem that this suggestion would avoid the difficulties just described, but this appearance is an illusion. One problem with Devitt's idea (to which I shall return in a moment) is that, if $E(T)$ is the event of someone's using a token of a term T, then there is a good sense of 'causal connection' in which *every* event in the backward light-cone of $E(T)$ is 'causally connected' to the event $E(T)$; but it will almost never be the case that the term T (or the token in question) *refers* to every event in the backward light-cone of $E(T)$ (and it will typically be the case that the term does refer to things with which the token is *not* causally connected, e.g., future things). Bracketing this objection for the moment, let us simply observe that 'A cat is on a mat' and 'A cat* is on a mat*' would normally be said to describe the *same* event. (Logically equivalent sentences do not seem to be descriptions of different events so much as equivalent descriptions of the same event; e.g., 'John put two apples in his pocket' and 'John put an even prime number of apples in his pocket' do not seem to be two different events which happened at the same time, but just two different ways of describing one event.) But, if this is right and 'a cat's being on a mat' and 'a cat*'s being on a mat*' are the same event, then they must *have the same causes and the same effects*. If so, then there is no way in which the event $E(T)$ can be causally connected to a cat's being on a mat without being identically causally connected to a cats*'s being on a mat*.

One can point out that, just as we do in the case of statements about what *explains* what, we require statements of causality to satisfy various pragmatic constraints. Such constraints – or simply, our interests in a particular context – may determine that it would be natural to describe the event one way, and to say 'A cat is on a mat' and 'weird' to say 'A cat* is on a mat*'. But when the question is not, what it is natural to *say* – that is, what *sentences* it is natural to utter – but what is the 'natural' way of describing the event *from the universe's point of view* – we run up against the difficulty that the very attribution of any point of view in the matter to the universe is nonsense.[12]

To come back to the objection I postponed: someone might suppose that the universe itself somehow 'factors' events into background conditions and bringers-about. And he might say that not every event in the backward light-cone of $E(T)$ is a 'bringer-about' of $E(T)$. (The problem of getting a *unique* description of the events which *are* 'bringers-about' still remains, of course.) But the distinction between bringers-about (causal agents) and background conditions is rather obviously an interest relative matter; again, the anthropomorphism of ascribing this distinction to 'the universe' is obvious.

One philosopher who has acknowledged this difficulty is David Lewis (1984). Lewis's solution is to give up the 'causal connection theory', and to postulate that certain classes of things are *intrinsically* natural. [What 'intrinsically' means in this connection is (i) not by virtue of what we *think* or of how things are described in language; and (ii) not by virtue of anything like the simplicity of laws – since the laws obeyed by the *-magnitudes[13] are formally the same as the laws obeyed by the 'standard' magnitudes.] In short, Lewis claims that certain classes are *natural from the universe's point of view*. While I compliment Lewis on seeing exactly what the problem is, I have to say that I do not see the advantage of adding to our conceptual scheme an unfamiliar metaphysical primitive like 'naturalness' over just taking the notion of reference itself as an unreduced primitive notion. Doesn't Lewis's account amount to saying that we-know-not-what fixes the reference relation we-know-not-how?

The metaphysical upshot

The upshot of the argument is not (or at least not without further argument) that 'realism is false' and 'anti-realism is true'. After all, there are many versions of both realism and anti-realism (and positions which may not be easily classifiable as 'realist' or 'anti-realist', e.g., Wittgenstein's). The upshot of *this*[14] model-theoretic argument is simply that semantic physicalism does not work. (However, physicalism seems to be the only sort of metaphysical realism that our time can take seriously.) The way reference is fixed is not intelligibly explained by any sort of physicalist account so far proposed. This conclusion leaves, of course, a wide variety of possibilities; not only the possibility of taking some notion other than reference (e.g., rational acceptability[15]) as the base for doing semantics, but also the possibility of taking reference as primitive.[16] What it rules out, if I am right, is the view that reference is fated to be reduced to notions which belong to the world picture of physics.

It is at this point that my discussion makes contact with Quine's philosophy. Quine has expressed qualified agreement with what he calls 'Brentano's Thesis' – with the thesis I just expressed by saying that 'reference is not fated to be reduced to notions which belong to the world picture of physics'. Moreover, his arguments in *Word and Object* and *Ontological Relativity and Other Essays* are, in significant part, model theoretic. (My own treatment differs from Quine's in (i) dropping the concern with 'proxy functions'; and (ii) – in *Reason, Truth, and History* – extending the argument to intensional logic.) But Quine has a way out of the problem very different from any I have ever considered accepting; a way out that involves a fundamental disagreement between himself and Noam Chomsky. Quine's way out is to *deny the existence of objective facts about reference, and also to deny the existence of objective facts about synonymy* (except in the case of observation sentences, and then only when the observation sentences are 'taken holophrastically'[17]).

In the remainder of this essay I want to explore the nature of this disagreement, using my own model-theoretic argument and its obvious relation to Quine's defense of 'ontological relativity' as an entering wedge. Let me begin by saying, however, that I did not perceive the relation of the arguments at the time the model-theoretic argument first occurred to me. The reason Quine's argument did not suggest my own argument to me is precisely that Quine's conclusion was so different – or rather, his conclusions (in the plural) are so different, for, as we shall see, Quine draws more than one conclusion from *his* model-theoretic argument.

Water imagery in Quine

One conclusion that Quine draws is expressed in a remarkable series of metaphors that all involve the idea of floating on water. That image has been used in philosophy before, of course, notably by Neurath in the famous anti-foundationalist image of knowledge-building as analogous to the task of rebuilding a ship while the ship is afloat on the open sea, but the point of the water imagery in *Theories and Things* is rather different. In that work, the upshot of the doctrine of the 'inscrutability of reference' is expressed by saying that all a translation scheme does is connect the 'free-floating reference' of the term being translated with the equally free-floating reference of its translation into the home language. When I say that *lapin* refers to rabbits I do not say what *lapin* refers to 'absolutely', Quine is telling us; I am only informing you that *lapin* and *rabbit* are coupled, they float together, presumably remaining side by side as they float. But Quine hastens to reassure us: even though our reference is floating, nothing goes wrong as long as we 'acquiesce in our home language' (which means, I take it, as long as we speak it without allowing ourselves to think about it as speculative philosophers) and *don't rock the boat* (1981, p. 20).

In the case of Neurath's image it is clear what the 'water' stands for: it stands for the pressures of life and experience which threaten to destroy our 'boat' (and with the boat, our very existence) if we try to replace too much of the boat at any one time. But what does the 'water' stand for in this passage in *Theories and Things*? As far as I can see, it can only stand for something like a *noumenal reality*.[18] Quine writes as if there were a noumenal reality, and what his model-theoretic argument shows is that our terms have an infinite number of ways of being modelled in it. I argue that at least the naturalistic versions of metaphysical realism land one in precisely such a conclusion as Quine reaches here – and I conclude that there must be something wrong with metaphysical realism! Of course, I am not accusing Quine of metaphysical realism; rather I am suggesting that the familiar Kantian image of our world as a 'product' with some kind of noumenal world providing the 'raw material' haunts Quine's thought. But metaphysical realism and that sort of Kantianism[19] are made for each other.

Inscrutability of reference and indeterminacy of translation

My emphasis on the model-theoretic route to Quine's doctrine of the inscrutability of reference may appear puzzling. After all, I said I would discuss the dispute between Quine and Chomsky over the question, whether there is a 'fact of the matter' as to the truth of (certain semantical) claims in linguistics. And, from a logical point of view, one might accept the picture of our terms as sliding freely over the surface of the noumenal waters, accept the picture of our terms as having no fixed 'absolute' reference, and not feel committed at all to accepting Quine's thesis of the indeterminacy of translation. That is to say, one might *accept* the doctrine that 'there is no saying what our terms refer to absolutely', while *rejecting* the inscrutability of ordinary 'relative' reference and the indeterminacy of translation. One might agree with Quine that *lapin* and *rabbit* have no 'absolute' reference at all (if a structured system of objects is a candidate for the interpretation of our words, any isomorphic system is an equally good candidate, Quine claims[20]), while insisting that there *is* a fact of the matter that '*lapin*' *refers to* rabbits (even though all that means is that the two 'free-floating references' are coupled in a certain way[21]).

While the objection would be correct as a point of formal logic, I think that one cannot understand Quine's picture of the situation if one simply takes his arguments one by one, independently of one another. Let us remember, first of all, that Quine partly inherits and partly rebels against a tradition, the tradition of Frege (the Frege of *Sinn und Bedeutung*), Russell, and Carnap, in which it is simply taken for granted that meaning (in the sense of 'intension' or *Sinn*) determines reference. Also, let us remember that for Frege and (at times) Russell (though not Carnap), meanings were supposed to be directly available to the mind (concepts are 'transparent to reason and reason's nearest kin', Frege wrote). Like Carnap, who explicitly rejected the idea that meanings can somehow be the objects of a mental faculty akin to perception, Quine thinks that *if* meanings can be retained at all in science, it must be by identifying them with equivalence classes of synonymous expressions. Meanings as entities whose existence somehow *explains* why it is that certain expressions are synonymous have to go.[22]

If reference is not fixed at all ('absolutely'), if saying that '*lapin*' denotes rabbits only tells us that the two words have the same 'free-floating' reference, then, in particular, the idea that reference is fixed by *meaning* is hopelessly wrong, and belief in anything like the traditional picture of the speaker as 'grasping' meanings which 'determine' reference is akin to belief in magic, to belief in noetic rays or whatever. What ontological relativity by itself tells us is not that synonymy is indeterminate – that requires, indeed, a separate argument – but that the traditional *philosophical* reasons for thinking it must be determinate were terrible reasons. It tells us that *if* the notion of synonymy is to be rehabilitated, it must first be rationally reconstructed.

What does it mean to rationally reconstruct the notion of synonymy? For Quine rational reconstruction has a very particular meaning. A rational reconstruction gives our 'first-class' scientific image of the world, the only image we should take with metaphysical seriousness, and it does so subject to certain constraints that are themselves seen as central to the scientific image, notably the principle of bivalence from classical logic and the maxim 'No entity without identity' – there must be statable criteria of identity for all entities admitted as values of variables. If synonymy is to be admitted as a notion of first-class science, if synonymy classes are to be admitted as values of variables, then there must be *criteria of identity* for synonymy classes, that is *there must be a set of criteria which fix precisely the conditions under which two terms may be said to be synonymous*.

It seems to me that *this* is the principle which really does the work in Quine's arguments for the indeterminacy of translation. Consider the structure of those arguments:[23] Quine lays down some criteria for synonymy (or, more precisely, for translation from one language to another). He observes that they do not determine a unique translation. The criteria he lists in the famous chapter II of *Word and Object* are so weak that this, in itself, is hardly surprising. But he also conjectures that no addition to those criteria would help the situation. And he adds that even if (contrary to what he expects) we *found* criteria which determined a unique translation, this would *still* not establish the factuality of translation-claims.[24] I want to postpone consideration of this last move for a little while, and consider the grounds for Quine's pessimism about the power of criteria to single out the 'correct' translation.

That scepticism, it seems to me, is fully justified – no matter what one's view on indeterminacy of translation. What Quine is saying here is something that, in fact, Noam Chomsky also believes – although most discussions of the debate fail to bring this out. Neither Quine nor Chomsky expects *mechanical translation* to succeed. That is, neither Quine nor Chomsky expects us to find a set of criteria which will function as an *algorithm* to determine when one has correctly translated an expression of one language into another language. The idea that *interpretative rationality can be fully exhausted by a finite set of criteria that we will actually succeed in writing down* is utopian on its face. But this is what Quine is, in effect, demanding – that we succeed in writing down such a set of criteria – before he will accept it that we have succeeded in rationally reconstructing the notion of synonymy.

To meet Quine's argument (as I have just interpreted it), to counter it *without* defending the possibility of success in the utopian project of completely formalizing interpretation, one must do one of two things: one must either show that the factuality of translation-claims does not require that there be exactly *one* rationally acceptable translation manual (and Chomsky has tried to argue that *given Quine's own epistemology* this *is* indeed a defensible position), or one must argue that translation can be determinate even though it is not a set of *criteria* that determines what the correct translation is. But if one takes the latter tack, Quine will, of course, ask how the position that something other than a set of criteria fixes correct translation differs from belief in mysterious 'meanings' – how it differs, except verbally, from what he calls the Museum Myth of meanings.

The question of the 'factuality' of semantics

According to Quine, even if we knew the totality of all possible correct observation statements, still it is possible that more than one theory would agree equally well with the whole totality. Certainly we do not possess *criteria* which would always single out exactly one theory of the world from the whole set of 'empirically equivalent theories' in every such case. Theory is, in this sense, 'underdetermined by evidence' – possibly underdetermined by the totality of all possible observations. So – various thinkers have asked Quine – how can you argue that the possibility of alternative translation schemes all equally in accordance with linguistic observation and the criteria of acceptability we are able to write down shows that there is 'no fact of the matter' as to which translation scheme is right, while at the same time arguing that *there is a fact of the matter* in physics? On your own showing, are not semantics and physics in the same boat?

In a generally excellent recent book, Christopher Hookway (1988) argues that such thinkers (he mentions Chomsky and Rorty) are 'misunderstanding' Quine. He writes, 'Although the misreading is understandable, it is clear that Quine's point is not primarily epistemological: his claim is not that correct translation is underdetermined by available evidence, but that it is underdetermined by the *facts*. In light of his physicalist conception of "the facts", he holds that correctness of translation manuals (and semantic claims generally) is not fixed by physics' (p. 137). But Chomsky (and Rorty) are perfectly well aware that Quine is making a metaphysical (and not just an epistemological) claim. The problem is that Quine's arguments for the metaphysical claim range from bad to worse. Again and again, Quine simply goes from the premise that all facts are supervenient on physical facts to the conclusion that all facts are identical with physical facts. For example, here: 'Full coverage is the business of physics and only of physics': 'nothing happens in the world, not the flutter of an eyelid, not the flicker of a thought, without some redistribution of physical states' (1981, p. 98). But supervenience does not imply identity[25] – not without further argument. And Quine supplies no such argument.

Were this all there was to say, it would have been charitable not to discuss Quine's position on the factuality of semantics at all. But when a great philosopher makes an *obvious* mistake, there is usually something behind it. Quine makes mistakes when a point is so clear to him, when the burden of proof is so obviously on his opponents, that he becomes impatient. (He has self-mockingly remarked that impatience is, perhaps, his main emotion.) What I am seeking is the line of thinking that makes it just *obvious* to Quine that semantics is not factual.

What I am suggesting is that the line that moves him (or, at least, the line that originally moved him to his present position) is the following. Although our fundamental picture of the world, the world picture of physics, may be underdetermined by the evidence, there is no *further* or *higher* picture from which we can stand back and say 'this is less than factual'. (Although there are tensions in Quine's view, this is how he himself, recognizing the tensions, sees the matter.[26]) Moreover, *within* our version of the world – even if it should turn out to be underdetermined by the evidence, and, in part, a radical choice – there are well-defined criteria of identity for all the entities we quantify over.[27] For example, although there are alternative systems of set theory available to us, yet *within* each system of set theory there is a simple and elegant criterion of set identity: x and y are the same set just in case they have the same members. But even after we have *chosen* a version of the fundamental facts, the facts of physics and mathematics, we are unable to state, in the language of physics and mathematics, a *criterion* for synonymy. If we still believed in 'meanings' as entities that *explain* synonymy, we could, at worst, simply *add them to our physics as additional fundamental entities*. But having given up the myth, that route is not open to us. We have to reconstruct the notion of synonymy if we are to employ it without lowering our standards of scientific rigor, and (for the reasons given above) the prospects for such a reconstruction are not good ones. I believe that this argument fits the text of *Word and Object* even if it does not fit all of the 'fall-back arguments' that Quine has developed since he wrote *Word and Object*. And it does not need the premise that *all* facts are physical facts (although Quine believes that premise), but only the premise that postulating irreducible 'semantic facts' represents a return to a way of thinking about meaning that has been seen not to make sense. It does not make sense, to repeat, because it requires 'meanings' to have properties that are quite magical, properties our scientific image of the world leaves us with no way of understanding.

Quine's fall-back argument

Unfortunately, there is another way in which Quine sometimes argues. Quine sometimes argues that *even if our canons singled out a unique translation* there would be no fact of the matter as to whether or not the *canons themselves* were correct. The only thing there is a 'fact of the matter' about is the 'verbal dispositions themselves'. (Recall: 'If [simplicity, charity, and "kindred canons of procedure"] suffice to weed out all conflicting codifications of the natives' verbal dispositions, which is doubtful, I would still say that they confer no fact on the matter.' Hahn and Schilpp, 1986, p. 155.)

Quine's argument seems to be that even if there were criteria of correct translation *C* which picked out a unique translation manual in each case, we could construct 'incorrect' but equally complete alternative criteria *C'*. Then (as long as the 'incorrect' criteria *C'* did not require us to ascribe verbal dispositions to the natives they don't actually have) we could ask: 'what makes *C* and not *C'* the correct set of criteria?' The answer couldn't be that criteria *C* are *analytic* of the notion of correct translation, for analyticity (within one language) was already 'debunked' in 'Two dogmas of empiricism'. Nor could it be any physical facts, since all physical facts are equally compatible with the statements (i) 'Criteria *C* are the correct criteria for selection of a translation manual'; and (ii) 'Criteria *C'* are the correct criteria for selection of a translation manual'. So (unless we are willing to accept 'non-physical facts', which Quine is not), we must regard our preference for *C* over *C'* as a matter of practical convenience (which can be explained in various ways, e.g., simplicity, utility, our past history and culture, etc.), without serious theoretical implications as to the Furniture of the World.

But this argument is more an immunizing move (in Popper's sense) than a serious argument. The model-theoretic argument against the traditional correspondence picture of meaning and reference is a serious and intricate argument, whether one finally accepts it or not. And it points to a real difficulty with a traditional notion of what a 'semantical fact' looks like. But this latter argument simply invokes the principle that all facts are physical facts: a principle for which, as we noted, Quine gives no real argument at all. (And it assumes that we cannot simply say, 'accepting *C'* rather than *C* would constitute *changing the meaning of the notion of synonymy*'; that is, it assumes that not only the notion of analyticity, but also the notion of synonymy has *already* been discredited. But in that case, we do not *need* any further argument against the factuality of assertions of synonymy.)

Again, Quine often points out that there is *one* kind of linguistic statement that he regards as fully objective: statements about our 'verbal dispositions' are fully scientific, in his view. How does my reconstruction of Quine's thinking square with this?

In his writing Quine has suggested that dispositional predicates refer to mechanisms which we presently do not understand, but which are perfectly physical in nature. 'We intend in advance that solubility consist precisely in those explanatory traits of structure and composition however ill-pictured or unpictured at the time, that do make things dissolve when in water.'[28] As Hookway (1988, p. 108) puts it, explaining Quine's view, 'While dispositional terms have an essential heuristic or regulative role in formulating ideas and problems as science progresses – and while they provide an excellent shorthand in alluding to great stretches of theory, and a useful means for covering up our relative ignorance – there is no reason to think they need have a role in formulating the true finished theory of reality.' There is no need, in Quine's view, for a general dispositional idiom in science; and if we do use individual dispositional predicates, this is only because we have not yet reached the stage at which they can be eliminated in favor of terms from more fundamental science. (In conversation, however, Quine has sometimes taken the line that it is all right to use dispositional predicates *even if it turns out that we cannot actually give necessary and sufficient conditions for their application* in the language of mathematics and physics. Perhaps this was only a slip; but if Quine were to stick to this line, it would represent another immunizing move in his philosophy of a most unfortunate kind.[29])

Alexander George's reconstructions of the Chomsky–Quine debate

Alexander George (1986) has suggested that the debate is, at bottom, an empirical disagreement about the future of cognitive psychology. And it is true that Quine has sometimes made statements about the nature of the brain processes involved in language learning.[30] But it is a mistake to think that discovering that these statements are wrong, and that the modularity hypothesis is right, would cause Quine to concede the factuality of semantic claims. Even if we imagine that every claim Jerry Fodor makes in *The Language of Thought* were empirically verified, for example, we would only have established the possibility of defining something called 'narrow content' in cognitive psychology. But Fodor himself emphasizes that 'narrow content' is not *meaning*[31] ('elm' and 'beech' may have the same narrow content, for example, but they do not have the same meaning). And Fodor's own suggestions for defining the non-solipsistic component of meaning – 'broad content' – run into a problem Fodor calls 'the problem of error' – a problem Fodor himself recognizes as a difficulty Quine raised as far back as 'Two dogmas of empiricism'. In any case, it is all but certain that the tremendously strong form of the innateness hypothesis defended by Fodor, which requires that 'every word in the Oxford English Dictionary' be innate (as Fodor has put it), is untenable – and untenable for reasons connected with Quine's meaning holism.[32] On *no* psychological theory – excluding ones made up by philosophers – is it going to turn out that whenever two speakers have the same belief the *identical* neurological or computational process is going on in their heads, because, for one thing, our actual notion of 'sameness of meaning' *discounts substantial differences in belief and in inference patterns.* So even if we allow criteria that invoke neurological or brain-computational evidence (as has also been urged by Michael Friedman [1975]), we will never be able to write down precise criteria for the selection of a translation manual.[33] True, the Chomsky–Quine debate is not a purely 'conceptual' debate; empirical facts are relevant, in the sense in which they are relevant to every philosophical debate; but it is certainly not a straightforward empirical disagreement about, say, modularity versus equipotentiality. Even were Quine to allow neurological, brain-computational, etc., evidence in linguistics, the most this *might* force him to concede is the possibility of defining some notion of narrow content (and I have argued in *Representation and Reality*, there are good Quinian arguments that such a notion would probably have *no* significant relation to the notion of 'sameness of meaning' that guides us in *translation*). To ignore the *conceptual* difficulties facing the program of finding a neurologically *cum* computationally based notion of 'narrow content' (one which makes it the case that narrow content is preserved in translation) is to fall for a 'scientific' version of the 'museum myth' of meaning.[34] And is this not what Quine has been telling us?

Concluding remarks

I have argued that Quine's argument (freed of various 'immunizing strategies' that Quine added later) has two parts: it consists of (1) an argument against the 'museum myth of meaning' which has interesting similarities to my own model-theoretic argument against (naturalistic versions of) metaphysical realism; and (2) an argument that a certain demand (one which Quine thinks we must impose before we admit such a term as 'synonymous' into our 'first-class' scientific language) cannot be met. An acceptable rational reconstruction of the notion of synonymy will not, Quine claims, turn out to be possible. We will not be able to give precise criteria for when two terms are/are not synonymous (criteria which are themselves statable in the language of fundamental science).

Although I have some problems with the first part – it is an inconsistency to speak of 'the free-floating reference of our own terms' if one also insists, as Quine does again and again, that there is no standpoint outside of or above our own language – I agree that the museum myth of meaning is untenable, and model-theoretic methods can help to bring this out. But my real difficulties are with the second part of Quine's argument. Asking for precise criteria (whether one also calls them 'behavioral' or not is a red herring, I think) for selecting a translation manual is, as I have said, utopian. And while the request for criteria statable in the language of 'fundamental' science has a certain appeal, it is ultimately indefensible. Quine's demands for such criteria lead him to reject not only the existence of an objective relation of synonymy, but also the existence of a fact of the matter as to whether or not two terms (in another language) are the same or different in reference. To avoid having to abandon the notion of reference as he has abandoned the notion of synonymy, Quine must then claim that in his 'home language' the situation is different. One can be a 'robust realist' with respect to one's home language, and give a non-realist or anti-realist account of the functioning of *every other language*.[35] Most philosophers would regard such an outcome as a *reductio ad absurdum* of the demand that leads to it.

In the end, then, I think Noam Chomsky is right in making this rejoinder to Quine's claims: the underdetermination of semantical descriptions (to the extent that there is underdetermination) has no more and no less significance – epistemologically *or* metaphysically – than the underdetermination of physical theory by evidence – or, for that matter, than the underdetermination of physical theory by sociology.

Notes

1   Quine and Chomsky have repeatedly discussed one another's views over the years. Here I focus on just one of their debates, namely, Chomsky's criticism in *Words and Objections* (1969) and elsewhere of Quine's claim that there is no fact of the matter as to the truth or falsity of semantic claims and Quine's reply in the same volume. I do not discuss their disagreement over Chomsky's innateness hypothesis, or over the status of generative grammar.

2   'Realism and reason' in my *Meaning and the Moral Sciences*, 'Models and reality' in *The Journal of Symbolic Logic*, 1980, XLV, 464–82, the book *Reason, Truth and History*, and the Introduction to my *Philosophical Papers, vol. 3: Realism and Reason*. See also my 'Information and the mental' in Lepore (ed.), *Truth and Interpretation* (1986) and chapters 12, 13, and 16 of *Realism and Reason*. 'Models and reality' is also reprinted in *Realism and Reason*, as chapter 1.

3   See, for example, Putnam, 1987.

4   More precisely, assume that we have succeeded in formalizing it up to some (possibly transfinite) level of the Tarskian hierarchy of metalanguages (to avoid semantical paradoxes).

5   Nor does my argument depend on this or any other particular list of theoretical constraints, contrary to what Richard Miller contends (1988). To see this, let C be any constraint on theory selection you like – even, if you think you understand the notion, 'realist truth'. Let ECC (the Epistemic Counterpart of C) be the constraint that *the world is an epistemic counterpart of a world in which C is fulfilled*. (The notion of an epistemic counterpart was introduced by Kripke, 1972.) The idea, of course, is that in any epistemic counterpart of a world in which p is true, one's experiences will fully justify one in believing that p is true.) Then ECC represents the part of the constraint C that is really *epistemic*. And any set of constraints that are *epistemic* in this sense will do for my argument. (Nor does this notion of the epistemic require the sense datum theory, or any other particular theory of what the objects of observation are – as was pointed out in 'Models and reality'.)

6   I am restricting attention to terms for physical objects in this example, of course.

7   The *locus classicus* for the deductive-nomological model is Hempel and Oppenheim, 1948.

8   Given an object language, both the construction of a metalanguage and the extension of the reference-relation of the object language to that metalanguage are completely straightforward procedures (given, of course, a sufficiently strong set theory – one which must be stronger than what is available in either the object language or the metalanguage). But if a reference relation has not been fixed for the object language, we cannot suppose that one is already available for the metalanguage, without begging the question.

9   For a considerably lengthier discussion of this point, see 'Beyond historicism', chapter 16 in my *Realism and Reason*.
10 I also raised this second difficulty in 'Information and the mental', 1986.
11 See the Appendix. (In his *Representing and Intervening*, Ian Hacking suggests that my model-theoretic argument may be flawed because it depends on the Skolem–Löwenheim Theorem, which does not apply to Second Order languages. Besides ignoring my discussion of just this point in 'Models and reality', Ian Hacking's suggestion ignores the fact that the model-theoretic argument of *Reason, Truth and History* – the book he cited – did *not* employ the Skolem–Löwenheim Theorem, but used a technique – permutation of individuals – which does apply to Second Order Logic, modal logic, tensed logic, etc.!)
12 For a much fuller discussion of the problems with the causal connection theory see my 'Is the causal structure of the physical itself something physical?', in *Causation and Causal Theories; Midwest Studies in Philosophy*, 9 (1984).
13 If M is the referent of any term under the 'standard' reference relation, M^* may be the referent of the same term under whatever non-standard reference relation we please (where the model-theoretic argument establishes that such non-standard reference relations exist). In particular, if $M_1, M_2, M_3 \ldots$ are the standard physical magnitudes, then $M_1^*, M_2^*, M_3^* \ldots$ will be magnitudes such that *the very same sentences that are nomologically true of the first lot, are also true of the second lot.*
14 Other model-theoretic arguments *do* bear against metaphysical realism, even in its non-physicalist versions, however. In particular, this is true of the argument from Equivalent Descriptions, explained in 'Realism and reason' (in *Meaning and the Moral Sciences*), and developed at length in Lecture One in *The Many Faces of Realism*.
15 This is the line I took in *Reason, Truth, and History* (1981). See, however, the last chapter of *Representation and Reality*, 1988, for qualifications and further explanation.
16 In *Representation and Reality* (1988), I argue that doing this does not commit one to viewing reference as 'simple and irreducible'.
17 The idea of taking observation sentences holophrastically – i.e., as unanalyzed wholes, thereby finessing Quine's own worries about whether to translate *gavagai* as 'rabbit' or as 'rabbithood exemplified again' – is emphasized in Quine's reply to me, in Hahn and Schilpp (eds), 1986, 427–31.
18 Speaking at a symposium on 'Ways the world is' at Harvard's 350th Anniversary Celebration (June 1986), Quine said that he does not believe in things in themselves, but added, 'I do believe in a world in itself. The world in itself is Nature.' Note the similarity to James's tendency to treat 'pure experience' as a pre-ontological noumenal reality.
19 That sort of Kantianism, I argue in *Reason, Truth and History*, and also in *The Many Faces of Realism*, is not the only sort. Much more of Kant than is commonly thought not only does not depend on the notion of a noumenal world, but is at odds with the notion.
20 Thus, after pointing out that 'it is quantification, with its variables, that embodies reification', Quine goes on to say, 'It is startling to reflect that this contribution is purely structural. *Other objects would have served the purpose as well as ours, as long as they were in one-to-one correlation with them.* No evidence, therefore, could be adduced for the reification of one lot rather than the other.' (My italics; the quotation is from *Quiddities*, 1988, 182.) While Quine speaks here of reification and evidence, rather than of reference, the underlying thought is model-theoretic: it is

magical, in Quine's view, to think that science can do more than fix the structure of the world up to isomorphism.

21 'Thus "London" designates London (whatever *that* is) and "rabbit" denotes the rabbits (whatever *they* are)' (Hahn and Schilpp (eds), 1986, 460).

22 'We could simply identify meanings with classes of synonyms ['if we could admit synonymy']. Ayer made the same point long ago and so did Russell . . . The point . . . is that the *prior* admission of an *unexplained* domain of objects called meanings is no way to explain synonymy or anything else' (Hahn and Schilpp (eds), 1986, 73).

23 For an analysis of the structure of Quine's arguments see my 'The refutation of conventionalism' in my *Philosophical Papers, vol. 2: Mind, Language and Reality*.

24 'If [simplicity, charity, and "kindred canons of procedure"] suffice to weed out all conflicting codifications of the natives' verbal dispositions, which is doubtful, I would still say that they confer no fact on the matter' (Hahn and Schilpp (eds), 1986, 155).

25 According to current physics, nothing happens in the world without a change in the gravitational field. But Quine himself would not argue that all facts are gravitational facts. To restate the point: 'all facts are supervenient on gravitational facts' is true; all facts *are* gravitational facts is false.

26 Cf. his reply to Roger F. Gibson, Jr. in Hahn and Schilpp (eds), 1986, 155–8.

27 Actually, this is not true in quantum mechanics. But I don't suppose that Quine's knowledge of contemporary physics reaches so far.

28 *Ways of Paradox*, 72. See also *Word and Object*, 222–5, *The Roots of Reference*, 4ff, 10–15, *Ontological Relativity*, 130–1.

29 See my discussion of Quine's use of dispositions in 'Is the causal structure of the physical itself something physical', in *Midwest Studies*, IV.

30 Quine believes that different people may acquire linguistic competence through entirely different means. 'Different persons growing up in the same language are like different bushes trimmed and trained to take the shape of identical elephants. The anatomical details of twigs and branches will fulfill the elephantine form differently from bush to bush, but the overall outward results are alike' (1960, p. 81).

31 As I understand it, Fodor's view is that meaning is something like the ordered pair of what he calls 'broad content' and what he calls 'narrow content'. And 'broad content' depends on what the utterer's words *causally co-vary with* – thus not just on what's 'in the head'. (Cf. his *Psychosemantics*, 1987)

32 See my 'Meaning holism' in Hahn and Schilpp (eds), 1986, and the first two chapters of *Representation and Reality*.

33 This is argued at length in my *Representation and Reality*.

34 As Ricketts remarked in his article on the Chomsky–Quine debate (1982): 'We simply have no idea as to how such distinctions are to be interpreted within any foreseeable extension of current neural theory' (p. 129).

35 Cf. Hookway, 1988, 208–10. See also my 'A comparison of something with something else' (a comparison of the views of Quine and Rorty).

References

Chomsky, Noam 1969. Quine's Empirical Assumptions. In D. Davidson and J. Hintikka (eds) *Words and Objections*, 53–68. Dordrecht: D. Reidel.

232 *Hilary Putnam*

1975: *Reflections on Language*. New York: Random House.
Devitt, Michael 1981: *Designation*. New York: Columbia University Press.
Fodor, Jerry 1987: *Psychosemantics*. Cambridge, Mass.: Bradford Books (MIT Press).
Friedman, Michael 1975: Physicalism and the indeterminacy of translation. *Nous* 9, 353–74.
George, Alexander 1986: Whence and whither the debate between Quine and Chomsky? *Journal of Philosophy*. 83, 489–99.
Hacking, Ian 1983: *Representing and Intervening*. Cambridge: Cambridge University Press.
Hahn, L.E. and P.A. Schilpp (eds) 1986: *The Philosophy of W.V. Quine*. La Salle: Open Court.
Hempel, C.G. and P. Oppenheim 1948: The logic of explanation. *Philosophy of Science*, 15, 135–75. Repr. in H. Feigl and M. Brodbeck (eds), *Readings in the Philosophy of Science*, 319–52. New York: Appleton-Century-Crofts 1953.
Hookway, Christopher 1988: *Quine*. Cambridge: Polity Press.
Kripke, Saul 1972 and 1980: *Naming and Necessity*. Cambridge, Mass.: Harvard University Press.
Lewis, David 1984: Putnam's paradox: In *Australasian Journal of Philosophy*, 221–36.
Miller, Richard 1988: *Fact and Method*. Princeton: Princeton University Press.
Putnam, Hilary 1975: *Philosophical Papers, vol. 2: Mind, Language and Reality*. Cambridge: Cambridge University Press.
    1976 and 1978: Realism and reason. Presidential Address to the Eastern Division of the American Philosophical Association (1976). Repr. as part four of *Meaning and the Moral Sciences*.
    1981: *Reason, Truth and History*. Cambridge: Cambridge University Press.
    1983: *Philosophical Papers, vol. 3: Realism and Reason*. Cambridge: Cambridge University Press.
    1984: Is the causal structure of the physical itself something physical? In French, P. and T. Uehling (eds), *Causation and Causal Theories: Midwest Studies in Philosophy*, 19, 3–17.
    1985: A comparison of something with something else. *New Literary History* (Fall).
    1986: Information and the mental: In E. Lepore (ed.), *Truth and Interpretation: Perspectives on the Philosophy of Donald Davidson*. Oxford: Basil Blackwell.
    1987: *The Many Faces of Realism*. La Salle, Il.: Open Court.
    1988: *Representation and Reality*. Cambridge, Mass.: Bradford Books (MIT).
Quine, Willard V. 1960: *Word and Object*. Cambridge, Mass.: MIT Press.
    1969a: *Ontological Relativity and Other Essays*. New York: Columbia University Press.
    1969b: Reply to Chomsky. In D. Davidson and J. Hintikka (eds) *Words and Objections: Essays on the Work of W.V. Quine*, 302–11. Dordrecht: D. Reidel.
    1973: *The Roots of Reference*. La Salle, Il.: Open Court.
    1981: *Theories and Things*. Cambridge, Mass.: Harvard University Press.
    1988: *Quiddities*. Cambridge, Mass.: Harvard University Press.
Ricketts, Thomas 1982: Rationality, translation, and epistemology naturalized. *Journal of Philosophy*, 79, 117–36.

12

Wittgenstein's Rule-following Considerations and the Central Project of Theoretical Linguistics

Crispin Wright

This is not the paper which I planned to write when I accepted Alexander George's invitation to contribute to this volume. Indeed, it finishes by posing the very questions which I had hoped to address. But a necessarily severely applied deadline has prevented me from attempting to take matters further. That I have felt willing nevertheless to see the paper published is owing partly to the great philosophical importance and interest which I believe the issues to have, and partly to the hope that it may be fruitful for others to think about the overall perspective which the paper accomplishes – if it accomplishes anything; but, mainly, I should have been greatly sorry not to have contributed to this celebration of the sixtieth birthday of Noam Chomsky, for whose accomplishments, both intellectual and political, I have the deepest admiration.

I

The Central Project of theoretical linguistics, for present purposes, is to achieve an understanding of one component in what Chomsky has termed the 'creative aspect'[1] of our language use – our ability, after exposure to the use of no more than a small part of our language, to recognise of indefinitely many unencountered strings both whether they constitute well-formed sentences and what, if anything, they could be used in a particular context to say. No doubt this ability admits of *some* kind of scientific theoretical explanation. What is characteristic of the Project is the thought that, in the first place anyway, it is appropriate to seek an explanation in, broadly, *cognitive-psychological* terms: it is an ability which we have because we are appropriately related to a finite body of *information* which may be inferentially manipulated in such a way as to entail, for each novel string on which we can successfully exercise our 'linguistic-creative' power, appropriate theorems concerning its grammaticalness and content.[2]

It is a basic and, familiarly, thorny question how the 'appropriate relation' which is to mediate between the contents of a suitable grammar, or theory of meaning, and the abilities of actual speakers may be best conceived – whether, for instance, it is happy to involve a notion of *knowledge*, however attenuated. But that is not now my immediate concern.[3] My question, perhaps even more basic, is whether, even in this inchoate and highly general formulation, the Central Project is not somehow already at odds with lessons to be learned from Wittgenstein's discussions of rule-following in the *Philosophical Investigations* and elsewhere.[4]

The tension is very immediate on Kripke's widely discussed interpretation (1982) of Wittgenstein. According to Kripke's Wittgenstein, all our discourse concerning meaning, understanding, content, and cognate notions, fails of strict factuality – says nothing literally true or false – and is saved from vacuity only by a 'Sceptical Solution', a set of proposals for rehabilitating meaning-talk in ways that prescind from the assignment to it of any fact-stating role. If that claim were correct, there would be nothing strictly and literally true to say about the content of a novel utterance nor, therefore, anything to be, strictly, known or recognised concerning its content. So linguistic creativity, conceived as the ability to *know* the syntactic and semantic status of encountered strings, would be a myth: there would be, simply, no such knowledge-forming power. The apparently remarkable, unbounded character of our linguistic competence would no more demand a deep, cognitive explanation than would a disposition to consensus about the *comic* qualities of an indefinite variety of situations (if indeed we were so disposed, and assuming, for the sake of argument, the non-factuality of judgments concerning comedy). It would still, no doubt, be possible to raise the question, what *does* explain our ability to communicate using novel linguistic constructions, if it is not that we deploy essentially the same store of syntactic and semantic information to arrive at the same answers to the same problems. Maybe the question could be so cast as to admit of some sort of natural scientific treatment. But we would have surrendered the vision which inspired the Project: the vision of basic English, say, as an articulate system of syntactic and semantic fact, whose mastery consists in the internalisation of a store of principles out of which all aspects of the system are generated. That vision calls for the existence of *truths* concerning the content of novel utterances, truths which Kripke's Wittgenstein repudiates. There would still be something, our 'agreement in semantic reactions', which might seem remarkable. But since it would be, precisely, no longer an agreement in *judgments*, properly so described, there would seem to be no legitimate project of enquiry into its cognitive provenance.

There is an additional, more specific point of tension between Kripke's Wittgenstein and the Central Project. The latter is a project in *psychology*, a project of explaining manifest abilities of the individual in terms of his cognitive-psychological (and ultimately, neurophysiological) equipment. Explanans and explanandum are thus both exhausted by characteristics of individuals 'considered in isolation'. By contrast, so Kripke's Wittgenstein argues, we can refashion the notion of meaning in the wake of the Sceptical Argument only by recognising that a proper account of the (non-fact-stating) use of statements essentially involving it and other cognate notions must make essential reference, one way or another, to the purposes and practices of linguistic *communities*. Meaning – what the Sceptical Solution saves of it – cannot lie within the province of individual psychology, so the methodological individualism which characterises Chomsky's work[5] is apparently guilty of a compound error. There are no facts of the kind which it seeks to explain by reference to (non-existent) states of individuals; and the concept of meaning, as entrenched in our (non-fact-stating) talk of meaning, has an essentially *social* character which the methodologically individualistic perspective imposed by the spurious explanatory project makes it additionally difficult to recognise.

Kripke's own remarks on the relations between the ideas of his Wittgenstein and the Central Project are somewhat low key. He writes (1982) for instance, that

> *if* statements attributing rule-following are neither to be regarded as stating facts, nor to be thought of as *explaining* our behaviour . . . it would seem that the *use* of the ideas of rules and of competence [in Chomsky's technical sense] in linguistics needs serious reconsideration, even if these notions are not rendered 'meaningless'. (pp. 30–1, n. 22)

Maybe such a 'serious reconsideration' might in the end succeed in conserving a use for the ideas of 'rules' and 'competence' in some kind of theoretical description of our linguistic practices. But Chomsky has conspicuously declined to take up the invitation, preferring a frontal attack on the Sceptical Argument and its alleged Sceptical Solution (1986, pp. 223–43). Concerning the first, the essence of his response, if I may simplify somewhat and presuppose some familiarity with Kripke's dialectic, is that the search for facts constitutive of what you formerly meant by a particular expression, or of its being a particular rule that it was your former practice to follow, is only improperly restricted by Kripke's Sceptic to the domains of your former linguistic behaviour and former conscious mental life. Rather, the claim, for example, that you formerly followed a certain specified rule, is a *theoretical* claim, and answerable, therefore, in the context of an appropriate embedding theory, to an indefinite pool of past, present *and* future evidence.[6] Any fact may seem fugitive if we do not look in the right place.

If that reflection rebuts the Sceptical Argument, there is of course no need for a Sceptical Solution. But Chomsky finds the Sceptical Solution 'far from descriptively adequate' (1986, pp. 227ff) in any case, demurring at what he takes to be Kripke's Wittgenstein's suggestion that the assertibility, by the members of a given speech community, that some third party is following rules, requires that 'his responses coincide with theirs' (p. 266). For this would frustrate the often unproblematic identification of practices governed by rules different to any pursued by the community in question. It is open to question whether this does justice to the resources of the Sceptical Solution.[7] But

Crispin Wright

whether it does or not, it would anyway now be widely accepted that no refinement of the Sceptical Solution can *be* a solution.[8] The crucial question concerns what is wrong with the Sceptical Argument – for it can only have the status of a paradox – and what relation it bears to (the real) Wittgenstein's discussion.

Chomsky's response to the Sceptical Argument is unsatisfying, it seems to me, for reasons which also apply to the dispositional response[9] effectively criticised by Kripke himself (1982, pp. 24–32). Kripke convincingly objects to the dispositional response that it cannot account for the normativity of understanding an expression in a particular way, intending to follow a particular rule, and so on. The reason for dissatisfaction which I have in mind, however, is not this. It is rather that Chomsky's suggestion, that the identity of followed rules is a strictly theoretical question, threatens, like the dispositional account, to make a total mystery of the phenomenon of non-inferential, first-person knowledge of past and present meanings, rules and intentions. The whole temptation to think of understanding, intention, etc. as mental states, against which Wittgenstein repeatedly inveighs in the *Investigations*, flows from this point of analogy with things which *are* genuine mental states and processes – sensations, after-images, having a tune go through one's head. Each of us is, for the most part, effortlessly authoritative, without inference, about our past and present intentions, about the rules we 'have in mind', about how we understand or have understood particular expressions. An account of the truth-conditions of such claims which, like Chomsky's or the dispositional account, makes a puzzle of this aspect of their first-personal epistemology should be rejected.[10]

The Sceptical Argument is flawed in any case and needs no response of the sort which Chomsky essays. For there is an explicit and unacceptable reductionism involved at the stage at which the Sceptic challenges his interlocutor to recall some aspect of his former mental life which might constitute his, for example, having meant addition by 'plus'. It is not acceptable, apparently, if the interlocutor claims to recall precisely that. Rather the challenge is to recall some *independently characterised* fact, in a way which does not simply beg the question of the existence of facts of the disputed species, of which it is then to *emerge* – rather than simply be claimed – that it has the requisite properties (principally, normative content across a potential infinity of situations). The search is thus restricted to phenomena of consciousness which are not – for the purposes of the dialectic – permissibly assumed 'up front' to have a recollectable *content*. (For to suppose that one could recall the content of a mental state would just be, the Sceptic will claim, to assume a positive answer to the question at issue – namely, whether there is such a thing as knowing one's former meanings.) If the Sceptic is allowed to put the challenge in this way, then it is no doubt unanswerable. But so put, it is merely an implicit prejudice against the ordinary notions of meaning and intention, according to which we may and usually do non-inferentially know of our present meanings and intentions, and may later non-inferentially recall them (see Wright 1984, pp. 771–8; 1987, pp. 395–403).

This somewhat flat-footed response to Kripke's Sceptic may seem to provide a good example of 'loss of problems'. (The phrase is Wittgenstein's own, of course, from *Zettel* 456.) In fact, though, and on the contrary, I think the real problem posed by the Sceptical Argument is acute, and *is* one of Wittgenstein's fundamental concerns. But the problem is not that of *answering* the Argument. The problem is that of seeing how and why the correct answer just given can *be* correct.

A central preoccupation of the *Investigations*, and Wittgenstein's other later writings on the philosophy of psychology, is with concepts which – like meaning, understanding, intending, expecting, wishing, fearing, hoping – seem to hover, puzzlingly and unstably, between two paradigms. To the left, as it were, stand genuine episodes and processes in consciousness: items which, like headaches, ringing in the ears, and the experience of a patch of blue, may have a determinate onset and departure, and whose occurrence makes no demands upon the conceptual resources of the sufferer.[11] To the right, by contrast, stand qualities of character, like patience, courage, and conceit, which are naturally viewed as constituted in the (broadly) behavioural dispositions of a subject, are fully manifest in things he is inclined to say and do, and advert to no inner phenomenological causes of these inclinations. Descartes's conception of the mental tended to draw everything towards the left-hand pole. The Rylean reaction, by contrast, attempted to colonise as widely as possible on behalf of the right. And the difficulty raised by the concepts with which Wittgenstein was preoccupied is that we are pulled in both directions simultaneously. Their first-person epistemology pulls us to the left – since explaining it seems to call for construal of such states as objects of consciousness. But, as Wittgenstein and his Kripkean ersatz both effectively argue, nothing strictly introspectible has, in the case of any of these concepts, the right kind of characteristics. We cannot, honestly, find anything to *be* the intention, etc., when we turn our gaze inward; and anything we might find would have no connection or, at best, the wrong kind of connection with those subsequent events – what we go on to count as fulfilment of an intention or expectation, etc. – on which the correctness of an earlier ascription to us of the intention, etc., depends. But if we accordingly allow ourselves to be pulled towards the right-hand pole – interestingly, Chomsky's response – we encounter the difficulties with normativity (at least in some cases), and with saving ordinary first-person epistemology, which have already been noted. We need, accordingly, some account or perspective on these concepts which is conservative with respect to the features which give rise to the difficulty – their combination of first-person avowability and 'theoreticity' – yet dissolves the temptation to assimilate them to cases which they do not fundamentally resemble.

Supposing that it is via provision of such an account that the Sceptical Argument can and must ultimately be defused, does any point of contact, or abrasion, remain between Wittgenstein's thought about rule-following and the Central Project? If there is no compelling argument to the conclusion that meaning, etc., are non-factual, is not the Project simply in the clear? Well, whether or not Wittgenstein's later discussions should be seen as issuing a challenge to the factuality of meaning and rule-following, they undeniably feature a recurrent, explicit discomfort with a certain conception of the *autonomy* of rules, the image of a rule as a rail laid to infinity, tracing out a proper course for a practice quite independently of any judgment of the practitioners (*Investigations*, 218). And it is hard to avoid finding this conception of autonomy in the picture of language and linguistic competence which drives the Central Project: the picture of language as a kind of syntactico-semantic mechanism, our largely unconscious knowledge of which enables us to compute the content which, independently and in advance of any response of ours, it bestows on each ingredient sentence. Chomsky wrote, almost thirty years ago (1959, p. 57):

> It is not easy to accept the view that a child is capable of constructing an extremely complex mechanism for generating a set of sentences, some of which he has heard, or that an adult can instantaneously determine whether (and if so, how) a particular item is generated by this mechanism, which has many of the properties of an abstract deductive theory. Yet this appears to be a fair description of the performance of the speaker, listener, and learner.

Note that the mechanism does the generating, and the competent adult merely keeps track of what (and how) it generates. The conception of language manifested in those remarks – a continuing fundamental theme of Chomsky's thought – is all one, it seems, in its implicit conception of the character of rule-following, with what Wittgenstein has in view in his remarks about mathematical rules in *RFM* IV, 48:

> But might it not be said that the *rules* lead this way, even if no-one went it? For that is what one would like to say – and here we see the mathematical machine, which, driven by the rules themselves, obeys only mathematical laws and not physical ones.

What motive could there be for such a view of, for example, the rules of multiplication which would not also motivate:

> But might it not be said that this sentence is grammatical, and has the meaning it does, even if no-one ever considers it? For that is what one would like to say – and here we see the language-machine which, driven by the rules of the language themselves, obeys only linguistic laws and not physical ones.

Unquestionably, Wittgenstein came to regard this conception as deeply misconceived.[12] But why? And is there any good reason for that verdict which does not in the end lead to the same place as the argumentation of Kripke's

Sceptic – the conclusion that there are, in truth, no such things as the requirements of rules? Anything which is genuinely an instance of rule-following, it is natural to think – rather than mere charade – has to consist in keeping abreast of certain objective requirements. If it is not that, if the requirements are not settled independently of the way I find myself inclined to go, then I do not *follow* anything – any more than, when walking in bright sunlight, I follow my shadow.[13] Is not the image of the syntactico-semantic engine simply a graphic expression of the rule-governed nature of linguistic practice? And if we reject it, are we not, in effect, rejecting the idea that proper linguistic practice *is* rule-governed – and thereby rejecting the notion of strictly *correct* linguistic practice, and with it the notion of meaning?

II

A reminder is desirable of the general gist of Wittgenstein's discussions of rule-following. I shall try, briefly, to provide one by concentrating (largely) on sections 185–219 of the *Investigations*, and paragraphs 23–47 of section IV of the *Remarks on the Foundations of Mathematics*.

The characteristic concerns of these passages seem to have nothing at all to do with the *reality* of rules. Rather, they are epistemological: Wittgenstein is preoccupied with the sense, if any, in which a rule is genuinely an object of intellection, something whose requirements we *track* – to use a more recent piece of jargon – by grace of some intuitive or interpretative power. Undoubtedly the intention – or one might better say, the suspicion – of these passages is negative. Wittgenstein thinks we badly misunderstand what the accomplishment is of someone who is a competent rule-follower, and that our misunderstandings lead us to over-dignify the nature of the constraint imposed by a rule, and the character of our accomplishment in following it. But there is, emphatically, no explicit denial of the existence of the constraint, and no consequential rejection of the very notion of accomplishment. It is not *impossible* that their absence is to be accounted for by Wittgenstein's failure to follow through all the way on his own thought; but I shall try to suggest a better explanation.

Four interlocking themes are prominent. First:

One's own understanding of a rule does not exceed what one can explain.
(Investigations 209–10; RFM VI, 23)

The temptation to suppose otherwise arises from the reflection that any explanatory process is finite and, hence, open in principle to an indefinite variety of interpretations. Yet explanation does usually – or so we suppose – secure mutual understanding. So, somehow, more is got across – the thought continues – than an explanation makes explicit. Correct uptake of an explanation is having the *right* 'something' come into one's mind as the result of the explanation; and the resulting informational state is then expressed in, but

essentially transcends, one's subsequent practice with the concept concerned.
   It is important to see that this picture of what is involved in successfully giving
and receiving explanations is a cornerstone for the thought that

> 'Once you have got hold of the rule, you have the route traced for you'.
> (*RFM* VI, 31; Wittgenstein's own scare quotes)

which is elaborated in the 'rules-as-rails' imagery of *Investigations* 218–19. For if
the rule governing a particular arithmetical series, say, really does determine its
every nth place quite independently of any judgment of ours, then – since any
feasible explanatory performance will allow of alternative interpretations
generating disputes about the identity of nth places which were not explicitly
covered – the every-nth-place-determining 'something' which someone who
follows the explanation correctly comes to have in mind – the 'essential thing'
which we have to 'get him to *guess*' (*Investigations* 210) – must somehow have
been at best clumsily and imperfectly conveyed. The idea which Wittgenstein is
opposing when he writes:

> If you use a rule to give a description, you yourself do not know more than
> you say . . . If you say 'and so on', you yourself do not know more than
> 'and so on'. (*RFM* IV, 8)

is hence a direct consequence of the rules-as-rails picture, joined with the
supposition that, by dint of ordinary training and explanations, we do indeed
succeed in perpetuating a community of mutual understanding of arithmetical
and other rules.
   The second theme is:

> *It might be preferable, in describing one's most basic rule-governed responses, to
> think of them as informed not by an* intuition *(of the requirements of the rule) but a
> kind of* decision. *(Investigations* 186 and 213; *RFM* VI, 24; *Brown Book* 5)

The point of contrast between the terms 'intuition' and 'decision'[14] is that the
former implies, and the latter repudiates, the suggestion that following a rule is,
even in the most basic cases when one can say nothing by way of justification for
one's particular way of proceeding, a matter of *cognition* of an independent
requirement. 'Intuition' suggests a primitive, unarticulated apprehension, a
form of knowledge too basic and immediate to admit of any further account.
Such an intuitive faculty would ensure that, once we have mastered, for
example, an arithmetical rule, our successive applications of it are disposed to
be appropriately sensitive to its requirements – either already in line or
bringable into line. But it seems there could be no further story to be told about
how the intuitive faculty accomplishes this harmony. For precisely that reason,
however, we have no means to resist a sceptical suggestion:

If intuition is an inner voice – how do I know *how* I am to obey it? And how do I know that it doesn't mislead me? For if it can guide me right, it can also guide me wrong. (Intuition an unnecessary shuffle.) (*Investigations* 213)

The reason why there is no response to this is because we have done, and can do, nothing to *fill out* the thought that, in the most primitive case of rule following, we track a set of independent requirements. But the sceptical thought is barely intelligible. For we have no accountable idea of what would constitute the direction taken by the rule by itself if the deliverances of our intuitive faculties were to take us collectively off track – 'no model of this superlative fact' (*Investigations* 192). That the sceptical thought makes no even apparent sense[15] but arises inevitably out of the intuitional epistemology of rule-following, brings out the cognitive pretentiousness of the latter, and the purpose of

It would almost be more correct to say, not that an intuition was needed at every stage, but that a new decision was needed at every stage. (*Investigations* 186)

The third theme is complementary to the second and elaborates Wittgenstein's doubts about the possibility of a 'tracking' epistemology of rule-following:

Supposing that grasping a rule is a matter of coming to have something 'in mind', how am I supposed to recognise what its requirements are? (Investigations 198, 209–13; *RFM* VI, 38, 47)

It is in the context of this theme that the 'paradox' is presented on which Kripke's exegesis concentrates:

'But how can a rule show me what I have to do at *this* point? Whatever I do is, on some interpretation, in accord with the rule'. – That is not what we ought to say, but rather: any interpretation still hangs in the air along with what it interprets, and cannot give it any support. Interpretations by themselves do not determine meaning. (*Investigations* 198)

I undergo some process of explanation – somebody writes down for me a substantial initial segment of some arithmetical series, say – and as a result, let us suppose, I come to have the right rule 'in mind'. But now consider any nth place in the series which lies beyond the demonstrated initial segment and which, in coming to a correct understanding of the intended rule, I nevertheless did not think about at all. How, when it comes to the crunch – at the nth place – does having the rule 'in mind' help? A natural response – because one tends to think of 'having the rule in mind' on the model of imagining a formula or something of the sort – is to concede that, strictly, merely having the rule in mind is no help. For it is possible to have a formula in mind without knowing what it means. So – the response continues – it is necessary in addition to *interpret* the rule. But then we immediately get the 'paradox' which Wittgenstein's interlocutor[16] blunders into in *Investigations* 198. *Any* selection for the nth place can be reconciled, on *some* interpretation, with the rule. An interpretation is of help to me, therefore, only if it is *correct*. But the fact that the idea of correctness has to be invoked at this point makes the play with interpretation idle. 'Knowing the correct interpretation of the rule' becomes just a piece of patter equivalent to 'knowing the rule'. Or if it is not – if we try to think of it as the having of something further in mind, some expanded account, for instance, of the content of the rule – then the problem will simply recur. That is: if having the expanded account in mind is having an uninterpreted object in mind, then I get no guidance; but if its guidance is conditional on interpretation, then I need to arrive at *its* correct interpretation, and an account is still owed of how I am to recognise *that*.

The relations between the three themes should, I suggest, be viewed like this. Suppose that what I take up from an episode of explanation, where it is successful, does indeed essentially transcend that explanation and any other that I might give in turn. I come to have the right rule in mind, but might, save for a kind of felicity, equally well have arrived at a wrong one despite having missed no overt feature of the explanation. This idea, challenged in the passages cited in connection with the first theme, connects with the second and third themes in that they jointly confront it with a dilemma. How does the explanation-transcendent rule which I supposedly have 'in mind' tell me what to do in novel cases? If I have to interpret it, that could be done in lots of ways. So how do I tell which interpretation is correct? Does that call for a further rule – a rule for determining correct interpretation of the original – and, if so, why does it not raise the same problem again, and so generate a regress? If, on the other hand, I don't have to interpret the original rule, then the only possible answer appears to be that I have some unmediated, intuitional contact with its requirements – the thought challenged by the second theme.[17] The upshot is, accordingly, that if we attempt to construe grasp of a rule as the presence in mind of an explanation-transcendent item, as the conception of the autonomy of rules expressed in the rules-as-rails imagery dictates, we are beggared for any satisfactory epistemology of step-by-step rule-following.

How do these ideas relate to those developed by Kripke? Several commentators[18] have challenged Kripke's interpretation on the ground that the second paragraph of *Investigations* 201 makes it plain that Wittgenstein did not accept the 'paradox' which Kripke makes pivotal. These commentators might also have emphasised the point, noted above, that the paradox is first presented, in 198, in interlocutor-quotation, as a suggestion for correction. And a third point of disanalogy, not generally noted, is that the focus of the regress-of-interpretations paradox of 198–201 does not coincide with that of Kripke's Sceptic. Kripke's Sceptic challenges his interlocutor to substantiate a claim to know what rule the interlocutor formerly followed – he is to call attention to facts concerning his former behaviour and/or mental life which nail the rule down. So the problem is to describe a cognitive pathway *to* the (former) rule. By contrast, the regress-of-interpretations paradox focuses on a particular conception of the path *from* the rule to a judgment about its proper application in a new case. The rule is assumed to be in place – 'in mind'; the question is, how does it help me to have it there?[19] And the problem arises only on a certain conception of what rules are, one which conceives of the relation between receipt of an explanation and successful ongoing practice as essentially mediated by cognition of the requirements of something interiorised. So not merely do the two paradoxes focus on ostensibly different – though of course connected – kinds of question concerning rules, namely:

How can I tell which rule I (used to) follow?

and,

How can I tell what the rule I grasp requires of me here?

In addition, while Kripke's paradox is directed at the very existence of rules and rule-following, Wittgenstein's paradox is directed, in intention anyway, at a misunderstanding of the epistemology of rule-following competences, which – he apparently believes – can be corrected without materially affecting their reality.

If that was Wittgenstein's intention, however, the question remains whether he succeeded in carrying it through. If the interiorised, explanation-transcendent rule, with its attendant, hopeless epistemological difficulties is, as I suggested, the inevitable upshot of a certain conception of the autonomy of rules, then that has to be a casualty too. So unless the thought that rules are nothing if *not* autonomous in that way is somehow disturbed, the upshot of the three themes which I have been describing is going to be the same as that of Kripke's Sceptical Argument. Does Wittgenstein manage to disturb that thought?

Disturbing it requires indicating an alternative: a conception of rules, and rule-governed practices, which allows sufficient distance between the requirements of a rule and the subject's reaction in a particular case to make space for something worth regarding as normativity, yet abrogates the spurious autonomy which generates the difficulties. It is clear enough what Wittgenstein regards as the *kind* of considerations that point us towards the right perspective on the matter. They are the considerations which constitute his fourth principal theme:

The foundations of language, and of all rule-governed institutions, reside not in the circumstance that we have internalised the same strongly autonomous, explanation-transcendent rules, whose requirements we then concur – or concur enough – about, but in primitive dispositions of agreement in judgment and action. (Investigations 211, 217, 242; RFM VI, 39)

There is no essential inner epistemology of rule-following. The connection between the training and explanations which we receive and our subsequent practices, although effected in ways which, no doubt, could be sustained only by conscious, thinking beings, is not mediated by the internalisation of explanation-transcendent rules that have to be guessed at. It is a basic fact about us that ordinary forms of explanation and training do succeed in perpetuating practices of various kinds – that there is shared uptake, a disposition to concur in novel judgments involving the concepts in question. The rules-as-rails mythology attempts an explanation of this fact. But the reality is the other way about: it is the agreement which sustains all rules and rule-governed institutions. The requirements which our rules impose upon us owe their existence to it.

This aspect of Wittgenstein's thought is familiar enough to need no further elaboration here – familiar, and ill understood. The great difficulty is to stabilise it against its natural drift to a fatal simplification: the idea that the requirements of a rule, in a particular case, are simply *whatever we take them to be*. That idea would, in effect, surrender the notion of a requirement. And Wittgenstein, it seems, explicitly cautions against it. (See *Investigations* 241; *RFM*, VII, 40.)[20] But then what is the upshot? We are told that the requirements of rules exist only within the framework of institutional activities which depend on basic human propensities to agree in judgment; but reminded that such requirements are also, in any particular case, independent of our judgments, supplying genuine norms in terms of which those judgments, even consensual judgments, may be evaluated. We have accordingly been told what does *not* constitute the requirement of a rule in a particular case: it is *not* constituted by our agreement about the particular case, and it is *not* constituted autonomously, by a 'rule-as-rail', our cognitive connection with which there would be no accounting for. But we have not been told what *does* constitute it; all we have been told is that there would be no such requirement but for the phenomenon of human agreement in judgment.

I believe that it would be vain to search Wittgenstein's texts for any more concrete positive suggestion about the constitutive question. His later conception of philosophy is, indeed, conditioned by a mistrust of such constitutive questions. Thus, consensus cannot constitute the requirements of a rule because we do, on occasion, make use of the notion of a consensus based on ignorance or mistake. But we must guard against the tendency to erect out of a practice in which that notion is given content the mythological picture of rule-following challenged by the first three themes. The mythological picture is at work in the platonistic philosophy of mathematics; and in the ease with which it comes to us to think that a private linguist could establish objective standards of correctness and incorrectness for himself. So it is important to expose it. But, once exposed, it does not need to be supplanted. Any further urge for clarity can be assuaged only by a kind of natural-historical *übersicht* of rule-governed institutions and practices.

I mean the foregoing to be recognisable as an 'official' Wittgensteinian line.[21] The most striking thing about it for present purposes is that it is hardly more hospitable to the Central Project than Kripke's Sceptical Argument. The Central Project is fuelled by the demand for a *deep* explanation of our ability to recognise the meanings of novel utterances. The Sceptical Argument entails that there is no such ability, since there is nothing to recognise. So the demand for deep explanation is misplaced; and insofar as candidate deep explanations advert to covert structures of tacitly known rules, they advert to nothing real. The 'official' response, by contrast, allows us to think, as we ordinarily do, that there is some fact about what a particular novel utterance, used in a particular context, means: a fact which it is possible to mistake, and which is normative with respect to appraisals of and responses to that particular utterance in that context. So facts about meaning are safe. But it does not follow that we may immediately raise the question which drives the Central Project. It may be granted that, in any ordinary sense, our agreement about the meaning of a novel utterance, like our agreement about a hitherto unconsidered *n*th place in some arithmetical series, is a rule-guided agreement. But it is quite another thing to accept that it calls for an account in terms of covert cognitive operations. The whole lesson of the negative parts of Wittgenstein's discussion was, wasn't it? that not *all* human agreement in judgments can coherently be thought of as a product of covert cognitive operations. Phenomenologically, at any rate, construal of a novel utterance is often immediate and spontaneous; what obstacle is there to the suggestion that agreement about content is, in such cases, in no way different to agreement about hitherto unconsidered places in simple mathematical series? If some of our judgmental agreement neither calls for nor admits of any further cognitive account, why should not our agreement about the content of novel utterances come into that case?

To stress: the transition from linguistic training to linguistic competence may be mediated in ways which are possible only for certain sorts of conscious, thinking beings. But that is not to say that it is informed by rules – whether put there by the training or, in part at least, in place already – of which linguistic competence works repeated but unconscious consultations. If we reject the constitutive question – what makes it the case that this is a correct application of the rule at this point? what makes it the case that this novel utterance means just that? – the phenomenon to be explained, it seems, can only be our agreement in judgments on the relevant point, and on similar matters. And if one message of Wittgenstein's discussion is that it is philosophically misguided to ask for an account of that in general, what is special about the particular case of agreement about the content of novel utterances? Can the sort of story which the generative grammarian tells be given without commitment to the mythology at which the negative part of Wittgenstein's discussion is directed? The 'official' Wittgensteinian view is apt to encourage a dismissal of the Central Project altogether.[22]

III

I want to canvass a third possibility: an account of the central insight of Wittgenstein's discussion of rule-following which is neither Kripkean nor 'official'. It may be that the 'official' view is exegetically correct, and that I do here part company with the intentions of the actual, historical Wittgenstein. But it seems to me that it is an important methodological precept that we do not despair of giving answers to constitutive questions too soon; if the accomplishments of analysis in philosophy often seem meagre, that may be because it is difficult, not impossible.

The rule-following considerations attack the idea that judgments about the requirements of a rule on a particular occasion have a 'tracking' epistemology, answer to states of affairs constituted altogether independently of our inclination to make those judgments. How can judgments lack a substantial epistemology in this way, and yet still be *objective* – still have to answer to something distinct from our actual dispositions of judgment?

A good example of a broadly parallel problem is provided by secondary qualities of material objects – qualities of colour, taste, smell, palpable texture, audible sound, and so on. It is an old idea that, in our judgments concerning such qualities, we respond more to aspects of our own affective phenomenology than to anything real in nature, and there is a corresponding perennial temptation towards an irrealist construal of such judgments.[23] But the irrealist response is, in this case, an overreaction. What may be true, I believe, is that (a large class of) judgments of colour, for instance, fail what I have elsewhere called the *order-of-determination* test.[24] Judgments of shape, by contrast, to take the most often discussed example of a Lockian primary quality, arguably pass the test. The order-of-determination test concerns the relation between *best* judgments – judgments made in what are, with respect to their particular subject-matter, *cognitively ideal* conditions of both judge and circumstance – and truth. Passing the test requires that there be some content to the idea of best judgments *tracking* the truth – the determinants of a judgment's being true and of its being best have to be somehow independent. Truth, for judgments which pass the test, is a standard constituted independently of any considerations concerning cognitive pedigree. For judgments which fail the test, by contrast, there is no distance between being true and being best; truth, for such judgments, is constitutively what we judge to be true when we operate under cognitively ideal conditions.

The contrast, then, is between judgments among which our best opinions *determine* the extension of the truth-predicate, and those among which they at most reflect an extension determined independently – henceforward *extension-determining* and *extension-reflecting* judgments respectively. So expressed, it is an intuitive and inchoate contrast, which can doubtless be elaborated and refined in a variety of ways. To fix ideas, let us look a bit more closely at the way matters might proceed first in the cases of (primary) colour and (visually appraisable, three-dimensional) shape; and then in the case of psychological characteristics.

Consider a plane surface one foot square. What conditions on a judge and circumstances of judgment should we impose in order to ensure that his/her (visual) judgment will be that the surface is, say, uniformly royal blue only if it is? Well, the surface must be in full view, and in good light, relatively stationary, and not too far away; and the subject must know which object is in question, must observe it attentively, must be possessed of normal visual equipment and be otherwise cognitively lucid, and must be competent with the concept *blue*. In addition, the subject must be free of doubt about the satisfaction of any of these conditions – for a doubt might lead to an unwillingness to make any judgment, or even to the making of some bizarre, compensatory judgment, in circumstances which were otherwise ideal for the appraisal of colour.

Now, it is presumably necessary, in order for our judgments, appropriately constrained (partially)[25] to *determine* the extension of some concept, that it be *a priori* true that the concept applies when, so constrained, we judge that it does. And it is, I suggest, *a priori* true that when all the foregoing conditions are met, the fact of the object's colour – at least at the level of refinement captured by a predicate like 'blue' – and the subject's judgment of the fact will, as it were, covary.[26] It is another question whether such *a priori* covariance is sufficient for the judgments to enjoy extension-determining status. But there are, in this case, three supplementary considerations which, if correct, arguably confer such sufficiency.

First, a priority in such a claim – a claim that, under certain conditions, C, a subject will hold a certain belief if and only if it is true (henceforward, a *provisional equation*) – may be the product of a certain triviality, consequent on the conditions' receiving no substantial specification but being described purely in terms of 'suitability', 'conduciveness', or, generally, as whatever-it-takes to appraise judgments of the relevant sort correctly. Clearly, we would have made no case for regarding best opinion as *determining* the extension of the truth-predicate among a given class of judgments if, although we had constructed an appropriate kind of provisional equation whose instances held *a priori* true, their *a priority* was owing to this kind of trivial specification of the C-conditions. For it is an *a priori* truth of *any* kind of judgment whatever that, if I operate under conditions which have everything it takes to ensure the correctness of my opinion, then it will be the case that P if and only if I take it to be so. But the conditions listed above for the appraisal of colour allow, it is plausible, substantial, non-trivial elaboration in a manner conservative of the *a priori* connection between their satisfaction and the correctness of the subject's opinion. We can, for instance, specify normal visual equipment on the part of the subject as: equipment which is actually statistically usual among human beings. Likewise, good lighting conditions can be specified as: conditions like those which actually typically obtain out-of-doors and out-of-shadow at noon on a cloudy summer's day.[27]

The second supplementary consideration is that the question whether the C-conditions, so substantially specified, are satisfied in a particular case is logically independent of any truths concerning the details of the extension of colour concepts. If this were not so, it would be open to question whether subjects' opinions, formed under these C-conditions, could be extension-determining; for satisfaction of the C-conditions would always presuppose some anterior constitution of colour facts. It is here that one disanalogy opens up with the case of shape, as we shall see in a moment.

The final supplementary consideration is that there is to hand no *other* account of what does determine the extension of the truth-predicate among simple judgments of colour, of which the *a priority* of provisional equations of the kind in question, whose C-conditions are substantially specified and, in the requisite way, free of logical presupposition about the extension of colour concepts, would be a derivable consequence. So there is, to put the matter another way, no *explaining away* the case which the other considerations supply for saying the judgments formed under the conditions in question are extension-determining rather than extension-reflecting.

The suggestion, in summary, is that there is at least a strong *prima facie* case for regarding a base class[28] of our best judgments about colour as extension-determining. The case consists in the circumstances (i) that we can construct *a priori* true provisional equations for such judgments; (ii) that the C-conditions in these equations can be substantially specified, in a manner free of the triviality associated with whatever-it-takes formulations; (iii) that the satisfaction of the C-conditions is, in any particular case, logically independent of the details of the extensions of colour concepts; (iv) that no other account is available of what else might determine the extension of the truth-predicate among judgments of colour, of which the satisfaction by the relevant provisional equations of conditions (i)–(iii) would be a consequence.[29]

Contrast now the situation of shape. Suppose x is some nearby middle-sized object, and consider the judgment, 'x is pear-shaped'. We will want to characterise the conditions which are cognitively ideal for the visual appraisal of x's shape in terms very similar to those suggested for the case of colour. But there are differences. One, relatively unimportant, is that the lighting conditions do not have to be as good; sodium street-lighting, for instance, is suitable enough for recognising shapes. But a second, much more important, consideration is that a single subject's *best* opinion about three-dimensional shape, if visually grounded, must needs be the product of *several* observations, from a suitable variety of spatial positions. And in order for it to be *a priori* true that, subject to whatever other conditions we wish to impose, such a subject's opinion about the shape of x will be correct, we need to ensure that no *change* in x's shape takes place through the period of these several observations. But that calls for some ingredient in the C-conditions of which it is an *a priori* consequence that whatever it is true to say of x's shape at any time during the subject's observations is also true at any other time within the relevant period. Some independent determinant is therefore called for of what it *is* true to say about x's shape during that period – independent, that is, of the opinion formed by the subject. There is accordingly, it seems, no immediate prospect of a provisional equation for 'x is pear-shaped' meeting both conditions (i) and (iii) above.

A natural response is that there is no reason why a particular kind of subject-matter might not dictate that the formation of a best opinion required *teamwork*. What if we discharge the single observer and consider instead the opinion concerning *x*'s shape which would be arrived at cooperatively by a number of strategically positioned subjects who observed *x* at the same time? That should filter out the problem of instability. But there is a deeper problem which brings out, I think, the real point of disanalogy between shape and colour. The application of shape predicates, even ones as rough and ready as 'pear-shaped', is answerable to a variety of considerations besides visual appearance. For instance, a solid is pear-shaped only if any maximal two-dimensional section of it describes two contiguous circles of substantially different sizes. But it cannot be an *a priori* truth that conditions of the kind which we regard as optimal for the visual detection of shape are adequate for the reliable visual appraisal of characteristics which are in this way answerable to such operational considerations. The operational criteria dominate the visual – that is why the Müller-Lyer illusion is a *visual* illusion. And we can well enough imagine starting out again, as if at the dawn of man's intellectual history, armed with the concepts which we have now but with no experience of the world, and finding that the cost of maintaining the thesis that reliable visual appraisals of shape are generally possible would be a disorderly plague of hypotheses about changes in shape, forced on us by the need to reconcile our visual appraisals with operational ones. It is an *a posteriori* courtesy of experience that the world in which we actually live is not of this awkward kind. And if that is right, then no kind of true provisional equation for visual judgments of shape, even if it invokes teamwork and thereby meets the independence condition (iii), can be both *a priori* and substantial.[30]

I am not, of course, presenting these remarks as establishing conclusively that (a base class of) judgments of colour fail the order-of-determination test, while judgments of shape pass it.[31] Nor is it clear that the considerations advanced, even as far as they go, will generalise to other instances of the primary/secondary distinction. My purpose is, rather, to indicate one framework for the discussion and development of the test; to give credence to the thought that there is a distinction here – perhaps a number of distinctions – and an explanatory programme of great potential importance.

Nevertheless, if the gist of the foregoing is correct, visual judgments of colour will emerge as an interesting mix of subjectivity and objectivity. They should not, at least in a basic class of cases, when appropriate C-conditions are met, be regarded as responsive to states of affairs which are constituted independently – our best opinions about colour do not, in that sense, *track* colour. But neither is it the case that there is no standard to meet, that whatever we say about colour goes or – what comes to the same thing – that there is no such thing as an object's real colour. Rather, it is a perfectly objective question what, in a particular case, the deliverance of best opinion would be; and that deliverence is something with which a majority, or even a whole community, may for some reason be out of accord.

IV

I pass now to the second set of potential examples which I want to air: that of self-ascriptions of psychological states like sensation, emotion, mood, belief, desire, and intention – the traditional category of *avowals*. The proposal that such judgments are extension-determining is an extremely attractive one. The traditional Cartesian epistemology attempts to construe avowals in general on the model of a certain conception of what is involved in competent self-ascription of *sensation* – a model which draws heavily on a comparison with perception of material objects, but with the crucial differences that the sensation, *qua* 'inner' object, is accessible only to the subject, whose gaze is conceived as all-seeing and error-proof. As a picture of knowledge of one's own sensations, this generates problems enough, principally by its presupposition of the operability of private schemes of classification – 'private languages'. But, even if we let the Cartesian account of sensation pass, it provides only the most feeble basis for an account of the self-ascription of other kinds of psychological states. For there are no plausible introspectible processes or states which are candidates to be, for instance, beliefs and intentions. And besides – and more important – to think of, for example, intention as an introspectible episode in consciousness generates no end of difficulties and contortions when we try to make sense of the necessarily holistic character of the scheme of beliefs, desires, and intentions by reference to which we explain subjects' behaviour, and of the notion of *fit* between an intention and the behaviour which implements it. One of the most central themes in Wittgenstein's later philosophy of mind is the idea that Cartesianism is based on a *grammatical* misunderstanding, a misinterpretation of the language-game of self- and other-ascription of mental states. The Cartesian takes the authority of avowals as a symptom of, as it were, a superlatively sure genre of detection. We should accomplish a very sharp perspective on the sense in which this is a 'grammatical' misunderstanding if it could be shown that avowals fail the order-of-determination test – in other words, that subjects' best opinions determine, rather than reflect what it is true to say about their intentional states, with the consequence that the notion of detection or 'inner tracking', as it were, is inappropriate. (Naturally, it would have to be part of a satisfying development in this direction that best opinions turned out to be relatively easily accomplished; otherwise, the authority of avowals would be unaccounted for.)

Can we, then, provide a set of conditions whose satisfaction will ensure, *a priori*, that subjects will believe themselves to have, for example, certain particular intentions if and only if they do? Well, how might a subject who had the conceptual resources to form a belief appropriate to the presence, or absence, of a certain intention, nevertheless fail to do so? Self-deception is one possibility, whatever the correct account of that puzzling idea. A subject may, as many people think, be simply unable to bring to consciousness the real intentions which inform certain of his courses of action. Conversely, we are familiar with the kind of weak-mindedness which can lead subjects into deceiving themselves that they have formed certain intentions – typically ones which are desirable but difficult of implementation – when in truth they have not done so.

In both these kinds of case, we typically regard the self-deceptive (lack of) belief as *motivated*. But in certain other circumstances it would be better to think of it as having a primarily physiological – perhaps a pharmacological – explanation. The cause of a subject's mistaken belief about his/her intentions need not reside in other aspects of his/her intentional psychology. Anyway, one way or another, an appropriate set of C-conditions will have to ensure that nothing of this kind is operative. And in addition, we need only include, it seems, a condition to the effect that the subject be appropriately attentive to the question what his/her intentions are. However, nothing in what follows will depend on whether these three conditions – grasp of the appropriate concepts, lack of any material self-deception or anything relevantly similar, and appropriate attentiveness – do indeed suffice.

The most salient difficulty, for our purposes, with the provisional biconditional which will emerge from these suggestions is that of making a case that it meets condition (ii) – the condition that the C-conditions be substantially specified. The motive for condition (ii) was not a distaste for triviality as such, it will be remembered, but rather for the particular kind of triviality involved in whatever-it-takes formulations. Such formulations are always possible and, by prejudicially representing matters in terms of the jargon of tracking, leave us with no way of getting at the distinction which it is the point of the order-of-determination test to reflect. And on the face of it, unfortunately, we are some considerable distance from a formulation of the no-self-deception condition which can count as non-trivial in the relevant sense. The problem is, first, that 'self-deception' covers, for the purposes of the biconditional, *any* motivated condition which might lead to a subject's ignorance or error concerning his or her intentions; and, second, we need, as noted, to allow for the possibility of unmotivated conditions – chemically induced ones, or whatever – with the same effect. So we seem to be perilously close to writing in a condition to the effect that the subject be 'free of any condition which might somehow impede his ability reliably to certify his own intentions'. And that, of course, is just the sort of insubstantial, whatever-it-takes formulation which condition (ii) was meant to exclude.

Perhaps it is possible to do better, to produce some description which excludes the relevant class of states but does so non-trivially. But none comes to mind, and it would of course be pointless to wait on the deliverance of empirical science if one is hoping for vindication of an extension-determining view of the beliefs expressed by avowals, and so requires something which will subserve the *a priority* of the resulting biconditional. So how to proceed?

We have, I think, to depart somewhat from the approach which emerged in the case of colour. But a possible variant of it is suggested by the reflection that the troublesome no-self-deception condition is *positive-presumptive*. By that I mean that, such is the 'grammar' of ascriptions of intention, one is entitled to assume that a subject is *not* materially self-deceived, or unmotivatedly similarly afflicted, unless one possesses determinate evidence to the contrary. Positive-presumptiveness ensures that, in all circumstances in which one has no countervailing evidence, one is *a priori* justified in holding that the no-self-deception condition is satisfied, its trivial specification notwithstanding. Suppose, then, that we succeed in constructing an *a priori* true provisional biconditional:

C(Jones) → (Jones believes he intends to φ ⟷ Jones intends to φ),

where C includes the (trivial) no-self-deception condition but no other trivially formulated conditions. Then if – lacking evidence to the contrary – we are *a priori* justified in holding the no-self-deception condition to be met, we are also *a priori* justified in believing the result of deleting that condition from the provisional biconditional in question. Likewise for any other positive-presumptive conditions listed under C. In this way we can eventually arrive at a restricted provisional biconditional in which all the C-conditions are substantially specified and which, in the absence of any information bearing on whether the conditions are satisfied which we have deleted from it, it is *a priori reasonable* to believe.

It is true that we are now dealing with something *a priori* credible rather than *a priori* true. But the question still arises: what is the *explanation* of the *a priori* credibility, in the relevant kind of circumstances of ignorance, of the restricted version if what determines the fact of Jones's intention, under the residual C-conditions, is something quite detached from his or her belief? The explanation cannot be that the C-conditions are trivially formulated, for they are all, by hypothesis, substantial.

Suppose that the three conditions suggested above – possession of the appropriate concepts, attentiveness, and lack of self-deception – do indeed suffice *a priori* for Jones's opinion about his or her intention to covary with the facts. But suppose also that possession of the relevant concepts and attentiveness raise, unlike lack of self-deception, no problems of triviality. Then the matter for explanation is: why is it *a priori* reasonable to believe that, provided Jones has the relevant concepts and is attentive to the matter, he will believe that he intends to φ if and only if he does? The key thought of the variant approach will be that the matter will be nicely explained if the concept of intention works in such a way that Jones's opinions, formed under the restricted set of C-conditions, play a *defeasible* extension-determining role, with defeat conditional on the emergence of evidence that one or more of the background, positive-presumptive, conditions are not in fact met.

To elaborate a little, there are, in contrast to the case argued for colour, no conditions which can be characterised non-trivially but independently – in the sense of condition (iii) above – whose satisfaction *a priori* ensures covariance of a subject's beliefs about his intentions and the facts. But there are such non-trivially, independently specifiable conditions whose satisfaction ensures, courtesy of no *a posteriori* background beliefs, that, failing any other relevant information, a subject's opinions about his or her intentions should be accepted. And the proposed strategy of explanation is, roughly, as follows. What determines the distribution of truth-values among ascriptions of intention to a subject who has the conceptual resources to understand those ascriptions and is attentive to them are, in the first instance, nothing but the details of the subject's self-conception in relevant respects. If the assignment of truth-values, so effected, generates behavioural singularities – the subject's behaviour clashes with ingredients in his/her self-conception, or seems to call for the inclusion of ingredients which he/she is unwilling to include – then the self-deception proviso, broadly interpreted as above, may be invoked, and the subject's opinion, or lack of it, overridden. But that is not because something is shown, by the discordant behaviour, about the character of some *independently constituted* system of intentions which the subject's opinions at best reflect. When possession of a certain intention is an aspect of a self-conception that coheres well enough both internally and with the subject's behaviour, there is nothing *else* that makes it true that the intention is indeed possessed.

The view proposed is minimalist. Nothing leaner has any prospect, so far as I can see, of accommodating both the avowability and the theoreticity of intention. To be sure, explaining the *a priori* reliability of a subject's C-conditioned beliefs about his intentions will do nothing to explain the reliability of his avowals – even assuming our right to regard him as honest – unless the C-conditions in question are likely to be met. But there seems no cause to anticipate problems on that score. Attentiveness – however precisely it should be elaborated – is presumably, like lack of self-deception, a positive-presumptive condition; and a subject's possession of the appropriate concepts is prerequisite for their being able to effect the avowal in the first place. So there is every promise of a straightforward kind of explanation of the authority which avowals of intention, *qua* avowals, typically carry.

Suppose, by contrast, that subjects' best opinions about their intentions are at most extension-reflecting. Then the *a priori* reasonableness, when nothing else relevant is known, of the restricted provisional biconditional needs another explanation. And providing one will require explaining how it coheres with the view that subjects' best opinions track independently constituted states of affairs to suppose it *a priori* reasonable to think, failing evidence to the contrary, that some of the conditions on an opinion's being best are satisfied. Why, in the absence of germane evidence, is *agnosticism* about the satisfaction of, for example, the self-deception condition not a preferable stance? The three conditions collectively formulate, on this view, what it takes to ensure a certain kind of cognitive accomplishment, a feat of detection. Why is it *a priori* warranted to assume, failing information to the contrary, that a subject satisfies any such conditions?

To avoid misunderstanding, I do not mean to present the question as rhetorical. There are various ways in which it might be approached by an opponent of the extension-determining view. Perhaps it could be made out that the warrant somehow flows from the subject's nature, *qua* subject, or from the nature of the states of affairs – the intentions in question are *his* or *hers*, after all – of which the conditions ensure his or her detection. Alternatively, perhaps other examples can be produced where best opinions are extension-reflecting and yet certain of the conditions on their being best are likewise positive-presumptive, for general reasons which might be argued to apply to the present case. But it is fair to say, I think, that the onus is now on someone who prefers to think that one's best opinions about one's own intentions, etc., are extension-reflecting. Why are we, apparently, so cavalierly optimistic about our general fitness for such detection? And what, fundamentally, when we succeed in holding best opinions, *does* determine the extension of the truth-predicate among the class of judgments in question, if not those opinions themselves?

My purpose in introducing the psychological was only the limited one of canvassing a second shape which the attempt to refine and apply the order-of-determination test might assume. Perhaps enough has been said to accomplish that. But note a prospective corollary, if the extension-determining character of subjects' best opinions about their intentions and similar states, and the authority typically carried by avowals of such states, can indeed be accounted for along the lines proposed. Earlier, I criticised responses to Kripke's Sceptical Argument which – like the dispositional conception, or Chomsky's own proposal – locates the called-for meaning-constitutive facts only at the cost of obscuring subjects' non-inferential knowledge of their own meanings. It would be appropriate to level a similar complaint against dispositional or theoretical construals of the notion of intention. But no such complaint is appropriate against an account of self-knowledge of intention further developed along the lines canvassed; one according to which subjects' best opinions about their intentions, *both past and present*, are properly conceived as provisionally extension-determining, and which explains how and why the opinions which they typically hold are indeed best. It will be, similarly, a perfect answer to Kripke's Sceptic to explain how judgments concerning one's own meanings, both past and present, are likewise provisionally extension-determining in the most ordinary circumstances. Challenged to justify the claim that I formerly meant addition by 'plus', it will not be necessary to locate some meaning-constitutive fact in my former behaviour or mental life. A sufficient answer need only advert to my present opinion, that addition is what I formerly meant, and still mean, and to the *a priori* reasonableness of the supposition, failing evidence to the contrary, that this opinion is best.

Responding to Kripke's Sceptic in this way does not require construal of meaning as a kind of intention; it is enough that the concepts are relevantly similar – that both sustain authoritative first-person avowals,[32] and that this circumstance is to be explained in terms of failure of the order-of-determination test. However, I can go no further into the matter here except to record the view that it is indeed with the conception of meanings as items which our best opinions may *reflect*, rather than with their reality *tout court*, that the Sceptical Argument engages.[33]

V

Correctly applying a rule to a new case will, it is natural to think, typically involve a double success: sensitivity is necessary both to the relevant features of the presented situation and to what, in respect of those features, will fit or fail to fit the rule. Correctly castling in the course of a game of chess, for instance, will depend both on apprehension of the configuration of chessmen at the time of the move, and on a knowledge of whether that configuration (and the previous course of the game) permits castling at that point. In this respect the simple mathematical examples on which Wittgenstein's discussion concentrates are apparently untypical. Knowing how to continue a series does of course require knowledge of what point in the series one has reached, and also in certain cases some knowledge about the preceding constitution of the series beyond the identity of the immediately preceding element. But there need be no *perceptual* input, corresponding to perception of the board configuration in chess. Wittgenstein's examples thus approximate as closely as possible to cases of *pure* rule-following, where only one kind of sensitivity – that concerning the requirements of the rule – is necessary for success, and failure has to be attributed to an imperfect understanding of the rule or to some technical slip in applying it. That is, presumably, why he selects just those examples. In order to focus on questions concerning the objectivity and epistemology of rule-following, it is obviously best to consider cases where our judgments about what accords with the rule are most nearly pure and unconditioned by the cognitive effects upon us of the prevailing circumstances.

Absolute purity is, however, impossible. The judgment that *this* move accords with a particular rule can never be informed only and purely by one's understanding of the rule. So much is clear when one reflects that aberrant performance, even in simple arithmetical cases and when there is no question of insincerity, can always in principle be explained in ways which conserve the hypotheses that the subject correctly understands the rule and, relative to what he or she took to be the situation, applied it correctly. The subject may, for instance, have lost his or her place, misremembered what he or she had done before, or misunderstood some relevant symbol not involved in the expression of the rule.

The ability successfully to follow a rule is thus to be viewed as, at each successive instance, the product of a number of cognitive responses which interact holistically in the production of the proper step. And some of these responses – correctly perceiving the set-up on the chess-board, for instance, or recollecting the expansion of the series to this point – do not strictly pertain to the rule but are possible for subjects who have no inkling of it. Where R is the rule or set of rules in question, let us call the others *R-informed*. Now, an R-informed response need not be encapsulable in any judgment which the subject can articulate distinct from the output judgment, as it were – the judgment into which his or her R-informed and non-R-informed responses conjointly feed. In that respect, the chess example, in which the R- and non-R-informed components could be respectively explicitly entertained as the major and minor premises for a *modus ponens* step, is untypical. I cannot always have concepts *other* than those whose governing rules I am trying to observe in a particular situation in terms of which I can formulate a separate judgment of the input to which these rules are to be applied. So I cannot always extricate and articulate a judgment which, conditionally on such a separate judgment of the input, formulates my impression of the requirements of the rules in a fashion which is neutral with respect to the correctness of my R-uninformed responses to the situation.

It is a platitude that the existence of a rule requires that some sort of content be given to the distinction, among responses which are informed by it, between those which are acceptable and those which are not. The fundamental question raised by the topic of rule-following concerns the ground and nature of this distinction. However, the points about holism and inextricability counsel caution in the formulation of this question. There is, for instance, because of the point about holism, no simple relation between questions concerning what makes for acceptable R-informed responses and questions to do with *truth*, as applied to the output judgments to which those responses holistically contribute. Indeed, we cannot always – because of the point about inextricability – equate the acceptability of a rule-informed response with the truth of any judgment made by the subject – at least, not if such a judgment has to consist in an articulatable belief.

Clearly, then, there is some awkwardness in attempting to apply the distinction drawn by the order-of-determination test to the question of the ground and nature of the requirements of a rule. The test, as so far considered, calls for a class of judgments about which we can raise the question of the relation between best opinion and truth. And the existence of such judgments is just what the inextricability point counsels us not to expect in general. Still, there are extricable cases. The example of castling in chess provided one. And, most significant in the present context, the comprehending response to a novel utterance provides another. Such a response will involve a set of beliefs about the utterance which someone could have who had no understanding of the language in question; but it will also involve a belief about what, modulo the former set, has been said – a paradigm, it would seem, of a rule-informed judgment. Rather than confront the awkwardnesses presented by inextricability, therefore, let me concentrate for our present purpose on such favourable cases: cases where the acceptability of a rule-informed response can be seen as a matter of the truth of a judgment which the responder may be thought of as making. Our question, then, is: what makes for the truth of such rule-informed judgments?

Irrealism is an option. One could hold that such judgments answer to nothing real, not even the deliverances of best opinion. Rather, making acceptable such judgments really is just a matter of keeping in step with the community of followers of the relevant rules. This would be, in effect, the opinion of Kripke's Wittgenstein.

A variation – no longer strictly irrealist – would hold that such judgments are true just in case there is agreement *in* them, and that this is the 'agreement in judgments' which is a pre-condition for the possibility of language serving as a means of communication (*Investigations*, 242). It might be thought that, as an interpretation of Wittgenstein anyway, this variant of the irrealist thought is ruled out by his explicit repudiation[34] of any identification of truth with consensus. But that would be a bad reason. Consensualism about the truth-conditions of R-informed judgments would be quite consistent with repudiating consensualism concerning the output judgments to which, in association with relevant non-R-informed judgments, they contribute on particular occasions.

Platonism is also a possibility. Platonism is, precisely, the view that the correctness of a rule-informed judgment is a matter quite independent of any opinion of ours, whether the states of affairs which confer correctness are thought of as man-made – constituted by over-and-done-with episodes of explanation and linguistic behaviour – or truly platonic and constituted in heaven. For the platonist, correctly following a rule in a particular situation involves a double-feat of tracking: one has to detect both all relevant aspects of the situation and the relevant requirements of the rule. But the principal negative point of Wittgenstein's discussion of rule-following was precisely that the ability to make acceptable rule-informed judgments allows of no coherent construal as a tracking ability, in the fashion which platonism requires.

That leaves the possibility for which I have been labouring to prepare. Abandoning platonism need not involve abandoning the objectivity of rule-informed judgments. There remains the option of regarding such judgments as extension-determining, of seeing *best* opinion as constituting their truth. I would like to be in a position to offer a supported opinion about whether this idea can be approached along the lines sketched for the cases of colour and intention. But I have, at the time of writing, no settled opinion to offer about that, let alone about whether the idea can ultimately be made good.

In summary: once it is agreed that the essential platonist thought is that best opinion about the correctness of rule-informed judgments is extension-reflecting, and that part of Wittgenstein's purpose was, in effect, to demonstrate the untenability of that view, the would-be interpreter of Wittgenstein on rules faces four broad choices. First, there is 'official' Wittgensteinianism, of which the hallmark is scorn of constitutive questions. Asked what constitutes the truth of rule-informed judgment of the kind we isolated, the official Wittgensteinian will reply: 'Bad question, leading to bad philosophy – platonism, for instance, or Kripkean scepticism.' If official Wittgensteinianism is rejected, on the other hand, and the constitutive question is allowed, there seem to be three options, each consistent with the repudiation of platonism. First, there is the thesis that *nothing* constitutes the truth of such judgments, and that this is an important and disturbing contrast which marks them off from judgments of other kinds. This inherently unstable view is in essence that of Kripke's Wittgenstein. Second, there is consensualism, as canvassed above. And finally there is the proposal that the truth-makers for such judgments – the facts in which their correctness consists – are constituted by the deliverances of best opinion.

VI

The concern of the Central Project was to explain our recognition of the syntax and sense of novel sentences. The judgments accomplished by such recognition are, as noted, naturally taken to be rule-informed judgments *par excellence*, which in turn contribute holistically, in association with other judgments of features of the presenting circumstances and with certain background beliefs, to opinions concerning the proper use, or specifically the truth or falsity, of the sentence in the circumstances. So, if the options are as just described, what now are the prospects for the thought that our recognition (agreement in judgment) of the meanings of novel sentences calls for a deep cognitive–psychological explanation, the *ur*-thought of the Central Project? Platonism might sustain it; but if that is the only way it can be sustained, then there is after all a real collision between Wittgenstein's thought and the Central Project, and one might well want to side with Wittgenstein. 'Official' Wittgensteinianism, as we have seen, and Kripkean Wittgensteinianism, by contrast, both undermine the thought. And the same is presumably true of the consensualist option. If the correctness of a rule-informed judgment is simply constituted by our agreement in it, there seems to be no call for a cognitive–psychological account of that agreement. On the contrary, the provision of such an account would immediately restore the idea that, since consensus in a rule-informed judgment would be the product of certain purely cognitive accomplishments, there ought to be some fact about what in any particular case, independently of our actual dispositions of response to it, the *proper* exercise of the relevant cognitive skills and informational states would culminate in; space, in other words, for the idea that an actual consensus might, in a particular case, be misplaced.[35]

With platonism out of the way, the Central Project, as a project in cognitive psychology, would thus appear to demand the view that the correctness of the relevant rule-informed judgments – semantic responses to novel utterances – is objective but best-opinion-determined – the view that semantic content is, if you like, secondary in Lockean terms. If that view can be sustained, then the cognitive–psychological project is properly seen as directed not at the description of the conditions for a certain kind of tracking-accomplishment – that conception has to fall with platonism – but at the detailed elaboration of the C-conditions whose realisation ensures that a subject's judgment of the content of a particular novel utterance will be *best*. The Central Project is thus *prima facie* compatible with Wittgenstein's thought-about rules, if the upshot of the latter is indeed (at least compatible with the claim) that judgments of content, and of the requirements of rules in general, are extension-determining.

Whatever the proper interpretation of Wittgenstein, the outstanding substantive questions are accordingly whether the order-of-determination test can be refined and developed sufficiently to allow a clear-cut application to judgments of content, with their failure – their classification as extension-determining – as the outcome; and whether the then emergent notion of *best* opinion will contain components whose proper description will require – or, less, allow – invoking the apparatus of theoretical linguistics. We are a long way from knowing what it is correct to think about either question. But it may be some advance to be a little clearer about some of the respects in which matters are unclear.[36]

Notes

1 The other component, as is familiar, is that uses of language are characteristically *stimulus-free*; language is 'undetermined by any fixed association of utterances to external stimuli or physiological states (identifiable in any non-circular fashion)' (1966(a), pp. 4–5). Chomsky speaks of the first component as '. . . the central fact to which any significant linguistic theory must address itself' (1966(b)).

2 Chomsky writes (1967, pp. 4–5), for instance

> A person's competence can be represented by a *grammar*, which is a system of rules for pairing semantic and phonetic interpretations. Evidently, these rules operate over an infinite range. Once a person has mastered the rules (unconsciously, of course), he is capable, in principle, of using them to assign semantic interpretations to signals quite independently of whether he has been exposed to them or their parts, as long as they consist of elementary units that he knows and are composed by the rules he has internalized.

Compare Dummett (1976, p. 70):

> A theory of meaning will, then, represent the practical ability possessed by a speaker as consisting in his grasp of a set of propositions; since the speaker derives his understanding of a sentence from the meaning of its component words, these propositions will most naturally form a deductively connected system.

A useful assembly of source material for this basic thought is provided, their deflationary purposes notwithstanding, by Baker and Hacker (1984a, chaps. 8 and 9).

3 I have considered some of the issues involved in Wright, 1986, chap. 6.

4 Both the present chapter and 'Theories of Meaning and Speakers' Knowledge' are attempts to pursue issues raised in the symposium I had with Gareth Evans (Wright 1981). The principal purpose of my contribution, (cf. chapter XV, Wright 1980), was to raise the question to which the present paper is addressed. But Evans's reply (1981), focused on the more specific questions to do with the notion of implicit knowledge which 'Theories of Meaning and Speakers' Knowledge' tries to pursue further. Somehow or other, with the obvious exceptions of Kripke's brief remarks and Chomsky's response (1986), there has been virtually no discussion of the present question since.

5 Cf. Fred d'Agostino (1986, chap. 1)

6 Which need not be restricted to aspects of behaviour and conscious mental life. See Chomsky, 1986, pp. 236ff.

7 See Alexander George (1987, pp. 158–60). Chomsky replies to George's criticism in the same number of the journal (1987, pp. 189–91).

8 For a variety of points of dissatisfaction, besides Chomsky's, see e.g., Baker and Hacker, 1984, pp. 429–32; Goldfarb 1985, 481–4; McDowell, 1984, 329–30; McGinn, 1984, 180–91; and Wright, 1984, 768–70.

9 Kripke (1982, pp. 22–3) characterises it like this:

> According to this response, the fallacy in the argument that no fact about me constitutes my meaning plus lies in the assumption that such a fact must consist in an *occurrent* mental state. Indeed the sceptical argument shows that my entire occurrent past mental history might have been the same whether I meant plus or quus, but all this shows is that the fact that I meant plus (rather than quus) is to be analyzed *dispositionally*, rather than in terms of occurrent mental states. Since Ryle's *The Concept of Mind*, dispositional analyses have been influential; Wittgenstein's own later work is of course one of the inspirations for such analyses, and some may think that he himself wishes to suggest a dispositional solution to his paradox.
>
> The dispositional analysis I have heard proposed is simple. To mean addition by '+' is to be disposed, when asked for any sum 'x+y' to give the sum of x and y as the answer (in particular, to say '125' when queried about '68+57'); to mean quus is to be disposed when queried about any arguments, to respond with their *quum* (in particular to answer '5' when queried about '68+57'). True, my actual thoughts and responses in the past do not differentiate between the plus and the quus hypotheses; but, even in the past, there were dispositional facts about me that did make such a differentiation. To say that in fact I meant plus in the past is to say – as surely was the case! – that had I been queried about '68+57', I *would* have answered '125'. By hypothesis I was not in fact asked, but the disposition was present none the less.

10 Cf. Wright (1987, pp. 393–5).

Of course, one will be inclined to play down, or query, the claimed feature of the first-personal epistemology of intentional states if one is independently convinced of the 'theoretical' view. And this, unsurprisingly, is what Chomsky does. See, for instance, the rebuttal of Dummett's claim that knowledge of meaning is conscious knowledge in Chomsky (1986, p. 271).

11 There are also genuinely episodic states whose occurrence is conditional on the conceptual resources of the sufferer. Having a tune run through one's head is arguably of this character.

12 Or better, the conception which someone who expressed themselves in this way would be likely to intend to convey. Wittgenstein's conservatism almost always leads him to fight shy of direct criticism of a problematical form of expression. Cf. *Investigations* 195:

> 'But I don't mean that what I do now (in grasping a sense) determines the future use *causally* and as a matter of experience, but that in a *queer* way, the use itself is in some sense present'. – But of course it is, 'in *some* sense'! Really the only thing wrong with what you say is the expression 'in a queer way'. The rest is all right . . .

The problems reside in our *interpretations* of what we say.

13 The comparison is James Hopkins's.

14 'Jntuition' and 'Entscheidung'.

15 Contrast, say, Cartesian scepticism about other minds, where we precisely do have an apparent conception of the truth-conferers for descriptions of others' mental states, based on a seemingly plausible projection from one's own case, which sets up an epistemological problem.

16 For note the quotation marks.

17 There is some question, I think, whether the third theme really strikes home at what someone is likely to be thinking who is working with the conception of the rule as explanation-transcendent but manifest to the subject. One is – I suppose this is a point of autobiography – much more likely to be thinking in terms of a kind of *inner illumination* than in terms of having the rule as, literally, an object of consciousness. But the connection between the 'inner illumination' and the step-by-step judgments involved in applying the rule remains irremediably intuitional, in the sense that opens it to the sceptical attack of the second theme. For an elaboration of the attack, see Wright, 1980, pp. 36–8.

18 For instance McDowell (1984), McGinn (1984) and Baker and Hacker (1984). See also Malcolm (1986, p. 154).

19 I am not, in presenting this contrast, forgetting that Kripke's Sceptic is a device for focusing on an *ontological* issue. It remains that the device works by raising, at the relevant stage of the dialectic, an epistemological worry. The transition to an ontological conclusion is mediated by the further assumption, disputed e.g. by the dispositionalist, that facts about (former) rules – if they existed – would have to be accessible, at least in principle, via reflection on (former) behaviour and conscious mental episodes.

20 But a distinction is necessary here. See p. 257 below.

21 I am thinking especially of Baker and Hacker's exegesis of the *Investigations* (1980). But it is a nice question how, if at all, John McDowell (1984), in his conception of semantic facts as a kind of bedrock, departs from the official line.

22 For elaboration, see Baker and Hacker (1984, pp. 345–56).

23 Famously succumbed to by Locke, of course, and recently by the late John Mackie (1976, pp. 17–20).

24 In my 'Realism: the Contemporary Debate – whither now?' in *Reality and Reason*, eds J. Haldane and C.J.G. Wright, Oxford: Clarendon Press, forthcoming.

25 'Partially' because we are, in effect, considering something of the form:

If S judges under conditions C, then (P if and only if S believes P),

which says nothing at all about the truth-conditions of P-type propositions under non- C-conditions. But we cannot plausibly consider, for present purposes, the stronger *basic equation* (to use Mark Johnston's term), namely,

P if and only if (if S judges under conditions C, S believes P)

unless we can foreclose on the possibility that bringing about conditions C might materially affect the truth-status of P. And that cannot be done with colour, or any characteristic sustained by a causally active and acted-upon base. Cf. note 26 in Wright, 1988.

26 Two possible doubts about the sufficiency of the listed conditions would need to be addressed before this claim could be finally sustained.

(I) Might a subject not be possessed of eccentric background beliefs – for instance, that there are no blue things at all! – which would prevent his formation of the appropriate belief about the object's colour, even though he met the conditions as stated? (I am here indebted to Paul Boghossian.) It is not clear. If the object is blue, it will look blue to him under the stated conditions; and then, if he believes that

Blue things look blue to *normally visually equipped* subjects in *good light*,

he is going to be constrained by the eccentric belief – if cognitively lucid – to doubt whether both those conditions are met. So he will violate the extremal condition, of being free of doubt, etc. But if he doesn't believe the principle connecting blueness and blue appearance, does he count as appropriately competent with the concept, *blue*? Still, that is just one kind of eccentric belief.

(II) Background colour affects colour appearance: a cream circle, for instance, may look pink, or eau-de-Nil, even in normal light, depending on the colour of the surface behind it. May we not need to strengthen the C-conditions to contain some stipulation of an appropriately coloured background? There would be great difficulties with the important independence condition, see text p. 248 if so. But does the phenomenon affect *royal blue, scarlet, emerald green, lemon yellow* to any extent which might result in a subject's erroneously judging (or withholding the judgment) that an object meets one of those descriptions? And would it anyway be absurd to think of colour as involving an element of situation-relativity – so that the judgments about, e.g., the cream circle are all correct?

27   The occurrences of 'actually' in these two specifications are to be understood as securing rigidity of reference to the status quo. So counterfactual situations in which other things are statistically usual are not C-conditions as specified.

28   A base class, rather than merely a proper subclass, because our beliefs about objects' colours under non- C-conditions are variously constrained by the characteristics of colours as determined by C-conditioned judgments. It is, for instance, conclusive justification for the belief that something is blue in the dark to justify the claims (i) that we would judge it to be blue if we saw it in good light and under the other C-conditions; and (ii) that bringing these conditions about would effect no changes in any determinable (contrast: determinate) aspect of the object which would need to be mentioned in an explanation of the form which our C-conditioned response would assume.

A connected point, which may help to forestall possible confusion, is that the relationship between the characteristic, being-judged-to-be-blue-under-C-conditions, and being blue is not to be compared to that between the characteristic marks of the instance of a natural kind and being an instance of that kind. It is true that the marks of gold, e.g. – its colour, lustre, heaviness, resistance to corrosion, etc. – are in some sense *a priori*; we do not learn what gold is and then discover that it has these characteristics. But in the case of genuine natural kinds we are (a) open to the discovery that some things which have the marks whereby we succeeded in identifying the kind are not actually instances of the kind; and (b) open to the discovery that actually no genuine kind of thing *is* individuated by those marks. By contrast, if what I have been suggesting about colour is correct, we are not open to the discovery that some objects judged to be blue under C-conditions are not blue; nor open to the discovery – should the microphysics of blue things prove bizarrely heterogeneous – that there is no such thing as an object's being blue.

29   It is not inconsistent with thinking of best judgments about colour as being extension-determining simultaneously to hold that the extensions of colour

concepts are determined by microphysical characteristics of objects – supposing that the physics *doesn't* prove bizarrely heterogeneous. For it will be best judgments about colour which determine *which* microphysical characteristics are fit to play a (supplementary) extension-determining role. And no obstacle to colour's satisfying condition (iv) is posed by this view of the relationship between colour and the microphysical, since the microphysical account of the determinants of the extension of 'blue' e.g., will not, presumably, entail that appropriate provisional equations can be formulated satisfying conditions (i)–(iii).

30 This train of thought is elaborated somewhat in Wright, 1988, pp. 19–20.

31 Various interesting further questions have to be negotiated which I cannot go into here. For instance, might best *operationally-determined* (contrast: visually determined) beliefs about shape arguably play an extension-determining role, or are even such beliefs at most extension-reflecting? One germane consideration would be that very many shape concepts – 'pear-shaped' is an example – are, while operationally constrained, subject to no obvious operational, as opposed to tactuo-visual, criteria of application. Another would be that we would expect to need stability provisos in the appropriate lists of C-conditions for operationally determined beliefs, since proper execution of the appropriate kinds of operation is essentially subject to invalidation by instability. It would be pleasant if that consideration were decisive, but I do not think that it is. For it may perhaps be mitigated by some play with the *positive-presumptiveness* of assumptions of stability, along the lines illustrated in the next section of the text for the role of lack of self-deception in the C-conditions for appraisal of one's own intentions.

32 Note that the most likely reservation about the claim that they do – the thought that certain elements of *convention*, which have no counterpart in the case of intending in general, sustain my ability to mean anything in particular by a word – will undercut the Sceptic's strategy in any case, since restricting the search for facts about my former meanings to aspects of my former behaviour and conscious mental states will precisely exclude the relevant conventional (presumably social) elements. I am here indebted to Bob Hale.

33 For further discussion, see Wright, 1987.

34 See references on p. 244 above.

35 Exactly the idea enshrined in the distinction between *competence* and *performance*, of course.

36 I am very grateful to Paul Boghossian and Bob Hale for helpful discussion of an earlier draft.

References

d'Agostino, Fred 1986: *Chomsky's System of Ideas*. Oxford: Clarendon.

Baker, Gordon and Hacker, Peter 1980: *Wittgenstein: Understanding and Meaning*. Oxford: Basil Blackwell.

1984a: *Language, Sense and Nonsense*. Oxford: Basil Blackwell.

1984b: On misunderstanding Wittgenstein. *Synthese*, 58(3), 407–50.

Chomsky, Noam 1959: A review of B.F. Skinner's *Verbal Behavior*. *Language*, 35.

1966a: *Cartesian Linguistics*. New York: Harper & Row.

1966b: *Current Issues in Linguistic Theory*. The Hague: Mouton.

1967: Recent contributions to the theory of innate ideas. *Synthese*, 17, 4–5.

1986: *Knowledge of Language*. New York: Praeger.

1987: Replies to Alexander George and Michael Brody. *Mind and Language*, 2 (2), 178–97.

Dummett, Michael 1976: What is a theory of meaning? (II). In S. Holtzman and C. Leich (eds), *Wittgenstein: To Follow a Rule*. London: Routledge & Kegan Paul, 99–137.

George, Alexander 1987: Review of *Knowledge of Language*. *Mind and Language*, 2, 155–64.

Goldfarb, Warren 1985: Kripke on Wittgenstein and rules. *Journal of Philosophy*, 82, 471–88.

Kripke, Saul A. 1982: *Wittgenstein on Rules and Private Language*. Oxford: Basil Blackwell.

McDowell, John 1984: Wittgenstein on following a rule. *Synthese*, 58 (3), 325–63.

McGinn, Colin 1984: *Wittgenstein on Meaning*. Oxford: Basil Blackwell.

Mackie, John 1976: *Problems from Locke*. Oxford: Clarendon.

Malcolm, Norman 1986: *Nothing is Hidden: Wittgenstein's Criticism of His Early Thought*. Oxford: Basil Blackwell.

Wright, Crispin 1980: *Wittgenstein on the Foundations of Mathematics*. London: Duckworth.

1981: Rule-following objectivity and the theory of meaning. In S. Holtzman and C. Leich (eds), *Wittgenstein: To Follow a Rule*. London: Routledge & Kegan Paul, 99–137.

1984: Kripke's account of the argument against private language. *Journal of Philosophy*, 81, 759–78.

1986: Theories of meaning and speakers' knowledge. In Wright, *Realism, Meaning and Truth*. Oxford: Basil Blackwell. Repr. in Shanker (ed.), *Philosophy in Britain Today*. London: Croom Helm (1986), 267–307.

1987: On making up one's mind: Wittgenstein on intention. In Weingartner and Schurz (eds), *Logic, Philosophy of Science and Epistemology*. Proceedings of the 11th International Wittgenstein Symposium, Kirchberg. Vienna: Holder-Pichler-Temsky, 391–404.

1988: Moral values, projection and secondary qualities. *Proceedings of the Aristotelian Society*. Supplementary volume 62.

Select Bibliography of Works by Noam Chomsky

1955   'Logical Syntax and Semantics: Their linguistic relevance', *Language*, vol. 31, no. 1.

1956   'Three Models for the Description of Language', IRE *Transactions on Information Theory*, vol. IV, no. 3; reprinted in *Readings in Mathematical Psychology*, edited by R. Duncan Luce, Robert R. Bush and Eugene Galanter, vol. 2, J. Wiley & Sons, New York, 1965.

1957   *Syntactic Structures*, Mouton, The Hague.

1958   'A Transformational Approach to Syntax', paper presented at the third Texas Conference on Problems of Linguistic Analysis in English, held at Austin, Texas, 9–12 May 1958 and subsequently printed in the proceedings of the title, edited by Archibald A. Hill, University of Texas Press, Austin, 1962; also printed in *The Structure of Language: Readings in The Philosophy of Language*, edited by Jerry A. Fodor and Jerrold J. Katz, Prentice-Hall, Englewood Cliffs, 1964.

'What is Said to Be?' (with Israel Scheffler), *Proceedings of the Aristotelian Society*, New Series 59, London.

1959   'Review of B.F. Skinner's *Verbal Behavior*', *Language*, vol. 35, no. 1.

1964   *Current Issues in Linguistic Theory*, Mouton, The Hague.

1965   *Aspects of the Theory of Syntax*, MIT Press, Cambridge, Massachusetts.

1966   *Cartesian Linguistics: A Chapter in The History of Rationalist Thought*, Harper & Row, New York.

Topics in the Theory of Generative Grammar, Mouton, The Hague.

1967   'Recent Contributions to the Theory of Innate Ideas', *Synthese*, vol. 17.

1968   *The Sound Pattern of English* (with Morris Halle), Harper & Row, New York.

1969   'Quine's Empirical Assumptions', in *Words and Objections*, edited by Donald Davidson and Jaakko Hintikka, D. Reidel, Dordrecht.

'Some Empirical Assumptions in Modern Philosophy of Language', in *Philosophy, Science, and Method: Essays in Honor of Ernest Nagel*, edited by Sidney Morgenbesser, Patrick Suppes and Morton White, St. Martin's Press, New York.

1972   *Language and Mind*, enlarged edition, Harcourt Brace Jovanovich, New York.

Studies on Semantics in Generative Grammar, Mouton, The Hague.

1974   'What the Linguist is Talking About' (with Jerrold J. Katz), *The Journal of Philosophy*, vol. LXXI, no. 12.

1975   *The Logical Structure of Linguistic Theory*, University of Chicago Press, Chicago (originally written in 1955–6).

Reflections on Language, Pantheon, New York.

'On Innateness: A reply to Cooper' (with Jerrold J. Katz), *The Philosophical Review*, vol. 84, no. 1.

1977   *Essays on Form and Interpretation*, North-Holland, Amsterdam.

1979   *Language and Responsibility*, based on conversations with Mitsou Ronat, Pantheon, New York.

1980   *Rules and Representations*, Columbia University Press, New York.

'Rules and Representations' (with Open Peer Commentary and Author's Response), *Behavioral and Brain Sciences*, vol. 3, pp. 1–61.

Language and Learning: The Debate between Jean Piaget and Noam Chomsky, edited by Massimo Piatelli-Palmarini, Harvard University Press, Cambridge, Massachusetts.

1981   *Lectures on Government and Binding*, Foris Publications, Dordrecht.

1982   *Noam Chomsky on The Generative Enterprise*, a discussion with Riny Huybregts and Henk van Riemsdijk, Foris Publications, Dordrecht.

'A Note on the Creative Aspect of Language Use', *Philosophical Review*, vol. 91, no. 3.

1983 'Some Conceptual Shifts in the Study of Language', in *How Many Questions? Essays in Honor of Sidney Morgenbesser*, edited by L.S. Cauman, I. Levi, C.D. Parsons and R. Schwartz, Hackett, Indianapolis.

1986 *Knowledge of Language: Its Nature, Origin and Use*, Praeger, New York.

1987 *The Chomsky Reader*, edited by James Peck, Pantheon, New York.

'Replies to Alexander George and Michael Brody', *Mind and Language*, vol. 2, no. 2.

1988 *Languages and Problems of Knowledge: The Managua Lectures*, MIT Press, Cambridge, Massachusetts.

'Language and Interpretation: Philosophical Reflection and Empirical Inquiry', ms., MIT, Cambridge, Massachusetts (to appear in University of Pittsburgh Series on Philosophy of Science).

Index

Austin, John, 23

Barwise, Jon, 31–5, 153
Benacerraf, Paul, 213
Berwick, Robert, 127–8
binding theory, 26–7, 30
Bowerman, M., 154, 163
Bresnan, Joan, 99–100, 107
Bruner, Jerome, 9–13, 20–1
Burge, Tyler, 32

Carnap, Rudolf, 222
Chomsky, Noam, 19, 20, 23–26, 28, 30, 27, 41, 42–3, 49, 50, 54, 60, 86, 97, 103, 112, 121, 128, 129, 139, 141, 150, 165, 171–2, 189, 190, 198, 209, 213, 221
  on acquisition of natural languages, 24–26, 127
  on the autonomy of meaning, 160–5
  on the creative use of language, 233, 238, 259
  on E-language and I-language, 62, 95
  on grammar, 94–5, 96, 104, 109, 125
  on knowledge of grammar, 104–5
  on Kripke's interpretation of Wittgenstein, 235–7, 254, 260
  on mental representations, 94–6, 108, 124
  methodology of, 176, 188
  on philosophy, vi–vii
  poverty of the stimulus argument, 19
  on the primary function of language, 200–1
  on Quine, 106, 222–4, 227–9
  on the social nature of language, 179–80
  on syntax, semantics and their interactions, 160–5
  on tacit knowledge, 131–5, 136, 140, 153, 171, 202

on universal grammar, 94, 126, 176
Churchland, Patricia, 18
Churchland, Paul, 13–14
Clarke, David D., 106
communication, language as an instrument of, 192–212; see also sense, the communicability of

Davidson, Donald, 41, 43, 44, 54, 160, 162–4, 200, 203, 204
Davies, Martin, 105–6, 129
Dennett, Daniel, 132–3
Descartes, Rene, 237
Devitt, Michael, 97, 107, 219
Dummett, Michael, 37, 106, 153, 160, 162, 164, 166–70, 260

Evans, Gareth, 104–5, 147, 195, 260

Fodor, Jerry, 96, 137, 141–6, 149, 160, 227
Frege, Gottlob, 23, 43, 45, 46, 54, 55, 195, 196, 198, 199, 200, 202, 203, 211, 222
Friedman, Michael, 227

George, Alexander, 227–8, 233, 259
Gödel, Kurt, 52, 56
government and binding theory, 42–3, 45, 48–9, 52–3, 55
grammar, 26, 90–102; see also Chomsky, Noam, on grammar
  inferential isolation of, 139–46
  psychological reality of, 97–8, 99–101, 108, 112–29
  tacit knowledge of, 102, 105–6, 131–51
  universal, 122–3, 126–9
Grice, Paul, 164, 197–9

Hacking, Ian, 230
Harman, Gilbert, 155–7
Higginbotham, James, 39, 102, 103, 108

Hookway, Christopher, 224, 226–7
Husserl, Edmund, 202

idiolects, 154–5, 175–87, 200–5
indexicality, 31–5

Katz, Jerrold, 95, 107, 157–8
Kenny, Anthony, 97
Kintsch, Walter, 99–100
knowledge of language
    ambiguity in the notion of, 96, 107
    tacit nature of, 131–51, 170–1
Kripke, Saul, 234–9, 241, 243, 245,
    257–8, 260, 261

Lakoff, George, 43
language of thought, 36, 102, 118, 124–5,
    143, 150, 157–8; see also
    representation, mental; thought

Lewis, David, 157–8, 220
linguistic explanation, 26–9, 31, 113–14
linguistic interpretation, effects of context
    on, 32, 34–5
Loar, Brian, 190
logical form, 26–31, 38, 41–53, 90
    alleged first-order nature of, 43–8,
        51–3
    coreference in, 45, 48–9
    as derivable from syntax, 41–2
    scope in, 45, 47
Lycan, W.G., 132, 135

McClelland, J., 123–4
McDowell, John, 197–9, 261
Marcus, Ruth, 104
Marr, David, 100, 112–14, 125, 144–5,
    189
meaning as use versus truth, 206–8, 211
mentalese see language of thought
Miller, Richard, 229
model-theoretic argument against realism,
    213–20
modularity
    Fodor on see Fodor, Jerry
    of language perception, 5–8, 120
    of visual perception, 3, 4
Montague, Richard, 54
music, 120

Neurath, Otto, 221

Palmer, F.R., 106
parser, 93, 96, 118
Peacocke, Christopher, 102, 108
perception, 1–21
    encapsulation of 9–16
    of language, 5–8
    as a species of inference, 3–4
    teleological arguments concerning, 9–
        13, 17–18
Perry, John, 31–5
Popper, Karl, 226
Putnam, Hilary, 106, 126, 154, 179

Quine, Willard Van Orman, 23, 41, 43,
    104, 106, 116, 131–2, 153, 190,
    213, 221–9, 230, 231

Ramsey, F.P., 206
realism see model-theoretic argument
    against realism
Reinhart, Tanya, 172
representation
    mental, 91, 94–5, 96, 102, 104, 107
    semantic, 93, 94
    see also logical form
Ricketts, Thomas, 231
Rorty, Richard, 224
Rumelhart, D., 123–4
Russell, Bertrand, 23, 41, 43, 45, 46, 54,
    55, 153, 222
Ryle, Gilbert, 237

Scott, Dana, 56
Searle, John, 97, 108
semantics, 35–7
    autonomy of, 159–60
    disquotational data for, 165–70
    game-theoretical, 46, 47, 49–50, 52–3,
        55–6
    social basis of, 175–87
    as theory of reference, or of knowledge
        of reference, 153–9
    translational view of, 157–8
sense
    the communicability of, 202–5
    a Fregean theory of, 199–203
Soames, Scott, 39–40, 99–101, 107–8
social nature of language see Chomsky,
        Noam; idiolects; semantics, social
        basis of
Sterelny, Kim, 97, 107

Stich, Stephen, 134, 141–2
Strawson, Peter, 147, 197–9, 209, 210, 211
syntax, 26–31, 38, 159–65

tacit knowledge of language see
    knowledge of language, tacit nature
    of
Tarski, Alfred, 203
thought, language as a vehicle of, 192–212
truth, 203

vision, 100

Weinberg, Amy, 127–8
Wettstein, Howard, 172
Wittgenstein, Ludwig, 23, 27, 41, 42, 49,
    54, 193–4, 206–8, 211, 220
  on rule following, 234–46, 250, 255,
    257–9
Wright, Crispin, 164

Ziff, Paul, 213